T0301989

# DESIGN FOR TRANSFORMATIVE LEARNING

The creative strategies in *Design for Transformative Learning* offer a playful and practical approach to learning from and adapting to a rapidly changing world. Seeing continuous learning as more than the periodic acquisition of new skills this book presents a design-led approach to revising the stories we tell ourselves, unlearning old habits and embracing new practices.

This book maps learning opportunities across the contemporary landscape, narrating global case studies from K12, higher education, design consultancies and researchers. It offers narrative context, best practices and emergent strategies for how designers can partner in the important work of advancing a lifetime of learning. Committed to driving sustained transformation this is a playbook of practical moves for designing memory-making, perspective-shifting, hands-on learning encounters. The book braids stories from design practice with theories of change, transformative learning literature, cognitive and social psychology research, affect theory and Indigenous knowing. Positioning the COVID-19 pandemic as a moment to question what was previously normalised, the book proposes playful strategies for seeding transformational change.

The relational practice at the core of *Design for Transformative Learning* argues that if learning is to be transformative the experience must be embodied, cognitive and social. This book is an essential read for design and social innovation researchers, facilitators of community engagement and co-design workshops, design and arts educators and professional learning designers. It is a useful primer for K12 teachers, organisational change practitioners and professional development facilitators curious to explore the intersection of design and learning.

**Lisa Grocott** is currently a Professor of Design and the Director of WonderLab at Monash University, Australia where she leads the Future of Work and Learning research program in the Emergent Technologies Research Lab. A mother of two children raised in multiple countries, Lisa grew up in Aotearoa New Zealand with a whakapapa to Ngāti Kahungunu on her mother's side and Pākehā from Waikato on her father's side.

# Design for Social Responsibility

*Series Editor: Rachel Cooper*

Social responsibility, in various disguises, has been a recurring theme in design for many years. Since the 1960s, several more or less commercial approaches have evolved. In the 1970s, designers were encouraged to abandon 'design for profit' in favour of a more compassionate approach inspired by Papanek. In the 1980s and 1990s, profit and ethical issues were no longer considered mutually exclusive and more market-oriented concepts emerged, such as the 'green consumer' and ethical investment. The purchase of socially responsible, 'ethical' products and services has been stimulated by the dissemination of research into sustainability issues in consumer publications. Accessibility and inclusivity have also attracted a great deal of design interest and recently designers have turned to solving social and crime-related problems. Organisations supporting and funding such projects have recently included the NHS (research into design for patient safety); the Home Office (design against crime); Engineering and Physical Sciences Research Council (design decision-making for urban sustainability).

Businesses are encouraged (and increasingly forced by legislation) to set their own socially responsible agendas that depend on design to be realised. Design decisions all have environmental, social and ethical impacts, so there is a pressing need to provide guidelines for designers and design students within an overarching framework that takes a holistic approach to socially responsible design. This edited series of guides is aimed at students of design, product development, architecture and marketing and design and management professionals working in the sectors covered by each title. Each volume includes the background and history of the topic, its significance in social and commercial contexts and trends in the field. Exemplar design case studies, guidelines for the designer and advice on tools, techniques and resources are available.

## 14. Design for People Living with Dementia
Interactions and Innovations
*Emmanuel Tsekleves and John Keady*

## 15. Design for Transformative Learning
A Practical Approach to Memory-Making and Perspective-Shifting
*Lisa Grocott*

For more information about this series, please visit: www.routledge.com/Design-for-Social-Responsibility/book-series/DSR

# DESIGN FOR TRANSFORMATIVE LEARNING

## A Practical Approach to Memory-Making and Perspective-Shifting

*Lisa Grocott*

Routledge
Taylor & Francis Group

LONDON AND NEW YORK

Cover image: Lisa Grocott

First published 2022
by Routledge
4 Park Square, Milton Park, Abingdon, Oxon OX14 4RN

and by Routledge
605 Third Avenue, New York, NY 10158

*Routledge is an imprint of the Taylor & Francis Group, an informa business*

© 2022 Lisa Grocott

*British Library Cataloguing-in-Publication Data*
A catalogue record for this book is available from the British Library

*Library of Congress Cataloging-in-Publication Data*
A catalog record has been requested for this book

ISBN: 978-1-138-36755-5 (hbk)
ISBN: 978-1-032-24625-3 (pbk)
ISBN: 978-0-429-42974-3 (ebk)

DOI: 10.4324/9780429429743

Typeset in Bembo
by codeMantra

# WEBSITE

The companion website for the book is a practical resource that connects you to many of the projects, activities, methods, designers and stories introduced here. The site includes links to downloadable activities, templates for digital learning encounters, additional reflective narratives on transformative experiences and the book bibliography.

www.designingtransformativelearning.com

# Dedication

To my Māori elder, Jonathon Mane-Wheoki, who changed how I show up in the world without me even noticing. To the young man in my Māori language class who in one sentence unsettled my understanding of learning. To Sonali Ohja, who shifted the trajectory of who I would become in the first twenty minutes of meeting her.

Poipoia te kākamo kia puāwai

*Nurture the seed and it will grow*

# CONTENTS

# FIGURES

# TABLES

# NARRATIVES

# PREFACE

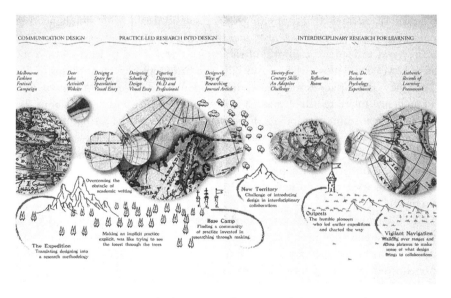

COMMUNICATION DESIGN       PRACTICE-LED RESEARCH INTO DESIGN                    INTERDISCIPLINARY RESEARCH FOR LEARNING

FIGURE 0.1 **Mapping Curiosity:** a visual map used for sense-making my own transformation journey.

I write this preface in 2020, in lockdown during a global pandemic. The economic, social, political and cultural disruption to billions of lives shows up in a multitude of ways. Black Lives Matter protests call attention to centuries of racism, inequity and oppression; businesses question what places of work might look like when people can return to offices; teachers pivot to online learning within a week's notice; people talk openly about grief, gratitude and loneliness, while governments finally find funding for mental health; primary school students experience school with no recess and play; students wonder the worth of a university education if there is no on-campus experience. The seismic nature of the disruption that occurred in 2020 might be unique, yet we can be certain that the future will repeatedly ask students and workers to unlearn, dismantle, adapt and imagine anew the ways we might live, work and learn. If we recognise that knowledge can be searched for in seconds or analysed faster by machine, we see how our mental models of learning as a process of knowledge acquisition are outdated. Many of our current practices around academic credentials, professional development or standardised testing are shaped by a different era in time. The focus of this book is on how we might design learning encounters that do not just fill us up, but that transform us. The work of this book is to interrogate what design might bring to and learn from the practices of transformative learning.

Let me start with a recent story of my own learning. A few years back, I was trying to work on a keynote address at a conference about Elastic Systems. There was little to show for the hours I was spending in front of a screen trying to make my case for considering the felt human experience of individuals within the scaled networks of systems dynamics. Instead, I was experiencing the cognitive overload that comes with trying to get my thoughts down while simultaneously engaging in a dialogue with my procrastinating self. On the surface, my easy excuse was to blame the timing of the event, I was about to leave New York after 12 years and move back to Australia and had more important things to do. Yet, below the surface-level excuse, my self-doubt had me questioning whether an audience interested in abstract systems would engage with a talk about the intra-personal realm of mindsets. Eventually, the internal chattering of procrastination was superseded by the well-worn narrative that this talk was stressful because I was a terrible public speaker. Given my presentation was about how we transform mindsets, I felt compelled to question whether this belief was fact or fiction. I decided to get curious about this story I tell myself and turn my research on myself.

To interrogate when I fixated on this idea of being a poor public speaker, I picked up a clear drinking glass and a Playmobil character. Improvising on an activity I had developed for a growth mindset workshop, I placed the avatar of myself inside the metaphoric glass prison. I then somewhat sheepishly explored (because somehow doing this alone in my apartment seemed more embarrassing than in a crowded workshop) the invisible yet forceful mindset that had me narrating this speaking engagement as a chore to push through as opposed to an opportunity to learn from. Given many of us find public speaking anxiety-inducing, I was looking to not just name the emotion but forage for the narrative that had seeded this limiting belief. The whole line of inquiry took only two minutes. As I began to play with the glass, I viscerally recalled a humiliating memory of my 11-year-old self standing on a stage. I used an unintentional pun in the opening lines of my impromptu speech. As a tween in an auditorium full of people laughing at a pun that was not only unintentional but unnoticed by me, I was next-level embarrassed. This was not a scenario where I could simply imagine the audience naked. Instead, I was the one exposed with nowhere to hide from the perplexing laughter that filled the remaining 55 seconds of my one-minute talk. Still, I somehow never made the connection between that old experience and my present belief that I hated public speaking. It took only another 30 seconds to dismantle the faulty story I had fixed on four decades earlier. Seeking disconfirming evidence from the past and the present, I recalled I was one of the first 11-year-olds to make the school's speech finals and I respected that my regular invitations to speak disprove the story that I am not good at this. This whole process took less than 5 minutes. I easily integrated my newfound perception that I actually might be quite good at public speaking and got back to writing my keynote address without the distracting backtalk. I walked away with new confidence, not just in my public speaking skills, but in the profound efficacy of my research.

Where is the learning in this tale? Is this really a story of transformation? What has this got to do with design? It is true that this story does is not represent learning as we typically think of it, there was no clear moment of instruction, no new information conveyed, or a new skill developed. However, I am aware of the ways my public speaking was elevated as a consequence of that 150 seconds of inquiry. I also know that in 40 years, I had not yet made the connection between my fixed mindset and the 1977 speech competition. I am not convinced that reflective rumination alone would have got me there. More than a thought experiment, the experiential encounter was designed to draw upon the material, haptic, affective engagement with the story I had been telling myself and the story the Playmobil and empty glass played back to me. The scaffolded interaction with the playful props helped me retrieve old memories and reclaim not just the humiliation of the fated 60-seconds but also the scripted speech I confidently gave on the stage an hour before. In stepping outside my head as a researcher, I was able to not think like an expert with answers but to instead feel like a learner with questions. In this way, the fleeting activity asked me to tackle a disorienting dilemma, to chase my own curiosity, to imagine how things could be different in the future. The experience was designed to shift my perspective so that I might be transformed by the encounter. Today, I think, feel and act differently than I did before that moment and that might be the simplest definition of transformational learning.

If the preface is where I make the case for why I should be the author of this book, then this is where I would document my credentials and win your trust. But again, this is not that kind of book. I could talk about how co-directing an interdisciplinary curriculum in small town New Zealand in my 20s led me to become a Dean at Parsons playing a leading role in shepherding the institution through an innovative reimagining of what design education might be. And yet, although my bias towards the interdisciplinary runs through the pages of this book and a commitment to envisioning new modes of curriculum and credentials has led me to interrogate every aspect of formal education, this book is not about the strategic moves or the structural shifts any more than it is about new technologies. The grand changes of this book are oftentimes granular, invisible and intangible. The transformative shifts operate in the margins – they are experienced at an intrapersonal level and can take their time to bloom.

The story of this book's evolution is a small example of one of those shifts. Just as I resist asserting my expertise, I also find the tone of declarative academic writing – the asserting of a fixed position – undesignerly. I spent years bucking against my perception that this type of writing would constrain me from writing a book that would align with the relational values I saw as core to the creative, fluid practice I was advocating for. To some extent, this was a mindset question like the public speaking tale. I see myself as a designer, not a writer, and my narrow preconceptions of what academic writing can be and my fixed narrative of my writing ability held me back. I was left to wonder: how could I be declarative if I understood a virtue of designing as being speculative? How might I fuel the readers' engagement if I were distractedly referencing the literature of others to assert the research's legitimacy? Why should I write a book because university cultures value publishing over designing? Slowly, I stopped deferring to conventions of academic authorship and began to creatively think about writing through the practice of designing engaging experiences. Might practice narratives draw the viewer in, in a similar way that experiential workshops engage the whole person? Could vulnerable stories where I humbly question my past practice assert the importance of interrogating assumptions? Could hosting a book workshop with international design and learning experts remind me of my intrinsic motivation to share our expertise with our community?

Once again, my way out was to put my own research into practice. I set out to design a manuscript that models the principles of an engaging, resonant, reflective, unsettling and creative experience. However, I struggled with the limiting assumption that the single-authored book could not model the social and reciprocal values the learning practices called for. Then, I thought to co-create a way to make it clear that this work sits within a rich community of PhD candidates, fellow academics and design practitioners. The professional case studies and the Design Rounds workshop offer alternative models and position the research practice in new ways. Making the participatory orientation of the practice visible, the WonderLab community gathered in the footnotes, offering plural perspectives and further reading. The diagrams and first-person narratives interleaved throughout the book invite you, the reader, to get curious about your perspectives and lived experiences. If you choose to surface your assumptions and question the practice implications of the ideas presented, you too can actively configure and reconfigure the material shared here. In this way, the book content, design and collaborative process resist declaring one way forward or a blueprint to follow. If the public speaking encounter represents the role of materials, motivation and reflection in learning new ways of being in the world, the design of the book illuminates the role of discussion, emergence and plurality. The book you are holding embraces multiple disciplinary, cultural and practice perspectives that make the designed workshop a social exercise in people contesting, affirming and wondering as they come together to learn.

My professional titles, degrees earned or the number of publications does not seem relevant for sparking your curiosity to read past this preface. Any quantification of my expertise is simply a shorthand for the wisdom gained from collaborating with colleagues and the mastery that comes from years of experience in research and practice. Alternatively, I would posit that for this book a reader should be looking for evidence of a life changed by a commitment to continuous learning. The insights surfaced from flawed collaborations with learning scientists, in turn, changed how I see the cognitive and emotional interplay of designing. Collaborating with ethnographers has taught me to see an alignment between their first-person narratives and my experiential sense-making. Partnering with experts in performance and play has granted me a sensorial understanding of the similarities between rehearsing and prototyping, between being vulnerable and being creative. These are a fraction of the life lessons that come from collaborating with other disciplines. Yet, decades of intentionally learning from not just the project but from the collaborations have helped me account for the value of the situated, experiential nature of design practice. The stories within this book illustrate what can be learned from geographic and disciplinary encounters and by reflexively examining our own failures, assumptions and interactions.

This positioning of myself as a learner came from a series of interviews I did with design practitioners. I was curious to understand how they had reinvented themselves from the focused field of graphic design to the diffused practice of transdisciplinary research. From these conversations, the primary insight was that each designer had found their own way to see research not as an output to be accounted for but as a process for re/search/ing. The inquisitive impulse to continuously search, to always be learning, helped explain the trajectory of their careers. Un/learning and re/learning what it meant to be a designer was a core part of the commitment to an inquiry-led practice, founded in principles of learning (13.1).

I recognise the attributes of this practice because I see them in my own journey from a graphic designer of fashion campaigns to a researcher working on transdisciplinary challenges exploring the future of work and learning. My quest has been to sense-make the contribution of design to interdisciplinary projects. My meaning-making practice explores through figuring, story-making, playing, co-creating and translating how design might amplify what it does well and address where it falls down. My practice shows up as interventions in the world of learning. For me, this world-making has traditionally taken the form of alternative learning transcripts, digital credentials or play-based curriculum. In this book, the focus is on designing engaged learning that leads to transformed selves.

What I have come to know is that if you, the reader, want this book to lead to real change, then you cannot just sit there and read passively. If you approach reading as information to acquire, precedents to glean, literature to cite, you are not really engaging and you will not build strong memory traces. This will diminish any hope of retrieving the content weeks or years from now. You will not walk away changed by your time reading this book. What you need to do is actively engage with the material. Lean into the areas when the content presents a disorienting dilemma. Go beyond the surface answer to deeply question how your assumptions or mental models are being affirmed or threatened. Create your own figuring diagrams to interrogate the intersections between ideas shared here and your own practice. Experiment with writing a story of a memorable learning moment in your life to recall the affective, sensorial feeling of that encounter. Yet, even with this research making the case for why you should take this approach, the chances are you will not embrace my suggestions. It is hard, very hard, for us to change what we do and how we do them. Our habits around how we read and consume books will not change simply because research tells us to. We know that already. The way we move through the everyday (our use of single plastic, our disuse of gym memberships) offer evidence that we do not shift our ways of acting in the world simply because our ways of thinking have been inspired.

May I make this more realistic suggestion instead? Before you turn to the pages ahead, pause to ask yourself why you are here. To adopt the stance of the book, you must find a way to prioritise chasing your own curiosity. Consider what it would take to let go of the extrinsic reasons for why you might have picked this book up and channel instead a personal motivation for engaging with this content. Are you here because disruptive technologies are changing what you teach? Are you curious about what practice mental models you are holding on to that might be redundant in a post-COVID world? Are you drawn to explore what you bring as a designer to research collaborations with learning scientists? Do you question how learning encounters might create sustainable change over time instead of elevating end of semester grades? Or are you wondering how design insights might improve your teaching by deepening your students' learning?

My personal motivation to write this was to make evident the value of design as a practice-informed mode of inquiry. I was intellectually motivated to spend weekends writing about how to better understand the contribution of designing with respect to transformative learning. In seeing this book as a conversation between you and me, I could shed the extrinsic motivations that had me feeling more obligated than motivated. A social contract and sense of purpose emerge from declaring my own motivations. I find hope that in sharing my insights with you here that together we can do the world-making needed to collectively nudge the role designers play in transforming how we learn.

Now, put the book down and return when you find whatever intrinsic motivation will keep you reading. I will wait for you.

# ACKNOWLEDGEMENTS

When you write a book about the relational orientation of transformative learning, it is a rewarding, reflective moment to pause and express gratitude for the many humans (and non-humans) who have shaped this book. There are the people who seeded the very ideas behind the book, the people who were integral to bringing it into being and the people without whom there would be no book.

I want to begin with the first group. Dominic Randolph, the Head of School at Riverdale Country School, is the person who introduced me to the overlapping Venn diagram that is design and learning. Dominic granted me not just the financial freedom to creatively and critically explore the potential of this space, but he also unlocked a community of teachers, students and interdisciplinary researchers with whom I could explore through the designing of encounters in the real world. As Dominic was introducing me to designing learning, Professor Meredith Davis of NCSU was generously sharing her decades of work in this space with me from a design perspective. Tim Marshall, then Executive Dean and my close collaborator at Parsons, and I were experimenting with what it meant to be designing the design school. My years working with Tim on considering the affordances of (re)designing design education are foundational to how I came to position the transformative role of designing in organisational change. Tim then introduced me to Rachel Cooper, the series editor of Design for Social Responsibility and President of the Design Research Society. The gracious invitation by Rachel to write a book on design for education is how this book literally came into being. I would like to especially acknowledge Rachel's patience as I went on to take years to deliver the actual book.

To the many collaborators, co-conspirators and colleagues whose work inspires me and challenges me, I am grateful to the chance to have learned from you and alongside you. To Roger Manix, Helen Chen, Kelly Schmutte, Annette Diefenthaler, Jamer Hunt, Mai Kobori, Maggie Ollove and Christopher Patten,

I can think of a concrete time each of you has shifted my thinking and changed my practice. To interdisciplinary colleagues Wesley Imms, Marian Mahat, Chris Bradbeer, Angela Duckworth, Todd Rogers, Greg Walton, Mia Perry and Lizzie Coles-Kemp, your adjacent, opposite and complementary disciplinary orientations have bought into sharp relief my perspective on the limitations and potential of design in this space. To my mentors Jonathon Mane-Wheoki, Desna Jury and David Thomas without your nurturing support in the early days of my career, I would never have found myself here.

The illuminating stories shared in the Part II case studies are testament to the wondering inquiry you bring every day to your work. To the practitioners: Deborah Parizek, Christopher Patten, Susie Wise and Tristan Schultz, thank you for showing us how this work can travel and evolve in professional practice. To the academics: Colleen Macklin, Nassim Parvin, Azad Naeemi, Aditya Anupam and Teemu Leinonen, thank you for exploring the translational agency of design research. To Dion Tuckwell and Claudia Garduño García, thank you for Ph.D. projects that telegraph the potential of designing transformative encounters to a new generation of design researchers.

When I look back to the transformative magic of the week of collaborative learning that we called the Design Rounds I believe the book would not be what it is without the deep wondering space that time opened up for all of us. To the busy people who gave us so much of their time I am forever grateful. To Penny Hagen, for modelling the professional practice I admire more than any in the world. To Tuuli Mattelmäki, for your quiet grace, inquiring mind and kindred spirit. To Elliott Montgomery, for your generosity and commitment to trouble my own assumptions. To Kevin Mattingly who, over the course of hundreds of hours of conversation, changed the very way I see the world. Your enthusiastic capacity to translate science, nudge design and challenge education is why this book has two scientific chapters. To Sonali Ojha, for showing us all how a contemplative design practice can embody ideas that we might otherwise only know intellectually. You are missed every day and yet you are also with us every day.

Without the WonderLab community, there might have been a book, but the practices and ideas within it would have been less engaging, less critical. WonderLab is the heart and soul of the book and I am grateful to my Monash colleagues Gene Bawden and Jess Berry for supporting this experiment in developing a community of practice orientation to Ph.D. education. To Dion Tuckwell, for the rewarding partnership as we navigated the Innovative Learning Environments and Teacher Change project. To Hannah Korsmeyer, your reflexive capacity to observe your own transformation has made it easier for me to observe my own. To Alli Edwards, for reminding me of the capacity of design materials as alibis for play. I am indebted to Myriam Diatta for all that I came to know through the journey of your Ph.D. and our collaborations, a rewarding, humbling experience in the teacher becoming the learner. To Sean Donahue, for always foregrounding the ethics of design practice and asking more of me in return. To Kate McEntee, for the critical acumen you bring to questioning our own positionality in ways that trouble my own thinking in profoundly useful ways. Ricardo Dutra Gonçalves, I love that I have gone from wanting to run away from your embodied work to deeply respecting this whole new way of being and knowing. To Yi Zhang, for your insightful critiques of academia and showing us how much there is to learn from the professional application of this work. To Kelly Anderson, for the most memorable of mid-workshop epiphanies. To Myfanwy Doughty and Alison Colwell-Matsuura, for reminding me there will always be new Ph.D. candidates opening up worlds I have never before spent time in. Lastly, to Wendy Ellerton, for engaging in the oftentimes unfocussed, yet always rewarding, wondering process of figuring the diagrams for the book. And Kate, Dion and Hannah, I have not forgotten that this book would never have been imagined into existence if it were not for the hours the four of us sat around conceptualising its orientation.

Beyond the Ph.D. candidates, there are the friends of WonderLab who lift the whole community up through their critical feedback, generous sharing, hard-won wisdom, excellent supervision and alternate perspectives. Ricardo Sosa, Kate Coleman, Shana Agid, Yoko Akama, Lina Patel, Ilya Fridman, Rowan Brookes, Nicholas McGuigan, Myra Theissen, Desiree Ibinarriaga and Leah Heiss, thank you for always showing up to WonderLab with care and respect. The learning community of WonderLab exists within the Emerging Technologies Research Lab at Monash University and I am lucky enough to work with colleagues Sarah Pink, Naomi Stead and Shanti Sumartojo every day. I especially want to acknowledge the joy that comes with imagining with Shanti what comes next...

I might be the director of WonderLab and yet we all know that Stacy Holman Jones is our leader. Stacy's scholarship, grace and generosity have come to define all that we do. If I could give a badge a decade for the person who had most transformed my knowing and doing, Stacy would be this decade's recipient. For sure. Stacy has shown me there is a different way to be an academic, to write, to reflect. To be. Thank you for your passion, commitment and love for this community. Above all, thank you for your friendship in the hardest of times.

Going back in time, there are others who have been in my life for so long I am forever shaped by their friendship. To Roger Manix for reminding me how to play and to Douglas Diaz for showing me how to be vulnerable. To Naomi Stead, Fiona Donald and Vicky Lam, for shepherding me through transitions, loss and pandemics. To Anne Burdick, my dear critical friend who has been there from the beginning,

Lastly, to my whānau, my family. My mother and father would have loved this book. Mum would have put it on her coffee table and Dad would have wanted to sit long into the night talking about the ideas. To my brothers, I thank you for standing by my side. You have both shown me different ways to own being Māori and different ways to be strong. Mark for your grounded counsel and small acts of care. Steve for the deep affection, brutal honesty and the hilarious memories I will forever cherish. To my sons, if I had not heard of intrinsic motivation,

I might have believed you got in the way of this book ever leaving my computer. Yet, Harper and Moss, what I know now is that without you, this work would have had no sense of purpose. Envisaging the worlds I want you to be custodians of, the professional opportunities I wish for you and the futures I want you to dream for yourselves, is all the motivation I needed to keep writing.

## Funding Acknowledgements

The research practice within this book would not have emerged without the funding *Riverdale Country School* gave Parsons and Monash in support of the development of the field of designing learning. Many of the projects referenced and the focus on transforming practice was a direct consequence of the research opportunities made possible from being a chief investigator on the *Innovative Learning Environments and Teaching Change (ILETC)*. My sincere thanks to Wesley Imms for inviting me to be part of this Australian Research Council (ARC) funded *Linkage Project (2016–2020*, project LP150100022). The views expressed herein are those of the authors and are not necessarily those of the Australian Research Council.

# PART I

# Designing Learning Encounters

An Introduction and an Invitation

FIGURE 1.0 **The Play Gym**: Embodied learning and affective engagement.

DOI: 10.4324/9780429429743-1

## An Introduction

With a goal to design learning encounters that lead to substantive, sustained change over time, this book makes the case for why a practice of transformative learning must be an embodied, affective, cognitive and social experience. The theory, scientific studies, ethnographic narratives and practice case studies referenced in the following pages speak to the potential roles designing can play in elevating and amplifying learner engagement that leads to transformational outcomes.

This book is not a philosophical theoretical text about learning or quantitative longitudinal case studies about learning interventions. This is a book grounded in a practice-evidence exploration of design research and transformative learning. The promise here is a generative text that shares practice stories, interdisciplinary insights, propositional frameworks, small moves and methods. You are invited to apply them to your practice. Whether you are a researcher, educator, designer or learner, the potential here is to read across and between the book's layered offerings in ways that align with questions you might be asking of your own practice.

There are no literal worksheets or step-by-step methodologies. I resist calling this book a 'toolkit'. Rather, I aim to provide an articulated set of paths for inquiry. You might question these ways of seeing, believing, making and framing. You might become unsettled when you consider your current practice. You might even be led towards new methods to consider in your own practice. The potential here is not to follow some predetermined route but to find your own off ramp by letting the research reveal a detour you would otherwise have driven past.

The focus here is on designing learning encounters that lead to transformed selves. This integrative work requires the learner to make over our interior worlds – to interrogate our mindsets, unsettle outdated mental models and craft future imaginaries that spark new habits of mind. I argue that this make-over is required of the designer too. To learn in parallel with the people whose transformation we are facilitating, we must position ourselves as learners too. We must always be wondering.

# 1

# THE DESIGN OF TRANSFORMATIVE LEARNING ENCOUNTERS

FIGURE 1.1 **Haptic Hands-on Learning**: This workshop from WonderLab's first public playdate has Alli Edwards and Kelly Anderson designing a metaphoric and haptic encounter that has participants considering their place and purpose within a local solar system, before moving on to declare their motivation to travel to adjacent systems within the shared universe.

## 1.1 Transformational Learning and Design Practice

You could say the 'why' of this book is straightforward. As we find ourselves transitioning into the fourth industrial revolution, the call for continuous learning over a lifetime becomes louder. As more tasks become automated, the stocks

DOI: 10.4324/9780429429743-2

of expertise – like being creative, adaptive and collaborative – overtake old skills more expeditiously done by algorithms. If we want to explore how humans learn, then this cannot be disentangled from the trend towards more automated decision-making. If we want to reimagine the learning futures of tomorrow, we must be cognizant of the industrial-historical context, the cultural institutional biases and the powerful technological forces that shape how we got here. This book does not attempt to forecast the future of education technologies but instead to zoom in on how transformative learning happens within the interior world of a learner as we find ourselves navigating increasingly uncertain futures. Artificial intelligence and machine learning are not the subject of this book, they simply set up the urgency by which we must ask different questions of what we learn, how we learn and why we are learning.

The focus on transformative learning does not presuppose that the transformation is in itself grand or disruptive. Yet, there is recognition that most learning is not transformative. In fact, most learning is assimilative to the extent that new experiences and information is internalised in ways that do not challenge our existing knowledge structures.[1] Jack Mezirow's Transformational Learning theory emphasises that the structures that anchor meaning for us are central to the work of shifting perspectives. Whereas Mezirow's emphasis is on transforming meaning schemes and meaning perspectives, the question I wish to explore is if the transformation leads to new ways of being and acting in the world. This might be a change in behaviour, but may also be less observable, like the change in mindset that allowed me to reframe my position on public speaking (see Preface). In this way, the stories in this book are often about small shifts that come from snapshots in time. Transformational Learning Theory recognises that a 'disorienting dilemma' in life or an assumption-busting activity can prompt re-examination of meaning structures: "the constellation of concept, belief, judgment, and feelings which shapes a particular interpretation" (2, p. 223). Disinterested in designing curriculum or learning technologies, the more pedagogical focus of this book explores design mindsets, moves and methods that engage people in experiential learning encounters.[2]

---

1  **Lisa**: Piaget made the distinction between assimilative and accommodative processes of knowledge acquisition. He notes assimilative processes have new experiences being made sense of by already confirmed, previously established knowledge structures. Think of an accumulative model where the knowledge keeps swelling yet never contesting what came before. In contrast, the more radical and rare accommodative process is when new experiences challenge existing knowledge. Think of an experience that requires renovations to make room for the new perspective surfaced by the disconfirming experience. (1)

2  **Dion**: It's interesting to situate this in relation to notions of transformative design; that is, how we might turn away from designing products or services and look towards a society-centred approach. Transformative Design focuses on the social dimensions and conditions of designing and how this engages with processes of creative inquiry into new potentialities – and how this might be designed and realised in new forms. (3, p. 9) What are design's potentials, instruments and contributions to shaping social change? (3, p. 9) And crucially, how might this be different when the transformation works at the level of the individual learner, the peer community, the social structure or the systemic infrastructure?

This book will elaborate in detail what these learning encounters might look like or feel like. The shorthand for now is that these are learning experiences charged with wonder. Like Sara Ahmed, I believe "wonder implies learning" (4, p. 183), and see that wondrous encounters need to be designed to fuel inquiry, invite introspection, spark better questions, illuminate relationships and forge connections. This act of 'wondering' will be a critical, embodied act – a space for doubt, amazement and curiosity. When we bring designing to the social and haptic experience of wondering, you have the animating force for creative, affective and cognitive exploration. These wondering moments might be fleeting, iterative, episodic, or they might be serendipitous, intentional or rhizomatic. This book does not define the form encounters take but instead shares design moves, methods and mindsets for planting seeds for wonder that will nurture personal and collective quests for meaning-making. To wonder new worlds into existence we must also make new scripts. It is in re-storying, narrating anew, that we can imagine, rehearse and adopt new ways of knowing, doing and being in the world.

If we are to resist the pull to return to normal in a post-COVID-19 world, we need to critique what was previously normalised. We need effective strategies for perspective shifting.[3] Here, we recognise the work of radically reimagining just, sustainable and equitable futures. It is a job that will be transdisciplinary, transnational and decades in the making. I humbly acknowledge the small part design might play in doing this difficult work. With consideration for how co-designing primes people to reflect, share and make, we explore design's contribution to engaging learners and citizens in projects that lead to transformation. The research frameworks come from questioning how the cognitive, constructed, relational, personal, experiential and imaginative nature of design might amplify our engagement in the unsettling of long-held meaning structures and the remaking of new constellations of knowing and being.

The verb 'designing' is central to the *doing* of inquiry called for in this research. The goal is not a designed artefact but designing as an inquisitive practice that shares the same experiential valence as the learning experiences being examined. The work is not always co-design, but there is an orientation to the social and a commitment to reciprocity that runs through the practices referenced. Furthermore, the invitation is to design encounters not just for the participants but to see our own learning as part of the co-design process of transforming "how we design our world, and ourselves, with others" (6, p. 31). The accounts

---

3   **Lisa**: There are many calls from climate crisis scientists, well-being experts, education academics. Yet perhaps poet Sonya Renee Taylor's call went viral because it is grounded in her social justice critique: "We will not go back to normal. Normal never was. Our pre-corona existence was not normal other than we normalized greed, inequity, exhaustion, depletion, extraction, disconnection, confusion, rage, hoarding, hate and lack. We should not long to return, my friends. We are being given the opportunity to stitch a new garment. One that fits all of humanity and nature" (5).

of my teaching, learning and designing practice, and those of my peers', are grounded in the pragmatism of research informed by a situational practice and a close engagement with the professional context of design. The design case studies in Part II include school-based, public sector, professional learning, PhD dissertations and academic research projects. Design research and creative arts literature examine the distinctions between practice-based, practice-led and project-grounded research. Some lines of inquiry are defined by a program grounded by real-world conditions and constraints. Alain Findeli would see this research engagement as thinking 'in project' (7). The PhD case studies offer examples of research led by questions of practice. These practice-led examples have the practitioner-researchers learning about themselves through the act of designing learning for others. (8; 9) The learning design projects explore the implications of evidence-based research, critical theories or Indigenous knowing as translated through the practice of design. (10)

The projects and practices included span from small scale, local explorations from within a research community, to longitudinal case studies scaled across Europe's education systems. There are projects that evidence the impact of the initiatives, and others that simply question what they would do differently next time. There are tactics familiar to many designers, and novel moves being shared here for the community to iterate on and improve. A prototypical ethos runs through the chapters, positioning the shared prompts, theories, frameworks and practices as a work-in-progress. There is an invitation to the broader community to continue to rethink, critique and co-create the role design can play in amplifying learner engagement and transformation.

## 1.2 Who Should Read This?

With the designing of transformational learning understood as a transdisciplinary challenge, this book has an entry point for many audiences: designers, researchers and educators. If you are interested in the potential of research through design, then this book exemplifies innovative approaches to a practice orientation to doing inquiry. If you are a researcher interested in how to motivate and mobilise people, or if you are working on research projects that implicitly ask people to shift their ways of being and acting in the world (and you probably are), then this book usefully distils socio-cultural and psychological change research from multiple disciplines into an extra-rational sequence conceived to drive sustained, individual transformation. If you are a design educator, the literature on the cognitive and social psychology of learning will be instructive in designing learning experiences for your students. It will also be provocative in asking you to reflect on your own beliefs around how learning happens. For the teacher somewhat familiar with design thinking or creative practices, you will find new imaginative strategies and conceptual frames for deepening experiential learning. That said, education or psychology researchers will recognise the introductory level of the learning sciences material. Hopefully seeing the literature through the novel application of the affective, design practice narratives will provide a perspective shift. To research methodologists, the translational value of material, visual, performative and narrative research methods is surfaced throughout. And if you are starting out your career in design research or if you are a design researcher interested in learning, then this book introduces many core tenets of a practice orientation to research.

First-person narratives, practice precedents, theoretical frameworks and interdisciplinary literature are interleaved throughout this book to make the reading experience more engaging and more transformative. With no linear sequence to how to read the book, many educators and non-design researchers may find what they are looking for in specific sections or chapters. I outline the content in more detail below. You can dip in and out of the book or read cover to cover, there is no prescriptive blueprint here.

A book on a topic as broad as design and learning could have had many orientations: the focus could have been on pulling out to critique educational structures and cultures of learning or examining the explicit and implicit systems that learning happens within (11) or zeroing in on the community interested in design thinking and education. (12; 13) The capacity for technological learning innovations to create more participatory and equitable learning experiences, systems and services is covered comprehensively in other books. (14; 15; 16) Similarly, the design of curriculum or designing learning spaces (17; 18; 19) are not the focus, although the principles introduced would resonate with these practices. While there are books that recognise the transformative potential of design in the social innovation sector, (7; 20; 21) this book centres the locus of transformation around pedagogy and the learner's experience. The scope of the research extends beyond the archetypal student sitting in a K12 classroom to the learner being a teacher, a graduate, a professional. The holistic focus on the learner is understood as personal and social, yet the unit of change, to be clear, is on the individual engaging, changing and learning.[4]

The following section of the introduction explicitly introduces the research paradigm, theoretical perspective and discusses the methodological approach. Later in the introduction, I will position myself as an author through stories of my lived experiences that surface some of my biases and values. However, before we go into more depth, the following table declares its territory by naming assumptions core to the positioning of the book (Table 1.1).

---

4   **Myf**: I like how slippery the term change is. Mortensen and Zalta (22) call out change morphs when observed from different angles. Temporal change can mean a bodily change; change in state. Change can be active – to change your outfit or change trains. It can also be affective, felt, experienced – moved to tears, or the sudden exhilaration of the 'light bulb' moment. To complicate things further, it is also tied up with notions of reciprocity and exchange – knowledge exchange, barter, the difference between the price of a thing and the amount paid. I sense that even when the focus here is on shifts in perspective; consciousness raising; an awakening or discovery of agency, there is something to be learned from also remembering change is temporal, felt and happens in relation to others.

**TABLE 1.1** Intersecting Assumptions: Positioning Transformative Learning, Collaborative Designing and Design-based Research

| | Learning | Designing | Researching |
|---|---|---|---|
| **Expansive Framing** | Learning is not limited to what happens in a classroom but can happen anywhere, anytime over a lifetime. | Designing is not defined by the artefacts produced but by the participatory process of creative engagement. | Design research is not limited to theoretical and historical scholarship but extends to practice-informed inquiry. |
| **Relational Practice** | A socially, co-constructed learning experience draws on the discussions, artefacts and activities of the group. | The participatory orientation of co-design scaffolds the conversation between people, place, prototypes and politics. | Design research is grounded by the situation-specific context and co-creative potential of a social applied practice. |
| **Lived Experience** | The learner always brings their inner world of beliefs and mindsets and their own world of experiences, people and place. | Designing for diverse lived experiences by resisting universal solutions and respecting pluriversal perspectives. | An ethnographic orientation to iteratively exploring the field potential of designs from proof of concept to pilot programs. |
| **Integrative Orientation** | Whole-self learning works with the integration of cognitive and embodied dimensions to transform future action. | A design practice that enmeshes past knowing and present-moment awareness with an always emerging future. | Future-focused, creative methodologies in support of the facilitation, translation and application of interdisciplinary research. |
| **Nature of Change** | Transformative, situated learning happens incrementally, suddenly and recursively by moving from the periphery to the centre. | Designing is a discursive, embodied, material practice propelled by generative moves of reflection and speculation. | An iterative, customised approach to design research interventions that embraces shifts in temporal dimensions. |
| **Ethical Call for Action** | Learning to be proactive not prescriptive, continuous instead of credentialed, transformative more than transactional. | To be critical of the social impact of design by interrogating and imagining how design can shape more equitable and just futures. | Disciplinary humility and reciprocity guiding research collaborations that cannot be solved by one discipline alone. |

## 1.3 How to Engage with the Book

Or should I say onto-epistemic? Karen Barad's feminist scholarship argues that a theory of knowing and theory of being cannot be separated, using the term onto-epistemological to account for how our constructions of the world are entangled with our experiences of the world. For Barad "Practices of knowing and being are not isolable; they are mutually implicated. We don't obtain knowledge by standing outside the world; we know because we are of the world. We are part of the world in its differential becoming" (23, p. 185). The explorations of my experiences as a teacher, designer and learner through auto-ethnographic narratives place value on subjective theorisations that are sourced from my lived-in ways of knowing, doing and being. They position me as a researcher of and in the world, where knowing/being are always in a state of becoming. As I stand by the value of wonder in learning, just as I adopt wondering, as described here by Fabiane Ramos and Laura Roberts, in my practice as way of "knowing-being-doing that fundamentally challenges binary and dichotomous colonial logics of knower and known" (24, p. 35). I contest any claim of scientific objectivity and own my privileging of storytelling, practice-evidence and situated knowledges. (25)

At the same time, I recognise there is a danger in a reflexive turn that operates as an echo-chamber with one's own thoughts. The book counters its affection for the integrity of subjective positions by valuing the cognitive diversity that comes with also integrating positivist research that lays claim to a truth by way of quantitative data and reproducible evidence.

To make sense of how the manuscript itself adopts a holistic, whole-self approach to learning, I propose a simple body metaphor. Think of the learning sciences research and critical theories included as the mind, the auto-ethnographic learning narratives as the subjective heart, and the practice-led design case studies as the action-oriented gut. If that is not helpful, intellectually grasp that transformative learning is not a discrete cognitive exercise. Integration between what we feel and what we think underscores how we act. The evidence-based scientific research illustrates the central role of embodiment and emotions. The auto-ethnographic narratives underscore the science of memory retrieval. The design of learning encounters is about more than the observable interactions. These intra- and inter-personal exchanges cannot be understood through quantitative data alone. Given we cannot easily access affective experiences, we need multi-modal approaches to make sense of what these encounters might afford. When we story our lived experiences, the narrative inquiry scaffolds the analysis of the experience itself. (26) The intentional decision to hold space in this conversation for stories *and* statistics is about more than the edict that stories need data and data needs stories. When designing for transformation, it is true, stories offer a pathway to understanding and integration. When designing for learning, it is also evident that psychology research upends assumptions about how we learn or verifies hunches that allow us to push what we instinctively believe to be true harder. Design inquiry here is explored through practice narratives and evidence-based research, with the understanding that learning and designing as integrative acts of the heart, mind and body. The learner's cognitive, emotive and performative engagement in learning is reflected in research methodologies that embrace plurality, affect and embodiment, respectively. In writing through and across design, it becomes possible to translate, integrate and ground education and psychology research into encounters conceived to engage the whole learner.

The learning scientist principles of retrieval practice, interleaving, spaced practice and encoding are introduced in Chapter 10 to offer concrete strategies for amplifying the stickiness of learning new ideas. The book design works with the scientific value of interleaving content, representing material in multi-modal ways and returning to ideas over time so the reader is primed to retrieve the book's insights when the situation arises. The threaded stories, interconnected theoretical positions, echoed refrains woven throughout and visual encoding of frameworks are not lazy repetition but an intentional implementation of what cognitive science teaches us about how we learn. The social psychology studies of Chapter 9 come from the research into our desire for belonging, the payoff of deliberate practice, the call for learner agency and the value of intrinsic motivation can also be applied by readers. See yourself in the vulnerable narratives that acknowledge failure and hubris as a move to minimise imposter syndrome, consider engaging with the footnotes as a reward that comes with extra effort, recognise that the countering perspectives made visible in the footnotes are an invitation to question your own position. Most importantly, consider what motivates you as you look for purpose between the lines of the practice case studies. These moves are an example of ways we can strategically design for intentional integration into future practices.

There are four parts to the book, each framing ideas from a different perspective that can help us design learning encounters that stick. The two following chapters in Part I frame the book with respect to authorship, methodology and literature. The next chapter zeros in on the book you are holding and why I am talking to you. Chapter 2 introduces the education and psychology literature on transformative learning so that the latter design sections are grounded by what has come before. The interstitial auto-ethnographic narratives sit between the chapters to make visible my own positionality but also a felt account of what it feels like to be in the middle of a transformative experience. I share these stories throughout the book but have foregrounded in this chapter the three encounters that most strikingly upended my core beliefs in ways that have stayed with me and forever shaped my teaching and designing practice.

The four chapters of Part II are grounded by case studies and practice vignettes that reveal the potential for design to change behaviour, mindsets and mental models. Starting with an expanded field of how we situate design, the chapters are not defined by the type of design. Design is not determined by project output – service design, interaction design, game design, experience design – but more by the dispositional orientation to inquiry. Is the design inquiry creating speculative spaces for imagining new futures, or is it more about offering solutions to real challenges on the ground? Does the learning experience amplify the conversation with the materials of the situation, or with the people living in that situation? By framing design through the meta objective of asking what the act of designing is seeking to create, expansive ways of thinking about making are opened. The case studies in Part II play with this to explore what it looks like to make sense by making never-before-seen ideas possible, to make unknowable futures visible so we can make people believe, to make fun so that new ideas might be made tangible and to make with others so we might make change.

Chapter 4 takes introduces early school-based case studies to offer a historical perspective on how the human-centred design process and design thinking initially entered the education sector. The PhD case studies in Chapter 5 explore design provocations that make the potential for discursive design to promote speculative inquiry and self-determination visible. The two game design case studies in Chapter 6 highlight the ways design experiences work with social, material and performative dimensions to translate complex ideas into playful learning encounters. The co-creative moves and participatory orientation of the case studies in Chapter 7 knits together projects that range in scale from a years-long, nation-wide professional learning project with teachers to a one-day water security challenge for hundreds of teenagers. Brief practice vignettes from design doctoral students and leading international practitioners working in the space of transformational change are woven between the case studies. The geographic and professional diversity of the projects allows highly visible professional projects in the United States, or system-wide initiatives in Finland, to sit alongside humble, profound, contemplative research stories from India, Uganda and Mexico. The epistemic and ontological shifts have practices that engage with Māori, Mayan and Aboriginal Indigenous perspectives to connect with feminist and queer principles that draw on play, embodiment and affect.

Part III pulls out from the grounded stories of practice to note the component parts that can support a drive for transformational learning. The first two chapters, focused on the science of learning, introduce research from social and cognitive psychology, respectively. The last two chapters speak to principles of abductive reasoning and learning through doing to highlight the contribution of designing in this space. Chapter 9 is concerned with learning mindsets, introducing research into belonging, effort, agency and motivation. Chapter 10 supplements this social orientation with a focus on building memories, through sections on retrieval practice, interleaving, spaced practice and encoding. Chapter 11 situates design as a creative practice through an exploration of reflective practice, allegorical imagining, kaleidoscopic thinking, emotions and affect. The final chapter, anchored by a call for embodied, multi-sensorial learning, highlights participatory prototyping, the importance of creating resonance and building relevance, the need to unsettle scripts and the value of novelty.

The concluding section of the book revisits threads introduced in the previous sections to reveal frameworks for translating the research into practice. In the first chapter, one framework speaks to how you can transform your own practice;

another revisits and revises the expanded field of making framework introduced in Part II; the third introduces worlds we live in as a way to navigate the liminal learning spaces between our interior and exterior, lived and imagined worlds. The chapter ends with a table that summarises transformational objectives and creative methods for designing engaging learning experiences. Chapter 14 distils the lessons from the research into SEED, an acronym for a design-led model for transformative learning. Situating SEED in relation to other disciplinary theories of change, the model draws on design practice's dual orientation to be creative and cognitive, while also being speculative and reflective. The concluding chapter reflects on how the book asks me to reclaim old practices and reimagine new ways forward. I am left at the end curious to better understand the relational complexity of a learning practice that is always in conversation with others and the self, with the body and materials, with the land and ethics, with the past and the future.

If this book were a large dinner party, many of the guests would be wanting to rearrange the seating plan behind my back. Of course, it would be possible to have different tables for different communities, to put the social and cultural psychologists together and make sure no neurobiologists ended up at their table. I could have the designers seated far from the Indigenous researchers and intersectional feminists. But this isn't a wedding and people are not here just to have a good time. This is a place for learning. This is a place to trouble our own positions, practices and beliefs. This is a place to get clearer about what designers might have to offer and a chance to be humble about what we might need to unlearn. It will be a loud dinner party; some people will shout over others. But we can also pay attention to whose voice is being heard. There is no one right way to learn. Just be sure that in this learning space, you chase your own curiosity.

Yet even though you are invited to follow the stories that engage you, it is important to note that you will not learn if you stay with the stories you are already familiar with. The challenge I put to you is that on your way to the bathroom, you stop by the table to introduce yourself to the people you do not normally hang out with. Cognitive diversity is useful when addressing complex problems. The more mental models we can hold in our mind, the more diverse perspectives we can acknowledge. Just as a designer uses sketches or prototypes to activate a feedback loop, the notion of cognitive diversity helps to evaluate a situation from plural perspectives. If we can get curious about how our own values sit in relation to those who make sense of the world differently, we can also see situations more holistically.

I say read the chapter that least interests you. Question why some ideas truly confound you. Just as designers resist recycling ideas, embrace experimenting with new materials, choose to apply the thinking you most disagree with as a creative constraint. Ask better questions of yourself, of your practice, of other disciplines. At the very least, you will walk away with greater clarity of your mental models for how the world works, how learning happens and why design matters. At best, you'll walk away with a shift in perspective that activates your practice in new ways and changes how you act in the world. That would be evidence of transformational learning.

## Narrative 1.1 Relational Learning: Belonging and Play

### 1992 – With my Te Atarangi Peers

*I am in Aotearoa, New Zealand, sitting in a group circle with more than 30 Māori peers. This is our first chance to speak English since our total immersion Māori language course began a week ago. It is also the one time we can share why we are here and how the week has gone. Since I am the only person who passes as white in the room I am excited, yet apprehensive, to introduce my Māori heritage so I might shed the Pākehā (non-Indigenous) label I have worn all week. This feeling won't last. The phrase check-your-privilege did not exist decades ago but within the hour I will get a life-changing lesson on privilege that will turn everything as I know it upside down.*

*My smug, educated self is excited to share with my peers how I want to improve my Māori pronunciation for interviews in a book I am working on. But as the conversation moves closer to me, I tune in to what my peers are saying. They are here because their children are coming home from Kōhanga Reo (Māori Kindergarten) assuming they can korero (talk) with their parents in the te reo, the language, of their ancestors. They are here because the elders who speak Māori in their communities deserve the assurance that the language won't die with them. Suddenly, my book sounds so...academic. When it's my turn to share I resist sharing the reasons I enrolled, aware of the ego-centredness of my motivations compared to the grounded-in-place and cultural reasons this community have come together to learn.*

*We move around the circle. The last person to speak is a guy in my learning team. He is the slowest learner I have ever spent time with. Shamefully, this is a challenge for me because the pedagogical approach of the course is committed to moving at the speed of the slowest learner. I am young, naive and a product of a meritocratic university system that has led me to believe that I am wasting hours of my day waiting for this guy to get his head around a concept in two hours that I can grasp in 20 minutes. As I wait for him to speak, I am bored, impatient and disengaged.*

*Yet, this story is not a pitch for ability groups or self-paced learning. It is the opposite, in fact.*

*Let's stop and listen to what the guy, let's call him Tama, has to say first. He is self-conscious as he stammers through the reasons he found himself in this class. He has returned to Aotearoa after being away for more than a decade. When he left, the fact he couldn't speak Māori was okay, normal even. But things are different now. Tama is telling us that before he returns to his turangawaewae (the place where he belongs) on the East Cape he wants to learn how to respectfully greet his iwi (his tribe) in Māori. Everyone nods — because, on some level, Tama's reason for being here is why we are all here.*

*Tama moves on to talk about his experience in my group. I listen to him describe how he dropped out of school the day he turned 15. He shares what it feels like, for the first time in his life, to be in a learning environment that is not leaving him behind. His voice cracks as he acknowledges that some people in his group are frustrated by having to wait for him. Then tears of gratitude come as he shares what it means to him that we are not running ahead without him.*

This all happened 30 years ago, yet I can still feel the intensity of the shame I experienced in that very moment.

Of course, there was the personal shame I felt for the self-absorbed, competitive narrative that had run through my head while Tama was simply striving to do his best. But there was also my institutional shame at an education system that accepts failing the Tamas of this world while serving the likes of me, a system that privileges not just personal success over collective thriving but also certain types of intelligence over other ways of knowing. If, as Edward Deming said, "every system is perfectly designed to produce the results it gets", then the education I had been a part of was designed to sacrifice one individual at the expense of the other.

I recognise that my retelling of this well-worn story might now bear little resemblance to what actually happened. Perhaps, when Tama was choking up, I defensively thought, "you've got to be kidding me?" Perhaps Tama spoke with less gratitude and more burning resentment. Yet, this is how I have come to remember it. Him benevolent, me forever changed. I have told this story to students, teachers, in pubs, at conferences, to white people, to Indigenous folks. I have told it lightly as a self-deprecating confessional and I have let myself feel and let others hear my shame and Tama's pain. Over the decades, the subject of critique has shifted in ways that ensure I have been changed by the retelling. Once I wondered how I had not seen other's potential, now I wonder how I had not seen my privilege. Whereas once I saw the Indigenous pedagogies as everything, I now see the transgressive data points that translate the wisdom of this whole-person, purpose-led approach. (27)[5]

I have retold this story countless times, and yet, it feels more embarrassing to publish these words. For when I 'perform' this story in person, it is easy to trick you, the listener, in being complicit. It is not hard to get people schooled in a meritocratic education system to nod in agreement at the foolishness of learning being set at the pace of the slowest learner. However, in this telling, I let you off the hook by taking on the role of the fall guy from the start. You are relieved of the burden of seeing yourself in me. With words on a page, perhaps it is easier to remember what it feels like to be on the periphery, to remember

5   **Lisa**: Elizabeth St. Pierre talks about "transgressive data" as the pieces of data that afford a new kind of sense-making. By being in reflexive conversation with emotions, dreams and other sensory experiences, we can begin to confound any belief in the "evidentiary warrant" that legitimises the production of knowledge. (28, pp. 177–79)

the anxiety that comes with simply not getting something, of holding others back, of being left behind, of being othered. We know education systems can promote inclusion while still leaving people feeling very much alone.

With gratitude, humility and vulnerability, Tama managed in one moment to remind us that we were in this together. My faulty memory has me instinctively, with certainty, apprehend that Tama's story exposes the very foundations on which my ideas about learning had been built. Lucky, this story doesn't end with his declaration and my ignorance, for this was just week one of a four-week program.

I left that day ready to dismantle what I had internalised from 15 years of institutionalised education. Today, my claim is that, over the weekend, I surrendered to the purpose-driven intrinsic motivations of the Indigenous-led, cooperative learning culture of the community. I committed to advancing the learning of my peers. In reality, I am sure I did not reinvent myself overnight. No doubt, I just reframed my definition of personal success. Probably with some white saviour hubris thrown in. Yet, in turning my reflexivity on myself (I resist any attempt to use this narrative to pretend to better understand Tama even if, of course, I would rather de-centre myself), for years I failed to attune to what else was going on at our table. My epiphany did not come from Tama's courage alone. We were taught Māori without a word of English through a material-based learning system that had us making pictures with blocks and rods.[6] The fact you didn't have to be physically confident, articulate, creative or a good writer, meant the prerequisite for learning was simply being curious and open. This play-based, community-grounded pedagogy supported taking risks and performed the importance of meeting people where they are at.

Come Monday our small group was back. We dived in together. As we came to individually grasp the concept being taught, we switched to become partners with our learning coach in supporting the whole group. Tama now had a team of peers dedicated to his personal and our collective success. Once the anxiety that he was holding us up was vanquished Tama only needed half-an-hour to grasp new concepts.

Predictably, my language acquisition was improved greatly by teaching others instead of passively waiting for my peers. Yet what stays with me is that it took this experience, a month after I graduated university, to glimpse the

---

6   **Lisa**: The *Te Ataarangi* methodology has the learning coach teaching with colourful rods, as we would sit like language detectives trying to guess if she was saying "For you…" or "Take this…" She would make a building with a few rods and we'd stumble over each other trying to guess if it is a library, a museum or the town hall. This hands-on way of learning together privileged the peer-learning environment and community resilience. The principle of not moving on until everyone had worked it out, gave Tama the confidence for his whole self to show up that Friday afternoon. (28)

promise of deep learning. I went on to grad school, got a PhD and have been an educator in higher education most of my life. And yet, I choose to never forget that my humble transformative epiphany happened in a small town continuing ed class. The disruption here did not come about from EdTech, smart classrooms or charismatic teaching. The perspective-shifting insight came from a deeply relational, social, embodied, reciprocal encounter.[7]

The integrity and candour of Tama's share that afternoon was a direct consequence of the sense of belonging he felt in that carefully curated learning environment. In hearing his truth, in seeing my complicit role in his story, I could use the weeks ahead to dismantle the narratives of my educated, white and economic privilege and rehearse a new way forward.

7  **Lisa**: For all the theorising, research evidence and transformative frameworks discussed in this book I acknowledge this 5-minute micro-intervention by Tama as the moment that most profoundly rattled my institutionalised beliefs. This is not an intervention I know how to scale. Nor do I imply that from that day my actions aligned with some vigilant critique of colonial, modernist education agendas. Yet I choose not to forget that an honest, humble young man, whose name I do not remember, spoke his truth and changed my life.

## Bibliography

1  Piaget, Jean. *The Construction of Reality in the Child*. Basic Books, 1954.
2  Mezirow, Jack. "Understanding Transformation Theory." *Adult Education Quarterly (American Association for Adult and Continuing Education)*, vol. 44, no. 4, 1994, pp. 222–32, doi:10.1177/074171369404400403.
3  Jonas, Wolfgang et al., editors. *Transformation Design: Perspectives on a New Design Attitude*. Birkhäuser, 2016.
4  Ahmed, Sara. *The Cultural Politics of Emotion*. NED – New edition, 2nd ed., Edinburgh University Press, 2004.
5  Brown, Brené. "Brené with Sonya Renee Taylor on "the Body Is Not an Apology"." *Unlocking Us Podcast*, September 16, 2020, https://brenebrown.com/podcast/brene-with-sonya-renee-taylor-on-the-body-is-not-an-apology/
6  Akama, Yoko and Alison Prendiville. "Embodying, Enacting and Entangling Design: A Phenomenological View to Co-Designing Services." *Swedish Design Research Journal*, vol. 9, no. 1, 2016, pp. 29–40, doi:10.3384/svid.2000-964X.13129.
7  Findeli, Alain. "The Research Project in Design, and the Question of the Research Question: An Attempt at Conceptual Clarification." *Sciences du Design*, vol. 1, no. 1, 2015, pp. 45–57, doi:10.3917/sdd.001.0045.
8  Smith, Hazel and Roger T. Dean, editors. *Practice-Led Research, Research-Led Practice in the Creative Arts*. Edinburgh University Press, 2009.
9  Grocott, Lisa. "Make Happen: Sense-Making the Affordances of a Practice-Based PhD in Design." *Practice-Based Design Research*, edited by Laurene Vaughan, Bloomsbury Publishing, 2017, pp. 165–74.
10  Vaughan, Laurene, editor. *Practice-Based Design Research*. Bloomsbury Publishing, 2017.
11  Charset, Brian and Kate Sjostrom, editors. *Unsettling Education: Searching for Ethical Footing in a Time of Reform*. Peter Lang, 2019.

12  Melles, Gavin, editor. *Design Thinking in Higher Education : Interdisciplinary Encounters*. Springer Singapore, 2020.

13  Gallagher, Alyssa and Kami Thordarson. *Design Thinking for School Leaders: Five Roles and Mindsets That Ignite Positive Change*. ASCD, 2018.

14  Bonsignore, Elizabeth et al., editors. *Participatory Design for Learning: Perspectives from Practice and Research*, Kindle ed. Routledge, 2017.

15  Tettegah, Sharon Y and Martin Gartmeier. *Emotions, Technology, Design, and Learning*. Academic Press, 2016.

16  Benson, Angela D et al. *Culture, Learning, and Technology: Research and Practice*. Routledge, 2017.

17  Camuffo, Giorgio et al. *About Learning and Design*. Bozen-Bolzano University Press, 2014.

18  Harrison, Andrew and Les Hutton. *Design for the Changing Educational Landscape: Space, Place and the Future of Learning*. Routledge, 2014.

19  Wiggins, Grant P and Jay. McTighe. *Understanding by Design*. Association for Supervision and Curriculum Development, 2008.

20  Manzini, Ezio. *Design, When Everybody Designs: An Introduction to Design for Social Innovation*. Translated by Rachel Coad, The MIT Press, 2020.

21  Azer, Daisy et al. *Design Thinking for the Greater Good: Innovation in the Social Sector*. Columbia University Press, 2017.

22  Mortensen, Chris and Edward N Zalta. "Change and Inconsistency." *The Stanford Encyclopedia of Philosophy*, 2020, https://plato.stanford.edu/archives/spr2020/entries/change/.

23  Barad, Karen Michelle and Duke University Press. *Meeting the Universe Halfway Quantum Physics and the Entanglement of Matter and Meaning*. Duke University Press, 2007. https://ezproxy.lib.monash.edu.au/login?url=http://dx.doi.org/10.1215/9780822388128.

24  Ramos, Fabiane and Laura Roberts. "Wonder as Feminist Pedagogy: Disrupting Feminist Complicity with Coloniality." *Feminist Review*, vol. 128, no. 1, 2021, pp. 28–43, doi:10.1177/01417789211013702.

25  Haraway, Donna. "Situated Knowledges: The Science Question in Feminism and the Privilege of Partial Perspective." *Feminist Studies*, vol. 14, no. 3, 1988, pp. 575–99.

26  Riessman, Catherine Kohler. *Narrative Analysis*. Sage Publications, 1993.

27  St Pierre, Elizabeth Adams. "Methodology in the Fold and the Irruption of Transgressive Data." *International Journal of Qualitative Studies in Education*, vol. 10, no. 2, 1997, pp. 175–89, doi:10.1080/095183997237278.

28  "Methodology." *Te Ataarangi*, 2011, www.teataarangi.org.nz/?q=about-te-ataarangi/methodology.

# 2

# AUTOMATED FUTURES, SOCIAL CHANGE AND FOREVER LEARNING FRAMING THE RESEARCH

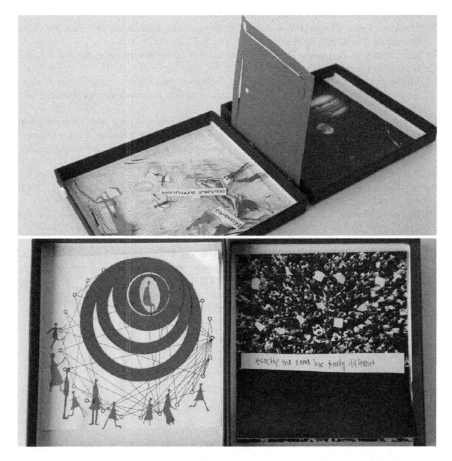

FIGURE 2.1 **Orienting Learning Dioramas**: These carefully crafted dioramas are a ruminating orientation activity conceived to invite participants to set learning intentions (Narrative 8.1). A social space for individually wondering where-I-am-today alongside where-I-hope-to-travel opens a space for speculation, creates connection and honours plural perspectives.

DOI: 10.4324/9780429429743-3

## 2.1 Why Transformative Learning

If you read the preface, and I am not assuming you have, then you already know that the case for this book could be laid out in relation to the broader techno- logical and economic trends in how we work and learn. The visible signals that education is no longer something you do in preparation for a lifetime of work in a single field is evident in the gig economy, the statistics around how often people change jobs and the received wisdom that people will have many careers over the decades.[1] The rise in automation of cognitive and physical labour and advances artificial intelligence correlate to these changes. These technological trends have underscored the need to reskill one-third of the world's workforce by 2030, according to the World Economic Forum. WEF has called for a 'reskilling revolution',[2] and with the onset of the fourth industrial revolution, the focus is now on those skills perceived to be less easily acquired by artificial intelligence and machine learning.[3]

When we interlace these two converging trends, the calls for continuous, just-in-time or life-long learning intersect with the calls to pivot away from core subject-specific literacies. This convergence future-proofs competencies that prioritise people learning and encourages critical and creative learning, solving complex problems and working collaboratively.[4] The practices in this book bring to the fore specific expertise: transdisciplinarity, design mindset, sense-making, social intelligence and novel and adaptive thinking that, in 2011, were projected be key work skills by 2020 (7). Yet, even if the naming of the competencies are slippery, there is a consistency to the underscoring of social and emotional skills in support of leadership and collaboration; creativity for complex problem solv- ing and innovation. Together, the economic and technological disruptions have employers more explicitly interviewing for the attributes that signal a person's capacity for intentional learning (8). In education, this might be accounted for as character attributes like curiosity and grit (9). But in professional practice, this looks like companies valuing humility and ownership as twin virtues (10) or assessing a person's capacity to be self-aware and proactive as evidence they

1   A report from the Future of Young Australians opens with the now familiar observation "By 2030, automation, globalisation and flexibility will change what we do in every job. We ur- gently need to prepare young people with the work smart skills they will need most". The report frames work smart skills as equal parts smart learning, smart thinking and smart doing. Alongside the call for an entrepreneurial mindset, the report argues that workers will spend one-third of their day learning on the job (1, p. 7).

2   The World Economic Forum declared a reskilling emergency in 2020 by claiming that one billion people, one-third of the world's jobs, will need to reskill by 2030 (2).

3   This research brief from MIT critiques the robots-are-coming-for-your-jobs narrative while acknowledging the import of governments and institutions preparing for and supporting the transition and disruptions that comes with artificial intelligence (3).

4   From World Economic Forum, to learning technology providers, to academic research there are countless reports, blog posts and books that might all use different language yet consistently speak to themes to highlight a shift towards a learning-integrated life (4; 5; 6).

will have the insight and motivation to keep up with ever-changing work ex-pectations (11). The many drivers for change have led schools, universities and workplaces to the shared conclusion that learning how to learn is an invaluable attribute for students, graduates, workers and employers.

Beyond the capitalist case for workforce readiness, there is an alternative pressing argument for the timeliness of this book. Let's assume for a moment that learning is bigger than the idea of work-readiness. We can then see a child's in-stinctive curiosity, the meaning-making of our adult brains, and our storytelling impulses as playful, interpretative, social orientations to learning in everyday life. Beyond formal education, we learn from the behaviour patterns that our families of origin model for us, the scripts we absorb from media and the lessons we inter-nalise from politics. As citizens, our minds are colonised in small and substantive ways from our daily interactions with society. Over time, our interior selves, i.e., our mental models, beliefs, scripts and values, come to shape our lived-in know-ing and internalise our perceived sense of agency.

Anyone who has failed to adopt new behaviour that would improve their own wellbeing or the health of the planet (which is everyone) knows transformative learning cannot be achieved with a cognitive realisation alone. It can be hard for us to make positive choices even when they have a direct impact on our own lives (like doing more steps) or to unlearn habituated behaviour (like sneezing into our hands instead of our elbows). As effective as it can be, the contribution of design explored here is not the techno-rational designs that motivate people to up their step count or the instructional designs that teach people COVID-19 hygiene practices. As hard as learning new behaviour is, the complex work of transforming mindsets and mental models involves a different magnitude of dif-ficulty. The question becomes how design can support the transdisciplinary work of unlearning scripts our unconscious holds on to, or intentionally shifting be-liefs that form part of our identity or interrogating the oppressive and destructive structures society upholds. If you are familiar with the iceberg model of systems thinking, then envisage that the focus on individual mindsets and collective mental models sit below patterns of behaviour, below systems structures. We are attending here to the very bottom of the iceberg, the place where, arguably, change can have the greatest leverage to transform what lies above (12).

It is critical to note that a caveat to this focus on interior work, is to under-score that there be no naive assumption that the shift work of revising internal scripts or letting go of obsolete mental models can alone transform the societal norms of our everyday. People do not equally have the power to change their external circumstances and this work must be understood as mutually implicated by the dominant structures, emerging patterns and episodic events also at play.[5]

---

5 **Sean**: The iceberg model reference is problematic to the extent that although it helps reveal what is not visible, the implication that the mindsets and mental models sit below the structures and systems does not make evident enough the extent the oppressive weight of what is further up the iceberg. Your caveat goes some way to underscoring the need for us to recognise that

The more urgent learning this research might inform is how we un/learn mental models of consumption so we might create new mental models for living sustainably.[6] The more challenging lessons might come from surfacing scripts of bias and privilege to transform our actions and advocacy with respect to racial equity. The harder shift might be reframing our beliefs around punishment and restitution to design systems and services for restorative justice. Learning from Indigenous communities' relational knowing or ancient contemplative practices will require us to surface what we already believe so we can consciously let go of old ways of acting to forge new ways of being (14; 15; 16).

Although the projects share a focus on the individual and their immediate learning community, the work of learning operates in a world of interdependent systems and structures. The practices might not be system change initiatives, but they work with a theory of change that believes that shifts in individual and community thinking can contribute to the dismantling of the structures that might limit our sense of collective agency and self-determination. In this way, these practices understand that the job of substantive, sustained change will never be complete. This is the ongoing work of policymakers and activists, scientists and storytellers. But it is also the work of designers. Or, at least it can be. Transformative learning theory respects that the pathway to change draws on rational and extra-rational troubling of the original perspective. To take better care of each other and of our planet, we need cognitive, affective and creative learning practices to understand the structures; biases and injustices, to feel the rage and oppression and grief, to channel hope, imagination and new tomorrows. Design is positioned here as an animating force that can contribute to the infinite project of navigating change. To do this work properly, we need to acknowledge the situated and subjective contexts, be attentive to positionality and relationality and embrace plural, diverse orientations to knowing.

## 2.2 Locating the Research

This book and the design projects within it share a theoretical perspective. Teaching and learning is understood here through theories of social constructivism which underscore the importance of the social interactions and artefacts of a group that support learning (17, pp. 3–14). Within the practice examples, there is a relational approach to questioning how we might design learning encounters

---

changing mindsets is not a project done in isolation. Approaching this from the opposite angle, my research wonders how attuning to the systems and structures can change mindsets.

6  **Desiree**: From an Indigenous perspective, I think it is critical to not reduce this to a question of mental models alone. To move to a place of living sustainably, we need to privilege place over people. My Ph.D. explores how a decolonising critical co-design methodology can support the privileging of Indigenous knowledge and with that biocultural diversity (13). **Lisa**: This links to Mississauga Nishnaabeg academic Leanne Betasamosake Simpson's idea that her people relate to land through connection. She shares an Indigenous practice of connection as "generative, affirmative, complex, overlapping and non-linear relationship" (14, p. 725).

by seeing designing and learning as always in conversation with the people, place and materials of a situation. The emphasis on transformation further brings into focus the psycho-social orientation to engage with what is happening at an intra-personal and inter-personal level for the learners. The kind of learning being designed here is more about belonging than behaviour, more about motivation and mindset than the activities and artefacts.

In undertaking this research, I came to question whether a book can apply transformative learning principles of engagement. Conventions of situating theory, documenting practice and sharing strategies support reading as a passive mode of knowledge acquisition. But can a humble book privilege transformative learning over transmissive or transactional learning? (18) For an experience to be perspective-shifting, it often begins with a 'disorienting dilemma' (19) and requires a certain level of desirable difficulty (20) for learning to stick (21). Knowing this, how might reading material prompt reader interactions that are productively disorienting, difficult and discursive? I began to wonder if narrative inquiry could help to situate learning as always nested in the individual, the social and community contexts (22).

The methodology of this book explores ways to be generative and improvisational, iterative and novel – akin to the disposition of many of the research case studies within the book. The ontological decision to resist the presentation of a tidy set of tools opens up space for a plurality of voices. From auto-ethnographic first-person accounts, to interviews with practitioners and sidebar conversations with colleagues, the text deploys narrative inquiry as its chosen methodology for finding out more about the embodied, material and mediated activity of practice (22). Inquiring through narrative allows life lessons to be expressed not just as data to be analysed but as felt experiences to be heard and respected (23). Creating a space where I could be in reflexive conversation with my emotions, dreams and other sensory experiences affords a new sensorial practice of sense-making that allows me to confound any belief in the 'evidentiary warrant' that legitimises the production of academic knowledge (23, p. 177). New ways of learning and unlearning become animated by the decision to stay with the story. By not defaulting to abstractions, an opening emerges whereby author and reader get to read and react through narratives of learning. The conversational structure is, however, about more than collecting stories of practice. Giving voice to first person, conflicting, subjective, critical positions is also a prototypical exploration of story-making as a social, creative, generative, sense-making practice. In sharing encounters that have transformed me, I recognise the story does more than reveal myself to you. I also discovered myself (24).

Refuting the promise of one reality, the design theories that emerge from the subjective narratives resist a strong provable theory, instead putting out into the world statements intended to be emergent, generative and negotiated. The research from cognitive and social psychology is not to be considered in isolation. The evidence-based learning science principles highlighted in Part II recognise the plethora of independent variables that influence a students' cognitive and emotional capacity to learn. These research findings might discredit a designer or educators' assumptions. Given real learning does not happen in a controlled environment, the science needs to be complemented with design's capacity to hold space for multiple interdependent variables. The empirical studies are intentionally juxtaposed with practice narratives and different worldviews to foreground the entangled social and personal context of learning. Tracing a line between Indigenous peoples' relationship to the land, human and non-human actors and psychology's understanding of social belonging and human connection, is one example of how diverse perspectives bumping up against each other might shift our understanding of relationality and learning (25). Folding the scientific data in with the provisional, contingent entanglements of design projects ensure the situated context is interpreted, not erased (26).

The elements and agents (human and otherwise) at the heart of designing for engaged learning cannot be reduced to simple scripts or prescribed activities. There is instead a theoretical shade tent floating over the material, relational and epistemic processes that comprise these provisional practices. The frameworks offered in each section, from key principles to figuring diagrams to conceptual metaphors, present tentative sketches of ideas always being critically re-examined. This final manuscript does not represent a fixing of my position any more than the prototype that goes into production is the ultimate solution to an adaptive situation.

Similarly, the case study projects and practice stories shared in the following chapters do not pretend to be exemplary. The playful experiential moves, the considered co-creation and the critical practitioner reflections are worthy of examination not because they lead to the 'right' solution but because they accept the feedback loops of practice that must be perpetually rethought and reconfigured. There is a pragmatism in each project for working with the situation, negotiating the constraints and making a move anyway (27). Echoing the sense-making of designing, the content is guided by questions of what would be useful for the reader, how reader engagement might be rewarded and how fellow contributors could be motivated to join the conversation.

Adjacent perspectives give voice to educators working in other spaces, designers with different backgrounds, practitioners engaging with different cultural contexts or researchers with alternate disciplinary values. In holding space for plurality, there is also recognition that there can be no generalisable framework. The theorising from the practice narratives and the conceptual and figurative frameworks grounded in design practice reflect the emergent premise of an abductive form of inquiry. The conviction here is not to code practitioner stories or my own past experiences to present the data as answers. The invitation is to chase abductive leaps across multiple data points so we might better make sense of what is being socially constructed and explore what is possible. The insights revealed through the practitioner case studies shape the *Making Design* constellation in Part II (Figure 4.3), that is reimagined again in Part IV (Figure 13.2). Yet, this constellation retrospectively shifted the language of Part I and is continuously confounded by the epistemic narratives that attune to affect in ways the case studies cannot. There is no linear process, positivist belief or clear methodological triangulation to declare "the data tells us" this. There is instead an informed, intuitive backtalk that scans and sense-makes through and across the theory, the practice, the stories and the frameworks. This interactive process evolves in parallel with the practice vignettes and the principles highlighted in last two parts of the book. The design theorising makes explicit that this holistic practice is equal parts cognitive, embodied, emotional and social. The relational, multi-modal methods for interpreting practice embrace an iterative process of framing, narrating, positioning, sensing, theorising, evaluating, starting over and, of course, unlearning.

In design research, we can understand the performative, creative process (28) of dialogic listening[7] as one of 'attuning' to the data. In the same way, the designer attunes to how someone interacts with a prototype or participates in a workshop, the sense-making within the book follows a disciplined attuning to embodied tales from the past, experiential stories of the present and imagining what this means for potential futures.[8]

## 2.3 Positioning the Researcher

Starting from a place of positioning the book's theoretical perspective and methodology is one way to situate the orientation of this book. Yet, the positions we claim are more than academic. Part of the process for transformative shifts comes from a place of critical introspection and self-awareness for what you as a person bring to a situation. A premise laid out in this book is that mindsets, beliefs and mental models shape our habits, behaviour and actions. Furthermore, our life experiences, (un)conscious biases, colonised minds and long-held values are reflected in how we show up in the world. The idea that transformation is wedded to holistic or whole-self learning recognises the reality that to shift how we live and act in the world is unlikely to be a solely cognitive act. To engage in the hard work of teaching others to examine their interior selves, we must first and foremost begin with ourselves.[9]

---

7   **Dion**: This interplay can lead to a greater respect for the story and the people telling those stories. According to Bakhtin, dialogical 'listening' requires three voices: the narrator; the theoretical framework which provides the concepts and tools for interpretation and the reflexive monitoring of the act of reading and interpretation (29). This last voice bears 'witness' to the storytelling, honing a self-awareness of the decision process that draws knowledge and meaning from the materials.

8   **Kelly**: The multiple interdependent variables and data points surfaced by a learning encounter can simultaneously leave a researcher paralysed by what to attend to. However, if the goal is to see, analysis is to capture the complexities of lived experiences in ways that value accessibility and respect emotions in the filters shift. The analysis phase can then be one of opening up new ways of seeing and broadening our collective understanding (30).

9   **Lisa**: Designers Yoko Akama, Penny Hagen and Desna Whaanga-Schollum (31) speak directly to this question of positionality in the social innovation sector, specifically when working with

I love the Māori word *turangawaewae*. The literal translation is 'the place where I stand', but it also speaks to one's relation to the land and to ancestors. You could say that a person's *turangawaewae* is not only reduced to the place where they are from but more holistically to the place where they belong. A complement to the previous section on positioning methodology the following candid introduction to the worlds I come from is generative for me to own, just as it might be productive for you to question your own positionality. Occasionally, my identity as an Indigenous woman from the global south defines my place in a room, on other days I hold all the power as the privileged white Dean from a top design school in the United States. On a rare day, those two selves collide. There are days I experience the marginalisation that comes with being the only woman on the stage and daring to talk about affect and emotions, other days I am the veteran educator aware that my expertise was shaped too long ago by a time and place that no longer exists. Plural voices are not something that happens just within a design workshop or the footnotes of this book. Multitudes live within us. Declaring my lived experiences as a learner, educator and designer is another way to declare the epistemic and ontological values that shape this book's research orientation. The positioning also extends an invitation to the reader to understand their own distinct stance and bring some explicit knowing to what we oftentimes only tacitly understand.

The biographical introduction to follow helps situate the auto-ethnographic[10] texts I share throughout the book. Introducing these multiple, oftentimes competing selves helps to make sense of why I am drawn to work across multiple research paradigms, to engage with designing as a research practice and to embrace multiple ways of knowing. Stacy Holman Jones, my colleague, would extend the ambition of the narratives, seeing a critical auto-ethnographic practice as a way

---

people of colour and Indigenous communities. In recognising that a white subject may not see how they move through the world, Akama and colleagues discuss what it means to disclose one's personhood as an act of accountability. Citing Sarah Ahmed's provocation that a white subject, ignorant of their own complicity, "by seeing their whiteness, might not see themselves participating in whiteness in the same way" (32, p. 179). The authors' call for a reflexivity, especially when the work is proximal and familiar, to turn the critical gaze towards ourselves and the worldviews we hold. Seeking to learn from the authors' performance in the paper to model accountability, I have rehearsed this new form of positionality in this section.

10  **Stacy**: Your commitment to include auto-ethnographic texts as a mode of positioning yourself in relation to design and learning practices is a way of, to use feminist philosopher Donna Haraway's phrase, 'becoming with'. Making room for – indeed, embracing – our personal stake and perspectives in design, learning and social innovation requires a commitment to bringing ourselves to our work and to each other in a process of becoming-with: other people, to be sure, but also other species, "things", environments and ways of thinking, making and doing. I like to think of auto-ethnography as a way of – again in Haraway's words – 'making kin' with the beings, objects, ecologies and epochs in which with live with the explicit purpose of co-existing in more compassionate, expansive and just ways (33).

"to embody and materialize the change we seek in ourselves and our lives" (34, p. 235).[11]

I am a Māori woman, of *Ngāti Kahungunu* descent. My mother's Pasifika ancestors came to Aotearoa on the waka (canoe), '*Tākitimu*', at the beginning of the last millennium. I am also a *Pākehā* woman, of Anglo-Saxon descent. My mother's ancestors came to New Zealand in the 1800s on a ship called the *Adelaide*. To look at me, you would believe the second story over the first, and you would rightly guess that my Father's ancestors are also very white. Although my most cherished childhood book was the well-worn *Māoriland Fairy Tales* and my teenage self proudly claimed my connection to legendary Māori activist Whina Cooper, it was not until university that I was meaningfully introduced to *Māoritanga* (culture). The fortune of having Jonathan Mane-Wheoki as a mentor and other Māori *kaumātua* (elders) as my guides allowed me to navigate a way into a world that was resoundingly unfamiliar yet strangely like coming home. My main memory of that period in my life was walking confidently into a Māori professor's office looking for answers that would help me come up with a visual dictionary of Māori symbols that would help avert cultural appropriation by *Pākehā* designers. I came in looking for answers. I had righteously entered the room, assured my white settler ideas of how we might categorise knowledge into tidy boxes would serve Māori and impress this professor. I remember my extreme frustration as the elder told me stories about my ancestors for an hour. I recall my impatience with his parable about grandchildren looking for answers in the wrong place. I wanted him to get to the point, to give me the information I was looking for, while realising on some level that his story was his point.

At the time, I could not see beyond my perception that his anecdotal tale was opaque and inconsequential. There was a cognitive dissonance that came with this professor intentionally not telling me where I could find the answers I was looking for. Mezirow would call this a 'disorienting dilemma'. A part of me sensed he was trying to teach me something. The child who grew up with Māori fables recognised these seemingly tangential stories were not vectors into nowhere but instead traces of inquiry curving inwards. If I could decode his anecdotes, I could answer questions I was not yet asking. Yet, I felt in that moment thwarted by the obtuse narrative and indignant of the work being asked of me left me. Decades later, I no longer recognise my 21-year-old self. It is hard to remember a time when I might wrestle with knowledge, ownership and respect being entangled. Today, when I participate in this kind of conversation, I would not experience it as a new way of knowing. I have fully internalised the

---

11 **Hannah**: Another dimension to the relevance of the narrative is if we understand the co-design activities of these learning encounters as not only the result of the reflective and negotiative "back-talk" between materials and an ever-shifting external context, but as also significantly shaped by the personal experiences of the designer. For then, attending to how the personal is in conversation with the preparation of co-design materials and methods can be an additional, crucial site of inquiry for reflexive practitioner-researchers.

critical, creative value of analogous storylines, subjective knowing and metaphoric thinking. I came to learn to not pre-determine the answer I was seeking; I got comfortable swimming in ambiguity. I have come to respect oral storytelling traditions as learning/knowing modalities for inquiry and translation. The narrative inquiry woven here represents the hard work of attuning to and interpreting my own stories and the stories of others as a critical meaning-making strategy for sitting with the shifts that are being asked of me and asked of my practice.

But I will forever need to work on unlearning my impulse to put things into boxes – because I am also my Father's daughter. I was raised by a philosophical father who loved conversations about ethics and compassion well into the small hours of the evening. Working in universities for decades, I have been surrounded by people who privilege cognitive intelligence over other forms of knowing. I can be seduced by the allure of empirical research and the intellectual acrobats required to work with other disciplines. I am drawn to propose frameworks that organise knowing into tidy parcels, even though I resist the deductive logic of hypothesis testing or the transferability argument that underpins calls for reproducibility. When I spend hours diagramming and labelling conceptual frameworks to make sense of multiple realities, I remember with affection the misguided 21-year-old who believed a visual dictionary was the solution. Coming of age in academic communities where who you cite and who cites you is more important than the social impact of your work is good training for asking critical questions, chasing rigour and interrogating assumptions. However, it is also a culture that fosters intellectual hubris. I am a researcher drawn to work in transdisciplinary collaborations; I am therefore a pragmatist. A consistent thread through decades of practice is to make the contribution of design known to other disciplines by exploring what methods are adaptable, what knowing is transferable and what design dispositions are learnable. Working with other disciplines asks of me to practice disciplinary humility and methodological generosity, accepting that the ontology of the collaboration will usually be determined by the dominant research paradigm. Still, I am not encouraging the designer researcher to be deferential to the quantitative paradigm. I believe in explicitly advocating for how creative methodologies, contingent methods and reflexive practice moves might complement the contribution of other disciplines.

This transdisciplinary commitment, grounded in a belief that the world's systemic challenges cannot be solved by one discipline alone, has led me to notice and attend to what rigour and new knowing looks like in a social practice of designing. As a student, I was more fascinated by the creative act of designing than the designed artefact. As a designer, I am more focused on how people experience an encounter than on the material props and prompts that stimulate engagement. As a researcher, I am paying attention to how I collaborate with partners and how the facilitation of the workshop is going in real time. Mine is a people-centred, relational practice of designing. My Fine Art Masters typographically played with incomplete sentences that asked the viewer to complete the unspoken conversation. My practice-based design PhD played with the tension between the speculative move of not knowing yet designing anyway and the grounded move to temporarily fix things to see what might be emerging. In a practice I called 'figuring', I used uncertain diagrams to draw the audience into navigating with me the push and pull between the known and the not-yet-known. Throughout my career as a design researcher, I have chosen to explicitly toggle between the pragmatic and the speculative, the grounded and the abstract, the material and the experiential. I hold dear the epistemic belief that there is a generative, productive slippage that comes with owning plural, subjective realities. This book takes the position that creativity operates at the nexus between the real and the not-yet-real, between this point of view and that alternate perspective, between the probable and the possible, between your truth and mine. This belief that we should inhabit the space betwixt and between the confines of disciplinary knowing also shows up in the catholic approach to theory that has citations from neuroscience, feminism and social psychology co-mingling in the same chapter.

My educator self also embraces the reciprocal exchange built into the interplay between learning and teaching. For almost three decades, I have taught in higher education and yet I have been a learner for longer. My position on education is largely informed by critiques of my own education. I was expelled from kindergarten because I was bored, and I loved my primary school teacher who made every subject an art class. I studied hard enough at high school and university to get good grades, only to forget the name of the units, the faces of the teachers or anything I wrote or read. Yet, I recall every assignment that required some kind of haptic engagement, a creative move on my part, any learning activity that asked me to take a risk. Sometimes the risk was intellectual (taking an oppositional position), other times emotionally vulnerable (putting my work out for critique), and other times technically challenging (trying something for the first time). The social construct and experiential orientation of studio learning led me to embrace the creative leap of learning. I believe that what keeps me focused, committed and inquisitive is starting at a place of emergence, rather than towards a place of certainty. I bring this unrelenting curiosity to my teaching practice. I began teaching in higher education at a young age and I often designed learning in reaction to what felt missing in the mentor-driven, authoritative, mastery art school model of learning design that I experienced. My early years were focused on how to drive a more student-centred, peer learning approach to pedagogy and a more interdisciplinary approach to curriculum. My leadership roles over the decades had me imagining new degree pathways, introducing research programs in design, reframing how we might design the design school for this century (35). Yet, beyond the large organisational change and field-building projects I have undertaken, I weigh the small moves that happen in the design studio as most important. I recall the shared revelation that came with the first time I asked a student to sketch their motivation through the arc of a project. I remember how long it took to get students to stop designing for what they believed I wanted. I came to know the why, what and the how of scaffolding for a class to build capacity to become excellent peer critics. The systems, the policies, the curriculum were an important part of the institutional shift work that needs to be done, but my deepest personal investment was always in the inter- and intra-personal work of peer-to-peer learning.

I could further introduce my queer self, my feminist self to explain the commitment to deviate from conventional disciplinary confines or to acknowledge the citational politics of including writers beyond the white male canon. I do know that my disposition to be a natural-born storyteller, a maker of frames, an embracer of change and a lover of metaphors also shapes how I author this text. No doubt even my middle-child, middle-aged, middle-class self is part of the story.[12] However, I lead with my ancestry, my vocation, my relation to place and people, as they situate the teacher, researcher and learner I am. I am a cultural product of the internalised learning, the lost learning and the unlearning that comes with my Indigenous ancestry and white settler class privileges from time spent in educational contexts in Aotearoa New Zealand, Australia, United States and India. It is this positionality that draws me to prototype the theorising of design in ways that resist the abstraction and quantification of what is known or knowable. Instead, I value attuning stories, competing positions and provisional frameworks that invite us to sit with the emergence, the situated-ness and the uncertainty inherent to a social practice of design.

To conclude, I want to acknowledge the generational and citizenship luck that means free higher education was not an election dream but an enshrined policy for me. Earning four post-graduate qualifications without accruing student debt has been the most extraordinary of privileges. I have often been aware that this fortune granted me choices in the world that similarly curious, dedicated learners did not have access to. For this, I am forever grateful and take seriously the reciprocal exchange of what I owe in return. The very idea of questioning how to give back to a field that needs to radically critique its own contribution to the climate crisis, decolonisation and mindless consumption has to be part of the equation.

In founding WonderLab, a doctoral learning community at Monash University, I was drawn to the word 'wonder'. A single word that spoke to being doubtful and in awe, to being curious and to pondering, to being lost for words and to eyes wide open. This most primary of emotions made me think of how my ancestors travelling on the *waka Takitimu* (canoe) across the Pacific centuries ago experienced wonder, as it did lead me to question how wonder can travel with me to craft new futures. Yet, even as we might optimistically see wonder as being the opening up of possibilities, we must also use wonder critically. For as Ahmed reminds us "wonder means learning to see the world as something that does not have to be" (36, p. 180).

---

12 **Stacy**: The primary assumption that undergirds all auto-ethnography is that personal experience is onto-epistemological. Ontological in that our senses, perceptions, embodiments constitute how we understand ourselves, other people and beings and our worlds and present us with particular challenges and privileges; epistemological in that we learn in relation to these others through our experiences.

In writing this book, I have defined four qualities of wondering: The wondering sparked by newness, a response to what is unfamiliar; the wondering that comes from being set adrift, the questioning that comes with being untethered and in doubt; the wondering that comes with resonance, a pattern-seeking urge to trace connections and lastly, the wonderous epiphany, the mind-body moment of awe when we sense a shift in perception and perspective. Together, these acts of wondering of getting lost and finding our way home are at the heart of how we make sense of the world, how we learn new ways of knowing-doing-being.

WonderLab operates on a social contract whereby our 'individual-shared wonderings', (37) seek to ethically contribute to our fields in exchange for our subsidised education. As one person, my scope is limited, my perspective partial, therefore I am indebted to the broader design research community whose work addresses the racial and gender equity, ethical and environmental sustainability and social justice work that is part of our collective project. Above all, I am grateful for how the informed and impassioned perspectives of my WonderLab peers, both PhD candidates and supervisors, travel beside me. With every sense, this book is better for bringing my everyday WonderLab conversations into the text. Working with my collaborators on the footnotes was a rewarding and apt way for this community to ask more of me, more of design and more of education. If you are curious to know the people joining me in the footnotes, they are WonderLabbers: Alli Edwards, Dion Tuckwell, Hannah Korsmeyer, Kate Coleman, Kelly Anderson, Myfanwy Doughty, Myriam Diatta, Ricardo Dutra Gonçalves, Sean Donahue, Sonali Ojha, Stacy Holman Jones and Yi Zhang, with special guest appearance by Christopher Patten.

The cynicism I felt standing outside only hours earlier was replaced by a deep sense of humility and wonder when I left that night. My 30-minute commute home gave me time to get curious about what had happened. If it's true, as Roger evoked, that "the way we play is the way we are", I could see I needed to deeply examine the cost of being so risk-averse, so cynical, so in my head, so un-attuned to my body. When I walked in the door, my partner bemusedly asked how my improv class had gone. I answered that I would never again see that the design I had been taught was an embodied practice. I shared that being asked to check in with my body, my feelings and my impulses had shifted my perspective on everything I thought I knew about learning. I dramatically declared that from this experience I would become a different person.[13]

13 **Lisa**: More than remember it, that evening shifted the trajectory of my design, teaching and research practice. Roger and I went on to run a design studio together, where he hosted the Play Gym and together we explored embodied learning and transforming mindsets (Narrative 12.1). The onto-epistemological shift in this tale is one where the secret of transformation lies in the act of repetition, of showing up and doing the hard work. If the Aotearoa narrative changed my mental model overnight, my embracing of embodied learning was years in the making. This Monday night evening class was simply the seed. Every time I engaged, I had to remember the energising, challenging, uncomfortable giddy feeling in my body to over-ride my intellectual impulse to negate the experience. Slowly, the aggregate moves led to unsettling old internalised habits that no longer served me.

## Narrative 2.1 Embodied Wondering: Performing and Becoming

### 2012 – with Roger Manix

*I am standing outside a classroom at Parsons, ready to enter a professional development workshop on how to teach collaboration. I have not come hoping to learn anything about collaboration. I am here because I am curious about the guy, Roger Manix, running the workshop. My students have had sessions with him and although incapable of finding words for what happens or why the sessions are so powerful, I am struck by their collective awe for what happens in his classroom. Somehow, Roger has managed to engage the thinker, the performer, the introvert and the maker in a workshop focused on play. Standing outside, I push down my anxiety and instead brandish my cynicism. I might be here voluntarily, but I am deeply wary that improv might be involved. Still, I am compelled to understand how work that seems so terrifying to me could somehow resonate for the whole student body.*

*My worst fears are realised within minutes of the class starting. Roger is getting us to play some kind of performative game to get our energy up. I fail to suppress my eye-rolling. The warm-up is over and Roger asks us to check in with our bodies. He asks how we are physically feeling, whether we are more awake, more ready to learn. I do not remember what happened next. The activity in the room fades into the background, the chatter quietens. In decades of institutionalised learning no one had ever asked me to check in with my body or even questioned whether I am ready to learn. I feel a sense of agitated consternation. Decades of being in educational institutions and no one has ever explicitly wondered how I am feeling. My disembodied, cynical self contests my felt, surprised observation that my body and mind are in fact more alert.*

Many activities that Monday night were distressingly awkward. My colleagues wilfully jumped in while I reluctantly held back. Still, almost a decade later, I remember the convulsive laughing (Figure II.1). I remember feeling present. I felt the opposite of checked out, bored or disinterested. I was exquisitely bewildered, but I was engaged.

*Toward the end of the session, we play a game that involves a person, 'Kitty', repeatedly and politely walking around a large circle asking people to swap places with her. The people being asked can only say "no," Beyond Kitty's peripheral vision, people in the circle are silently swapping places. When Kitty is fast enough, she can jump into a vacant spot and just like musical chairs the last person standing becomes the new Kitty. I quickly read this game as all about strategy. Calculating the right time to swap places easily minimises my risk, ensuring I never need to endure being Kitty. As the game drags on I watch colleagues make crazy last-minute dashes across the circle and inevitably get caught. It is beyond my comprehension that they cannot be more strategic, less impulsive. I am convinced that because I am yet to be Kitty, I am 'winning'. The game drags on. When the rules change, and we are now allowed to say "yes" when Kitty asks to trade places, I am bored enough to tentatively say yes and relive every school gym nightmare. Eventually someone stumbles, I get to grab a spot in the circle. The anxious beating heart is suddenly overwhelmed with the giddy, joyful relief of being safe again.*

*At the end of each activity, Roger sits with us on the floor to debrief the play. The "tell me, tell me..." prompt is prefaced with a stream of questions, an invitation to tell him: why are we doing it, what did we learn, what came up for us? It is clear to me that Kitty is about strategy, non-verbal communication and risks. To communicate this, I offer the example of a guy who I couldn't even chance looking at given because he was taking such great risks.*

*The guy looks at me incredulously. Genuinely perplexed, he asks, "What was the risk?"*

*There are no words to express how exposed I feel.*

*One minute ago, I smugly believed I had nailed the game. It was self-evident that being Kitty was the risk. Until his question, it had never crossed my mind that people might enjoy being Kitty. Roger nudges me to reflect on what it might feel like to let go of the assumption that being Kitty for five minutes would be losing. What might it feel like to exchange my tense, focused, anxious, risk-averse strategy for the playful, teamwork, empathic, risk-embracing game play embraced by many of my peers?*

## Bibliography

1 "The New Work Smarts: Thriving in the New Work Order." Foundation for Young Australians, Report, July 2017, www.fya.org.au/wp-content/uploads/2017/07/FYA_TheNewWorkSmarts_July2017.pdf.

2 "Reskilling Revolution." *World Economic Forum*, 2020, www.reskillingrevolution2030.org.

3 Malone, Thomas et al. "Artificial Intelligence and the Future of Work." Research Brief, 17 December 2020, workofthefuture.mit.edu/research-post/artificial-intelligence-and-the-future-of-work.

4 "Schools of the Future: Defining New Models of Education for the Fourth Industrial Revolution." World Economic Forum, Report, 14 January 2020, www3.weforum.org/docs/WEF_Schools_of_the_Future_Report_2019.pdf.

5 "The Future of Lifelong Learning: Designing for a Learning-Integrated Life." D2L Corporation, White Paper, 20 January 2020, www.d2l.com/wp-content/uploads/2020/02/Future-of-Lifelong-Learning-D2L-2020-Digital-Edition.pdf.

6 Bellanca, James A. and Ronald S. Brandt. *21st Century Skills: Rethinking How Students Learn*. Solution Tree Press, 2010.

7 Fidler, Devin. "Future Skills: Update and Literature Review." Institute for the Future for ACT Foundation and The Joyce Foundation, July 2016.

8 Christensen, Lisa et al. "The Most Fundamental Skill: Intentional Learning and the Career Advantage." *McKinsey Quarterly*, 7 August 2020.

9 "Step Outside." *Character Lab*, 2021, characterlab.org/tips-of-the-week/step-outside.

10 Friedman, Thomas L. "How to Get a Job at Google." *New York Times*, 22 February 2014.

11 Zhuo, Julie. "How to Impress an Interviewer: The Two Traits That Speak Most to Future Potential." *Medium*, 23 April 2015.

12 "Systems Thinking Resources." *The Donella Meadows Project, a project of the Academy for Systems Change*, 2021.

13 Ibinarriaga, Desiree. *Critical Co-Design Methodology: Privileging Indigenous Knowledges and Biocultural Diversity*. Deakin, 2020. http://hdl.handle.net/10536/DRO/DU:30136596

14 Simpson, Leanne Betasamosake. *As We Have Always Done: Indigenous Freedom through Radical Resistance*. Kindle ed., University of Minnesota Press, 2017.

15 "Country Centered Design." *Old Ways, New*, n.d., www.oldwaysnew.com.

16 Scharmer, C. Otto. *Theory U, Leading from the Future as It Emerges: The Social Technology of Presencing*. Berrett-Koehler, 2009.

17 Richardson, Virginia, editor. *Constructivist Teacher Education: Building a World of New Understandings*. The Falmer Press, 1997.

18 Svensson, Oskar H. et al. *Transformative, Transactional and Transmissive Modes of Teaching in Action-Based Entrepreneurial Education*, ECSB Entrepreneurship Education (3E), May 2017.

19 Dodson, Constance T. *Negotiating Disorienting Dilemmas and the Transformative Learning Process in a Complex Society*. Umi Dissertation Publishing, 2009.

20 Bjork, Elizabeth L. and Robert A. Bjork. "Making Things Hard on Yourself, but in a Good Way: Creating Desirable Difficulties to Enhance Learning." *Psychology and the Real World: Essays Illustrating Fundamental Contributions to Society*, edited by Morton A. Gersbacher et al., Worth Publishers, 2011, pp. 56–64.

21 Heath, Chip and Dan Heath. *Made to Stick: Why Some Ideas Survive and Others Die*. Random House, 2007.

22 Schatzki, Theodore R. et al. *The Practice Turn in Contemporary Theory*. Routledge, 2001.

23 St Pierre, Elizabeth Adams. "Methodology in the Fold and the Irruption of Transgressive Data." *International Journal of Qualitative Studies in Education*, vol. 10, no. 2, 1997, pp. 175–89, doi:10.1080/095183997237278.

24 Lieblich, Amia. *Narrative Research: Reading, Analysis, and Interpretation*. Sage Publications, 1998.

25 Kwaymullina, Ambelin. "Seeing the Light: Aboriginal Law, Learning and Sustainable Living in Country." *Indigenous Law Bulletin*, vol. 6, no. 11, 2005, pp. 12–15.

26 Grocott, Lisa. "Make Happen: Sense-Making the Affordances of a Practice-Based PhD in Design." *Practice-Based Design Research*, edited by Laurene Vaughan, Bloomsbury Publishing, 2017, pp. 165–74.

27 Agid, Shana. *Making Anyway: Education, Designing, Abolition*. Cultural Studies Association, 2014.

28 Grocott, Lisa and Ricardo Sosa. "The Contribution of Design in Interdisciplinary Collaborations: A Framework for Amplifying Project-Grounded Research Grocott." *Associations: Creative Practice and Research*, edited by James Oliver, Melbourne University Publishing, 2018, pp. 35–52.

29 Bakhtin, Mikhail. *The Dialogic Imagination: Four Essays*. University of Texas Press, 1981.

30 Clarke, Charlotte L et al. "A Seat around the Table: Participatory Data Analysis with People Living with Dementia." *Qualitative Health Research*, vol. 28, no. 9, 2018, pp. 1421–33, doi:10.1177/1049732318774768.

31 Akama, Yoko et al. "Problematizing Replicable Design to Practice Respectful, Reciprocal, and Relational Co-Designing with Indigenous People." *Design and Culture*, vol. 11, no. 1, 2019, pp. 59–84, doi:10.1080/17547075.2019.1571306.

32 Ahmed, Sara. *On Being Included Racism and Diversity in Institutional Life*. Duke University Press, 2012.

33 Haraway, Donna J. *Staying with the Trouble: Making Kin in the Chthulucene*. Duke University Press, 2016.
34 Holman Jones, Stacy. "Living Bodies of Thought: The "Critical" in Critical Autoethnography." *Qualitative Inquiry*, vol. 22, no. 4, 2016, pp. 228–37, doi:10.1177/1077800415622509.
35 Marshall, Tim and Lisa Grocott. *Figuring Design: Mappings of the Design Process {a Visual Essay}*, Design Perspectives: Envisioning Design for the XXI Century, 2005.
36 Ahmed, Sara. *The Cultural Politics of Emotion*. NED – New edition, 2nd ed., Edinburgh University Press, 2004.
37 Ramos, Fabiane and Laura Roberts. "Wonder as Feminist Pedagogy: Disrupting Feminist Complicity with Coloniality." *Feminist Review*, vol. 128, no. 1, 2021, pp. 28–43, doi:10.1177/01417789211013702.

# 3
# PERSPECTIVE SHIFTS AND NEW WAYS OF BEING

FIGURE 3.1  **Sense-making Materials**: A toy box of convivial tools deployed in Dion Tuckwell's *Making Space* workshop with teachers about innovating learning environments (5.2 and Figure 6.1). In these early sense-making encounters, the focus was on the allegorical potential of materials as the more-knowledgeable-other, before moving on in later workshops to teachers working with architectural plans and furniture.

DOI: 10.4324/9780429429743-4

## 3.1 Transformative Learning Literature

During the COVID-19 pandemic, it is not only teachers, facilitators and managers wondering how to create an environment that motivates and engages learners. Parents and carers home-schooling children have been drawn to consider how learners form a connection with what they are studying. Yet, education reformers have been asking similar questions for at least a century. The ideas outlined in this book synthesise many ideas seeded decades ago by educators and researchers driven to explore ways of learning that go beyond the practices of rote learning through memorisation. Friedrich Froebel, the German educator who invented kindergarten in the 1830s, understood play to be the highest expression of development (1). He believed play enables us to construct our understanding of the world. Progressive reformer Maria Montessori further pushed for a more child-centred approach to education. An early proponent of decoupling learning from accreditation, Montessori learned from the students' phrase "Help me do it by myself!" that the inner evolution of children can be stoked by scaffolding support for the self-directed learner (2). This experiential orientation is echoed in American philosopher and psychologist John Dewey's emphasis on experimentation by learning through doing. Dewey understood that all learning is social and interactive. He critiqued formal education and teacher training for encouraging passive engagement and emphasising the mastery of facts. He believed that citizens arrive at social truths by engaging in critical and intersubjective discourse. More than a century after Dewey wrote Democracy and Education, his call for an education that prepares students to be reflective, autonomous and ethical is as relevant as ever (3). However, Dewey was not solely focused on childhood education. He also had an interest in life-long learning, which was not limited to 'continuing education', whereby an adult goes in and out of periods of formal learning but centred on a paradigm shift that asked us to see learning as integral to life (4). These pioneers of progressive education call a designer's attention to consider concepts that will echo through this book. There will be a particular focus on the idea that intrinsic motivation can drive an inquiry-led approach – a whole-self, experiential orientation to support learners to make connections across subjects and into life. There are also signs in these decades-old insights that design has something critical to offer. For example, there is Froebel's reference to the materials we use to mediate play as "gifts", and Dewey's belief that knowledge comes from the impressions made upon us, claiming, "it is impossible to procure knowledge without the use of objects which impress the mind" (3, pp. 217–18). The emphasis on experimentation and hands-on learning aligns strongly with the designer's capacity for prototypical thinking and reflective conversation with the materials of a situation (5).

Design potentially has a lot to contribute to the space of formal education – from intuitive learning management systems, to the design of innovative learning environments and smart furniture. However, that work might best be served by research into the technologies, materials and affordances of user experience, spatial design and furniture than the specific context of learning. This book is more specifically framed by what design can bring to learning and how learning can inform what we design. Here, we connect design's move towards addressing wicked problems and Dewey's claims around the importance of life-long learning. This work, contextualised by the designer who increasingly engages in complex, knotty projects, often calls for system (re)design, mindset shifts and/or behavioural change. The premise of this book is that although this work might not be understood as learning in a formal education sense, there is value in design seeing the remit of this work as more complicated than a transactional behaviour nudge. The straight transmission of knowledge – to learn the right answer – is defined by its narrow quest. In contrast, it can be more transformative to take the more meandering route of helping learners' wrestle with their own assumptions so they might question the mental models they hold before engaging with new material (6, p. 18). Even when studying physics, research shows it is best to first grapple with the student's current mental representation of a law before expecting a new understanding to be internalised (7). Even then, does a new reconstruction of knowledge alone lead to acting differently? When we ask people to change the way they act or behave, the challenge is not in asking people to have shorter showers or to teach differently. Rather, the challenge lies in asking people to care enough in the change asked of them, to let go of old thinking. The challenge is in finding the motivation, to acknowledge what is getting in the way of them acting differently in the future. This is why I introduce the literature of transformative learning to introduce how designers and educators considering the dimensions of this work. This chapter introduces the theory of transformative learning with a focus on the potential affordances of design to amplify the potential of a learning experience to lead to transformation.

## 3.2 Mezirow's Transformative Learning Theory

Jack Mezirow accounts for transformative learning as "learning that transforms problematic frames of reference to make them more inclusive, discriminating, reflective, open, and emotionally able to change" (8, p. 22. Author's emphasis). From this definition, we can see the journey that Mezirow argues the learner needs to go on to come out the other end of their transformation. Mezirow understood the pathway as one that involved sequential phases – beginning with a "disorienting dilemma" (when an inner conflict surfaces for people) and ending with "reintegration" (when there is a revision of both beliefs and behaviour). This perspective transformation is supported by providing a space for ideas to be interrogated, a forum for social interactions with others going through the same process and a place for experimenting with changing practices. One way for design to make sense of the overlapping moves of transformative learning is to see the process as critical, connected and creative or for designers perhaps the more resonant alliteration might be: purposeful, participatory and prototypical.

Within the field of Education Mezirow's transformative learning theory has been the focus of many international conferences, led to the Journal of Transformative Education, is the subject of dozens of books and hundreds of scholarly papers as well as doctoral dissertations that have advanced the theory and explored the translation of theory to practice (9). Over decades, the theory of transformative learning has been critiqued and modified to incorporate new constructs for considering learning praxis in relation to various disciplines. The narrow focus here on the practical implications for, and contributions of, designing transformative learning encounters, is grounded by Mezirow's early writing, while acknowledging that Mezirow's own ideas evolved in conversation with other scholars in the field. Valerie Grabove sees that even though researchers' debate to different degrees the extent to which transformation takes a cognitive or affective path, there is a shared commitment to: "humanism, emancipation, autonomy, critical reflection, equity, self-knowledge, participation, communication, and discourse" (10, p. 90). Carolyn Clark notes that transformative moves engage with three dimensions: psychological (changes in understanding of the self), convictional (revision of belief systems) and behavioural (changes in lifestyle) (11). Here, I take the position that lifestyle change (like committing to 10,000 steps each day) can be more reductive than the more ineffable invitation to act and be in the world differently. The transformative focus here is on the shift work itself. The design emphasis then explores how affective, creative and analytic paths might converge to inspire the labour required to rewrite scripts, find motivation and shift how we show up. Showing up differently, in a collaboration for example, might well be an observable behavioural shift like delegating differently, but it could also be a mindset shift that has you reframe the success of others as a learning moment not a threat, or perhaps a subtle yet driving ontological shift to stay true to your convictions.

Transformative learning theory began with adult learning yet connects with contemporary calls for access to life-long learning and continuous education. Compared to just-in-time learning, which recognises the imperative for professional development opportunities that allow people to gain on the job training, the focus of transformative learning is on the emancipatory potential of seeing learners as agents of change. The distinction here is not that transformative learning is unrelated to workplace preparedness but that the motivations are not potentially grounded in skill acquisition. Mezirow's early ideas came from observing women returning to study who were looking for a transformation in perspective as a way to better understand events changing around them (8, p. 3). The relevance of this social orientation to engaging in perspective transformation today is in part due to the recognition that the acquisition of skills, information and knowledge does not alone empower people to drive change, fight prejudice, adapt old habits, create equitable systems or imagine a new reality. The emphasis on transformation locates the individual learner's agency at the heart of the project.

The epistemic shifts that come with noticing, sensing, figuring, grappling with and realising are integral to the practice of seeding transformation. Just as the ontological changes that emerge from a period of troubling, experiencing, experimenting, envisaging and integrating are key to settling transformation. The onto-epistemic stories I share narrate the shifts of what I come to know by reflecting on how my lived-in ways of being continue to shift my perspective and evolve over time (12).

If we seek to design learning encounters that foster this liberatory potential within citizens, we must hold front of mind the idea that transformative learning is not something done to someone else. We can explore how design materials and the design process might scaffold the surfacing, questioning and revising of current perspectives. We must critically evaluate how these materials and processes impact the realisation of the perspectives, imagining and prototyping that comes with transforming how one might act in the world. Yet, we must remember that the learner is the person doing the active transformation. The design of the encounters will be stronger for working with Robert Boyd and Gordon Myers recognition that "the journey is not for the weak nor to be travelled in isolation" (13, p. 283). In humbly understanding our position as facilitator of the learning, we can direct time towards encounters that grant a sense of agency, offer peer support and the intrinsic motivation to engage. With the goal of ensuring the learner is an equal and willing partner in the process (10). The thesis presented here is that design offers creative ways to support the reflexive, affective, cognitive and speculative process of engaging in this challenging yet rewarding journey. The *Making Design* constellation (2.0, Figures 4.1 and 13.2) proposes how design might surface by making visible, question by making sense, revise by making possible and integrate by making change.

In considering the question, "what must happen for a person to change their view of the world?" Mezirow argues that it all begins with the "disorienting dilemma" (14). The auto-ethnographic narratives speak to this concept of disorientation (or "cognitive wobble"), as James Nottingham calls it (15) – the moment someone is faced with a situation that does not fit with their beliefs. We can often find ourselves in a situation that is disorienting because it troubles our beliefs, and yet that experience can leave us only more certain of our current position.[1] The dilemma part is key here; it is when the new experience disconfirms a previous belief or, at the least, prompts us to question the worldview we currently have.

As you read in the previous narrative (Narrative 2.1), I went into Roger's improv class wary and cynical. If I had left that night still convinced there was nothing to be gained from the experience, there would be no dilemma. If, however, I keep front of mind my students' expressed value of the experience, I am primed to sit with my discomfort and attend to my bias. I might be unsettled by

---

1   **Kathryn:** This slippery space of cognitive disequilibrium interests me as practitioner-researcher and teacher in initial teacher education. With the Secondary Visual Arts and Design teachers and we have had many discussions about navigating this point in the process of inquiry. How long you can stay in the uncertainty of not knowing and unknowing before you find yourself somewhere other than where you began?

the experience, but I might find myself wondering why the space is one I chose to immediately reject. This leads to a cognitive dissonance between my beliefs and the students' experience. Consequently, maybe I attune to the physiological dimensions of the disorienting dilemma. I remember the waves of anxiety, but I also recall the experiences that invited me to move more, to laugh more. I own that I left feeling ineffably more awake, more present. My colleague, Dion Tuckwell, uses the phrase "exquisite disorientation" to recognise the affective quality of this kind of dilemma (16).[2] "Exquisite" captures the more nuanced experience of being drawn into a state of discomfort that is simultaneously painful to experience yet irresistible to ignore. I appreciate how this first phase of Mezirow's theory hints at the journey ahead, signalling the dilemma as the critical driving motivation behind what will inevitably be a felt, neurobiological and cognitive exercise. Yet, I also observe the times when the catalyst for transformation was one more of an orientation towards something, a moment of coming home. I see the potential in both an unsettling moment of disorienting, or an orientating moment of resonance. The experience of (dis)orientation in the embodied and social practice of design expands Mezirow's cognitive dissonance to a place of wondering between mind and body. For Ahmed, "disorientation could be described here as the 'becoming oblique' of the world, a becoming which is at once interior and exterior, as that which is given, or as that which gives what is given its new angle" (45, p. n.d.). Aligned with the animating force of wondering-as-learning (1.0.1) and the tensions I describe as inherent in wonder (1.1.3), I see *wondering disorientation* as core to the shift work of transformative action.

From the outset, the initial point of departure signals how this experience will be different to other learning experiences. Arguably, all learning leads to change. I once did not know the research behind risk-taking, and creativity and then I did. I learned the craft of synecdoche and began to apply it in my writing. In reading the first half of this chapter, the neural pathways in your brain have changed. That said, transactional or transmissive learning encounters do not necessarily lead to changes that shift our beliefs or transform the way we act, even if the learning introduces a new skill, concept or awareness. Sitting with disorientation allows an internal motivation to steep and the change begins to emerge in ways that will seek to reconcile the dilemma we face.

Travelling home that night from the improv class, I reflected on how different my body felt, I noticed how I resisted more than my peers the invitation to take risks. I observed my strong dislike for being vulnerable in a learning environment. In sitting with this discomfort, I came to question who I might be if

---

2  **Dion**: Exquisite disorientation was my term for the process of disorientation that takes form within a design practice. This picks up on Mezirow's disorientating dilemma and Kegan's argument that without form, there is no transformation (17). The suggestion of an 'exquisite' disorientation evokes the wonder inherent in being bewildered by the proximal form of transformative learning and what that might look like for a designer learning through complex research processes – labelling the affective experience of inhabiting this complex formation.

I did not need to be in control, if I were more able to be playful. This dilemma now poses the more unsettling question: could I be more creative if I were more willing to be vulnerable?[3] This exquisite disorientation, a compelling yet fraught challenge to a current world view, is the catalyst that can fuel a learner's conviction to engage in the subsequent phases and hard work that Mezirow identified as supporting transformative learning.

I stand with the researchers who underscore that access to extra-rational ways of knowing can be an invaluable source in seeking to disorient (19–22). There is value in connecting Mezirow's rational, cognitive and analytical approach to a more intuitive, creative and holistic view of transformative learning. A lecture on play would not have granted me the perspective the performance-based class did. Mezirow acknowledges: "Intuition, imagination, and dreams are other ways of making meaning. Inspiration, empathy, and transcendence are central to self-knowledge and to drawing attention to the affective quality and poetry of human experience" (22, p. 6). Mezirow's original ten phases appear to outline a rational, sequential process.[4] Yet as Grabove underscores, there is courage and authenticity required in the effortful work of undermining our own beliefs, challenging our assumptions and enacting newly formed perspectives. She accounts for how both the rational and the affective play a role in transformative learning. This is work that must engage with "the cognitive and intuitive, the rational and imaginative, the objective and subjective, the social and the personal" (10, p. 95). This push and pull between the known and the experienced echoes the creative tension in design between the reality of the current situation and the not-yet-knowable tomorrow. It is this tendency of design to forever negotiate what *is* with what *might be* that can productively scaffold this tension within the learning process.

3   **Yi**: This process and these questions describe a lot of what happens during a coaching session. A client brings in a topic, which might already be some sort of exquisite disorientation. There is a dilemma and an interest in reconciling the disorientation. In the coaching session, there is the opportunity to reflect more deeply on what occurred, to interpret the current mental maps before positing questions about alternative futures that allow the client to see possibilities for responding differently. The transformative adult learning literature maps onto and accounts for the cognitive shifts affected through the more behavioural orientation of coaching (18, p. 112).

4   **Lisa**: Early in his career, Jack Mezirow in a study with Victoria Marsick distinguished ten phases of transformative learning (23). Those ten phases are: (1) a disorienting dilemma; (2) a self-examination with feelings of guilt or shame; (3) a critical assessment of epistemic, sociocultural or psychic assumptions; (4) recognition that one's discontent and the process of transformation are shared and that others have negotiated a similar change; (5) exploration of options for new roles, relationships and actions; (6) planning a course of action; (7) Acquisition of knowledge and skills for implementing one's plan; (8) provisional trying of new roles; (9) building of competence and self-confidence in new roles and relationships and (10) a reintegration into one's life on the basis of conditions dictated by one's perspective. In 4.3, I revisit these phases to propose design-led ways of supporting transformative learning.

## 3.3 Interdisciplinary Research into Affect and Transformation

It is interesting to consider the ways in which Mezirow's sociology and adult education position on transformation might be understood through the lens of other disciplines. Sarah Pink, an ethnographer, posits that engaging with the "embodied, emplaced, sensorial and empathetic" can lead to a disarming disorientation (24). Pink argues that the sensorial disorientation invites the researcher/learner to attune to new knowing that would not be accessible through observation or participation alone.

Edward W. Taylor, Mezirow's co-author on "Transformative Learning in Action: A Handbook for Practice", (25) highlights the potential for neurobiological research to help understand which brain systems are activated during disorienting dilemmas. Modern neurobiological technology can make the role of implicit memory visible, illuminating how rationality and emotion can be recursively negotiated through the process of transformative learning (26).

Neurobiology also helps map the connection between emotions and memory in ways that explain why people are more likely to remember emotionally charged events than emotionally neutral ones. Wrestling with the battle to maintain students' attention in lectures, John Medina introduced a 'hook' every ten minutes. For a hook to successfully get the students' attention, it needs to (1) trigger an emotion, (2) be relevant and (3) summarise or foreshadow the content (27).[5] The emotions that could arouse the students could be incredulity, fear, laughter, nostalgia. Neurobiology offers a different way of understanding our impulse towards meaning-making through a process of pattern-matching. Disorienting situations and experiences can heighten learner engagement by fuelling the desire to get back to a place of understanding.

These insights also intersect with the discipline of psychology. Robert and Elizabeth Bjork's research into learning conditions that establish a desirable difficulty affirm that making learning challenging in the short term is effective in the long run (28). Studies into emotions signal the importance of emotional granularity and the learner's capacity to understand and label specific emotions. Psychologists who study affect talk about emotional granularity as the capacity to describe emotions with a level of specificity that allows them greater agency to predict, categorise and act upon those sensations more deliberately (29, p. 180; 30; 31).

If I walk away from the improv class and the only word I have for describing how I feel is awkward, then I might not have seen a disorienting dilemma worth chasing. Being able to see that I felt threatened, vulnerable and apprehensive, at the same time as feeling content, inspired and a little joyful gives me pause to go deeper. Psychologist Lisa Feldman Barrett confirms that the way our brains

---

5  **Yi**: Not only is this a tactic to engage students' attention in general, in formal coaching training these hooks ensure participants do not slip into passive listening mode. The premise being that active engagement is essential to the potential for transformation in coaching workshops.

simulate responses to situations upends any dominant Western narrative that thinking, perceiving and dreaming are distinct, different mental events (29, pp. 27–28).[6] As an example, simulation, as the default mode for all mental activity, would have me projecting a negative association in anticipation of the improv class beginning at the same time as me simulating a joyful emotional response when the games connected with memories of childhood play.

Valuing the capacity to label and express affect as part of the transformative process of learning is a recurring point across disciplines (32). Lyle Yorks and Elizabeth Kasl trace the connection between affective dimensions of learning and the import of emphasising the whole person (33). Offering a phenomenologist's perspective on whole-person learning they understand experience as a verb (not a noun to reflect on cognitively). Critical of Mezirow's pragmatic thought-based orientation towards reflection-on experience (as a noun), they alternately evoke a whole-person approach that privileges the feelings and emotions of the encounter. Drawing on multiple ways of knowing – the affective, imaginal, conceptual and practical – is necessary to support the important work of learning-within-relationship.[7] This relational orientation seeds the affordances of convivial tools to facilitate the mutual attunement necessary when seeking to sit with one's own whole-person knowing while interacting with the whole-person knowing of your peers.

These fields of inquiry help us better understand what happens when participants are making, sensing, imagining and thinking their way through a designed encounter. Engaging with multiple ways of knowing allows the learner to more implicitly trust what they know. If we can design learning experiences that draw on the cognitive, affective, somatic, intuitive and spiritual dimensions, there is a greater chance the participant learner can move from a place of disorientation to form new perspectives that reorient future action.

The interdisciplinary research gives us clues as to how we can further simulate rich experiences that capitalise on a creative approach to sense-making our way

6   **Lisa**: This new science has emotion scientists speculating that simulation is a mechanism for understanding language, feeling empathy, remembering, imagining and dreaming, among other psychological phenomena. Those from a Western cultures might want to parse out thinking, perceiving and dreaming as distinct mental events, yet simulation is the one process that describes them all. The more we understand simulation, the more we will understand how the brain creates emotions.

7   **Lisa**: Yorks and Kasl speak directly to what they call the paradox of diversity when it comes to the challenge of learning-within-relationship. They caution that Mezirow's recognition of the importance of "trying-on" other's experiential knowing as a foundation for empathy and transformation comes from a place of presuming a level of homogeneity. The researchers believe "the more diverse the perspectives among a group of learners, the more likely it is that they will challenge each other's habits of mind and habits of being. Thus, diversity is directly and positively related to possibility for growth and transformation". The paradox lies in the recognition that the more diverse the learning community, the less likely it is that they will be able to create an empathic field that enables them to understand each other's point of view. This in turn blocking their capacity to lead each other towards growth and transformation (33, p. 186).

through transformative learning. Design already has moves and methods that can be redeployed to engage the whole-self to help label emotions and to negotiate the tension between the objective and the subjective, the intuitive and the rational. The typical script for learning – the transmission of cognitive information – needs to be augmented with what Robert Boyd and J. Gordon Myers call 'extra-rational sources', such as symbols, images and archetypes (20). The opportunity for design is in harnessing how creative methods and speculative moves can do the integrative work of enacting and envisioning new ways of being human.

## 3.4 Emancipatory Learning and Paulo Freire

Mezirow was deeply influenced by the pedagogical and philosophical theories of Brazilian educator Paulo Freire. Perspective transformation was a journey towards emancipation. For Mezirow, this was about the development of new abilities *and* the removal of internalised restraints (20, p. 265). If the focus of transformative learning is on the journey from disorientation to integration, then Freire's Critical Pedagogy laid the foundation for why the world needs to rethink pedagogical practices. Grounded in anti-colonialist thinking, Freire's seminal text, "Pedagogy of the Oppressed", was first published in 1968 (34). Ali Nouri and Seyed Mahdi Sajjadi introduce Freire's commitment to humanising the world through dialogue (35, p. 79). They underscore that the conditions of love, humility, faith, trust, hope and critical are more than a consideration for engaging critically and expansively with content. The quality of dialogue present when one shows love for others brings humility to learning, or has faith in humanity, is elevated to a dialogue that promotes mutual trust and the potential for hope. Indigenous scholar Linda Tuhiwai Smith ties the anticipatory move of (re)imagining to the motivating potential of hope and the transformative act of posing alternative futures. Tuhiwai Smith argues that the imagining of a different world allows people to believe in the possibility of transcending "material, empirical realities" while also disclosing "the reasons why the world we experience is unjust" (36, p. 259). This aligns with Freire's emancipatory belief that a quality of critical thinking can emerge if the dialogue understands reality as a process of transformation (34). Again, we see affect and imagination entwined with critical, cognitive moves. Bringing an extra-rational, affective lens to the dialogic allows us to consider how Feldman Barrett's interleaving of thinking, perceiving and dreaming might align with Freire's notion of a "thinking which does not separate itself from action, but constantly immerses itself in temporality without fear of the risks involved" (34, p. 81). The potential of designing to aid the transformative process is aligned here to the backtalk of prototypical thinking, a bias to action and the capacity to imagine the never-before-seen.

Alongside the commitment to humanising dialogue, Freire asserts the importance of conscientisation as key to integration. Emancipation comes from a reflexive understanding of how one is positioned within the institutions and structures that might limit or empower a sense of agency, freedom and future action (34). The emancipatory potential of such a pedagogical approach is based upon a set of principles researchers ascribe to Freire. The true dialogue of education must be political and empowering, for only then can the student's view of reality be broadened and perceptions transformed (35, p. 81). To engage in the social justice agenda that underpins these practices, design is asked to do more than solve problems. Freire argues that critical consciousness comes from moving between reflection and action. His case for a recursive flow between dialog and problem-posing has influenced the development of Participatory Action Research by offering an alternative to the limiting lens of problem solving (36). Here, I question how precedents from discursive design, speculative design, design fiction or design futures might amplify design's capacity to pose problems. In what ways can design lead to making waves, making visible, making tangible, making trouble and making possible?

The field of design will continue to question how to do the work of decolonising design, how to interrogate who gets a say in the futures we design and how to design for a plurality of futures that deviate away from oppressive structures. This social justice orientation needs to increasingly be part of the remit and critical discourse of design schools and professional practice. The focus here on transformative learning is seen as a middle step in the complex, ongoing work of redesigning social systems and services through a lens of care and equity. There is a professional opening, a space where design can contribute to the capacity building work of transformative learning (37). In this way, it becomes possible for the design profession to contribute to the crucial step of preparing people for disruptive system-level change by supporting them in the work of reassessing assumptions, predispositions and values. In doing so, employees, citizens, leaders and learners can begin to connect the consequences of how these beliefs, mental models and cognitive scripts shape their actions. This more ineffable, often invisible work feels smaller, less ambitious and harder to evidence than large-scale physical projects. Yet, we also know we cannot drive substantive change by only attending to the visible tip of the iceberg. For the more ambitious work to gain traction, we need to not only shift habits of mind but also habits of being (33). Reacting to observable events and behaviours alone will limit the potential for sustained, designed transformation to take hold.

## 3.5 Transformation Theories outside Education

Building on the learning theories introduced and the psychology chapters to come, it is worth situating how the work of designing for transformative learning can also be informed by, and departs from, literature on behaviour change and theories of change. Rather than adhering to a specific mental model of change that might bring a singular disciplinary lens to the challenge, this research is drawn to an integrated approach that recognises the lessons from various models.

The Transtheoretical Model of Behaviour Change (TTM) was a stage-based framework that incorporates an interdisciplinary approach to healthy behaviour based on a meta-analysis of peer-reviewed journals (38). Compared to techno-rational theories of change often found in design (for example, the theory that if I quantify patterns around my sleep better, sleep habits will follow), the stages of TTM productively acknowledge the phases that exist before any action to change behaviour is enacted. The five-stage model moves from pre-contemplation, to contemplation, preparation, action to the final stage of maintenance (with recognition that there can be relapse phases that loop back to the action phase again). This text emphasises the potential of design to navigate the cognitive, affective and evaluative processes, therefore prioritising the first three stages that support someone moving from not-ready, to getting-ready, to ready to change. There is here an acknowledgement that design's contribution to systems and behaviour change is more readily articulated. As already mentioned in the introduction, the emphasis here on the mental models and mindsets (at the bottom of the iceberg) still supports the critical, more visible, structural and behavioural change. The TTM processes of consciousness-raising, self-re-evaluation, dramatic relief and social liberation in this way present to design new ways to creatively engage in scaffolding the shift work of transformation.

Immunity to Change is another transformation model that works from the premise that we are immune to change because there is always a powerful pull back to how we have always done things (39). An immunity map (a worksheet) is the primary applied tool for navigating a dialectical approach that asks the individual to move from complaining to committing and from blaming to personal responsibility. Core to this work is owning the competing commitments and assumptions that lead the pull to homeostasis. The less sequential and more recursive invitation for design here is to explore how convivial tools can support the self-reflective inquiry and commitment to *make aware* and *make visible* the limiting beliefs and assumptions that hold one back.

Behavioural science further illuminates the value of an approach that works holistically, resisting a pure cognitive approach to change. The thesis behind Daniel Kahneman's *Thinking, Fast and Slow* is that people have two complementary systems of thinking: systems 1 is fast, instinctive and emotional, systems 2 is slow, deliberative and logical (40). The decision-making heuristics and biases Kahneman notes illuminate diverse ways people might defer to systems 1, against all logic, for example, being overconfident or irrationally optimistic. For Kahneman, a question that has evolved is how to see the idea of someone moving from A-B as a less transactional journey.[8] Kahneman acknowledges his debt to Kurt Lewin's Force Field Analysis work and how considering the social forces in a situation can shift how we think of eliciting new behaviour (42). He queries

---

8  **Lisa**: This podcast interview with Kahneman highlights how his thinking has evolved since writing his Nobel Prize winning book. His acknowledgment that it is almost impossible to have expectations of behaviour change is instructive (41). The limitations of bringing cognitive analysis to a Systems 1 and 2 problem, potentially illuminates the ways in which design can bring a more integrative approach that works between the cognitive and creative.

whether we can shift our focus from the driving forces that might nudge behaviour change, to instead acknowledge the restraining forces that get in the way of people adopting desired new behaviour. Lewin's popular Unfreeze, Change, Freeze model of change (43; 44) further acknowledges not just the structural forces but the temporal dimensions of this work.

---

## Narrative 3.1 Indigenous Knowing-Doing-Being: Reciprocity and Resistance

### 1991 – with Jonathan Mane-Wheoki

*I am sitting in his office, confounded and a little bemused. It is the first month of my last year as an undergraduate design student and I am meeting with a professor who I hope can help me with my major project on the appropriation of Māori motifs in New Zealand graphic design. Not wanting to waste the professor's time, I have arrived with a list of questions. I walk in certain in my belief that if I could find out the meaning behind each Māori symbol, I could confidently classify those marks so Pākehā (non-Māori) designers would understand their meanings and use them respectfully. Simple.*

*I have only been in the room for ten minutes and already I can tell this is not going to be simple.*

*The professor is not being dismissive or unhelpful, he is however responding to my request for a taxonomy of sorts with a lengthy, animated parable of a grandmother's feather cloak. I am confounded because the record of symbols must exist – surely – so why would he not share it with me? I am bemused because I sense this oblique story is the lesson – clearly – but what am I to do with this rambling tale?*

*In my timeline for this year-long project, I have put aside a week to get hold of the 'knowing' I need. I am already impatient to get to the 'doing' part where I am visually designing a beautiful dictionary of Māori symbols. The professor is now telling the part of his story where the grandchildren are not automatically allowed to wear their grandmother's feather cloak to their graduation ceremony. I want him to hurry up and get to the point, at the same time as sensing with a heavy heart that this is his point. I have not earned the right to walk into his room and ask for this knowledge. He is showing me that other to a possessive notion of knowing I had sought to claim, there is another way of 'being-with' what I am seeking.*

I will walk away from this meeting disoriented in more ways than one. I will come to see that the knowing-doing-being of this encounter telegraph a construction of meaning-making different to the one I have known. Decades later I do not recall if he was a professor of geology, economics or politics. His academic credentials are not relevant here, I was in his office because his people are my people. This elder's stories are not abstract parables. He is sharing stories of my ancestors and distant cousins. Knowing-doing-being in this room values different relationships to time, people and land. Knowing is not a transactional commodity to be traded. The wisdom woven into narrative and shared through metaphor is to be hard-won and respected. The cognitive dissonance I feel as I leave his office is both disarming and captivating. I recognise that there is something new being asked of me here and I am challenged yet curious. Over the coming months I will go head-to-head with my design professor, I will mourn my loss of certainty, I will come to embrace interpreting obtuse tales and I will learn that I am of these stories and yet these stories do not centre around me. The stories present a generational perspective about the past and the future that I must respect in the present.

*It is the final day of my undergraduate studies. I have hung my not-a-dictionary project on the wall for examination.[9] I leave campus for the last time exhausted by all that I have had to unlearn and by the painful, political battles with the institution. Yet, I walk away proud of how radically my thinking has shifted, mindful of how many beliefs I unsettled to get to this place.*

I was not there the day of my examination. However, as a Māori student I could request a Māori academic to represent me, ensuring the process has cultural integrity. It is Jonathan Mane-Wheoki, the mentor who has shepherded me through this transformative and tumultuous year, who tells me months later that the jury of white male peers unanimously concluded that my project did not give designers' the answers they are seeking. In the context of the dominant Western knowledge systems, my major project deserved to fail.

While I had come to trust a knowing-doing-being process that respects the inherited wisdom and acknowledges the local context of this living culture, my design professor had held on to his idea of a visual dictionary that would analytically fix the meaning behind the Māori motifs. To my design professor, my subjective, intuitive, visual and metaphoric stories were not a critical provocation but an empty exercise. As the jury made the case for me failing, Jonathan counterargued that I had respectfully reframed the project

---

9   **Lisa**: Three decades later, I bring new perspectives and a greater vocabulary to the seven posters I hung on the wall that day. At the time I knew I was proposing a pathway for working respectfully with knowledge that was not mine to appropriate or to colonise. The posters modelled fictitious design process case studies to illustrate what a respectful process might look like. Today, I see the relational dimensions of the work. In making visible the internal dialogue between the designer, their material moves and the socio-cultural context I was in turn proposing an ethical approach to positioning Māori as the custodial partner in this work. Yet, in situating the designer within this respectful relationship with the cultural motifs and community elders, I could not ignore the import of examining one's own unconscious bias. With the posters externalising the designer's hubris and assumptions, the messy, inquisitive process made visible the lesson that there are no right answers, only better questions.

away from providing answers for designers to asking questions of the designer. What the examiners saw as meandering and vague, he presented as inquisitive and contingent. What they saw as a meaningless and non-productive project Jonathan positioned as a meaningful and powerful provocation.

Not surprisingly, Jonathan failed to dismantle the judges' modernist constructions of knowledge during the debate. Yet, I did walk away with a passing C-grade after he threatened to appeal to the university if they were to let their Western bias shroud my Indigenous knowing with disrespect. My year of resistance and anger came from reckoning with the Eurocentric knowledge system, so I am grateful that it was also the university's policies that stopped me from failing. Still, I recognise that in my year of purpose and meaning it was the Māori elders, professors and community members who taught this young designer how to wonder in three dimensions.

## In Conclusion

Although the term 'Transformative Learning' starts with Mezirow, by intersecting with design, it evolves into a practice more than a process. This section proposes that in designing encounters that lead to transformation, a multidimensional practice is involved. It is disorienting yet meaning-making, cognitive yet personal, constructed yet relational, experiential yet integrative, and intentional yet imaginative. Initial disorientation drives meaning-making creative activities that prime, unsettle and engage with extra-rational and affective ways of knowing. The cognitive yet personal dimension acknowledges that the socially constructed scripts we carry and personal stories we tell ourselves shape our mental models and mindsets. If we learn to attune to the intra- and inter-personal, social and ethical aspects of the relational dimension, we are better able to consciously decide what narratives drive our actions. In return, the performative, situated and playful nature of the experiential work supports the long-term integration of new ways of being in the world. Lastly, the imaginative realm of design grants an energetic charge to the import of intentionally evoking agency and purpose when motivating the learner.

Mezirow might have favoured a more causal reasoning compared to design's impulse to follow a more abductive path to perspective transformation. Drawing on extra-rational sources, like visual metaphors and co-creative processes, the act of designing can scaffold how we come to examine our current practice in light of past beliefs, so we might craft intentions for how to act differently in the future. The writing of a love letter or a break-up letter illustrates how a creative exercise can have a learner amplifying emotions and imagining desirable scenarios that seed future intentions. The written expression of holding on or letting go of love creates a conceit by which the writer weaves her past beliefs into how she will make future meaning. This letter writing is unlikely to direct a change in future behaviour, and yet drafting a transformation narrative can lay a foundation for future exploration (46).

Almost analogous to letters to myself, the auto-ethnographic narratives[10] interleaved here position how I came to care about this practice. Designing learning encounters is understood as about more than a world of tangible artefacts and convivial tools. The narratives ground the embodied, reciprocal work in the realm of play, belonging and different ways of knowing. Yet, the glimpses into my inner world colliding with other's inner worlds also reveal multiple ways the dominant script of design education is founded on a notion of progress inseparable from a modernist agenda. For design to be an ethical partner in creating more just social futures, we need to make amends for the roles we have played in crafting the dystopian, unjust worlds some populations already live in. We must commit to designing futures that serve not just the industrial, capitalist model of modernity. The focus on transformation cannot be reduced to design's embedded relationships with business, for example, using this work to shift people's beliefs around digital privacy or creating deeper belonging in a company so employees work longer hours. In weighing the ethical, sustainable and socio-cultural consequences of our decisions and actions, we must consider what it means to be accountable to ourselves, the well-being of others, the more-than-human as well as our planet.

A pervasive intellectual bias runs deep in Western academic institutions that privilege cognitive knowing. This makes the choice to talk about feelings and emotions, vulnerability and courage an inherently risky decision. Whole-body, play-based, affective learning is polarising work to practice in the academy. As a woman, this work has at times been a liability. The act of writing the auto-ethnography narratives in this section helped me see how the privilege of passing as a white woman allowed me to shamefully, unconsciously choose at some point to not honour the Indigenous provenance of the lessons I carried forth into my practice. I instead turned to neurobiology, emotional studies and psychology to help explain why whole-self learning might be key to the challenge of designing encounters that lead to transformational change. These narratives helped me see, with clarity, where the wisdom originally came from. There is in this redirect a deferential nod to the sciences as the dominant paradigm. Yet, there is also a nod to appreciating plural ways of knowing in adopting a polyvocal

10  **Stacy**: Carol Hanisch's idea that 'the personal is political' is an important touchstone for auto-ethnography. Though if we take seriously the idea that auto-ethnography is relational, we see how the political and the personal are co-constituted and co-determined. Our focus turns to how we become-with others to compose what Haraway describes as a "common liveable world" (47, p. 40). Auto-ethnographies of becoming-with like this one show our entanglements and encounters with others in terms of how we think and act across similarities and differences, constraints and freedoms. They focus on the compositional work of how and why worlds-in-relation come to be, rather than the product(ivity) of what we compose. These texts also ask us to "seriously attend to and recognize the constitutive power of the stories through which we come to understand the world, and, when necessary, give our all to reorganize them" (48, p. 22).

approach to the voices I listen to. The transdisciplinary content within this book does more than legitimise what designers might intuitively believe to be true. The case studies of Part II share practice knowing that emerges from applied contexts, as the practice vignettes translate applications of lab-based evidence and field work insights. The designer's investment in honouring peoples' lived experiences (or the narrating here of my lived experiences) surfaces a rich vein of insights that invite us to more intentionally integrate new ways of being and doing into old ways of thinking.

## Part I Wonderings

In these wondering sections, I pause to ruminate on and synthesise pieces of 'transgressive data' from the narratives. These wonderings seek to make sense of the extent to which these somewhat fleeting encounters led to perspective shifts, seeded everyday evolution of my practice and, with time, led to substantive and sustained transformation (49).

In the present moment my flawed memory has me walking away from Tama's Friday afternoon speech ready to dismantle what I had internalised from 15 years of institutionalised education (Narrative 1.1). I package up this narrative as if, in one weekend, I could surrender to the purpose-driven intrinsic motivations of the Indigenous-led, cooperative learning culture of the community. Even if I did become immediately committed to advancing the learning of my peers, I did not reinvent myself overnight. A reflexive examination invites me to do more than make amends for the role I played then, but also to consider the roles I continue to play. I have no doubt that my intention to show up for Tama was laced with some white saviour hubris. Yet, in turning the reflexivity on myself (as much as I would rather not centre myself, I must resist speaking on behalf of Tama), I see my epiphany did not come from Tama's courage alone. We were taught Māori without a word of English through a material-based learning system that had us making pictures with blocks and rods.[11] The prerequisite rested on an openness to get curious, not on being physically confident, articulate, creative or a good writer. This community-grounded pedagogy met people where they are at by playfully asking them to jump into learning together.

11  **Lisa**: The Te Ataarangi methodology has the learning coach sit with us in role as language detectives trying to guess, as she passes us a rod, whether she is saying "For you..." or "This is green..." She would make a building with rods and we'd stumble over each other trying to guess is it a library, a museum, the town hall. This hands-on learning privileged peer interactions as much as the principle of not moving on until everyone had worked it out (50).

In the Māori language class, material play was the alibi that ensured learning together would look different to formal school. Yet, Roger's check-in-with-your-body play called for another level of valuing different ways of knowing and learning. Beyond my mind, hands and sight, as a designer, I was able to develop an extended physiological grammar for attuning to the human interactions I was designing for. Did what we were designing quicken the heart? Could that look of apprehension be channelled into anticipation?

I see now how I had to go back to my final year of undergraduate (otherwise known as my introduction to *mātauranga Māori*, Māori knowledge), to define my critique of educational institutions and to get me curious about learning (Narrative 1.1). My wariness of didactic knowledge seeded the idea that there was something to explore in the peer learning space. Being seduced by experiential knowing in the Māori language class further fertilised the belief that knowledge is dynamic, contingent, integrated, subjective, situated and political. The value of stories, material metaphors and embodied knowing in turn set me up to sit with the disorientation of Roger's physical play (Narrative 2.1). The realisation for me, in writing these three foundational narratives, is that the Māori perspective introduced to me in 1991 was not located in Indigenous content but in the Indigenous ways of knowing and being that gave me the permission to act otherwise when it came to designing learning encounters.[12] When you add the experience of a performative practice like design, then it becomes clear how in the mutually implicated relationships between knowing and being can also not be separated from the doing of making. This extends to an embodied orientation to transformative learning, where the doing is implicated in the work of shifting what we know and how we are in the world (53).

What is your position in the worlds you live in? What ways of knowing, doing and being are still contested, still up for negotiation? When you turn your gaze away from how to design transformative encounters to how you have been transformed by experiences, what are you left wondering...?

---

12 **Desiree:** The relatedness at the heart of Indigenous ways oftentimes sees environment-people-cosmos as ontologies and epistemologies that cannot fundamentally be differentiated (51). **Lisa:** Just as the onto-epistemologies of Indigenous ways of designing and researching locate the knowing in being, so do new materialists. Problematically for Karen Barad "The separation of epistemology from ontology is a reverberation of a metaphysics that assumes an inherent difference between human and nonhuman, subject and object, mind and body, matter and discourse" (52, p. 185). This dichotomous splitting needs to be acknowledged yet critiqued, so in Barad's terms we can begin to understand our "ethico-onto-epistemologies" (p. 381) as always in "intra-action" (p. 128).

# Bibliography

1 Provenzo, Eugene F. "Friedrich Froebel's Gifts: Connecting the Spiritual and Aesthetic to the Real World of Play and Learning." *American Journal of Play*, vol. 2, no. 1, 2009, pp. 85–99.

2 Montessori, Maria. *The Secret of Childhood*. Translated by Barbara Barclay Carter, Orient Longman, 1978.

3 Dewey, John. *Democracy and Education: An Introduction to the Philosophy of Education*. WLC Books, 2009.

4 Cross-Durrant, Angela. "Lifelong Education in the Writings of John Dewey." *International Journal of Lifelong Education*, vol. 3, no. 2, 1984, pp. 115–25, doi:10.1080/0260137840030205.

5 Schön, Donald. "The Theory of Inquiry: Dewey's Legacy to Education." *Curriculum Inquiry*, vol. 22, no. 2, 1992, pp. 119–39.

6 Bain, Ken. *What the Best College Students Do*. Harvard University Press, 2012.

7 Halloun, Ibrahim Abou and David Hestenes. "The Initial Knowledge State of College Physics Students." *American Journal of Physics*, vol. 53, no. 11, 1985, pp. 1043–55.

8 Mezirow, Jack. *Transformative Dimensions of Adult Learning*. Jossey-Bass, 1991.

9 Kitchenham, Andrew. "The Evolution of John Mezirow's Transformative Learning Theory." *Journal of Transformative Education*, vol. 6, no. 2, 2008, pp. 104–23, doi:10.1177/1541344608322678.

10 Grabove, Valerie. "The Many Facets of Transformative Learning Theory and Practice." *Transformative Learning in Action: Insights from Practice. New Directions for Adult and Continuing Education*, edited by Patricia Cranton, Jossey-Bass, 1997, pp. 89–96.

11 Clark, Carolyn M. *The Restructuring of Meaning: An Analysis of the Impact of Context on Transformational Learning*, 1991. University of Georgia, Unpublished Doctoral Dissertation.

12 Boehnert, Joanna. "Transformative Learning in Sustainable Design Education." EKSIG 2011: SkinDeep – Experiential Knowledge and Multi Sensory Communication – Proceedings of the International Conference 2011 of the DRS Special Interest Group on Experiential Knowledge, University for the Creative Arts, 2011.

13 Boyd, Robert D. and J. Gordon Myers. "Transformative Education." *International Journal of Lifelong Education*, vol. 7, no. 4, 1988, pp. 261–84, doi:10.1080/0260137880070403.

14 Welton, Michael Robert. "Transformation Theory of Adult Learning." In *Defense of the Lifeworld: Critical Perspectives on Adult Learning*, edited by Michael R. Welton, State University of New York Press, 1995, pp. 39–70.

15 Nottingham, James. "James Nottingham's Learning Challenge (Learning Pit) animation." YouTube, uploaded by Challenging Learning, 23 November 2015, www.youtube.com/watch?v=3IMUAOhuO78.

16 Tuckwell, Dion. "Joining Practice Research." PhD Thesis, Monash University, 2020.

17 Mezirow, Jack. *Learning as Transformation: Critical Perspectives on a Theory in Progress*. Jossey-Bass, 2000.

18 Bennett, John L. and Francine Campone. "Coaching and Theories of Learning." *The Sage Handbook of Coaching*, edited by T. Bachkirova et al., Sage Publications, 2017, pp. 102–20.

19 Taylor, Edward W. and Career ERIC Clearinghouse on Adult, and Vocational Education. *The Theory and Practice of Transformative Learning: A Critical Review*. ERIC Clearinghouse on Adult, Career, and Vocational Education, 1998.

20 Dirkx, John M. et al. "Musings and Reflections on the Meaning, Context, and Process of Transformative Learning: A Dialogue between John M. Dirkx and Jack Mezirow." *Journal of Transformative Education*, vol. 4, no. 2, 2006, pp. 123–39, doi:10.1177/1541344606287503.

21 Cranton, Patricia. *Understanding and Promoting Transformative Learning: A Guide to Theory and Practice*. 3rd ed., Stylus Publishing, 2016.

22 Mezirow, Jack. "Learning to Think Like an Adult: Core Concepts of Transformation Theory". *Learning as Transformation*. Jossey-Bass, 2000.
23 Marsick, Victoria and Jack Mezirow. *Education for Perspective Transformation: Women's Re-Entry Programs in Community Colleges.* Columbia University, 1978.
24 Pink, Sarah. *Doing Sensory Ethnography.* Sage Publications, 2009.
25 Mezirow, Jack. "Transformative Learning Theory." *Transformative Learning in Practice: Insights from Community, Workplace, and Higher Education*, edited by Jack Mezirow and Edward Taylor, Jossey-Bass, 2009, pp. 18–32.
26 Taylor, Edward W. "Transformative Learning Theory: A Neurobiological Perspective of the Role of Emotions and Unconscious Ways of Knowing." *International Journal of Lifelong Education*, vol. 20, no. 3, 2001, pp. 218–36, doi:10.1080/02601370110036064.
27 Medina, John. *Brain Rules: 12 Principles for Surviving and Thriving at Work, Home and School.* Pear Press, 2014.
28 Bjork, Elizabeth L. and Robert A. Bjork. "Making Things Hard on Yourself, but in a Good Way: Creating Desirable Difficulties to Enhance Learning." *Psychology and the Real World: Essays Illustrating Fundamental Contributions to Society*, edited by Morton A. Gersbacher et al., Worth Publishers, 2011, pp. 56–64.
29 Barrett, Lisa Feldman. *How Emotions Are Made: The Secret Life of the Brain.* Kindle ed., Mariner Books, 2018.
30 David, Susan A. *Emotional Agility: Get Unstuck, Embrace Change, and Thrive in Work and Life.* Penguin Books, 2016.
31 Brackett, Marc A. *Permission to Feel: The Power of Emotional Intelligence to Achieve Well-Being and Success.* Celadon Books, 2020.
32 Sveinunggaard, Karen L. "Transformative Learning in Adulthood: A Socio-Contextual Perspective." Adult Education Research Conference, New Prairie Press, 1993.
33 Yorks, Lyle and Elizabeth Kasl. "Toward a Theory and Practice for Whole-Person Learning: Reconceptualizing Experience and the Role of Affect." *Adult Education Quarterly*, vol. 52, no. 3, 2002, pp. 176–92, doi:10.1177/07417136020523002.
34 Freire, Paulo. *Pedagogy of the Oppressed.* Continuum, 1989.
35 Nouri, Ali and Seyed Mehdi Sajjadi. "Emancipatory Pedagogy in Practice: Aims, Principles and Curriculum Orientation." *The International Journal of Critical Pedagogy*, vol. 5, no. 2, 2014, pp. 76–87.
36 Smith, Linda Tuhiwai. *Decolonizing Methodologies: Research and Indigenous Peoples.* 2nd ed., Zed Books, 2012.
37 Yee, Joyce et al. "Transformative Learning as Impact in Social Innovation." *Design and Culture*, vol. 11, no. 1, 2019, pp. 109–32, doi:10.1080/17547075.2019.1567984.
38 Prochaska, Janice M et al. "A Transtheoretical Approach to Changing Organizations." *Administration and Policy in Mental Health and Mental Health Services Research*, vol. 28, no. 4, 2001, pp. 247–61, doi:10.1023/A:1011155212811.
39 Kegan, Robert. *How the Way We Talk Can Change the Way We Work: Seven Languages for Transformation.* Wiley, 2001.
40 Kahneman, Daniel. *Thinking, Fast and Slow.* Kindle ed., Penguin, 2011.
41 Parrish, Shane. "Daniel Kahneman: Putting Your Intuition on Ice." *The Knowledge Project*, Podcast, www.fs.blog/knowledge-project/daniel-kahneman.
42 Lewin, Kurt. "Defining the 'Field at a Given Time'." *Psychological Review*, vol. 50, no. 3, 1943, pp. 292–310, doi:10.1037/h0062738.
43 Lewin, Kurt. "Frontiers in Group Dynamics: Concept, Method and Reality in Social Science; Social Equilibria and Social Change." *Human Relations*, vol. 1, no. 1, 1947, pp. 5–41, doi:10.1177/001872674700100103.
44 Hussain, Syed Talib et al. "Kurt Lewin's Change Model: A Critical Review of the Role of Leadership and Employee Involvement in Organizational Change." *Journal of Innovation & Knowledge*, vol. 3, no. 3, 2018, pp. 123–27, doi:10.1016/j.jik.2016.07.002.
45 Ahmed, Sara. "Feminist Wonder." *Feminist Killjoys*, vol. 2014. https://feministkilljoys.com/2014/07/28/feminist-wonder/

46 Kligyte, Giedre. "Transformation Narratives in Academic Practice." *International Journal for Academic Development*, vol. 16, no. 3, 2011, pp. 201–13, doi:10.1080/13601 44X.2011.596703.

47 Haraway, Donna J. *Staying with the Trouble: Making Kin in the Chthulucene*. Duke University Press, 2016.

48 Loveless, Natalie. *How to Make Art at the End of the World: A Manifesto for Research-Creation*. Duke University Press, 2019.

49 St Pierre, Elizabeth Adams. "Methodology in the Fold and the Irruption of Transgressive Data." *International Journal of Qualitative Studies in Education*, vol. 10, no. 2, 1997, pp. 175–89, doi:10.1080/095183997237278.

50 "Methodology." *Te Ataarangi*, 2011, www.teataarangi.org.nz/?q=about-te-ataarangi/methodology.

51 Martin, Karen and Booran Mirraboopa. "Ways of Knowing, Being and Doing: A Theoretical Framework and Methods for Indigenous and Indigenist Re-Search." *Journal of Australian Studies*, vol. 27, no. 76, 2003, pp. 203–14, doi:10.1080/14443050309387838.

52 Barad, Karen Michelle and Duke University Press. *Meeting the Universe Halfway Quantum Physics and the Entanglement of Matter and Meaning*. Duke University Press, 2007. https://ezproxy.lib.monash.edu.au/login?url=http://dx.doi.org/10.1215/9780822388128.

53 Nohl, Arnd-Michael. "Typical Phases of Transformative Learning: A Practice-Based Model." *Adult Education Quarterly*, vol. 65, no. 1, 2014, pp. 35–49, doi:10.1177/0741713614558582.

# PART II

# Making Learning

## Narratives and Case Studies from Design Practice

FIGURE 4.0   **A Value Exchange Map**: Meaning-making through sensing, narrating and mapping.

DOI: 10.4324/9780429429743-5

## An Introduction

Years ago, I read Nigel Cross's argument that scientists were in search of truth, humanities researchers were on a quest for justice and design research was framed by a commitment to…appropriateness. (1) I felt disheartened. Appropriateness seemed insignificant and unromantic alongside truth and justice. The term reeked of compromise. And yet, many times over the past decades, I have returned to consider the term, as I have observed the impulse of the designer to make change, to make together, to reframe, to negotiate, to learn from failed moves. I can now see there is something in a designer's commitment to seeking, exploring and iterating in search of the appropriate way forward that I can uphold and respect. In wondering what an 'appropriate' approach to a book about experiential, transformative learning might be I concluded the work had to enact the practice. The experiential orientation led me to sit with my lived, yet subjective, experience. Critical theory asked me to be reflexive to my own position within these encounters – to be attentive to the authority and privilege I often have, as well as the bias and assumptions that show up in what I design. Transformative learning invites me to further trace the journey from my initial disorientation to my settled integration of new ways of being.

In Part I, I laid out my position, the literature and my transformative learning experiences to foreshadow the ethos of belonging and relationality that runs through this book project. Here in Part II, we look at case stories and practice vignettes where the teller is speaking from another position, in another place, through another project. There is no attempt here to spin a cohesive narrative but to instead propose a plurality and intra-connectivity across different practices, geographies and contexts. The entanglements between theory, research and practice captured in these stories recognises the transformative process of knowledge production as inherently situated, subjective and ethical.

In this part of the book, the design and learning narratives shared have been chosen to reflect different cultural contexts, professional applications and research agendas. Not all examples fit under the narrower frame of transformative learning but they do all share lessons and insights around what design has to offer school-based education and adult learning. Each chapter has two project case studies, as well as brief vignettes from a WonderLab PhD candidate's research and a design researcher. The case studies represent international professional and research projects developed over years. In contrast, the practice vignettes bring a granular (single moment, situated context) focus to stories from public sector engagements. I continue to share transformative auto-ethnographic narratives interleaved between the chapters. This time, I move away from stories of how learning has shifted to times when my perspective on design has been reframed. I have internalised many of these stories and treat them as lessons of unlearning from my design education, and they fed into the next project I worked on. The act of sharing serves to reveal the structures, assumptions and values of design that I have actively dismantled over the years.

It would perhaps be critically instructive to share the stories where colleagues, collaborators or context pushed back.[1] However, these stories are ethically harder to share, given I cannot speak, with integrity, to the perspective of the people experiencing my poorly conceived lesson. Instead, here I share stories where I am the learner, not the designer. The goal is to learn from my own reluctance, discomfort and vulnerability as I engage, resist and am drawn towards getting curious again about what design is and can be.

The assumptions introduced at the beginning of the book (Table 1.1) declare an orientation to nothing being static, and everything being under consideration and open to new interpretations. If you have come here to learn, not just to know, then I invite you to engage in questioning your own position as you read the tales of practice in this section. It is appropriate in a book about perspective taking that we receive a diversity of opinions that counter, contest and confirm not just my, but also your lived experiences.

## Bibliography

1   Cross, Nigel. Designerly Ways of Knowing. Birkhäuser, 2007.

---

1   **Lisa**: There are many times where learning encounters fell flat for being too radical, too uncomfortable, not necessary or simply misguided. Sometimes the ask of the people was just too little or too much. There was my colleagues' eye-rolling when I used solely affective language to critique a Master's project, the stonewalling that came with making visible the patriarchal bias of the curriculum, the disengagement when I asked peers to engage in play instead of standard fare professional development. I do not withhold these stories because they did not succeed, as I recognise reflecting on failures is key to developing better encounters and deeper understanding (11.1).

# 4

# DESIGNING MAKING

## Expanding the doing of Design

### 4.1 The Making Design Constellation

Thirty years ago, I had to repeatedly explain to my grandparents what I was studying at university. Presumably, they felt about design the way I feel when my kids tell me they want to be YouTubers when they grow up. Today, the litmus test for what people think design might be comes up every time I get into a cab. Telling the driver I am a design professor always leads to a follow-up question. Most commonly, what kind of things do you design? The assumption is always that I design a 'thing'. If I say "communication design", no further explanation is required. If I feel like conversing, I share that I design experiences and interactions by comparing what it feels like to hail or order a cab, or how different it feels to have bullet proof glass between us versus complimentary mints.

Through my modernist undergraduate design, I saw myself as a functional problem solver. Decades later, our ideas on what design does are more expansive. The idea of designer-as-facilitator can sit alongside the designer-as-futurist. We can reconcile the philosophical belief that design operates in the realm of possibilities to craft preferred tomorrows with the pragmatism of co-designing with stakeholders as a strategy for community engagement. Today, I see design as an inclusive practice that accommodates powerfully complementary orientations.

Ever since I read Terry Rosenberg's *The Reservoir* decades ago, I have conceptually held on to the idea that there is a push and pull at the heart of designing (2). Rosenberg presented the creative tension between the pragmatic push towards seeking solutions for real-world challenges and the poetic pull towards speculatively imagining never-before-seen worlds. Drawing on affective neuroscience, educational psychology and creativity theory Ross Anderson considers similar tensions but through the lens of learner engagement and embodiment.

DOI: 10.4324/9780429429743-6

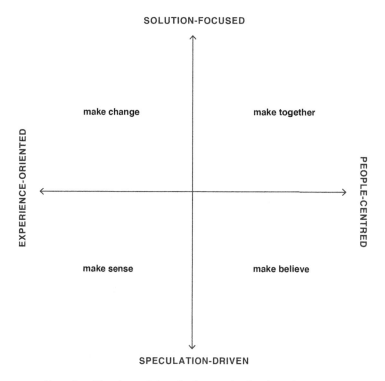

FIGURE 4.1 **Creative Tensions**: Ricardo Sosa and I developed in a paper the 4DRO
Framework, (1) proposing four design research orientations that are
mapped to underscore the push and pull between the two axes. The
human-centred orientation learns through co-creating with stakeholders. The opposing force of the experiential orientation learns from engaging with multi-modal artefacts. The speculation-driven orientation
offers divergent moves for learning through imaginative thought experiments that question what might is possible. While the solution-focused
orientation counters with the convergent move of learning from tentatively fixing ideas to assess their potential appropriateness.

Observing the body-mind yearning to make meaning from environments that
are always in flux, Anderson posits that:

> meaning making relates the present moment to past and future experience
> in an anticipatory forward-feeling sense of direction. The felt distinction
> between furtherance and hindrance, openness and scepticism, and fluidity
> and resistance emerges in the mind from emotional responses seated in the
> body's viscera.
>
> *(3, p. 75)*

The Creative Tensions diagram (Figure 4.1) reveals the productive tug-of-war to
the act of navigating between a material-oriented practice and a people-oriented

one. In an interdisciplinary context, I have seen this push and pull as what locates design as between art and psychology, between engineering and science fiction. Yet, through the process of writing this book, I find myself wondering about this tension narrative I have held dear for so long. What would a perspective shift on this look like? What might I be missing in this conceptual framing of design as a discipline wrestling with opposing forces? One obvious consideration is that there is a dualism at the core, even if this explanation of design is not trying to reconcile the binary in some tidy way. This makes me curious about how I was always attuned to the wrestling. For it is the troubling of a problem-solving narrative that I find compelling. Yet, I wonder if framing the tensions as the catalyst for designing (Figure 4.1) is to pay too much attention to the dualities and not the liminal space designing activates.

## 4.2 Animating Sites for Making

Language around design's turn towards the social, a dematerialised practice or simply a shift in scale from objects to services to systems all help designers to consider the shifts in practice the field is responding to or engaging with (4). However, I am particularly interested in a shift in mental model that allows the designer to recognise the relevance of much of their experience and education while nudging them to be curious of the gaps in a design education. To do this, I explore how the shift is still tethered to the creative, physical concept of making. The question becomes, beyond *things*, what are we making?[1] Here, the question becomes more focused, what are our encounters making for the learners' who engage? We make a thing, the thing makes a move, and the move makes action (for better or for worse). This is how we make change.

The following chapters are organised around a constellation of what designers are doing when we are making. The constellation has evolved, conceptually and linguistically, to account for how we narrate and understand the expansive field of contemporary design practice. Emphasising my always-becoming disposition to theorising, I note that I have iterated on these making concepts for years and continue to wrestle with these ideas that subvert any attempt to tidily fix my thinking (1; 5; 6). In the final section of this book (13.2) I expand my thinking further based on the wondering the case studies evoke.

Across this expanded field of 'making', I position a contemporary orientation of design as a liminal practice. I understand liminality here as a site that exhibits

---

1   **Sean**: I appreciate the shift to questioning what is being made. Yet, it seems that in de-centring the made artefact, there is also a negating of the role materials can still play in this expanded constellation. For me, the unique conditions that emerge from making happen when material, practice, bodies and context come together. From a place of making-with, questions give way to more questions, and the multiple worldviews of the moment change again, and again, and again. The use of the form and grammar of design need not privilege physical outputs but it can shape the next iteration and direct the nature of engagement.

an 'in-betweenness', or a bordering position, that invites adjacency, porosity and intermingling. The ambiguous nature of a liminal practice affords a multiplicity of formalised and informal cultural dimensions of practice to co-exist (7, p. 351).

To leverage the dominant, enduring perception of designers as makers of things, it is illuminating to see this tension not as a binary to be negotiated, but as sites of making to be animated and reconfigured. In this way, we start to understand how convergent thinking drives solution-seeking and is complemented by divergent, speculative thinking (Figure 4.2).

The openness of the make terms feels analogous to the visual practice of figuring. I define 'figuring' as a creative method conceived to amplify the backtalk of designing in the service of evolving one's understanding of a situation (8). This negotiative method configures and reconfigures the concepts

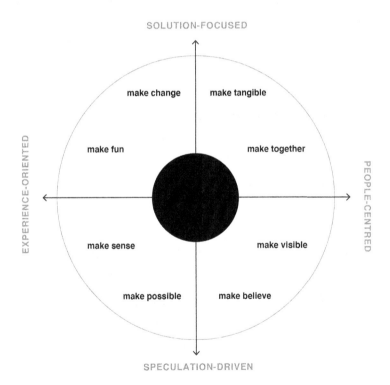

FIGURE 4.2 **Expanded Field of Making**: A further iteration on earlier models, this diagram represents an expanded field of 'making'. The proposition is that to make meaningful change, we need to make (and unmake) from multiple perspectives. Similarly, we see how a people-centred orientation complements, rather than opposes, the material orientation of piloting and prototyping. Here, it becomes possible to imagine a participatory design practice where bespoke artefacts leave sticky notes behind.

designers wrestle with through a reflective conversation made up of ambiguous moves and interpretative gestures. A story from practice introduces figuring, revealing how the paradox, and agency, lies in this commitment to temporarily fix ideas still in flux (Narrative 6.1). The inquiry agitates Rosenberg's push and pull by simultaneously taking a position while resisting the tug to lock in a solution (9).

With the *Making Design* constellation that emerged, the poetic ambiguity of the language allows new meanings to emerge and new phrases to surface. In pandemic times, *make space* conjures different interpretations if we are talking about social distancing or arrested grief. *Make trouble* might be radicalised in the context of Black Lives Matter or playful in a creativity workshop. The words chosen in the above constellation diagram emerged from the lessons the case studies reveal at this moment in time. The decision to pair two *makes* (like *make together* to *make change*) with two case studies follows my resistance to highlight the tension and not imply some causal relationship, but to instead promote the liminal space between (Figure 4.3).

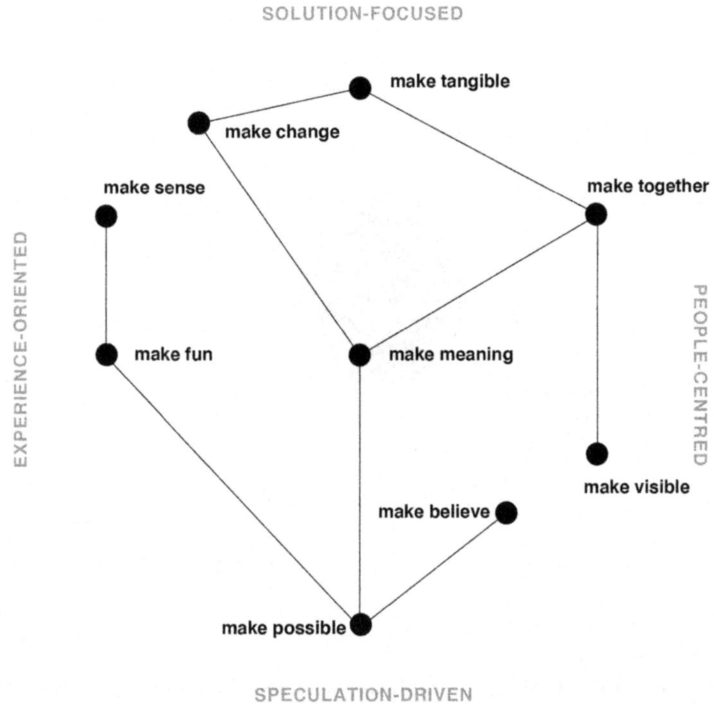

FIGURE 4.3 **Making Design Constellation**: As I explored different configurations of Making Design, I sought to capture the fluid relationships between the makes. The visual metaphor of the constellation felt a more honest dynamic representation of a conceptual framework where lines will be redrawn and new stars discovered.

## 4.3 The Research Stories

There is no correct sequence to read the chapters, dip in and out of the ones that resonate with you. As you read, consider the ways in which the different practices offer glimpses into Mezirow's ten phases of transformative learning (10, p. 105). There is no case study that moves sequentially through Mezirow's phases. None of the practice vignettes seek to comprehensively move from disorientation to reintegration. Yet, each story illustrates at least one way the field of design might contribute to the practice of transformative learning.

Chapter 5 is on human-centred design process and methods that support a people-centred orientation. These design process professional case studies, drawn from the United States, discuss how designers *make sense* to *make possible*. Design provocations and the conditions that promote a reflective/speculative orientation are the focus of Chapter 6. The two early career research case studies (one based in Mexico, one in Australia) characterise the potential to *make visible* to *make believe*. The game design case studies in Chapter 7 of this section, both from the United States, reveal the social, material and performative interactions that shape a learning from doing orientation. This focus on design experiences calls out how designers might *make fun* to *make tangible*. Lastly, Chapter 8 examines co-design sensibilities that support a participatory orientation to design from an Indigenous Australian and a Finnish perspective. This chapter draws our attention to how the designer's moves support the work to *make together* to *make change*. The case study projects and the practice vignettes themselves are by no means defined by the chapter they have ended up in. The boundaries between them are not as discrete as their placement in the framework might imply. Each case study has something to reveal about design as a process, a provocation, an experience and a collection of moves.[2] Temporarily fixing them within these chapters is simply a conceit by which it is possible to focus our attention on how an expansive orientation to making might be animated.

The practice vignettes at the end of each chapter draw from two different communities of practice. The WonderLab vignettes are a snapshot of a granular moment in one doctoral candidate's research, offering a glimpse into specific practice-led orientation to applying this research.

If the WonderLab tales came from us translating this research into practice, the Design Rounds vignettes came from us intentionally creating a transformative learning environment where we could experience for ourselves other approaches to designing learning. Using the concept of medical rounds as an analogous space for how interns learn in a teaching hospital, we created a platform by which a small team could go from project to project (like patient to patient) to learn by being in conversation with each other. A WonderLab team that included

---

2  The majority of case studies are from interviews between the project leads and design researcher Kate McEntee. The exception is Chapter 5 which uses the doctoral dissertations of the two lead researchers as source material.

Dion Tuckwell, Hannah Korsmeyer, Kate McEntee and Kelly Anderson helped co-create and co-analyse a learning encounter that could appropriate the practice-oriented, immersive nature of medical rounds. We invited five international designer/researchers together so the ten of us could engage directly with the practice of others. We sought to remove the hierarchical, diagnostic component of the hospital setting and instead framed the invitation as a chance to experience another's practice up close. The goal was to collectively discover what design has to bring to the space of learner engagement and what it could learn from education and learning sciences literature. The coming together of different cultures – from the learning sciences to co-design, from Scandinavia to the Global South, from working with marginalised communities to privileged universities – ensured each design round was profoundly distinct. Joining us at Monash University in Melbourne, Australia, were Penny Hagen from The Southern Initiative (Aotearoa New Zealand), Sonali Ojha from Dreamcatchers (India), Tuuli Mattelmäki from Aalto University (Finland), Elliot Montgomery from The New School and the Extrapolation Factory (USA) and Kevin Mattingly from PLUSSED+ and Columbia Teachers College (USA). The Design Rounds vignettes shared here reference the workshop each person facilitated during the week. There are links to download for free the Design Rounds activities at the book website: www.designingfortransformativelearning.com.

The focus in this part of the book is on offering a kaleidoscope of ways to situate and frame accounts of design practice creating impactful learning encounters. The diverse topography of this landscape presents the breadth of potential applications for this work.

---

### Narrative 4.1 Inquiring: Learning as Research-wondering

#### 2015 – with Anne Burdick, Sean Donahue and Yoko Akama

*I do not remember the day, years back, when I chose to shed the title 'graphic designer' and call myself a 'communication designer'. Yet I recall that it was an easy decision made with seemingly no immediate consequences. In contrast, the evolutionary steps that have seen me evolve from design practitioner to practitioner-researcher feel acutely hard-won and never-ending.*

*I am a few weeks into a research study I initiated with three colleagues and I can already tell the study might go nowhere. Yesterday, my plan was to take a design-led approach to gather insights into the ways in which our late 20th-century communication design education has shaped our current research practices. Today, I sense my colleague's disinterest in my questions and a wariness of my methods. I have recruited long-distance colleagues who belong to a tribe of academics who previously called themselves communication designers. Our collaborations with people in the digital humanities, human and land rights, learning sciences, and disaster preparedness space have taken our practices in different directions. Our communication design history sits in the background now we have moved into these more transdisciplinary fields. Yet, today I am attuned to my colleague's resistance to the study I have designed. Although 'attuned' feels too gentle a word for something explicitly enacted. It is not like I am reading subtle body language or reading between the lines of what was left unspoken. I have given them a task and every one of them has overridden my instructions.*

*It is evident that my colleagues believe the visual prompts designed to scaffold our virtual conversation between our locations in New York, Los Angeles, Kampala and Melbourne are charting our inquiry in the wrong direction. I know that the next day I will have the detachment to examine what went wrong in the task, refine my hunch and respond with a new way forward that seeks to be more resonant for my participants. But in that moment, I just feel...blah (I am yet to learn the value of labelling my emotions).*

The prompts are matrices that sought to locate our orientations to practice. These simple two-by-two matrices are here to help each of us plot a decade's worth of projects into the relevant quadrants. This priming activity was conceived to get us reflecting on whether projects had been or had become more expeditionary or instrumental; more representational or discovery-led; about designing artefacts or experiences or about designing with or for others. I should have foreseen that these binary choices would not be engaging. One colleague undermines the data by diving into the more interesting graphic challenge of visualising patterns between and across projects, another hacks the exercise by overwriting the words on my continua. The implicit critique leaves me swinging from defensive to defeated, struggling to detach enough to listen to the visual feedback.

The wondering disorientation for me is that I, somewhat bemusedly, internalised some objectivist notion that in messing with my visual data, they are messing with the research integrity of the study. I am yet to defend the troubling of my methods as evidence of a robust process. I do not yet see that attending to *why* my colleagues had subverted my intentions might reveal the next move.

*Walking away from the diagrams I turn to papers my colleagues have written and the transcripts of our conversations. My thoughts twist and pause like a kaleidoscope as I try to synthesise ideas prompted by the biographical details, the stories shared, and the annotated matrices. A new question slowly emerges. My colleague Yoko Akama's research position declares her quest for design to be located within a world attentive to politics, ethics and the environment. Anne Burdick shares the compelling, urgent nature of unanswered questions as a motivation for attending graduate school, while acknowledging the quest for new knowing is not easily sated. Sean Donahue writes about how possibility for him lies in using the qualities of design to construct new types of engagements, exchanges and understanding.*

My priming activity was not engaging because it did not ask them to go deep enough. There was no desirable difficulty. Whatever the quest, journey or impulse, there is a restlessness to not be limited by the current paradigm in their practice. Their explicit commitment to keep exploring, questioning and learning explains why the activity needed to address their own questions, not just disclose something to me about practice. It was this practice of remaining open to 'continuous learning' that led me to see the study of our evolving practices through the lens of a curious learner instead of an interdisciplinary researcher.[3]

I go on to chase the hunch that there is something in my colleagues' itch to critique my methods, to challenge themselves and to learn from participating in the research. The paper I write is the first time I grasp how an inquiry-led design practice can offer a framework for forever learning. Once I started channelling the iterative orientation of designing to my research practice, I could use my design capacity to tune into the backtalk from the methods, and use participants to inform my next move as a researcher. The sense-making acts of attuning, noticing, reflecting and wondering came together to facilitate the emergence the designer in me holds dear. To be in a state of always-becoming is essential to an inquiry-led practice. Emergence dilates the omnipresent instinct to pre-determine where we are going or to hold tight to what we already know. This shape-shifting energy is what renders it possible for never-before-seen pathways to take hold in our imagination.

---

3 **Lisa**: I felt apprehensive about casting our hard-won research profiles as a consequence of being ever-curious learners. Back then, I still compartmentalised learning as something that happened in formal education. In our collective commentary on newfound understandings, insights and new methodologies, my peers and I never mentioned 'learning'. I wonder what would happen if we did? What if our capacity to reinvent ourselves was due to the incremental transformative moves we were making along the way?

## Bibliography

1 Grocott, Lisa and Ricardo Sosa. "The Contribution of Design in Interdisciplinary Collaborations: A Framework for Amplifying Project-Grounded Research Grocott." *Associations: Creative Practice and Research*, edited by James Oliver, Melbourne University Publishing, 2018, pp. 35–52.
2 Rosenberg, Terry. ""The Reservoir": Towards a Poetic Model of Research in Design." *Working Papers in Art and Design*, vol. 1, 2000.
3 Anderson, Ross C. "Creative Engagement: Embodied Metaphor, the Affective Brain, and Meaningful Learning." *Mind, Brain, and Education*, vol. 12, no. 2, 2018, pp. 72–81.
4 Krippendorff, Klaus. *The Semantic Turn: A New Foundation for Design*. CRC/Taylor and Francis, 2006.
5 Grocott, Lisa. "Make Happen: Sense-Making the Affordances of a Practice-Based Phd in Design." *Practice-Based Design Research*, edited by Laurene Vaughan, Bloomsbury Publishing, 2017, pp. 165–74.

6 Grocott, Lisa. "Making It Up: What Do You Design?" *NiTRO*, 24 August 2018.
7 Rantatalo, Oscar and Ola Lindberg. "Liminal Practice and Reflection in Professional Education: Police Education and Medical Education." *Studies in Continuing Education*, vol. 40, no. 3, 2018, pp. 351–66, doi:10.1080/0158037X.2018.1447918.
8 Grocott, Lisa. "The Discursive Practice of Figuring Diagrams." *TRACEY Journal: Drawing Knowledge*, 2012, pp. 1–15, www.lboro.ac.uk/microsites/sota/tracey/journal/edu/2012/PDF/Lisa_Grocott-TRACEY-Journal-DK-2012.pdf.
9 Grocott, Lisa. *Design Research & Reflective Practice: The Facility of Design-Oriented Research to Translate Practitioner Insights into New Understandings of Design*, 2010. RMIT University, PhD Thesis.
10 Kitchenham, Andrew. "The Evolution of Jack Mezirow's Transformative Learning Theory." *Journal of Transformative Education*, vol. 6, no. 2, 2008, pp. 104–23, doi:10.1177/1541344608322678.

# 5

# DESIGN PROCESS

## Make Sense to Make Possible

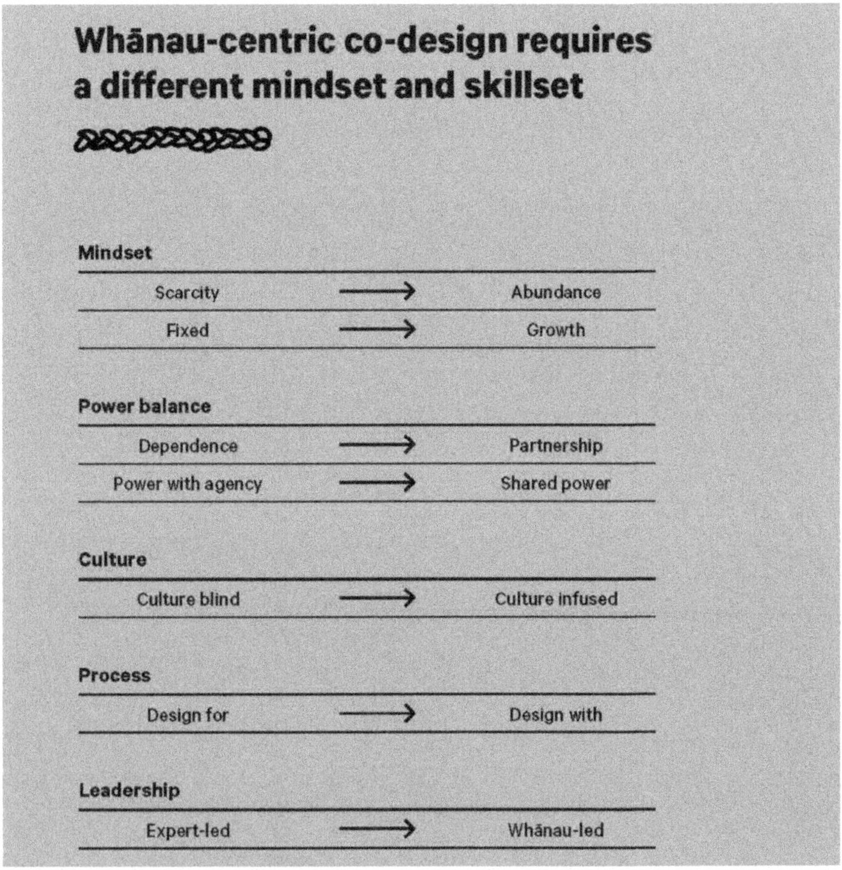

**Whānau-centric co-design requires a different mindset and skillset**

| Mindset | | |
|---|---|---|
| Scarcity | ⟶ | Abundance |
| Fixed | ⟶ | Growth |

| Power balance | | |
|---|---|---|
| Dependence | ⟶ | Partnership |
| Power with agency | ⟶ | Shared power |

| Culture | | |
|---|---|---|
| Culture blind | ⟶ | Culture infused |

| Process | | |
|---|---|---|
| Design for | ⟶ | Design with |

| Leadership | | |
|---|---|---|
| Expert-led | ⟶ | Whānau-led |

FIGURE 5.1 **Alternate Worldviews**: In this Practice Shift Card from the Auckland Co-Design Lab a one-size fits all approach to designing with others is contested. Indigenous ways of knowing and respect for cultural perspectives are explicitly telegraphed. In under 50 words the card foregrounds a relational orientation that calls for a reimagining and reframing of how to do shift work with integrity.

DOI: 10.4324/9780429429743-7

This chapter looks at two projects from the United States that bring a historical perspective to the introduction of design thinking to the K12 school environment. With a focus on the design process, the case studies explore the connection between making sense and making possible. Considering the potential of design in revealing complicated or complex conditions as precursors to transformative change, the WonderLab and Design Rounds vignettes pull sense-making into the space of co-design practices. Together the projects and practices explore different strategies for surfacing possibilities not yet realised.

The case studies come from the IDEO/d.school Californian ecosystem of programs and practices that packaged design thinking as the most teachable and learnable aspects of the human-centred design process. Design thinking, as framed by IDEO, is grounded in deploying a designer's toolkit to bring the needs of people to the potential of technology, for the requirements of business. The instructive process at IDEO evolved to be applied to the education sector through early initiatives like the Design Educator's Toolkit for Educators[1] and went on to include system-wide education projects. A study of initiatives from multiple continents commissioned by WISE identifies three key takeaways with respect to the potential of using design thinking in the K-12 sector: reimagining systems and models for schooling; transforming school culture by getting educators working together differently and supporting the student development of 21st century skills (2). The Hasso Plattner Institute, commonly referred to as the d.school at Stanford University, further explores the potential of design thinking through workshops that seek to engage stakeholders directly by working through ambiguity using tangible materials (3). This term 'design thinking' existed before IDEO popularised it (4; 5). There exists a critique of the codified process for its reductive simplicity, (6) while at the time recognition that the simple narrative is what helped commercially package the process to non-designers. Although the projects are positioned within a world that championed the application of design thinking in K-12, the practitioners interviewed continuously critique the limitations and learn from failed traction. In acknowledging the ongoing evolution of the field, the practitioners wrestle with or resist the temptation to package design into a linear five-step process.

The co-design practice vignettes operate at a different scale. These snapshots counter the case studies impulse to package the design process with moments from design practice that represent the antithesis of a formulaic process. The practice vignettes adopt a more relational process that reflects the nuances of sensing and the possibilities-seeking aspect of co-creating. They operate in the charged, liminal state of becoming. Through this unfolding and enfolding, the

---

1  **Lisa**: Commissioned in 2013 by Dominic Randolph, the Principal of Riverdale Country School and lead by Annette Diefenthaler from IDEO, this toolkit introduced the idea of how design thinking might be used by teachers not as content but as a process for designing school-based experiences for students (1).

designer and the learner are asked to attune to the here and now, while being in negotiation with what comes next.

## 5.1 *Henry Ford Learning Institute*

### 5.1.1 *A Make Sense Case Study*

*Henry Ford Learning Institute (HFLI)* was founded in 2003 by The Henry Ford and Ford Motor Company Fund to model new ways of teaching and learning for ambitious student outcomes and positive social change. *HFLI* has developed charter schools, professional development for educators and out-of-school programs dedicated to helping underserved youth in urban areas achieve equitable educational outcomes (7).

When *HFLI* was founded, the application of design thinking to education and learning was a relatively new concept. These schools were forerunners in many initiatives that sought to address challenges in classrooms by adopting design processes, tools and attitudes. The ways in which *HFLI's* programming has developed and changed over the years illustrate an evolution in the application of design thinking in education. This case study serves as an example of an iterative approach to continuous learning when it comes to applying human-centred approaches to structured learning.

Deborah Parizek, Executive Director of *HFLI*, tells us that at the time design thinking was introduced, *HFLI* schools were successfully preparing students for college and/or careers upon graduation from high school, but not effectively developing higher order thinking skills in students, such as creative problem solving. There was a growing understanding that students needed to be better equipped with critical and creative thinking skills needed for an emerging economy centred around values of innovation and technology (8).

*HFLI* developed an education model based on five developmental areas and at the core of these sits design thinking (7). For Parizek, putting design thinking at the centre meant infusing the spirit of empathy at every level of the system, using making as an important tool for learning and embracing iteration and feedback (Ibid). *HFLI* defines design thinking in their schools as "a collection of mindsets and methods that allow us to creatively explore problems, then reframe and act on them" (7). The desire to equip students with critical thinking and creative thinking skills to *make sense* was not only forward thinking but also came from a place of seeking to unsettle an "educational system that was designed for the industrial age, that was designed to segregate, that was designed to create social classes in the United States" (8). Christopher Patten, a previous Associate Director of Design Thinking at *HFLI*, laments the need to tell a story of how effective design thinking is in the schools. In his three years at the Institute, he recognised the extraordinary and challenging goals of what *HFLI* is trying to accomplish with this ambitious yet complicated agenda.

Initially, teachers attended summer workshops in design thinking, based on the traditional double-diamond approach popularised early on by IDEO and the d.school. The process Parizek described started with a relatively simple idea that teachers could be trained in design thinking each summer before the school year began. Design Thinking was *HFLI's* identified process for developing critical and creative thinking skills. The theory of change was that teachers could use this new process to structure lessons within their classrooms, as well as develop skills in design thinking for their own professional development. Early on, decisions were made to evolve the d.school's original five-step design thinking process into six steps. This involved repositioning the test phase into feedback and introducing a new reflection phase. This approach sought to promote a more human-centred, empathy-oriented approach to both teaching and learning by introducing concepts like need-finding, project-based learning and creating mechanisms for feedback throughout the schools. However, *HFLI* faced challenges in trying to teach the design process as content to be transmitted. It soon recognised there was a need to address the more nuanced skills and mindsets that support a design process if the experience was to be transformative.

Patten describes being frustrated that bringing design into the school system was initially framed so tightly. Rather than thinking expansively about framing and understanding user needs and insights, the packaged process offered a prescriptive set of tools and very specific application of design thinking. As an example, in creating point of view statements about user needs and insights, the teachers focused on the outcome (the statement) and lost sight of the perspective-taking objective (to uncover unmet needs and co-create insights based on what is discovered).

In some instances, this transmissive orientation to learning led to a shallow execution and limited teachers' ability to adapt the processes into their curriculum. This was largely based on a lack of deeper understanding of the principles or the type of unlearning needed to adopt this new mindset. Parizek describes an 'aha' experience for the organisation in realising teachers did not have to follow a complete step-by-step design cycle, but could integrate different design thinking tools into their teaching and learning. To this end, *HFLI* evolved its approach to emphasise identities and mindsets. Teachers can now define how, when and where to implement design thinking into their classrooms and professional tasks. Working with the three identities *HFLI*[2] saw as critical in supporting the professional development of teachers and administrators, the institute scaffolded the integration of these mindsets with new workshops, coaching support and the summer workshop series.

---

2  **Lisa**: The three identities were: a *Design thinker* who uses design thinking as a default approach to understanding and framing problems and exploring potential solutions; the *Facilitator* of learning experiences for students developing design thinking mindsets and skills, as well as assessing and reflecting on growth overtime and the *Content expertise* educators bring to the subject they teach (8).

*HFLI* realised in developing these academies that focusing on the educators and classrooms was not enough. Realising the challenges that surface if you don't have a principal or a school system that supports a change of approach, *HFLI* began to focus on leadership. Consequently, a new set of questions emerged:

> How do you bring design thinking into education leadership? What are the behaviours that a leader needs to understand and enact? What kind of culture does that leader support? What kind of partnerships does that leader need to initiate and nurture? (8)

*HFLI* is constantly learning and developing how to best use design thinking in their quest to develop and nurture critical and creative thinkers. Over time, the schools have iterated on different models of how to introduce, facilitate and measure design thinking learning outcomes with students, from engaging in classroom design challenges, to school-wide challenges, to simply implementing discrete tools and approaches at specific moments in a curriculum. They define their approach to design thinking, "...in a way that: Is open to and inclusive of other disciplines and methods; acknowledges the complexity involved in the process and doesn't oversimplify; and, continually evolves and expands" (7). Beyond this case, there is an evolution of bringing design thinking to schools that has shifted from the application of step-by-step processes and tools, to a deeper and more nuanced understanding of what it might mean to shift cultures and mindsets through an application of a human-centred, action-oriented approach to teaching and learning.

## 5.2 School Retool

### 5.2.1 A Make Possible Case Study

*School Retool* is a fellowship program implemented by the K12 Lab Network at Stanford d.school in collaboration with IDEO and school leaders across the country. It focuses on working with school leaders around specific mindsets that underlie the design process. The mindsets *School Retool* focuses on are framed as bias towards action, starting small and failing forward to learn. This highly regarded United States-based program continues to support school principals throughout the three-month program. The focus on working with school leaders echoes the *HFLI* lesson, that to anchor creativity and innovation at the core of the school system involved a complete cultural shift in leadership and administration.

Susie Wise, the founding director of the K12 Lab Network and a co-creator of the *School Retool* program, helped shepherd the move from the network's initial focus on introducing educators to the power of design thinking as a process to the charge of *School Retool* to champion three design mindsets for school leaders. (9) Susie describes this shift in orientation to design thinking: "We need to move much more into not the what, but the how of learning. I think that's a really powerful place where design plays a critical role because design is a process of learning" (9). One of the powerful moments of design and learning for Wise is the connection it creates to learning by doing, emphasising making and the need to use 'materials', whether internal (like feelings) or external (like data) to play with both your head and your hands to create deep learning (10). This is where sense-making intersects with action learning.

*School Retool* is modelled on the belief that "big changes start small".[3] Wise describes the goals of the program as, "very much about those outcomes which are creative, critical thinking, communicating, and knowing who you are as a learner" (9). However, the nature of the project is focused on challenging and shifting underlying mindsets and approaches in school leadership, rather than facilities or curriculum. The culture change program embedded in *School Retool* was focused on helping leaders design changes that would promote greater belonging for students, a key contributor to students' own learning mindsets. Education researcher Daniel Wilson highlights the need for changes in school systems to be supported by the culture and mindsets of the community and says that otherwise the changes will fail. He gives the example of a maker space. If a school funds a maker space, without a culture and mindset to support experimentation and making as a tool for learning, it will not succeed. If a school instils experimentation and making as core values, learning activities which embrace that shift in practices will emerge (11). The act of introducing a design thinking mindset into a school community cannot be understood in isolation.

The activity often referenced from the *School Retool* project is the 'small' action for a principal to shadow a student for the day, which gives an immediate experience of what it might mean to be a human-centred school leader. In the *Shadow a Student* Challenge, principals are tasked with spending a day seeing their school through the eyes of a student, going to classes, spending breaks and eating lunch together. There is a multi-step process to encourage principals to first question their assumptions before the activity, record observations made during the day and follow up with time to reflect on what they experienced, and develop ideas for making small changes in their school.[4] In the early days of exploring the potential of design thinking in schools, pioneer Dominic Randolph,[5] shadowed his students. Dominic, principal of Riverdale Country School, Bronx, NY, wore a backpack filled with weighty textbooks, travelled on the school bus for an hour each way and stayed up late doing hours of homework after sport.

---

3  www.schoolretool.org/.

4  www.dschool.stanford.edu/shadow-a-student-k12.

5  **Lisa**: Dominic Randolph experimented with incubating many design initiatives within the Riverdale, the United States and Internationally. He understood the importance of supporting research and resources that would have an impact on the education sector beyond the grounds of the exclusive, private school campus. Randolph went on to co-found The Character Lab with fellow educator Dave Levin and psychologist Angela Duckworth, to partner with IDEO on the Design Thinking for Educators Toolkit and The Teachers' Guild initiative. Riverdale also funded and supported my research into professional learning at both Thrvng and Wonderlab.

These are just some of the embodied memories that stayed with him from that experience early on in his tenure. Yet, the empathy that came with trying to stay awake in classes after little sleep further compelled him to not only question the homework load and advance placement (AP) classes but also had him keenly aware of what it means to design engaging learning experiences. Christopher Patten, also a facilitator of the *School Retool* workshops, cites in his experience that principals love the opportunity to reconnect with their original passion and inspiration for their job – to be there for students (12). The popularity of the *Shadow a Student Challenge* has grown into a world-wide challenge with school administrators across the globe participating annually. In making sense of the student experience, small yet powerful insights emerge, *making possible* new education futures.

These experiences and reflections underscore a common learning outcome from early adopters of design thinking. The translation of design thinking into a palatable and easy to consume concept made it accessible. Many people in the education space immediately resonated with the powerful methodology design thinking offered, and what it might enable for learning. The simplified process, illustrated through diagrams such as the double diamond, allow for the ideas of design thinking to be shared easily through social media and packaged into a three-day design sprint. Yet, following a five-step model of a design thinking process does not guarantee empathetic, human-centred, action-oriented approaches. The ability to learn, embody and integrate this work takes time, and the ability to apply and iterate different ways of working offers space for rehearsal and experimentation of how new ways of practicing can be integrated into everyday routines. However, once the field began to mature, it became more obvious that the simplification of the process also led to challenges around skilled application.[6]

By 2020, the term Design Thinking has faded – neither IDEO nor the K12 Lab reference the term anymore. The K12 Lab has a more overtly political project now: to obliterate opportunity gaps in elementary and secondary education by designing more equitable models (14). This evolution of thinking is indebted to lessons learned from *School Retool* and marked by the focus of recent projects. Moving beyond teaching a process, the leaders participating in the *School Retool* program and the *Shadow a Student Challenge* were asked to concretely explore and examine the equity challenges in their schools. The imploration to use design mindsets to address their most pressing challenges, like disproportionate suspensions to lower graduation rates for students of colour, bought into sharp focus questions of equity. This directly informed the K12 Lab's follow-up work on *Liberatory Design* (15) and Susie's later work on *Design for Belonging* (16).

---

6   **Lisa**: Daniela Rosner offers an excellent critique of how we might reframe some of the assumptions of design thinking. In 12.3, I reference her research in a discussion around how to unsettle dominant narratives (14.1).

## 5.3 Co-Design Practice Vignettes

The first eulogy to Design Thinking was delivered in 2011 by an early protagonist in Fast Company, based on a critique of the framing and the assumption a process trick could lead to change (17). Years later, Natasha Iskander's critique in Harvard Business Review is more pointed: "Design thinking is, at its core, a strategy to preserve and defend the status-quo". Critical of how design thinking privileges the designer and limits participation Iskander advocates for an alternative engagement where the designer is decentred and participation allows for different stories to be heard. For Iskander this move away from the more imperial "step-by-step march through a set of stages" would open up a transformational space for people to together. The practice vignette's in this chapter align with Iskander's call for a place where people can interpret how "changing conditions challenge the meanings, patterns, and relationships that they had long taken for granted" (18, p. nd). In different ways, the two vignettes explore how communities might make sense of the possibilities of working differently? The WonderLab snapshot is from a moment in Alli Edwards's research practice when she led a co-design regional workshop as part of the *Innovative Learning Environments and Teacher Change* (ILETC)[7] described in more detail in the next chapter. The Design Rounds vignette is an activity Penny Hagen and colleagues developed at Auckland Co-design Lab (19). This design-led learning Lab sits within *The Southern Initiative,* an organisation that builds participatory and collaborative capacity in the public sector to advance equity and intergenerational well-being in Aotearoa. Both co-design activities represent an unbundling of design thinking. They offer an approach to engaging with an orientation to co-creating that promotes a relational exchange between community members and that encourages an attunement to the self, the systems, the struggles and the potential.

### *5.3.1 Magical Mystery Change Contraption*

The fifth in a series of regional workshops for the ILETC research program, Alli's *Magical Mystery Change Contraption* activity, is designed for a peer community of teachers to collectively consider the component parts that would need to come together to create systems-wide change. Before the activity begins, the participants were shown a playful Rube Goldberg video to introduce a system thinking approach to their teaching practice – helping to connect the dots that teacher motivation, student sense of purpose, feedback loops and modes of assessment are all inter-related. The following hands-on visual activity has the teachers play with the visual metaphor of a boiler room of pipes, furnaces, gauges, gears and thermometers to fundamentally consider what fuels their practice. In starting from this place of internal motivation, allowing them to explore what drives

---

7  A case study in the next chapter is also nested within the ILETC program. You can find out more about the whole program at www.iletc.org.au and the *Making Space* case study (6.2.).

them as a teacher, the groundwork is laid for teachers to *make sense* of what levers to pull in an innovative learning environment that might amplify their commitment to student learning. The first part of the activity has teachers working independently introducing visual components (like oil to lubricate challenges) and annotating what is there (like what is the gauge for measuring deep learning) before getting into small groups to share their individual change machines. The second half has the groups co-creating a response that is shared with all workshop participants. The quiet yet creative, contemplative yet challenging first half creates space for critical reflection and ownership of what learning matters for the individual, helping to seed a commitment to change whilst acknowledging that change is complex, vulnerable and hard. The co-generative, discursive and playful second part invites people to laugh about and debate the different ways they interpreted the metaphors. This is a theme within Alli's research that explores materials as co-facilitators (Figures 3.1 and 15.1). The shared individual machines work as boundary objects that bridge ways to come to a shared understanding of the oftentimes unspoken practice values, beliefs and motivations that can get in the way of school-wide cultural change.

### 5.3.2 Co-design Capabilities and Conditions Framework

If the *Magical Mystery Change Contraption* brings creative energy to the discovery phase, Penny's *Co-design Capabilities and Conditions Framework* brings an analytical lens to evaluating the situation. The framework calls for a critical, candid assessment of the current conditions, so a team or organisation can create a plan for growing capability and the conditions for co-design (9). During the Design Rounds, Penny facilitated the discursive activity that sits alongside the flexible framework that helps teams to create a tailored approach and action plan. To support discussion among team members, labelled cards are introduced to engage participants in evaluating their organisational capacity. Four streams help scaffold consideration for: how they work with people, how they innovate, how responsive they are and how the structural conditions support the mission. The 50-something cards, colour-coded to the four streams, offer specific ways into examining an organisation from the perspective of these fundamental questions. How are whānau (extended family) and other stakeholders involved in the design and delivery of outcomes? How do we apply design and evaluative approaches to identify, iterate and embed responses and the capacities needed to deliver them? How do we manage responsively and work together to build our learning? How do our structures, policies, funding, resourcing and measures enable participatory and whānau-led approaches? Once the initial deliberation is over, the capacity cards are placed against a five-point rubric that goes from undeveloped, through developing, to leading. Following this, mapping phase is the task to design a capability-building action plan.

These capabilities and conditions sit within a framework that brings a more participatory, collaborative orientation to the process of design thinking than the earlier models adopted by *HFLI*. The initial discovery stage is described as a moment to *frame* and *engage*, the interpretation stage similarly values the relational in its description to *explore* and *connect*. However, the overall framework works with the shared observation that an individual learning the design thinking process is only one component part. A holistic approach is required to prepare for the kind of cultural and systemic changes necessary to successfully transition into a learning organisation that embodies core co-design principles (Figure 5.1). The specificity of each card makes blind spots, strengths, gaps, biases and potentials clear. The vulnerable, negotiative act of debating the rank productively exposes different expectations of what is acceptable versus what is desirable.

Where the *Magical Mystery Change Contraption* leaned on playful engagement to motivate the teachers for the work ahead, the *Co-design Capability and Conditions Framework* illuminates the complexity of the expertise required and a way to prioritise the capability-building work needed. Together, these make-sense-to-make-possible practice vignettes offer complementary strategies for motivating, evaluating and making together pathways for charting new territories and framing commitments to change.

These stories above offer a window into how we might prime the learner to attune, to notice, to be with what is and how to attend to what might be. The *make sense* lens and the idea of making possible are further elaborated on Part III where concepts of abductive thinking, allegory and sense-making are connected to the reflective and affective orientation of designing (11.2).

## Narrative 5.1 Improvising: A doll workshop

### 2010 – with Maria Foverskov and colleagues from DAIM

*I am more apprehensive than curious. The wooden manikin on each table has made me timorous. The visitors from the Royal Danish Academy, School of Design (DAIM) have pitched this event as a Doll Scenario Workshop. I want to shudder on their behalf. I do not realise yet, but I am about to participate in my first co-design workshop. I am wary. There is no hint that one day I will host my own play-based workshops. No sign this is the person I will become.*

My memory of the workshop exists in fragments. I do not remember the names of our hosts, other than our facilitator, Maria. Yet, I remember that our accomplished hosts deftly shepherded us through the co-creative encounter. I more recall my sensory, affective memories of the day. This truly experiential lesson stood out in contrast to the conventional lecture and Q&A we used for exchanging intellectual ideas with people passing through Parsons. The great insights sparked by these world-class presentations oftentimes became sequestered away in my notes app. However, the conscious choice by Maria and colleagues to pass over the passive presentation came from their belief it would be stickier for us to engage with the felt experience of co-creating a strategy for driving civic engagement. Their decision is why I have a strong memory of this experience. It is also why it jumped out of my notes and transformed my perspectives of designing.

The flashes I can retrieve from that day illuminate how memories privilege multi-sensorial, affective experiences. I cannot recollect anything strictly cognitive: the workshop overview, the prompts or the content that framed our inquiry.

Instead, I recollect how the invitation to each of us to share an experience opened up space for everyone to talk. I remember the pressure of time compressing on us to follow our gut, to be decisive. I remember the permission these hastily made decisions gave us to be less precious. I remember feeling fond of two colleagues playfully performing their story. As if I have never really *seen* them before. I remember scrambling for materials and realising I had no time to make anything look 'good'. I remember calculating, in real time, how to signify with the limited materials what I was telegraphing.

*The rush of the activity washes over me. The stress of the temporal urgency and the liberating high that comes with play collide in an animating force that drives the invitation to propose ideas not-yet-formed. The atmosphere is energetic. Laughter fills the room. The levity nurtures the vulnerability to take risks. My colleague throws a feather boa necklace around one of the wooden manikins and declares the doll the Australian Prime Minister. I am laughing on the outside. On the inside I am lost.*

*Throughout this embodied workshop, I continue to feel wary, self-conscious, in my head. I find it hard to be fully present as a deep disorientation pulls me out of my comfort zone. My design expertise draws me into wanting to own the materials, to control them, to perform my expertise. But how am I to do this with cheap craft supplies and no time? I am an Associate Dean, so I mistakenly believe I need to embody confidence, yet I feel untethered. In this space my authority as a designer is as irrelevant as my institutional title.*

*After the workshop, I walk toward my office still laughing with my colleagues. The dark stairwell seems lighter. I feel energised and connected. In two hours, I feel a deeper relatedness to the people I have worked alongside for years. Even still, I am not won over.*

Decades later, it seems self-evident that the person I was would fall hard and quickly for this kind of practice. I was never an authoritative leader, nor a form-driven designer. Yet, I do not wish to sanitise that in this uncertain space the vulnerability of positioning myself as inexpert as the next person was equal parts terrifying and humbling, unsettling and liberating. If my Indigenous knowing had not already primed me to be open to a more collective, performative, story-making way of designing, perhaps I would have walked away closed off to the door the encounter opened.

Upending ways we have shown up for years is never easy. The true disorienting dilemma of this experience for me was to understand that the tightly held form-making practice of my design education limits the capacity for others to co-create alongside me. To de-centre my expertise, I needed to reconsider the practices and tools that were leading me to colonise the conversation. The intellectual dismantling of what I had held dear was not too hard to shift. The real challenge finding the courage to teach from that uncomfortable, uncertain place where vulnerability and play live side by side. It was six months before I was able to.

## Bibliography

1 "Design Thinking for Educators." *IDEO*, January 2013, www.ideo.com/post/design-thinking-for-educators.
2 Diefenthaler, Annette et al. "Thinking & Acting Like a Designer: How Design Thinking Supports Innovation in K-12 Education." Qatar Foundation and IDEO, Commissioned Research Report, 23 September 2017.
3 Plattner, Hasso et al., editors. *Design Thinking Research*. Springer, 2016.
4 Buchanan, Richard. "Wicked Problems in Design Thinking." *Design Issues*, vol. 8, no. 2, 1992, pp. 5–21, doi:10.2307/1511637.
5 Lawson, Bryan. *How Designers Think: The Design Process Demystified*. 4th ed., Elsevier/Architectural, 2006.
6 Kimbell, Lucy. "Rethinking Design Thinking: Part I." *Design and Culture*, vol. 3, no. 3, 2011, pp. 285–306, doi:10.2752/175470811X13071166525216.
7 "About." *Henry Ford Learning Institute*, 2021, www.hfli.org/about-hfli/.
8 Parizek, Deborah. "Book Interview, Online." Interview by Kate McEntee, 22 January 2018.
9 "Susie Wise Says Traditional Education Deserves a Design Revolution." *Core77 Design Awards*, 2018, www.core77.com/posts/73421/Susie-Wise-Says-Traditional-Education-Deserves-a-Design-Revolution.
10 Wise, Susie. "Book Interview, Face-to-Face." Interview by Kate McEntee, 25 August 2017.
11 Wilson, Daniel. "Book Interview, Online." Interview by Kate McEntee, 15 November 2017.
12 Patten, Christopher. "Book Interview, Online." Interview by Kate McEntee, 21 November 2017.
13 Rosner, Daniela. *Critical Fabulations: Reworking the Methods and Margins of Design*. The MIT Press, 2018.
14 K12.Lab. "K12 Lab Overview." 2021, https://dschool.stanford.edu/programs/k12-lab-network.
15 Anaissie, T. et al. *Liberatory Design*, 2021, www.liberatorydesign.com/.
16 Wise, Susie. *Design for Belonging*. Ten Speed Press, 2022.
17 Nussbaum, Bruce. "Design Thinking Is a Failed Experiment. So What's Next?" *Fast Company*, vol. 2021, 2011. https://www.fastcompany.com/1663558/design-thinking-is-a-failed-experiment-so-whats-next.
18 Iskander, Natasha. "Design Thinking If Fundamentally Conservative and Preserves the Status Quo." Harvard Business Review, 2018, https://hbr.org/2018/09/design-thinking-is-fundamentally-conservative-and-preserves-the-status-quo.
19 "Practice Development." *The Auckland Co-Design Lab*, nd, www.aucklandco-lab.nz/practice.

# 6

# DESIGN PROVOCATIONS

## Make Visible to Make Believe

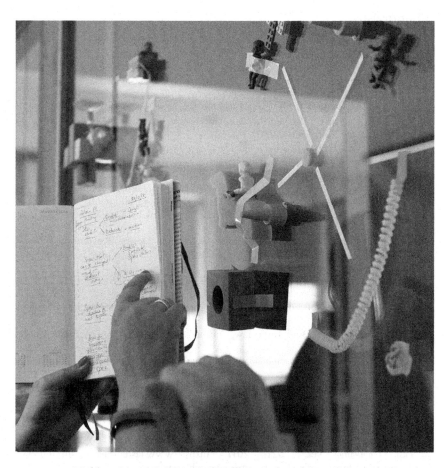

FIGURE 6.1   **Making Space**: In Dion Tuckwell's second workshop (5.2), teachers explore what would motivate them to shift their practice. Participants first create the world they wish for, then they connect to their peers imagined worlds. The playful galaxy of potential makes visible the elements of innovative learning environments teachers believed would deepen student learning.

DOI: 10.4324/9780429429743-8

The case studies of this chapter speak to Design Provocations that *make visible* and *make believe*. Two community-led research projects are explored: the first together Finnish, Mexican and an Indigenous Mayan community in Mexico, the other a peer community of teachers in Australia. The first case study makes the importance of equal and reciprocal relationships visible by positioning a co-design approach as a mode for navigating a longitudinal engagement with community. The emphasis on the designer as co-learner drives an agenda that ensures everyone holds a mirror up to their own biases and assumptions. The unsettling of the designer's beliefs runs through these case studies and the practice vignettes – as the encounters explore novel ways of making learning desirably difficult. The practice vignettes illustrate how the role of discursive and speculative design is not wedded only to the simulation of utopian or dystopian futures. The WonderLab vignette proposes a game designed to highlight the importance of reflexively questioning our positionality as learners and researchers when designing for tomorrow. The Design Rounds activity explores material, and embodied strategies for critically and creatively rehearsing and improvising the future. Toggling between *making visible* to *make believe*, the speculative provocations collectively and individually ask participants to try on different roles, to become aware, so we can imagine future actions.

Distinct from the professional projects in Chapter 5, here two research case studies intentionally complicate the messiness of doing research ethically and respectfully within communities. Working with Bruce and Stephanie Tharp's term "discursive design", this chapter recognises that design can be used productively to target critical thinking, prompt self-reflection and ignite the imagination (1). Tharps' thesis offers a unifying theory for the breadth of methods that might fall under critical design, speculative design, design fiction and adversarial design. These case studies model strategies for how interaction and participation can be brought to place-based, community projects so we might see the potential of discursive design at the intersection of social criticism and social change. The reciprocity between designer and participant that reverberates through both case studies further highlights how a discursive practice is inherently bi-directional, with the learning flowing in both directions. In this way, a commitment to discursive inquiry troubles a notion of experts as separate from learners. The reframing that comes with positioning everyone as a learner breaks open the potential of new socio-cultural scripts.

The practice vignettes take these ideas further by paying close attention to the role of speculation and anticipation in crafting these futures. The WonderLab PhD project uses a discursive game to stage a design team's exploration of potential biases that might unconsciously foreclose yet-to-be-imagined futures. The Design Rounds activity scaffolds a line of inquiry that opens up never-before-seen ways to imagine futures. Together, these practice moments ask us to examine the intrinsically interconnected moves of speculation and reflection.

## 6.1 *Design as Freedom*

### 6.1.1 *A Make Visible Case Study*

When design brings a social orientation to a project, there can be an impulse to position the interventionist designer as the saviour. The ethical and social critique of the designer parachuting in to help a community market their crafts, solve their water delivery problem, or introduce a better ride hailing service has been made elsewhere.[1] The criticism of the design intervention for its imperialist motivations stands with the real, and at times harmful, consequences of interventions that naively ignore the layered nuances of the local context (7.3).

Herbert Simon's claim, in the late 1960s, that "Everyone designs who devises courses of action aimed at changing existing situations into preferred ones" was not a capitalist argument (3, p. 55). Yet, design's pitch to business is often framed as an economic return on investment. This capitalist position oftentimes prioritises increased profit margins over improving the client's future. As outsiders to the communities we partner with, we must ethically consider the implications of what we are saying when advocating for the emancipatory potential of transformative learning. We can begin by acknowledging that a morally grounded practice of design would critically question whose 'preferred futures' are being designed. Only then can the imagined futures we are creating meaningfully unsettle the dominant paradigm (12.2).

The following research case study presents a place-based design project where design students and researchers from Aalto University, Finland, partner with an Indigenous Mayan community in Mexico over several years. ALM (Aalto LAB Mexico) served many agendas but the case study shared here focuses on the research component accounted for in Claudia Garduño García's PhD dissertation *Design as Freedom*.[3] This research project seeks to bring a moral orientation to design. The ethical principle upheld is that "if designers can imagine better futures and ways to achieve them, the lack of profit-making does not seem like sufficient reason to withhold those potential contributions" (4, p. 63). With reference to political philosophy, Garduño García's thesis argues that designers are morally obliged to act to reduce injustice. The philosophical critique uses an ethical argument to deflate the dominant paradigm where economic growth is privileged above all else. With reference to Amartya Sen, a fight for freedom is presented

---

1 **Lisa**: The story of the *PlayPump* is an excellent cautionary tale of an idea full of promise that fell short in reality. The *PlayPump* was a merry-go-round type device installed and connected to a water pump allowing children to play on the merry-go-round while pumping water into a storage tank. Reporter Amy Costello, who introduced the *PlayPump* to a broad audience (leading to significant raised capital) returned for a follow-up story five years later (2). The second story illustrates the challenges and assumptions that led to a failed rollout across Africa. Harvard Business Review, among others, use the case study as an example of how we might learn from failure.

as the path to a more just and sustainable future (4, p. 146). For Garduño García, the narrative of design around boosting economic growth restricts the potential contribution that might be realised by an expansive notion of sustainable futures that account for not just financial capital but also human, social, natural and physical capital (4, p. 265).

Putting this theoretical frame into practice, the research adopts an experiential approach to exploring the claim that the collaborative and empathic potential of design lies in the critical and creative practice's capacity to imagine better futures. Productively troubling who decides what 'better' looks like, *Design as Freedom* presents the challenges, assumptions and insights that come with the intent to *make visible* the prospect of better futures.

This longitudinal study adopted multiple methods and moves for creating a collaborative, participatory environment for rich insights to emerge and methods to be refined. The conception of design as a way to exercise freedom evolved in reflective conversation with the literature, grounded by an iterative practice and refined through the social learning context of the communities that came together. Here, the focus is on the experiential learning that had co-participants from different social and cultural contexts putting *Design as Freedom* principles into practice. Design students were recruited from Finland and Mexico to visit with the Mayan Indigenous community El 20, in Campeche, Calakmul. The study tour model, at the core of the ALM mission, needed to find a way to rise above the normal, yet oftentimes uncritical, social good educational adventure. A familiar tension of such programs is navigating the imperialistic promise of visiting a site to improve the lives of others while recognising the imposition of hosting students so they might learn from the community. Two methods of note addressed how to ethically form a social learning community: first, the idea of agenda-as-method reframed design objectives away from what the designer creates towards an agenda for what the designer *should* create; (5) second, the double-sided mirror perspective established a method for co-learning community conversations (6). These methods unsettle an assumption that design is there to serve/save the local community. The participants came to recognise how collaborative exchanges need to be designed to empower both the Mayan and student community.

The agenda to expand peoples' freedoms was a method for driving the design of the learning encounters that worked with key aspects of participatory design, democracy and empowerment. This political agenda believes that if a design object, service or system brings greater freedom to people, then design has succeeded in its goal of empowerment. This agenda setting promotes a provocative and discursive engagement in a process that asks different questions of designers and prompts reflection by stakeholders. In the situated context of ALM, the students were primed to see designing for freedom as a way to exercise people's right to live the life one values (4, p. 222). This curbed some underlying assumptions as to what a 'better' life might look like, engaging the visitors to wonder what type of life a Mayan Indigenous community would have reason to value.

The students became aware to the extent their personal values (and discontent) were founded on a consumerist worldview that entwines financial wealth and well-being. The complex and nuanced Mayan worldview that there are plural notions of impoverishment had students examining their own beliefs. Listening to reflections on the freedom to stop and have a break at work whenever you wish, observing the connection that comes with regularly playing football with extended family, and sensing the richness that comes with a community raising children together all served to deepen the students' wondering.

Many conventional human-centred design tools are designed to turn the focus on the community member as a research subject. The double-sided mirror perspective countered that stance, ensuring that the tools also reflected back on the students. Akin to Freire's concept of conscientisation, the double-sided dialogue with community reflected to the students' how their lived experiences in global, urban, industrial Western societies might go some way towards explaining why the Mayan people seemed oftentimes happier than the people they knew (4, p. 372).

To learn from putting *Design as Freedom* into practice, Garduño García adopted the role of participant observer, facilitator, designer and educator. Yet, in adopting a design-led approach to figuring out what it would mean to empower people to exercise freedom, the applied research study also made exposed the entanglements and assemblages at play in designing more preferred futures. Theoretical and abstract concepts of ethics, morals, values, trust, dignity, integrity, poverty and empowerment, to name a few, were accessible to debate, enact, contest and question when located in the lab environment. The double-sided mirror perspective metaphorically captures how design can *make visible* even without the tropes of visual form-making. The explicit framing of the mirrored exchange as a mutual learning experience reveals what groups can learn about themselves by looking at each other. In turn, the experience elevates new affective attributes like vulnerability, humility and trust as a critical way of joining with and learning from a community (11.4).

In this work, the term co-design is used to convey a longitudinal process in which designers and participants acknowledge each other as equals, enabling the emergence of reciprocal relationships, causing both parties to learn from each other. The notion of adaptive preferences is used to explain how all participants in the study have learned to adapt and accept the situations they are in over time. Here, there is recognition that in learning to adapt to contemporary urban Western life, we have adapted to living with less meaningful social interactions, fewer restorative social rituals and ultimately less social connection. The reciprocity woven through the encounters made clear how current life is lived and valued by different communities.

## 6.2 Making Space

### 6.2.1 A Make Believe Case Study

When I think of 'professional development', I envisage brief 'drive-by' sessions that focus on a transmissive mode of instruction. The most instrumental of these are workplace compliance courses delivered online. In the case of teacher professional development, top-down educational reforms add an additional challenge, prescribing methods of teaching to people with informed opinions on what good teaching looks like. A core tension here is when evidence-based academic research disconfirms the practice-based expertise of the classroom teacher. The *Making Space* case study introduces how a participant-centred, discursive approach to teacher professional learning might model a way to support more sustained, transformative changes in teacher practice.

*Making Space* is a design-led study situated within the 'Innovative Learning Environment and Teacher Change (ILETC) research project funded by the Australian Research Council.[2] The research broadly investigates how teachers can use the untapped potential of 'Innovative Learning Environments' (ILEs) to improve learning outcomes for students. With a focus on the teacher change aspect of the ILETC project, this study designed peer-to-peer social encounters that assisted teachers in the process of adapting teaching practices to maximise the affordances of new learning environments.[3]

Conceived as a learning exchange between researchers and teachers, *Making Space* innovatively paired co-design with Participatory Action Research (PAR) (8; 9). The study was a critical place for the ILETC to generate new knowledge in partnership with teachers given PAR and co-design's orientation to research that foregrounds the participant as a researcher. The reciprocity built into the methodology mobilised the co-researchers to actively create and codetermine through "co-generative dialogue" (10, p. 133).

The co-design approach was consistent with the PAR goal (8) to change people's understandings of their own practice and the conditions under which they practice. The workshop encounters primed people for a transformative agenda by considering how to envisage sustainable shifts in practice. As co-researchers, the teachers were involved in planning, enacting and reflecting upon pedagogical development amidst the process of shifting into new learning spaces. Fieldwork was conducted at two Sydney secondary schools seeking to develop new pedagogical practices amidst the process of transitioning into ILEs. By engaging

---

2 **Lisa**: The Innovative Learning Environment and Teacher Change program was funded by the Australian Research Council. 978 0 7340 5503 3, ARC Linkage project (2016–2019). www.iletc.com.au/. I was a Chief Investigator on the project but did not work directly on the *Making Space* study. Dion Tuckwell was the PI and his collaborator, Fiona Young, was the architect researcher leading the PAR aspect of the multi-site school-based study.

3 **Dion:** Teachers as Designers of Learning Environments, a report published by the Organisation for Economic Co-operation and Development (OECD) makes explicit the relationship that teachers could have with design: "It is precisely through the idea of teachers as designers of learning that innovation at the level of practice can be seen as a normal side of the teaching profession to solve the daily challenges in a context which is in constant change" (7, p. 133). The report declares the clear relationship between the role of design in schools that lends itself to teacher expertise: "Teacher learning—collaborative, action-orientated, and co-designed—is fundamental to change" (7, p. 43).

with sites of social practices, this methodological pairing was able to capture the teachers' lived experience, surface local tensions and respect teachers' expertise.

Over an extended period, the lead design researcher, Dion Tuckwell, joined with the participants as they explored where the teachers wanted their practice to go (11). The teachers as co-researchers determined what directions to explore and where they would like to make changes. The material heuristics of the co-design workshop offered 'designerly' modes for giving voice to the teachers, and in turn scaffolded reflection on their sites of practice. In this way, the PAR-led co-design workshops ensured the designed outcomes resonated with the teachers' particular change motivations.

The six workshops sequenced activities to make the learning principles the teachers valued visible to each other, then gave clarity around where individuals wanted to take their practice. The workshops also aligned the affordances of innovative learning environments with individuals' teaching philosophies, and showed how teaching practice can use an ILE to deepen student learning. Far from a drive-by professional development experience, the commitment to the teachers as a professional learning community was explicitly fostered. Inverting an experience that might have begun with the ILE as the solution, the agency granted to the co-researchers ensured the teachers' internal motivation was driven by what resonated with them (Figure 2.1).

Early workshops involved aspects of *making sense* of current beliefs and *making visible* the potential of new learning spaces. However, the focus in the second workshop on creatively envisaging a future practice speaks to the goal to *make believe*. The speculative orientation was not used in this context to bring into being a futuristic internet of things learning environment. Instead, the prompt was for teachers to identify a desired future practice through an affective lens.[4] Rather than dreaming of technological solutions, they were asked to imagine what would quicken their heart and drive their purpose. In channelling this internal motivation (9.2), it became possible for teachers to believe in a different future and let go of well-established, yet potentially redundant or maladaptive practices.

This *make believe* exploration worked with the metaphoric framing of a solar system where the planet was practice and orbiting objects were the affordances of an ILE (Figure 6.1). The teachers got to 'play dress-up' with representations of the learning environment affordances orbiting their practice. Participants identified enabling affordances, such as 'space stations' (a metonym for teacher planning/collaboration zones), and constraining affordances, such as 'black holes'

---

4 **Dion:** Distinct from speculative design or design futures approaches to social dreaming, this speculative approach aligns with the social sciences look to *inhabit* research processes through experimentation. This directs a constructive process that resists pre-determined research questions and instead actively formulates an experimental and emergent mode that seeks alternative questions and methods – to re-situate concepts and "to relaunch them again as propositions capable not of poisoning the present but of cultivating a different kind of future" (12, p. 22).

(a metonym for students unable to cope with excessive noise). After discussing each group's planet and orbiting objects, participants were asked to visually link their planets to the other groups' orbiting objects. This allegorical mode of inquiry showed new ways of seeing current tensions and the materially-led exploration allowed the co-generative conversations to trigger metonymic connections between the integrated elements of practice. Workshop two concluded by locking in the starting place for next workshop, with the teachers as co-researchers taking a polaroid next to their constructed worlds. Each teacher noted how they hoped to adapt their solar system in the future. In pulling back to see the assemblage of their colleagues, the more-than-human architectural and spatial affordances of new learning environments make change more possible, more desirable, more believable.

Over an 18-month period of coming together to deepen their thinking and imagining, a personalised learning community evolved. Seeing each other as learning partners and Tuckwell as an advocate of their evolution allowed the expansive universes the teachers' generated to reveal new affordances. As facilitator, designer and researcher, Tuckwell was mindful he was joining a social field that came with its own history, power relations and social dynamics (11). Like Garduño García, he intentionally positioned himself as a participant observer in the study. In a participant-led studies, researchers must continuously return to the question 'who learns from this research?' For Tuckwell it became useful to see re/search, for himself and the teachers, as a kind of systematic learning. Seeing the participants as co-learners and co-researchers helped to give meaning and context to the explicit reciprocal commitment for the research to benefit all participants first and foremost. The mutual learning saw the insights teachers-as-researchers generated about their future practice exchanged for what the designers-as-researchers learned about designing for transformative learning and architectural affordances. Yet beyond that, Tuckwell, like Garduño García, was changed by the experience of joining this learning community of practice (4, 11).

Attending to how the experience of being a participant observer led to his own perspective transformation, Tuckwell noted the shift as "seeing how prototyping practice with teachers has led to how I prototype my own practice as a designer". Tuckwell respected that the years-long transformation was a practice of becoming in which emergence was embraced, whereas his initial moves to join the community were shaped by a belief that his primary job was to facilitate in a co-design context. However, as he attuned to the capacity of the material and metaphoric activities, he designed to mobilise new insights he came to confidently own and integrate his antecedent practice as a communication designer. As the principal investigator in study not about teacher change, Tuckwell may not have noticed how the experience was changing his practice. However, research into professional development shows that the active and collaborative learning environment of these co-design workshops, alongside the move to return to the conversation over an extended period of time, increases the chances such experiences will lead to deeper learning for all co-researchers (13).

## 6.3 Design Futures Practice Vignettes

How might the speculative orientation of design support the emergence of more just, safe and sustainable future trajectories? This question is approached from different sides in the practice vignettes – with one activity more reflexive the other more generative – yet both aware of the creative, critical contribution design can play in averting the pull towards the already prescribed future. In the WonderLab vignette, Hannah Korsmeyer shares a card game designed to engage a design research team in the work of considering how their beliefs and biases might inadvertently direct design outcomes and default towards an established future. In the Design Rounds activity, Elliott Montgomery of The New School in New York City, took us through a scaffolded strategy for escaping well-worn ideas by moving away from the predicted towards never-before-imagined scenarios. Both snapshots of practice highlight that the role of discursive and speculative design is not wedded to the creation of utopian or dystopian futures.

### 6.3.1 Make-shift Feminist Futures Game

Hannah's PhD research brings feminist principles to the task of deviating from dominant futures. This practice vignette presents a learning encounter for the designer researcher by way of a feminist twist on Stuart Candy and Jeff Watson's open source *Thing from the Future* card game (14). The card game began as a design sprint for a team of researchers moving into the data analysis phase of a large-scale public sector co-design project. More than an instrumental activity for translating insights into outputs, the bespoke feminist re-boot of the game also brings a double-sided mirror perspective to unsettling the power the designer holds once the workshops are over. Taking the place of the 'Arc' cards, 'Change' cards reminded the design team that there are plural possibilities for how to steward in new and more equitable futures. While not an exhaustive list of all possibilities for enacting change, a description of each of the change cards (inspired by Candy's original language) provocatively explored how an intervention might Improve/Amplify, Remove/Make Way, De-Centre/Include, Discipline/Enforce or Transform/Resist. Candy's 'Terrain' cards were also replaced with 'Themes' cards containing key data and insights from the co-design participants, which served to de-centre the researcher's own assumptions in translating the participatory data into final design outputs. By challenging the researcher/players to go beyond corroborating or defaulting to their 'expert' experiences, the playing cards put the participant insights and lived experiences back on the table as a physical presence through the final design phase.

Similar to the agenda behind the *Design as Freedom* case study, this pluralistic, intentional encounter seeks to scaffold the challenging work of deviating from the dominant and expected 'solutions' of the most powerful or expert stakeholders. The game operates at the level of a productive design sprint within the arc of the larger project. The learning encounter asks the design research team to reflexively interrogate how bias, assumptions and established cognitive scripts or 'orientations' can slip into practice and inadvertently foreclose the possibility of certain futures.

## 6.4 Future Anachronisms Activity

Elliott brought his commitment to experimental, participatory methods for designing futures to the Design Rounds. Elliott's research explores the ways hypothetical future props might be deployed in the service of imagining, prototyping and evaluating visions of possible futures. The snapshot of practice Elliott facilitated for us was a workflow designed to introduce students, teachers and administrators to a process by which one's experience of today can spark speculations of what is possible in the future. The learning objective was to instil in students a speculative sensibility that grants them, as citizens, a greater sense of agency to shape the future they wish to inherit.

Elliott began the *Future Anachronisms* process by underscoring the importance of seeing the future through multiple dimensions. The STEEP framework introduces dimensions by which to consider the future: Social, Technological, Ecological, Economic and Political. Priming learners to be self-aware about which dimension(s), they lean heavily on has people question whether, for example, they typically see technology as the salvation while ignoring political pathways to change. Scanning for signals in contexts outside of our go-to dimensions immediately revealed our biases and illuminated pathways less travelled.

The worksheet has a clear procedural elegance. Although designed for elementary through to secondary school contexts, the participants determine the level of complexity of their prompts. Similarly, the flexible co-creative exercise could be a 30-minute generative task or a deep dive two-day long activity. The four-step process has pairs of participants creating a prop, a future anachronism, by way of reflecting, imagining, envisioning and embodying different potential futures.

**Step 1 – Select a Signal**: This step begins with identifying a signal, an event that exists now that could be scaled or disruptive in the future. The speculative move here is to see the signal as the possible future hiding in plain sight today. The caution, however, with respect to Hannah's critique, is to question if this is a future we should actively deviate from.

**Step 2 – Imagine the Consequences**: Ensure that a critical perspective is brought to the future already seeded. A meshwork-like diagram, called a Futures Wheel, radiates out from the original signal and participants fill in multiple circles to consider the direct and indirect consequences if this future were to come into being. Here, the learner conceptualises concrete yet fictional forms of this not-yet-realised future by asking what behaviours we would see, what businesses might pop up and what social movements might make headline news.

**Step 3 – Envision a Document**: The visual move also serves to make this future believable.[2] The instruction to create a prop from this future world brings to life the scenario that is emerging. The prop, a metonym for this future scenario, introduces a situated yet speculative provocation of what this future might offer or threaten. Whether a passport, psychotropic or permit, the discursive prop sets up how to debate, refine or evaluate this future.

**Step 4 – Detail a Scene**: This step navigates the transition from envisioning to enacting. The instruction to create and perform a scene using the prop draws on the value of experiential engagement and the lessons that come not just from prototyping but from performing the physical, social and emotional interactions the prop instigates.

Beyond the evident deployment of activities that *make visible* to get to a place of *making believe* the four steps also integrate an analytical, critical approach with a performative, creative one. In partnering an analysis of the cause and effect of dynamic, interconnected systems with making and embodying the relational future artefacts new feedback loops are engaged. Reminding us again that for fine points to be fleshed out, assumptions to be troubled and new lessons to take hold, the act of rehearsing the implications is the bridge for exposing what needs to be believed.

The focus in both practice vignettes on the contribution of speculative thought to design's capacity to imagine the future offers an alternative to data-led algorithms that might calculate or simulate the future. As designers, world-makers, researchers and citizens, there is an ethical caution in these stories of practice to consider the epistemic, social, ecological politics of imagining.

I return to the insights uncovered in these projects and practice narratives in Part III. The section on the importance of designing interaction (3.4) reinforces the importance of establishing resonance, prototyping with others, unlearning and unsettling the never-before-seen, by way of embodied learning. Woven through these stories is the importance of the personal as it sits alongside the relational as introduced in Part I. The provocation here is that being in conversation with others might be the easiest bridge by which to turn the conversation inward to examine ourselves. If we receive a disorienting dilemma as an invitation to attune to others, it just might *make visible* our positions in ways that help us to reframe our individual worldviews and critically question what we believe now so we might interrogate what we believe is possible in the future.

---

## Narrative 6.1 Figuring: an Ambiguous Move

### 2005 – with Tim Marshall

*The room is windowless, of that I am certain. I remember the walls as painted grey, a fluorescent light flickering in the ceiling. That is probably not true. I have lost track of time in this place with no sun, absorbed in the process of designing I don't know what. For now. I am alone with Illustrator, the application. We are absorbed in conversation. I am moving shapes around in ways that anyone observing might read as directionless. This aligns with my perception that I have no clear intention.*

*My education led me to understand that the designer designs communication, objects and interactions. This productive practice comes with a set of decisive moves and sacrificial prototypes that scaffold a process of iteration and feedback. Yet, today I am lost in flow as I aimlessly move form around to see how the materials respond to me.*

*You see, I am lost. I am new to this country, to this university. As I sit with the abstract forms on the screen, I am thinking more conceptually than concretely. I do not know the context well enough to begin addressing any meaningful challenges here in my new job. I am not trying to imagine what a new curriculum might look like as much as sitting with how a new orientation to design education might feel. At this point I have no words for what I am doing. I just know I am not trying to solve a problem as much as sense a way into what I do not know.*

I came to call this a practice of figuring. In that bleak room, displaced from anything familiar, it became possible to use my form-making, propositional thinking and abductive sensing to not fix a solution but to be abstractly, yet deliberately, in conversation with my own ideas, assumptions and values around curriculum design. Until that moment, my mental model of communication design would construct the artefact as a mode of communicating to others, like Figure 0.1 of a scientific text. In this new space, figuratively and metaphorically, I am unconsciously exploring whether this act of figuring could be as an end in itself.

*On this day, my conversation is with threads of colour on a screen. I am wondering how different ways of conceiving Parsons curriculum might be visualised – do the ribbons represent fields of design practice or transdisciplinary thematics? The meandering curves in the paths remind me of aerial views of New Zealand's braided rivers. It makes me question what would braid the strands together and what directs the ever-shifting flow of the water. The backtalk in my mind is further animated by the serendipitous moves the computer makes, drawing me into a conversation that asks what happens when scales unsettle, opacity promises and forms collide. Are the marks on the screen proposing bridges or tunnels, crossings or intersections? Suspending the impulse to interrogate the consequences of these ruminations I try to stay in the realm of the potential.*

*Now, Tim has joined me. It is late and we both should be heading home. But this is enticing work, provocatively generative. There is an intimacy in this interpretative process that feels other to the daily schedule of meetings that trade on decisive and persuasive wordsmithing. Together we weigh what the ambiguous marks of the screen might hold for how we conceive of design education this century. This feels different, I am not presenting an idea, nor persuading him of my pitch. I am inviting him to share how he is reading the still-to-be-made-sense-of marks. Now we are designing together, side-by-side, playing with the forms to see what surfaces. Resisting the pull to figure it out and operationalise the ideas, we stay drawn into figuring out the possibilities. The design backtalk in my head is amplified by Tim's interpretations animating my ideas and the marks on the screen. We do not know it yet, but these nascent moves in the office that was once a storage room office are Tim and I designing a way of collaborating, a way that will shape how we work together for years to come.*

The images we were co-creating were not communication design as I knew it. The new visual grammar – neither diagram, nor visualisation, nor sketch – was harder to classify. This was a visual conversation that opened up spaces for negotiation, interpretation and revelation.

My intent had never been for these visual interior ruminations to be made public. Yet, Tim could see the democratic potential of the Parsons community engaging in the interpretative, speculative process we had. Tim sensed that talking to design educators through design might bring more people along than a white paper or bullet points on a slide deck. With the images out in the wild, I notice the captivating engagement that comes with evocative diagrams that scramble any easy reading. Working with desirable difficulty, I visually framed the confounding tensions and curious questions the figuring diagrams elicited.

This was transformation by stealth. There was no unsettling dilemma as much as an invitation to act otherwise. The tacit, familiar moves of the mouse and the aesthetic decisions I made came from decades of practice. At my computer, I knew what I was doing, even if in the room in the other hemisphere I was stumbling in the dark. The interplay between the knowing and not-knowing cracked open a way for me to amplify the reflective backtalk between my porous ideas, Illustrator's mark-making, Tim's slippery interpretations and the emerging question of what it might take to design the design school for a new century.

## Bibliography

1  Tharp, Bruce M. and Stephanie M. Tharp. *Discursive Design: Critical, Speculative, and Alternative Things.* The MIT Press, 2018.
2  Costello, Amy. "Southern Africa: Troubled Water." Online Documentary Episode, PBS Frontline, 2016, www.pbs.org/frontlineworld/stories/southernafrica904/.
3  Simon, Herbert Alexander. *The Science of the Artificial.* The MIT Press, 1969.
4  Garcia, Claudio Garduño. *Design as Freedom.* Aalto ARTS Books, 2017.
5  Keinonen, Turkka. "Design Method – Instrument, Competence or Agenda." *Multiple Ways to Design Research: Research Cases That Reshape the Design Discipline,* Swiss Design Network, 2009, pp. 280–93.
6  Berg, Theresa et al. *Benefits of Design Practice in Fieldwork: How 'Artesanía Para El Bienestar' Emerged in the Field as a Concept to Improve Access to Healthcare in a Mayan Community in Campeche, Mexico,* 2014, OCAD University, 15 Oct 2014.
7  Paniagua, Alejandro and David Istance. "Teachers as Designers of Learning Environments: The Importance of Innovative Pedagogies." Organisation for Economic Co-operation and Development, 9 April 2018.

8 Kemmis, Stephen and Robin McTaggart. "Participatory Action Research: Communicative Action and the Public Sphere." *The Sage Handbook of Qualitative Research*, edited by Norman K Denzin and Yvonna S Lincoln, 3rd ed., Sage Publications, 2005, pp. 559–603.
9 Cohen, Louis et al., editors. *Research Methods in Education*, 6th ed. Taylor and Francis, 2007.
10 Elden, Max and Morten Levin. "Cogenerative Learning: Bringing Participation into Action Research." *Participatory Action Research*, edited by William F. Whyte, Sage Publications, 1991, pp. 127–42.
11 Tuckwell, Dion. *Joining Practice Research*, 2021. Monash University, PhD Thesis, doi:10.26180/14533521.v1.
12 Wilkie, Alex et al., editors. *Speculative Research: The Lure of Possible Futures*. Taylor and Francis, 2017.
13 Darling-Hammond, Linda et al. "Professional Learning in the Learning Profession: A Status Report on Teacher Development in the United States and Abroad." National Staff Development Council, 2009, edpolicy.stanford.edu/sites/default/files/publications/professional-learning-profession-status-report-teacher-development-us-and-abroad_0.pdf.
14 Candy, Stuart and Jeff Watson. "The Thing from the Future." Situation Lab, 2017, www.situationlab.org/project/the-thing-from-the-future/.

# 7

# DESIGN METHODS

## Make Fun to Make Tangible

FIGURE 7.1 **Crafting Attunement**: This Trojan Horse was initially conceived as a speculative, playful prop for facilitating a conversation around how to smuggle social psychology research into schools. Our conversations revealed the affordance of the improvised method lay less in the horse's capacity to imagine future tactics and more in its capacity to hold attention (Narrative 7.1). Watching interview subjects being pulled back in by the horse's presence, as if the crafted artefact was the one asking questions, was to witness the value of materials as co-facilitators of generative conversations.

DOI: 10.4324/9780429429743-9

The focus on designing experiences does not touch on complex digital games or simplistic gamifying of learning. Instead, this is more about play. Resisting getting to answers, play as an engagement strategy prioritises spirited curiosity over getting to the next level. Brian Sutton-Smith, a play theorist, notes that many of the rhetorics of play are framed around productive modernist narratives of progress and creativity (1). For example, we understand the rhetoric of play-as-identity when we ascribe child's play as a form of developmental progress, we make the case for play-as-the-imaginary to drive innovation and we see how hobbies weave a consumerist angle through play as a form of relaxation for the self. These *productive* narratives of play are steeped in the justification for bringing play to learning.

Seen through the lens of *make fun* and *make tangible*, this chapter's two game design case studies, *Budgetball* and *Particle in a Box,* acknowledge the limitations of play as a discrete solution to educating players and more as a gateway to making abstract concepts more accessible. In these stories lies a caution in espousing the educational value of a game. Alternatively, the call is to follow the fun the game play creates. This emergent approach allows the game to speak back to the players and designers to reveal what lesson there is to be learned.

The practice vignettes rely less on game play yet advance the idea of social interactions for priming people to see situations from another perspective. The WonderLab vignette presents a haptic orientation to data analysis. The co-creative process has workshop participants creating themes from the participants stories of their lived experiences. *ATLAS,* from the Design Rounds, is a design game that brings a hands-on approach to project teams constructing the scope and focus of a new initiative. The non-linear process undermines any sense of a prescriptive sequence by granting each player a moment to chase the aspect of the project they are motivated to examine next. Together, the case studies and the snapshots from practice draw the connection between priming people to be curious, allowing ideas to emerge from the social interactions and letting play help translate unformed ideas into tangible topics for discussion.

## 7.1 *Budgetball*

### 7.1.1 *A Make Fun Case Study*

PETLab is a research lab inside Parsons School of Design that explores the learning potential of games to create more critically informed citizens. With an emphasis on creating games for social impact, the projects create novel ways for people to learn about issues in their community through digital and physical interactions and engagement. The founder and co-director of PETLab, Colleen Macklin, who is committed to making learning more playful, says,

We know learning creates impacts. And when you know more about a specific topic, you become a more informed citizen. Our goal is to work with partners who are trying to contribute to a better world in some form or another.

*(2)*

In examining the value of games as a tool for public engagement, PETLab extends its work beyond digital environments to include physical engagements that deepen learning experiences.

Macklin finds a key component of game design is in 'finding the fun'. You iteratively build a system and put it out there, so you can watch people play it. The feedback that comes with watching people play comes from noticing what people enjoy doing, from finding the intrinsically rewarding moments that keep people playing. Macklin describes the learning value that comes from making a game: "When you're making a game, you're tinkering. You're taking apart a system and putting it back together. You're changing components of it, you're changing connections between the things and then seeing what happens" (2). It's not about simply adding a point system or badges to a process to engage people, it's a holistic making exercise, "a caveat for well-designed games is being able to go deeply into systems to find the intrinsic pleasure" (2).

A call from a Washington D.C. think tank asking creative practitioners to imagine new ways to teach citizens about policy, led to the development of *Budgetball*. Designed for university students to learn about federal debt, *Budgetball* was designed by PETLab in collaboration with design firm Area Code. *Budgetball,* a team 'sport', takes an embodied approach to creating a learning experience that makes citizens 'fiscally and financially fit'. Modelled on intercollegiate sport, players engage in a competitive event organised around understanding the relationships between debt, savings, interest and taxes. The design of the game forces people to make choices about spending money to gain different competitive advantages, or saving money and having less resources than other teams. In order to get out of debt, a team has to make sacrifices, such as being forced to play while holding a tiny egg or wearing oven mitts. In playing the game, students go through the 'budgeting' process. Players have an embodied experience of the benefits and challenges that come with making choices around debt, resources and strategising to manage the longer-term implications of near-term decisions.

In 2009, a final tournament of *Budgetball* was hosted on the National Mall in Washington D.C. where university teams competed against staff from the White House and Congress, (including congresspeople and the US Secretary General). The physical, playful gameplay made tangible concepts that are oftentimes conveyed mathematically. In strategising how and when to spend, the game turns the fairly abstract problems of the national debt into tangible and physical realities (2). However, Macklin is quick to acknowledge that bringing in more detail, particularly how different sectors might spend money to go into debt, dragged the game into minutiae that had diminishing returns. The design team decided it was more important players walked away with a stronger conceptual model than detailed knowledge. Designed to understand the challenges around spending, budgeting and paying back debt, the game does not take a side, but rather wants players to grapple with the abstract and emotional levers. The game play leads to a felt reckoning with and embodied memory of how seductive or empowering it feels to gain resources and how overwhelming or despairing it can feel to know you have to pay them back.

*Budgetball* allows players to learn the emotional push and pull that comes with sacrificing and negotiating in their whole bodies. This embodied, affective encounter is what helps players not just grasp but remember the abstract financial lesson. The game as a gateway to future learning (3) sparks interest in the issue, and provides an entry point to go deeper and ask more questions. In positioning games as portals into understanding larger systems and actively experiencing complexity, we can focus on using play to seed further inquiry.

## 7.2 Particle in a Box

### 7.2.1 A Make Tangible Case Study

Professors Nassim Parvin and Azad Naeemi both teach at Georgia Institute of Technology (Georgia Tech), in the School of Digital Media and The School of Electrical and Computer Engineering, respectively, while Aditya Anupam is a Ph.D. candidate in Digital Media at Georgia Tech and is supervised by Parvin. In the Fall of 2013, Naeemi found himself lamenting to Parvin about the challenges of teaching quantum mechanics in his introductory courses. Parvin had been an electrical engineer before transitioning into design, so the difficulty of teaching quantum mechanics resonated with her immediately. When teaching classical physics, you can relate concepts in mathematical equations back to our lived experiences of the world. Understanding physics through our understanding of what happens when we go down a hill or throw a ball is infinitely easier than asking learners to grasp a world they have never experienced.

Even more disorienting is the idea that in many cases, quantum mechanics contradicts a learner's experience of the physical world. Research studies confirm that secondary and lower undergraduate students regularly have difficulty relating quantum physics to physical reality (4). It is common for students to pass introductory courses in quantum mechanics with an ability to solve its mathematical equations and yet also maintain significant misconceptions about its conceptual frameworks. Many introductory courses focus on mathematical formalism and less on the conceptual understanding of the subject (5), leading to a surface learning that fails to shift a learner's mental model. The early focus on mathematics has students believing that understanding lies in the mechanics of solving equations, with understanding the relationships between systemic parameters and their physical significance requiring a different kind of inquiry (5).

Seeing an opportunity, Parvin and Naeemi considered how a student might be able to experience a world ruled by quantum mechanics. If a student was able to experience the behaviour of particles in the quantum 'world', might they more readily grasp the conceptual frameworks supported by the mathematical formalism? The potential for the learner to move beyond the mathematical seeded the idea for a digital game. The leap to designing a game was not informed by the gamification trend in education which they saw as arguably flawed and misguided. Instead, the decision to design a game was based on the probabilistic nature of the quantum world. The team recognised that "the best way to understand this nature is to experience it over and over. The naturally repetitive nature of gameplay is thus suitable for understanding probabilistic quantum phenomena." (5)

The work began as, and is still today, an experiment in multidisciplinary collaboration, seeking to understand how and what an environment ruled by quantum mechanics might be. The research group that emerged from this project is led by PhD student Aditya Anupam, who after completing an undergraduate and Master's degree in electrical engineering, pursued a doctorate in the School of Literature, Media, and Communication (LMC) around the design of digital games and digital media to foster learning. Students from across disciplines at the University have participated in myriad ways in the creation of this game, from game and character design, offering skills in illustration and coding, to working with physics students to structure and clarify content.

Today, the platformer game *Particle in a Box* asks the player to navigate a world ruled by the laws of quantum mechanics. Offering insight into how differently physics operates at the quantum level has helped the game become a supplemental learning tool for students in introductory quantum mechanics at Georgia Tech, as well as other schools and universities around the world. At the same time, the team asserts you could never teach advanced quantum mechanics through a digital environmental representation and gameplay alone. *Particle in a Box* could not supplant students learning the necessary mathematics to advance through a course. Instead, it works alongside traditional methods of teaching and learning to develop a curiosity for discovery and inquiry in students through an experiential environment and engaging gameplay. Even though *Particle in a Box* has become a useful experiential learning tool used by other universities (it can be downloaded or played online), the team quickly noted the parallel learning space the game opened up. The researchers recognise the significance of the game inspiring a spirit of inquiry amongst the interdisciplinary team who continually develop the game. The deep learning opportunity presented by students and professors from different disciplines collaborating on the quantum environment led to the development of a cooperative online game for teaching quantum mechanics called Psi and Delta (6).

When transmissive education prioritises 'knowing' the content rather than learning how to question, the capacity to be curious is not correlated with getting to the answer. Yet, curiosity is what helps the learner ask different and better questions. Parvin sees a Science education fuelled by questioning, scepticism and reflexivity as core to the development of a scientists' practice. Part of learning the ways of science is to bring to science and math equations a degree of the reflexivity and scepticism. "They are not models of the world as it is... the process of science itself is messy, and how these are different paradigms for seeing the world, not like, unlike poetry." An assumption in this project is that science is not a set of absolute facts that represent the world as it is. Naeemi acknowledges that "Many mistakes are made. Debates are never resolved... The sooner we can communicate this to the students, the more prepared they are to be better researchers." (7)

This collaboration between design and physics demonstrates an open, iterative and curious approach to designing learning. The experiential elements of game play construct a reality that acknowledges it as just one way to make sense of the world. The play orientation trades in its ability to operate outside of the real-world constraints and encourages players to explore, question and experience the abstract principles they are grappling with in classroom textbooks.

## 7.3 Design Framing and Analysing Practice Vignettes

How might a social, playful encounter infuse creativity into the planning and analysis phases of co-design projects? These practice vignettes explore creative material modes for participants collaborating on the design move of co-evolving different project phases at the same time. The *Storymaking Engagement Framework* and the *ATLAS* game take the idea of co-evolving the problem/solution in new directions (8). In the Storymaking Engagement Framework, making sense of the problem space by proposing potential solutions works at the level of participants' simultaneously co-realising and co-analysing the data. In the *ATLAS* design, game players co-evolve the planning and ideating phases of a new project. Both snapshots reveal how a playful push and tangible pull work together to generate new insights.

### 7.3.1 The ATLAS Design Game

Tuuli Mattelmäki, the Director of Encore Lab at Aalto University, introduced *ATLAS* to us in the Design Rounds (9). *ATLAS*, a game conceived to help cross-disciplinary teams scope and plan service design projects, is a collaboration between Encore, SimLab and BIT – three research labs at Aalto University in Helsinki. Tuuli and her team brought co-creation to the scientific research the business and innovation partners contributed. *ATLAS* is grounded in empirical findings and theoretical reflections from 13 research projects and it scaffolds how players-as-stakeholders come together to develop a project plan. The game offers a vocabulary for the dimensions that co-creation projects are built on – supporting players in charting how a project might take shape by identifying the key design decisions that need to be made (10). The game translates a framework of design choices so that the players can work through what influences the formulation of projects and what informs the selection and development of methods. The game is designed to support teams in coming together to assess and plan co-creation projects.

The game play has teams go through various dimensions essential to planning and conducting service co-creation projects. With a facilitator at each table, small teams take turns selecting cards to focus the planning around one of those dimensions. For example, a player might choose to focus on who gets to participate, followed by the next player choosing the dimension of what objects could be designed. The non-linear game rules support a co-evolution that affords divergent, focussed inquiry alongside convergent opening up of the decision-making sequence (Figure 9.0). The coded design materials, shaped in a hexagon, present a specific kind of convivial interaction. Although quite analytical and solution-oriented, there is a playfulness imbued in the random unfolding of the sequence. Design games, like John Carse's (11) notion of the infinite game, stage participation not around winning or losing but around the value of continuing to play. Design games (12) have rules (like finite games) but also a playful gameplay that invites a porous boundary between what needs to be planned and what might be allowed to unfold in its own time. In this way, the design game as a workshop offers a mutual learning platform for sharing current and past experiences that deepens insights for the designer, the player and the game designer. In *ATLAS*, this play mindset is brought to the task of making tangible decisions about future services and systems.

### 7.3.2 The Embodied Enquiry Workshop

WonderLab Doctoral candidate Kelly Anderson works with these mindsets at another phase of the co-design process. Kelly's research engages participants in sense-making workshop insights as they emerge. In doing so, she wrestles with similar concerns to those in Hannah's PhD about what happens to participant data post the workshop event and to Tuckwell's interest in seeing participants as co-researchers. In extending the remit of the workshop to include co-analysis, it becomes possible to inclusively engage people in interpreting their own data. The storymaking of the workshop has participants move through form-making, sense-making and meaning-making as embodied modes for coding and interpreting stories-as-data. The workshop facilitates ways to co-evolve the sharing of an individual's lived experiences while collectively interpreting and analysing each other's stories. The work is framed as an extended period of co-realising, rather than as an additional step. Workshop attendees transition from co-realising insights in pairs, to co-realising the themes emerging from the data. The co-evolution here shuttles between the surfacing of the individual's lived experience (what this tells me about myself) and analysis of the collective experiences (what this tells us about what works and doesn't work). The tacit insights to be mined from reflecting on a personal experience are made thicker when seen in the social context of others' stories. Echoing Garduño Garcia's methods (6.1), the analytical insights to be gained from theming the collective data serve to hold up a mirror to the original shared experience. The transformative potential of the workshop is heightened by this co-evolving of the meaning-making.

In the four-step workshop, the first two steps, *reflect* and *translate*, outwardly align with common co-design practice. Feeling their way through a lived experience, participants are asked to recall the affective qualities (the emotions, the atmosphere, the physiological and the interpersonal, to name a few) over the observable facts. They then use everyday household materials to translate the indeterminate, subjective experience into an abstract or metaphoric form. Focused on how people are left *feeling* by an experience (for example, like waiting for healthcare results), there is no intention in this workshop to design solutions or gather objective evidence. Kelly is agnostic about the specifics of someone's story and instead drawn to how designers can put to work the nuanced, affective data buried within the experience.

In steps three and four, the request to *interpret* and *analyse* departs from the usual co-design script. The introduction of an evaluative mindset[1] manifests in a series of analytical moves conceived to detach from the affective story made physically tangible in steps one and two. After sharing the story with a partner, the participant places the tangible story on the ground to examine from a bird's eye view before stepping back to observe the form from afar. Throughout the *Interpret* step, the pair are attentive to more than how the physical reframing is shifting their perspective. In constant verbal and non-verbal conversation, the pair sense how seeing the other person's story from multiple angles shifts their own story. The embodied backtalk between making, sensing and storying extends to talking back to the emerging data. This is mutual learning in action. The *Analyse* step has the pair identify a shared theme the previous step has surfaced. This act of distancing seeks to leave behind a longer story, located in a specific time, by picking up a grander theme about trust, hope or injustice. The final step has participants fill in incomplete sentences to code how an identified theme might show up outside the specifics of their story. As an example, a couple who identified curiosity as a theme might use the prompts to analyse that curiosity *overshadows* despair, curiosity *creates* motivation or curiosity *allows* for engagement.

These practice vignettes are not as traditionally fun as *Budgetball* or as game-like as *Particle in a Box* but there is a whole-self, big picture sensibility to the *ATLAS* game and the *Embodied Enquiry* workshop that circles back to the hands-on,

---

1 **Lisa**: The Southern Initiative (TSI) has developed an evaluative framework designed to deepen practice by scaffolding learning. *Niho Taniwha* seeks to foster a culture of 'learning in complexity' by embedding evaluative mindsets and activities within all levels of TSI. In the quest to amplify transformation an approach to evaluative learning possible respects multiple sources of evidence including emergent outcomes for whānau, practice knowing, system change impacts, strategic learnings, quantitative and qualitative data (13, pp. 19–20).

felt, interactive social context of learning alongside others. The material props, experiential learning and open-ended playfulness trace a connection between the potential to create fun through tangible interactions with yet-to-be-realised ideas. Together, the stories of this chapter cast a light on the relationship between social interactions and the emotional experience of a learning encounter. Consideration for embodied engagement is foregrounded even though the objective might prioritise introducing quantum physics or federal budgets.

This chapter deepens the relational dimension introduced in Chapter 5 by emphasising the value exchange of the social experience. The call to *make tangible* reminds us how learning is deepened when grounded in simulation or placed in context in ways that invite the learner to see the situation from another perspective. The social context goes further to ask the learner to make sense of how their understanding sits in relation to others. Co-creating with physical artefacts, whether moving cards around or creating an artefact from household materials, supports the making ideas tangible, so they can be laid down, debated and respected by peers. In Part III, you can trace connections between this commitment to *make fun* with the chapter on Designing Interactions (3.4). The chapter explores novelty and embodied learning and the section on participatory prototyping reminds us that engaging encounters only come into being after endless rounds of prototyping, playtesting and piloting (14, pp. 105–17).

## Narrative 7.1 Co-realising: a Convivial Metaphor

### 2014 – with Mai Kobori

*I am aware of the weight of the origami horse I hold in my hands. It is made of kraft paper, so it is not the physical heft I am weighing. There is a weight to the care my collaborator Mai Kobori put into crafting it, the light touch that comes with its fragility, and the weight of the risk we are about to take (Figure 7.1). This is a design move we have not made before. I sense the vulnerability in the playfulness of what we are asking of people. I have no confidence this will work. I do know I want to learn from peoples' lived experiences, and I do not want to do an empathy map.*

*We will embrace the fragments of knowing, partial insights and productive ambiguity that comes with people seeing something in this horse that Mai and I had never considered. I learned to become comfortable with making it up as we go along.*

*The first person walks in for his interview. He is a school principal. I have no relationship with him and no experience interviewing people. Yet still, I find myself sitting across the table from a stranger with just a beautiful origami horse as the only prop between us.*

*We engage in small talk. This man's time is precious and yet I am hesitant to begin. With time, I share why we want him to do this not-an-interview with us. For all the research declaring the economic and social benefits of teaching social and emotional learning, there is little support for a curricular solution. We are left wondering how experts in this space might imagine could help get this content into schools. I deliberately, somewhat ceremoniously, place the horse in the middle of the table. I ask the principal that, if delivering social and emotional learning is the goal, what, metaphorically, might be the Trojan horse that opens the gates?*

That day, we had two other metaphoric props similarly poised to generate new avenues of inquiry. A football playbook conceived to surface tactical insights as to how we might teach these skills, a compass and a blank map that spoke to how we might orient students on this journey. Still, I mainly recall the grace with which the inanimate yet assertive, playful yet earnest Trojan horse uncovered rewarding insights and opened up our thinking.

*The epitome of a convivial tool – the horse, as co-facilitator – engages the interview subjects and focuses the conversation. More comfortable now, I let the horse do the hard work. The principal returns to the Greek myth and questions if there is a war between the curriculum and students' emotional development? The teachers' college professor wonders what the stealth move might be to get social and emotional learning in past the guards. The teacher pauses mid-sentence and picks up the horse. Sensing the carefully crafted object might calm the rational trajectory of her reasons as to why things cannot be, she holds the horse in her hands to imagine what might be. A student repeatedly centres the horse on the table as a reminder to keep circling back to why we are here. Throughout the day, we riff on the material qualities of the horse: its unstable footing, its fragile appearance and its intimate scale.*

*There is an improvisational lilt in our conversations. The ideas we came in with are quickly disregarded and any notion of structured questions abandoned; the horse leads the discussion. We enjoy the ride. We find ourselves letting go of any pretence that we are objective bystanders. With the horse unashamedly influencing the conversation, we shift our own stance too. More like an asynchronous studio critique, we allow the artefact to centre the ideas. We weave comments from the earlier interviews into the discussion, we celebrate the plural interpretations and we let the generative co-realising build on what came before.*

I found the horse last week. It has been lying flat in a file box for seven years. I feel neglectful, almost ashamed. Like a collapsed puppet, silent and alone, the horse has none of the vital presence we granted it in that interview room on the other side of the world. I was wrong to focus on the horse's weight. The statuesque ever-present metaphor took up space on the table and in our minds. The care taken to craft the unique form commanded our engagement, focussed our conversations and bundled together our collective ideas.

## Bibliography

1 Sutton-Smith, Brian. *The Ambiguity of Play.* Harvard University Press, 2001.
2 Macklin, Colleen. "Book Interview, Online." Interview by Kate McEntee, 21 February 2018.
3 "James Gee's Principles for Game Based Learning." Legends of Learning, 16 November 2016, www.legendsoflearning.com/blog/james-paul-gee-game-based-learning.
4 Krijtenburg-Lewerissa, Kim et al. "Insights into Teaching Quantum Mechanics in Secondary and Lower Undergraduate Education." *Physical Review Physics Education Research,* vol. 13, no. 1, 2017, p. 010109, doi:10.1103/PhysRevPhysEducRes.13.010109.
5 Anupam, Aditya et al. *"Particle in a Box*: An Experiential Environment for Learning Introductory Quantum Mechanics." *IEEE Transactions on Education,* vol. 61, no. 1, 2018, pp. 29–37, doi:10.1109/TE.2017.2727442.
6 Anupam, Aditya et al. "Design Challenges for Science Games: The Case of a Quantum Mechanics Game." *International Journal of Designs for Learning,* vol. 11, no. 1, 2019, pp. 1–20, doi:10.14434/ijdl.v11i1.24264.
7 Anupam, Aditya et al. "Book Interview, Online." Interview by Kate McEntee, 18 January 2018.
8 Dorst, Kees and Nigel Cross. "Creativity in the Design Process: Co-Evolution of Problem–Solution." *Design Studies,* vol. 22, no. 5, 2001, pp. 425–37, doi:10.1016/S0142-694X(01)00009-6.
9 Lab, Service Design. *Atlas* Game, 2012, www.servicedesignlab.net/service-co-creation-game.
10 Lee, Jung-Joo et al. "Design Choices Framework for Co-Creation Projects." *International Journal of Design,* vol. 12, no. 2, 2018, pp. 15–31.
11 Carse, James. *Finite and Infinite Games.* Free Press, 1986.
12 Vaajakallio, Kirsikka and Tuuli Mattelmäki. "Design Games in Codesign: As a Tool, a Mindset and a Structure." *CoDesign,* vol. 10, no. 1, 2014, pp. 63–77, doi:10.1080/15710882.2014.881886.
13 "Review of TSI 2020: Strengths & Opportunities." Yunus Centre, Griffith University, Review Report, 2020.
14 Macklin, Colleen and John Sharp. *Games, Design and Play: A Detailed Approach to Iterative Game Design.* Pearson Education, 2016.

# 8
# DESIGN MOVES
## Make Together to Make Change

FIGURE 8.1  **Together/Alone Diorama**: This is my wondering from the Design
Rounds diorama activity designed to affirm our encouragement of plural
parallel paths of inquiry. The Design Rounds week was dedicated to an
experiential exploration of the contribution of design to create spaces for
transformative learning. As hosts, we wanted this initial activity to reflect
the valence of the types of embodied, vulnerable, relational experiences
we believed would support our guest's plural selves showing up (also
Figure 2.1). My narrative shares how my conversation with the bespoke
materials drew me into figuring, wondering and futuring a new way
of understanding how we would be together and alone (Narrative 8.1).

DOI: 10.4324/9780429429743-10

The proliferation of human-centred design toolkits was a strategic response to the claim that anyone can be a designer. The accessibility of free design methods in the toolkits allowed people introduced to design thinking in a one-day workshop to continue building capacity. The design mindset (as noted in Chapter 4) nudged this practice a little and yet there is still oftentimes an emphasis on the deployment of the tool as the solution. Participatory design researchers Yoko Akama and Ann Light critique design's emphasis on methods, contesting the principle that design methods are transferable or generalisable (1). This chapter stands with their call for methods to not be decoupled from the ways a practitioner negotiates and facilitates the application of a method. It is not that all methods are inherently flawed, even if some, like the persona, are perhaps more reductively insidious than others. It is the ethically questionable suggestion that methods can be applied by an outsider entering a community. Akama and Light reference moments from participatory design workshops to highlight that although methods aid negotiation, it is the more nuanced moves of the designer that address the need for socio-cultural consideration for place and context, mindful consideration for the values and motivations of the people and responsive consideration for complex, in-the-moment social interactions (2).

It is in this final chapter of Part II that the lenses of *make together* and *make change* are examined through culturally specific projects from Finland and Australia. The co-creative angle of making with shows up in the participatory case studies that interweave autonomy and agency with politics and ethics. Grounded in the values of participatory design, the *Edukata* and *Relative Creative* case studies show an attentiveness to attune to how the moves of the designer can support the cultivation of knowledge communities. This commitment to *make together* grants participants the agency to co-create learning goals and to discover the breadth and depth of expertise amongst the participants (3). In partnership with participants, the designer learns how the constraints and opportunities participants face might be reconfigured, reframed and reimagined.

The call to *make change* draws us back to the transformative learning frame of the book. Pelle Ehn, one of the founders of participatory design, reflects on how the approach to learning that emerged in the early days of participatory design (the second half of the 1970s) was an interplay between Freire's pedagogy of the oppressed (2.3), Marxist strategies of local knowledge production and Kurt Lewin's theories on change.[1] Interdisciplinary academic theories were interlaced with practical strategies for honouring a bottom up liberating pedagogical agenda, a decentralised approach to how knowledge is enacted and steps for supporting the transition phases that lead to real change. Back in the 1980s and 1990s, Ehn's ideas on the intersection between learning and participatory design were informed by Suchman's ideas on situated knowledge and action, Lave and

---

1   **Lisa**: Pelle Ehn's chapter on "Learning in Participatory Design as I Found It" gives a first-person account through the decades on the theories and practices that have shaped the field of participatory design today (3, pp. 7–21).

Wenger's seminal work in communities of practice, Engström's cultural-historical framing of activity theory and Schön's theories of the reflective practitioner.

Signalling how participatory design might design for change, action and emancipation, Ehn links Lewin's sentiment that if you want to truly understand something then try to change it, to Karl Marx's observation that philosophers interpret the world but the point is to change it (3, p. 10). From here, Ehn posits the import of reframing expertise so we might engage the community in the active, situated work of making change. This chapter respects the historical perspective that the participatory orientation to *making together* is deeply connected to a quest to make meaningful change.

The WonderLab vignette exemplifies the notion of small moves by considering how an individual might, to use Freire's term, bring a conscientisation to their own positioning. Sean Donahue's vignette speaks directly to Ehn's troubling of expertise and echoes threads made explicit in the *Relative Creative* case study. To illustrate the cultural and political complexity of *working with*, the international development practice snapshot reveals an intentional coming together with the community before any designing begins. Alternatively, Sonali Ojha's Design Rounds snapshot finds its ethical footing in the connection between designing for emotions and priming people for their own liberation. Here, the role of affect and the move to enlist vulnerability in facilitating the learning encounter emphasises how designing for transformation is a cognitive, emotive and behavioural act.

## 8.1 *Edukata*

### 8.1.1 *A Make Together Case Study*

As digital tools become more prevalent in education and classrooms, designers are increasingly playing a role in defining how learning is delivered. This case study explores how a project reframed the question of *how* to deliver, to *what* should be delivered. *Edukata* is a Finnish program which enables and supports teachers to collectively design new learning activities for the classroom (4). The participatory design model challenges the idea that technological advancements will define the future of learning and classrooms, and instead promotes a system in which teachers collectively define future learning innovations, with or without new technologies.

The program came out of a research project within the Learning Environments Research Group (LeGroup), a design lab at Aalto University in Helsinki. It was part of an EU-wide research consortium to develop effective learning tools to help define future classroom technology. The process underlying the *Edukata* program is based in LeGroup's participatory research model that ensures educators are included in the process. *Edukata* was the most well-received and successful outcome from research groups across the EU looking into building tools for future-oriented classrooms. However, the formalised program that evolved into

*Edukata* started out as yet another digital tool. The pivot in the project came from the researchers noticing the ways co-creating the learning activities was driving teacher engagement and classroom innovation. By attuning to what resonated with teachers, LeGroup was able to reframe the participatory process for collectively designing learning as the focus of the *Edukata* model.

The model begins with bringing a team of dedicated educators within a school together with a trained *Edukata* facilitator. The team creates a 'Design Studio' environment and through a series of workshops over several months explores new possibilities for how learning might happen in their specific school. Initially, the team is presented with pre-defined design challenges, developed through previous design and piloting cycles by LeGroup. From these prompts, they collectively frame design opportunities, identify resources that are useful and ultimately create new learning activities for their education environment.

The scenario-based workshops invite teachers to collectively create learning activities for specific, relevant situations. These responsive learning activities are described through templates that detail underlying motivations, necessary resources, how to prepare and provide inspiration for the activity. The activities can be shared with peers to promote generative thinking, but teachers are encouraged to adjust activities for their specific environment. Research demonstrates that well-designed learning activities are a valuable tool for teachers, especially when the teachers are "supported to design their own Learning Activities with proper facilitation and guidance, the results are even better" (5, p. 42). Educators are empowered to let their lived experiences inform the learning activities and resources they create.

The *Edukata* model is based on the belief that each educational environment has unique situation-specific challenges and opportunities. The *Edukata* Facilitators Guide proposes the anchoring of new tools within each individual school, "Participatory design means that the people who are likely to be affected by a design are invited to participate in the design" (4, p. 9). The model's capacity to transform learning communities lies with this decision to privilege a teachers' expertise and grant them the autonomy to decide what, how and when they will implement learning in their classrooms. In addition to teacher participation, the activities are also test run with students, iterated on and then codified by a group of teachers in the school.

*Edukata's* lead researcher, Teemu Leinonen, describes how this ethos is a deep part of Finnish society, "We don't get any change in the Finnish schools if you don't get the teachers" (6). The socio-cultural context is relevant here. *Edukata* was translated into seven languages and disseminated across the EU, yet it never reached the level of traction it had in Finland. This raises the question of context-specific interventions and to what extent models for innovation and transformation can be scaled across cultures and demographics. There are also systemic considerations. *Edukata's* reception in Finland is potentially tied to teachers having post-graduate degrees, high salaries and a corresponding status similar to that of attorneys or doctors. *Edukata* leveraged the strength of the culture within which it was developed to identify teachers as the key stakeholders in a system in which teachers are given a lot of respect and autonomy.

The agency the teachers are granted in the process trusts in teachers' capacity to navigate uncertainty and messiness within a creation process. Rather than providing a simplified schematic of a step-by-step 'design' process to follow, it purposely avoids dictating specific directions or naming specific examples. Instead, the model scaffolds the imaginative process of envisioning ideal learning scenarios and classroom practice for participants while attending to the critical step of implementing the new practices. A prototypical commitment to iterate, pilot, co-create and learn from experiential feedback is woven into the process from beginning to end.

In embracing the messiness and complexity of teaching and learning, there is a commitment to deviate from the value placed on a suite of scalable yet homogenous learning activities. In avoiding reductive schematic representation of teaching, the participatory research method and the *Edukata* model invite teachers to complete as they see best. By valuing diversity over transferability, a huge variety of activities are generated (5). Leinonen describes this as an 'open source' way of thinking as opposed to a 'lesson plan' way of thinking (6). As an innovative, participatory model, it highlights ways in which place-based, people-centred design can bring a school community together to catalyse and support transformational change.

## 8.2  Relative Creative

### 8.2.1  A Make Change Case Study

*Relative Creative* is a design studio based in Brisbane, Australia co-run by Tristan Schultz and Bec Barnett. Much of the studio's work is concerned with bringing attention to critical social and environmental issues, such as the impacts of colonialism and climate change. The studio runs interactive learning experiences across a spectrum of topics and audiences, which seek to address critical challenges for their community and the world. Working with children, students and adults, they host learning events on restoring and repairing furniture, learning about e-waste and workshops on critical issues such as food security. Schultz and Barnett frame the value of design as a way to educate people differently, using their design practice to build awareness and catalyse change (7). The studio uses interactive practices, visualisation tools, system-level analysis and multimedia engagement in their quest to create transformative learning experiences. The *FutureBNE* challenge case study embodies *Relative Creative's* belief in making as a critical and political pedagogical tool that can help people "see the world differently" (8).

*FutureBNE*, designed and facilitated by *Relative Creative*, is Australia's largest one-day educational event. At the time of writing the latest event hosted 650 children aged 11 and 12, selected from Brisbane and South East Queensland schools. Students come together to learn about specific challenges, early topics explored water security until 2019 when the topic shifted to carbon neutrality.

In pitching the educational event to the Brisbane City Council and participating schools, Schultz and Barnett made it clear students would not be reading about water security or hearing someone speak about the challenges, but rather students would be using design techniques to engage with this topic. They would be learning through making. Like *Edukata*, using design techniques as pedagogical tools was a strategy to grant the students agency in the learning process. Giving the students tools to think about the challenges of water security and create something in response to how they are thinking, gives the students a sense of agency to affect their present and create the future that can travel with them beyond the event itself. This perspective on learning is focused on a systemic impact, rather than a focus on an individual or technical learning outcome. The designers' critical position approaches "designing events with an emphasis on designing into both the unfolding and the message taken home, the notion that design is both an enabler and disabler of serious future challenges" (9, p. 1). Barnett and Schultz highlight the importance of "empowering children to recognise their power as social change agents, the power inherent in the privilege of their geopolitical location and the power inherent in the geographical unsettlement of their region" (9, p. 1).

Over the years, Barnett and Schultz have designed a specific structure for the event to facilitate an engaged, maker-driven learning process with the students. In many ways, this structure is in parallel to a classic design process: beginning with knowledge gathering and building insights, then moving to a rapid phase of sketching ideas within a team and collaboratively converging these ideas into design fictions, and then from the design fictions building systems model of a complete idea. What is distinctive about the learning experience is the ethical, Indigenous, conscientisation moves that wrap around the design process.

Barnett and Schultz characterise their agenda as "decolonial and social-democratic" (9, p. 1). In their work to de-colonise design practice, they consider how the event itself comes to be, how participants are supported throughout and the tools used to transmit information during the event. The first step of knowledge gathering in *FutureBNE* is facilitated with prepared collateral. 'Knowledge cards' provide key information about water security challenges and prompt students to engage with mini-challenges. The students are not asked to understand the information presented on each card simply by reading it, rather, the mini-challenges on the cards ask students to engage with the information through discussion, inquiry and making.

From the outset, the knowledge cards mobilise the de-colonial agenda by unsettling dominant narratives. First, the information on the cards avoids neo-liberal, Western framing of water security issues and rather references knowledge from Indigenous water practices around the world. Secondly, the cards highlight 'the darker sides' of technology and industry and serves as a caution against solution-seeking, neo-liberal 'answers' to problems. By recognising the pitfalls of designing our way to answers, students are primed to think more holistically and systemically about the long-term consequences of their ideas. The knowledge cards demonstrate Barnett and Schultz's belief that design work should be informed through theory (7). While the mini-challenges are not related to the final models, the students are tasked with making, and the engagement process is consistent in activating learning through the making. Yet, deploying design to activate a learning experience is not simply about learning through doing. A deeper, more expansive understanding of praxis is asked of the students: how might they put specific worldviews or knowledge systems into action through a critical practice of making?

Next up, a peer-to-peer learning session has the students sharing and processing what they learned from the knowledge cards together. This social learning move primes belonging, supporting the collaboration to create a design fiction based on what they have learned. Set in 2100, the future fiction teleports students into a world that asks them to understand contemporary issues through a temporal lens (7). These longer time spans disrupt modernity's focus on immediate progress and short-term solutioning, evoking instead a different generational and custodial notion of time.

From these design fictions, students build models. Discouraged to think about their models in a user-centred way, the students consider them through a systems lens. Barnett and Schultz discuss expanding ideas around what a 'model' could constitute. Students are asked to think about whether their design is an artefact, an experience, an art installation or an event. This expansive framing of design communicates the breadth of possibilities and posits a transdisciplinary practice where the output is based not on 'users' but on the design's ability to affect ontological agency" (9, p. 6).

Like *Edukata* and *Making Space*, the event seeks to make explicit that knowledge production is a messy process. Schultz recognises that his Gamilaroi Aboriginal and European Australian heritage inform his design, driving an ethical commitment to being critically informed and concerned with ecological and social responsibilities. Core to the design of the reciprocal and relational learning exchange is a belief in revealing the many entanglements, embracing different ways of knowing and respecting radical positions as valuable (8). The goal is not for students to feel they are able to create a viable solution to water security from a day-long event, but as Schultz puts it, to leave with a 'politics'. He describes this as a politics based on what modern Western educational systems have negated. Schultz's aim is for them to leave with a newfound understanding that beyond scientific positivism, true and valid knowledge "can come from hermeneutic analytical, interpretive messy processes" (8).

The ongoing, political tension between the neo-liberal and politically 'safe' agenda of the council who host and fund the event, and the de-colonial and social-democratic agenda of the designers, are made explicit by Barnett and Schultz (9). Drawing on the educational philosophies of Ivan Illich and Paulo Freire, Barnett and Schultz organise the event explicitly to raise critical consciousness of the students and directly contest industrial models of education (9). The ethico-political moves of the *FutureBNE* challenge critiques dominant productivist forms of education. The challenges of water security or carbon neutrality are the content but not the lesson. The not-so-hidden curriculum lies in leveraging the making process for active knowledge production. This transformative commitment to agency and conscientisation is the difference between simply learning and building capacity for youth to be agents of change.

## 8.3 Embodied and Relational Practice Vignettes

How might poetic and physical ways of coming together invite connection, promote self-determination and create a platform for co-learning? The two following practice vignettes by Sean Donahue and Sonali Ojha explore very different embodied, relational strategies for making with others and changing ways of coming together. Deviating from a conventional co-design approach that has people working on an artefact together, these designers explore ways of learning, not in collaboration, but in parallel. The design move captured in Sean's *Making Bricks* vignette offers an approach that prioritises relationships over outcomes. Set in the fraught socio-cultural space of international development, the contextualised moves confront the colonising history of this field of work. Sean, a white designer from the United States, explores how to position himself as the novice in the group. Sonali's contemplative moves offered an inclusive whole-body strategy based on the invitation to everyone to come as they are. Sonali, a social innovator from India, shows how a practice forged at the intersection of social work and emotion-led design, might use the body as an instrument for sense-making the how and why of transformation. These encounters designed for non-Western contexts remind us of the universal importance of paying attention to emotions and relationships and the antithetical yet corresponding situational knowing shaped by unique lived experiences and local cultures.

### 8.3.1 Dreamcatcher Facilitating

Sonali, from *Dreamcatchers* foundation, joined the Design Rounds as someone working in the shadows of traditional design. Not trained as a designer, she had, over the years, come to see the potential of design in her social and educational work with vulnerable and under-represented youth in India. Sonali's non-Western, new-to-design practitioner perspective introduced startlingly different ways of conceptualising how one might design for transformation. From the outset, Sonali made explicit that this kind of practice is grounded in designing for emotional needs, specifically emotional safety. If agency and empowerment are central to the goal of emancipatory transformation, then for Sonali, the only way to get to that is to design for hope. In this way Sonali's lived experience echoed the education mantra to first 'start where people are at'. Other case studies have acknowledged the messiness of teaching and learning. Sonali's facilitation-led practice is not just comfortable with messy contradictions, but also with tears, trauma and long silences.

The transformation session Sonali deftly hosted in the Design Rounds cannot be reduced to an academic framework or easily digestible steps. Analogous to a yoga class, the session unfolded as a sequence flowing from one activity into the other. The overarching felt experience of the slow-paced encounter was that this was more ritualistic. The contemplative atmosphere felt opposite to the high-energy, structured design sprint. The session began with Sonali privileging belonging as the essential move for making participants feel included and safe. Each individual was invited to place a rock on a blanket in the middle of the table to make tangible: I am here, I am present, my voice counts. The moves that followed ensured participants' whole selves showed up. One activity had participants taking minutes to closely examine the lines and structure of their hands. After reflecting on what the hands had held, healed, made, created, nurtured, carried, written and cherished, participants shared a sentence that began with the prompt: 'these hands have…'. For homeless youth in Mumbai, that might be children sharing 'these hands have fed my little brother', 'these hands have stolen food to survive'. In Melbourne, what people shared was oftentimes more prosaic and yet inevitably intimate. A similar move, later in the session, had participants attune to how their feet touched the ground. With eyes closed, people stood on tiptoes before settling their heels on the floor in search of the point of connection that confirmed the earth was there for us. The embodied act grounded participants in the present and acknowledged a connection to what has come before.

Beyond the body work, a guided visualisation had participants bring to mind a well-placed structure strong enough to withstand the wind and rain, attractive enough to draw in people passing by and welcoming enough to be a place where people want to spend time. The structure was to represent a way of revealing how a participant might wish to leave their mark in the world. This meditation purposely primed participants for the making phase. We created the kind of structure we wanted to build with inexpensive stones. When it came to share the bridges, sanctuaries and shelters, the reflective prompt was not to describe the structure but to share what we discovered about ourselves through making.

Towards the end, Sonali invited participants to walk as slow as they could. In paying close attention to all that had to come together to simply take a step, participants were invited to notice the effort required to build momentum. The walking feet needed to lift away from the supportive earth if we hoped to travel somewhere new. This performative metaphor gifted learners an experiential understanding of the challenges of transformative work. In observing their bodies, participants were introduced to a physiological, emotional, cognitive respect for the energy, muscles, faith, bones and intention that need to align for an individual to take a step forward. To mobilise these reflections into action, the last task had participants bring paper cut-outs of their footprints to the stones placed at the beginning of the session. The final prompt was to contemplate the path one wished to make alone and to make together.

Antithetical to modernist productive principles of resolution, solutions and answers, this inclusion-driven practice was committed to holding space for shame, fear, sorrow and pain. From the first call for belonging to the last invocation to set an intention, this close attention to the affect of place, time and emotions shaped the session. These new ways of *being with* transcend Western notions of co-creating at the same table. Just as the moves to *make change* consciously created a shared, if not collaborative, space for honouring that whole-hearted work is challenging for a reason.

### 8.3.2 Making Bricks Relational Activity

Sean Donahue is core faculty in the Graduate Media Design Practices program at ArtCenter, principal of RCD/LA and a WonderLab PhD candidate. The social justice orientation to Sean's design research practice has him working in different international contexts. For Sean, the ethics of such a practice cannot be marginalised as an academic concern. This snapshot examines one way that Sean ensures his initial encounters with community bring a performative orientation to the charged context of the white foreign consultant arriving in a new land. Committed to sustainable ongoing relationships, Sean played the long game. In contrast to an introductory co-design sprint that would privilege and prioritise the literacies and expertise of the visitors, this vignette begins with Sean embarking on a day trip to build bricks with the locals. In different contexts, Sean had heard reference to the sentiment that every man in Uganda knows how to make a brick. There was, in this truism, not just a recognition of the labouring expertise of such a practice but also the literal and symbolic importance of one's masculinity being tied to a proven ability to sustain, shelter and support loved ones. Even the invitation to go to the fields to make bricks was a more welcoming gesture than onsite training; the vulnerability of stepping away from one's professional expertise and stepping towards the local know-how of the hosts is a significant relational move.

At a WonderLab PhD intensive on exploring affective narrating on design practice, Sean spent time sitting with the background behind this day trip in Uganda. Through the process of remembering his embodied experience, emotional response and ethical orientation, Sean came to see the encounter through multiple dimensions. His praxis narrative[2] explored how he was saying yes to culturally learning from the natural resources from which the brick is made, to learning from the multi-dimensional knowledge of the elders who have been digging for bricks for decades, and to learning from the rituals and practices of this land. However, Sean saw that he was also saying yes to performing his position as someone not-from-there. In doing this, he was saying: I will let myself be comic relief, I will feel in my bones what I do not know, I will be humble, I will feel my foreignness. This move is clearly about more than learning from others. It is also learning through positioning oneself in relation to others. Sean's parents owned a landscaping business, so he knew how to use a shovel. Yet in owning his Muzungu status (the Bantu word for white foreigner or aimless wanderer), he could honour that there the land was not the same, the soil was unfamiliar

---

2  Sean's Making Brick's praxis narrative is on the book website: www.designingtransformative-learning.com

and the objective different. The act of trying to strike the soil in the way his body knew, only to know that this was not what was being asked of him, was an appropriately humbling reminder of the limits of his practice knowledge in this place. In this situation, his fellow collaborators were the shovel and the land.

This guest status was not, however, a singly affronting position even if it was othering. The men noted his commitment to show up, they observed his pained expression as he walked barefoot across the hard land, and they witnessed to his lack of skills. They gave him the nickname Baby Feet. The name was simultaneously a description, an endearment and an insult. More than a participant observer, Baby Feet is also the subject of observation.

Like the *Relative Creative* hidden curriculum, this field trip was never about the bricks. Before stepping into their future shared work together, the act of being seen allows for difference to be acknowledged and respected. Sean has his expertise, brickmaking and understanding this land is not one of them. When establishing connection and building relationships are the priority then this is a good place to start.

The case studies here assert the value of co-creating, co-realising and co-learning whether between a teacher or student peer community. The practice vignettes present more deviant moves for learning not through collaboration but through adjacency. In creating embodied, situated moments of learning these vignettes offer a less clear distinction between learner and facilitator, collaborator and host. Like parallel play, there is an understanding that the adjacency of proximal intimacy, as opposed to direct collaboration, can foster social learning.

There is a risk in a practice that unsettles the conventional script of international development engagements or the choreographed high-octane performance of a design workshop. If something were to have gone wrong on the brickmaking expedition it would not have been Sean who was compromised. If past trauma or unprocessed grief for one person were to surface in Sonali's workshop, all the participants have to find a way to sit with that pain. Dismantling the Western civilisation model is hard because we have internalised many of the scripts, the model is designed to protect itself and we inevitably will find ourselves in unfamiliar land. Yet, neither individual nor societal transformation can come without an active commitment to unlearn, to be uncomfortable or to take a risk (12.2). It is in the courage and vulnerability that comes with not trying to control each interaction that a space for new relationships to self and others are forged. Sara Ahmed says that "the magical and mundane can belong in the same horizon". Whether labouring in the fields or closely examining your own hands, these practice stories hint at how a seed for transformation can be planted in everyday, mundane activities.[3]

---

3   **Hannah**: Sara Ahmed notes that deviating from dominant scripts is intentionally made hard. However, in 'What's the Use: on the uses of use' she notes the interplay between the magical and mundane (10, p. 6). Potentially, there is something transcendent that can happen if design steps away from the modernity script of productivity and output to alternatively prioritise connection, trust and humility.

## Narrative 8.1 Facilitating: Making as Caregiving

### 2018 – with Hannah Korsmeyer

*My eyes might be cast downward, yet I am attuned to the people in the room. As I hold my diorama in my hands my senses are alert to the furtive moves of others' hands, to the curious, tentative creating happening around me, to the feeling of the quiet, generative energy. My heart quickens. There is something about the contemplative yet creative atmosphere of these people, in my home, that feels simultaneously transgressive and yet domestic.*

*Although we are in my house, working on an activity I co-designed, this situation is as novel to me as it is to everyone else in the room. It is clear that all ten of us are at sea; wavering, wandering and wondering. This is day one of a week-long gathering of practitioners coming together to explore new ways of learning alongside each other. This short activity is freighted to carefully, subtly, constructively signal what is being asked of us all over the coming days. Beyond the specific aim of the activity there lies a desire to help people land, metaphorically and physically. We anticipated that for some participants their bodies might be here, but their thoughts may be in another time zone. As the landing runway we have settled on this self-guided session that prompts reflection on why you here are and anticipates what do you long for. The primary goal of this hands-on activity is to channel participants' internal motivations so they can set their personal intentions. And yet. As hosts we are acutely aware that although I know some people in this room well, others have flown half-way around the world on the promise of an email from a near stranger. Beyond any academic agenda, we hope that in materialising our dioramas and sharing our dreams, this activity might just as critically forge connections and foster belonging.*

We know that for this week to work, we as the designers of this relational learning space, must attend to more than peoples' physical needs and intellectual curiosity. We must care for their sense of safety, belonging, agency and investment in our shared mission. For only then will we collectively be comfortable with owning what we don't know, have the courage to give embodied, critical, formative feedback to each other and embrace the intellectual risk of humbly questioning practices we once held dear. The paradox here is that for people to commit to the week's agenda, we need to invite them to find their own purpose for being here, and yet for this learning experience to be transformative, the price of admission is disorientation. To create a safe place that can hold space for discomfort, we need a program that embraces deviation and plurality. This is how we came to be creating personalised dioramas by layering crafted bespoke materials, onto a selected visual metaphor, into a linen box.

*The materials I am holding in my hands activate an internal chatter that animates multiple paths of inquiry (Figures 2.1 and 8.1). I stand here choosing the background image for my diorama. I reach out for the universe metaphor, given I chose the images I have a head start, an idea already formed. I soon realise others are already working with the stars, I hesitate to let go of the material conversation I have already anticipated. I reluctantly choose the bridge metaphor, surrendering to the idea that the stars are their stories now. Unsure of my next move, I tentatively look at the bridge for a clue. Even if I do not know where I am going, I find I trust the materials to get me back to shore.*

To scaffold the diorama-as-intention-setting we have shared four worlds of learning to frame our exploration (13.3). This activity is designed to prime each of us to consider what worlds will we travel to over the next week. The collective dioramas help us see where our individual wonderings align and where they depart. The design rounds of the week will have everyone leading workshops, experiencing them, critiquing them, learning from both the public program and the personal work we set out to do. Care has been taken to ensure each person plays every role. We will return five days from now to iterate, annotate and evolve our dioramas to reflect how our lessons diverged from what was initially anticipated.

*I pick up some miniature laser-cut people, I wonder where they are going, how they want to get there. I tentatively place a person on the bridge. Frustrated I note that the scale is off. I search through the images for smaller people, settling on a child playfully running. I wonder what this might mean. What would skipping feel like in the week we have (un)planned? How would it show up? I sense how my contented present-moment-self, signals the anticipatory optimism my future-self feels about skipping my way through the week. I check in with my body and wonder when my heart quickens if it is skipping. I sneak a look at the engaged faces of the people around me. The depth of concentration, the fleeting smiles affirm they too are deep in reverie, talking through the materials, to their selves. Out of the corner of my eye I see Hannah has chosen a paper silhouette of a seated person. My eyes travel between the skipping child to the seated man. Suddenly, it is clear why we are here.*

*The bridge is in perspective. The child skips in the background, a man sits in the foreground. Patient, waiting. I am assured we are all where we are meant to be. Before people even start sharing their dreams for the week ahead, I am secure in my conviction we simply meet people where they are at. I can see now that sometimes I will be the one running to catch up. Maybe for a moment everyone will be on the bridge but me. Another day I might be ahead. I nudge the seated man. Is he being patient or passive? This mediation of my inner back-talk has me questioning whether my future-self will wait for others to join or whether I will go to them. Perhaps I will meet them in the middle. Better still, could I skip alongside them? I exchange the seated character for a person with a hand outstretched. My eyes smile. I see now how in caring for how my peers might find their path into the week ahead I have found my own place on the bridge.*

## In Conclusion

These practice narratives of Part II reveal that the reframing capacity of designing operates at the interplay between making and critiquing, co-creating and reflecting. Distinct from a dialogic practice, the act of meaning-making in design is facilitated by the iterative, recursive act of constructing things. Nowadays, it is quite possible that the 'things' may never get to role play being refined artefacts. The increasingly dematerialised practice of contemporary design shows us how objects might not be fixed solutions addressing a defined problem. Still, even if the goal is not to solve a problem, the applied orientation and seeking of appropriate solutions still propels the creator-as-seeker to analyse the information (sensorial and cognitive, pragmatic and conceptual) that the different design moves reveal. Yet, we also see in the case study stories from the field that many of the everyday moves of design – even those not focused on producing refined artefacts – are grounded in the material, the visual and the tactile. From change machine contraptions, to design games, to polaroid portraits, these tangible moves directly inform and shape the kind of knowing[4] an activity might surface, seed or synthesise.

In Part IV, I elaborate on what it looks like when designing and Mezirow's theories of learning intersect. For now, consider how the case studies and the practice vignettes connect back to Mezirow's ten phases of transformative learning (Chapter 15). The *FutureBNE Challenge* case study and the Make-shift Feminist Futures praxis narrative make explicit the propelling force of a declared disorienting dilemma. Sonali Ojha's contemplative practice and Kelly Anderson's use of affect in embodied enquiry show how everyday material engagement can support the work of self-examining feelings. The working with Indigenous perspectives at *Relative Creative* and *The Southern Initiative* and in *Design as Freedom* all reveal new paths into Mezirow's fourth step commitment to interrogate epistemic and socio-cultural assumptions. Every project on some level, but explicitly the *Innovative Learning Environments and Teacher Change* projects and *Making Space* and *Magical Change Machine* narratives, seek to normalise by making visible the discontent and transformation journey. A crucial move in Mezirow's steps is making space to explore new relationships and actions. This is observed in the detail-a-scene embodied phase of Elliott Montgomery's *Future Anachronism* vignette.

---

4  **Myriam:** I wonder how the teachers, caretakers, scientists or artists that designers work with make sense of the 'material, visual, tactile' 'kinds of knowing'? As designers we make things with people. In our paper, *A Family of Sensibilities: Toward a Relational Design Practice Grounded in Materiality and Embodiment*, we presented six case studies ranging from a dementia care unit to a public playground. For me, it was in laying the cases side by side that we managed to get at these different kinds of knowing. Writing the poems in the paper did more than just help us access new ways of knowing, they also encourage a reader to tap into poetic and artistic ways of seeing that get closer to material, visual, tactile kinds of knowing (11). **Ricardo:** This makes me think more specifically about how making visible shows up in the context of creating democratic learning environments. To me, there is something about design moves that are in their nature *multidisciplinary*.

Similarly, Sean Donahue's haptic brickmaking experience presents an alternative ethnographic strategy for considering the role of competence or self-confidence to *School Retool's* process. Tuuli Mattlemäki and colleagues *ATLAS* project explicitly navigates how a design game supports planning a course of action, as *Particle in a Box* and *Budgetball* bring a game-like exploration to the acquisition of new knowledge. One consistent area flagged by Mezirow and poorly considered by these design examples is the need for people to try out new roles. The *Henry Ford Learning Institute* case study observes this criticism, as do the other teacher interventions (*Edukata, School Retool* and *ILETC*) which intentionally stage the learning encounters over time to make space for real time implementation and experimentation. Mezirow's tenth step is to complete the transformation cycle by internalising and embodying the new knowing into your world of expertise. Even though many of the examples shared here do not purport to complete this full cycle, there lies in all the stories notes for how lessons prime people for the final step of integration.

To see beyond what we design to what we are creating, we need new stories, new moves, new knowledge systems. To step back from the field-situated case studies and practice vignettes, the keywords of Part III offer old and new ways to signal what we are doing when we are designing learning. Familiar phrases like 'reflective practice' and 'public prototyping' are context-tied to learning. More novel concepts like 'unsettling' and 'kaleidoscopic thinking' speak to new ways of sense-making design, and interdisciplinary terms like 'retrieval practice' and 'intrinsic motivation' introduce psychology research primed for translation into the practice space of designing learning encounters. In the bricolage of words that mash together different theories and even epistemic positions, remember as you intuitively seek out the words that resonate, to also intentionally linger on the words that you resist. Let yourself be disoriented, for with that tension comes a path to transformation.

---

## Part II Wonderings

The stories of my practice illuminate how my own understanding of design practice has shifted. It would perhaps be critically instructive to share the stories where colleagues, collaborators or context pushed back. Learning encounters can fall flat for being too radical, too uncomfortable, not necessary or simply misguided. Sometimes the ask of the people was just too little or too much. There was my colleagues' eye-rolling when I used solely affective language to critique a Masters project, the stonewalling that came with making visible the patriarchal bias of the curriculum, the disengagement when I asked peers to engage in play instead of standard fare professional development. I do not withhold these stories because they did not succeed, as I recognise that reflecting on failure is key to developing better encounters and deeper understanding (11.1).

However, these stories are ethically harder to share, given I cannot speak, with integrity, to the perspective of the people experiencing my poorly conceived lesson. Instead, here I shared stories where I am the learner, not the designer. The goal was to learn from my own reluctance, discomfort and vulnerability as I engage, resist and am drawn towards getting curious again about what design is and can be.

Years back, my idea of what design is making would have been defined by the artefact. This question became alive for me when the research-wondering study had me exploring the nexus of world-making, sense-making and meaning-making (12). Now, an elaborate ecosystem of relational moves and material methods, creative processes and critical acumen stands before me. I knew immediately after my first co-design workshop that I now had new tactical moves (like sharing a video with stakeholders as a tangible reminder of what they had co-created) and new strategies for co-creation (like the sequenced process that made it less likely one person could co-opt the direction). I instinctively held tight to Maria and her colleagues' framing of the work as creating a space for rehearsing the future for the people whose lives will be most changed by the work (13). Yet, my recollection of how I felt walking down the stairs post-workshop was not due to my being adept at tuning into my embodied feelings. I was not. I can replay my memory because my body remembers. This writing made clear how possible it is for me to sense in the present moment, what at the time, I did not grasp cognitively.

There is a similar story with the practice of figuring. I spent my PhD theorising what the practice of figuring meant for design more broadly, and more personally what aspects of my cognitive script of the affordances of design needed to be revised and restoried. This theorising needed a language if I hoped to not just articulate the shifts in practice to the Parsons community, but to ask them to engage in figuring with me. Naming this becoming practice of figuring helped me to get familiar with the potential force of the not-yet-known, to respect the defiantly non-declarative, the intentionally ambiguous, the productively open-ended. I did not see, until I wrote the narrative, how my life in a new country, new institution and in a new century also primed me to be looking for a new mode of the inquiry. By the time I was playing with origami horses, the choices to take risks felt more intentional and I was beginning to be more disciplined in noticing the affective realm. I can easily bring to mind the scene in which the horse taught me that the negotiative, generative, interpretative act of figuring is not limited to the back-talk between me, my peers and a computer mouse. It was the same day the metaphoric artefact taught me that co-realising, learning with and in conversation with others, can happen outside the cacophony of a convivial workshop. The horse showed us that if we held the metaphor lightly in our hands, we could deliberately, playfully weave together and carry over creative insights from one conversation to the next.

We know that today's designers create services, experiences, interactions, games and systems as well as products. Yet, we still limit our understanding of the social impact of our work in the world if we do not consider new ways of storying, noticing and accounting for what happens when we design. If we do not attune to emotional states and the affective dimensions that seed resonance or surface resistance, how do we learn? If we do not question how remembering and forgetting happen, how do we go about memory-making? If we let old language lock us in and stick too closely to familiar scripts, how do we create change? The *Making Design* constellation reminds us that we cannot reduce design practice to the outputs we produce, nor the stories we tell ourselves about design. How would practice be changed if our tangible designs (the card game, the teaching app, the learning encounter) were more clearly understood as manifestations of what happens when we design for connection, for well-being, for justice, for clarity, for engagement and for play? If the brief were not to design an app but to design for connection, how might the outcome shift? To make sense, to make with, to make fun, to make visible is the foundation by which the designer can further explore the potential to make believe, to make tangible, to make possible, to make change.

When you reflect on your latest project, what did you think from the outset you were making? What can you now see you were making? Does an expansive framing of making change anything? Which case study or practice vignette left you wondering what would happen if you were to intentionally make differently?

## Bibliography

1  Akama, Yoko and Ann Light. "Readiness for Contingency: Punctuation, Poise, and Co-Design." *CoDesign*, vol. 16, no. 1, 2020, pp. 17–28, doi:10.1080/15710882.2020.1722177.
2  Light, Ann and Yoko Akama. *The Human Touch: Participatory Practice and the Role of Facilitation in Designing with Communities*, 12th Participatory Design Conference, August 2012.
3  Bonsignore, Elizabeth et al., editors. *Participatory Design for Learning: Perspectives from Practice and Research*, Kindle ed. Routledge, 2017.
4  Keune, Anna et al. *Edukata Facilitator Guide Book*. Aalto University School of Arts, Design and Architecture, 2014.
5  Toikkanen, Tarmo et al. "Designing Edukata, a Participatory Design Model for Creating Learning Activities." *Re-Engineering the Uptake of Ict in Schools*, edited by Frans Van Assche et al., Springer, 2015, pp. 41–58.
6  Leinonen, Teemu. "Interview." 26 June 2017.
7  Schultz, Tristan. "Interview." 18 October 2018.
8  "Design Lab." *Relative Creative*, 2018, relativecreative.com.au/design-lab.

9 Barnett, Bec and Tristan Schultz. "Decolonising Approaches to Designing with Children: Futurebne Water Security Challenge." *Relative Creative*, Case Study, January 2018.

10 Ahmed, Sara. *What's the Use?: On the Uses of Use.* Duke University Press, 2019.

11 Diatta, Myriam et al. "A Family of Sensibilities: Toward a Relational Design Practice Grounded in Materiality and Embodiment " *Design and Culture*, Forthcoming.

12 Grocott, Lisa. "Chasing Curiosity: Inquiry-Led Practice in Communication Design." *One and Many Mirrors: Perspectives on Graphic Design Education*, edited by Luke Wood and Brad Haylock, Occasional Papers, 2020, pp. 136–47.

13 Halse, Joachim et al., editors. *Rehearsing the Future.* The Danish Design School Press, 2010.

# PART III

# Designing Learning

## Keywords and Stories from Psychology and Design

FIGURE 9.0 **ATLAS Design Game:** Memory-making as the residue of haptic, social interactions and critical thinking.

DOI: 10.4324/9780429429743-11

## An Introduction

My research practice affirms my belief that our capacity to address transdisciplinary societal challenges (1) would benefit from researchers inhabiting the liminal space betwixt and between the confines of disciplinary knowing. The interdisciplinary citations and a catholic approach to theory in the following chapters respond to this belief. Here, the premise of exploring the literature of different disciplines is to consider what new ideas might emerge from the new perspective these disciplinary lines of inquiry open up. I recognise this superficial scanning of what other fields have spent decades researching is more analogous to the generative approach a designer brings to practice precedents than it is to the deep analysis a qualitative researcher might bring to a systematic literature review. There is no pretence on my part that the themes identified are comprehensive. Although the keywords can operate as breadcrumbs to be followed up in academic literature, best-selling publications or countless education blogs and industry reports, that is not the aim. The intention behind only fleetingly introducing science, learning and design concepts through 17 keywords is to amplify the incidental, not accidental, serendipity of you, the reader, intentionally tuning into the bricolage potential of these interdisciplinary themes being remixed in practice (2).

However, studies in cognitive diversity and team learning caution there are limits to our capacity to learn from each other without shared planks of understanding (3). I have therefore organised this section primarily around psychology and design, with links back to the learning literature. From the sciences, evidence-based research from cognitive and social psychology are inflected with complementary notes from neurobiology. From design, specifically the fields of participatory and co-design research, practice-evidence is considered alongside literature from affect theory, queer and Indigenous studies.

The following chapters deepen our understanding by offering specific disciplinary understandings of how learning happens. I do not pretend to understand (or have read) the breadth of cognitive science and social psychology journal articles, but share the content based on a translation of what design can bring to the topic of how we learn. My perception of where the contribution of design lies is informed directly by my collaborations with research psychologists, discussions with my learning science collaborator, Kevin Mattingly, our research with Riverdale Country School and our practice experiences at WonderLab. For a more comprehensive introduction to these concepts, I suggest you read some of the books. Yet, even a rudimentary comprehension of these core concepts can help translate, from an education and psychology research perspective, the ways a multi-sensorial, designed approach to learning can contribute to this interdisciplinary applied space.

Quantitative and qualitative studies are foregrounded in the two social science chapters. They present to the designer of learning an array of considerations we might normally be blind to. The final two chapters work with the situated practice-evidence (including WonderLab project vignettes) to consider the design potential of creative, abductive reasoning and learning through when it comes to onto-epistemic shift work. The evidence-based psychology research potentially signals opportunities for how this research gets translated into practice, just as the practice-evidenced projects propose implications for designing learning. The design chapters begin with situated practice vignettes from WonderLab to make clear that although the chapters atomise these principles and practice into keywords, the learning encounters bring these works back together again. Seen as a whole, this keyword bricolage invites the reader to make do what they might with this complex interplay of moves, knowledge, capacities, principles and practices.

The interconnectedness of the ideas assembled proposes how we might explore the doing and being involved in designing memorable and productive learning experiences. As an interdependent ecosystem the component parts (the keywords) illustrate the role each plays in sustaining a thriving environment for learning. The first chapter – a primer on research from social and educational psychology – speaks to the influence of the learner's mindset. Concepts of social belonging, deliberate effort, learner agency and intrinsic motivation are positioned as holding up the learner so they can focus on the learning at hand. If this first chapter scaffolds learning, the second is the fertiliser. This chapter identifies four primary practices from the learning sciences that support how the brain encodes and retrieves memories and introduces keywords from cognitive psychology that effectively multiply learning performance. The sense-making and meaning-making practices outlined in the design Chapter 11 feel analogous to a practice of turning over the soil to keep the ground fertile and generative. This chapter remixes familiar design capacities like reflective practice and allegoric thinking with new terms like kaleidoscopic moves and less known literature like affect and emotion studies. The final chapter, like seasonal transitions, respects the iterative nature of a process that moves through embodied, exploratory and emergent phases of doing, knowing and becoming. Here, the assemblage mixes together known design aspects of participatory prototyping and novel imagining, with the importance of establishing relevance while unsettling scripts when it comes to designing engaging experiences.

Earlier, the idea of transformative learning was summarised through broadbrush stroke concepts such as disorienting yet meaning-making, cognitive yet personal, constructed yet relational, experiential yet integrative and intentional yet imaginative (Chapter 3). These multiple dimensions resonate with some of our anecdotal lived experiences of how we have come to learn something over time. The transformative learning literature introduced in Part I, was then bought to life by the applied practice context of the design case studies in Part II. The purpose of this section is to propose the ways in which a designer might draw on this interdisciplinary research to deepen learning experiences. The keyword collisions between these scientific theories, design capacities, creative practices and psychological principles further open up paths for imagining the transformative contribution of design to learning. The final section Part IV encapsulates the transformative capacity of designing learning to seed unfamiliar ways of seeing and being, and reconfigures the themes introduced in the following chapters into a set of four commitments (Chapter 14).

## Bibliography

1 OECD Directorate for Science, Technology and Innovation. "Addressing Societal Challenges Using Transdisciplinary Research." OECD Publishing, Report, 16 June 2020, www.oecd-ilibrary.org/science-and-technology/addressing-societal-challenges-using-transdisciplinary-research_0ca0ca45-en.
2 Markham, Annette. "Bricolage." *Keywords in Remix Studies*, edited by Eduardo Navas et al., Routledge, 2018, pp. 43–55.
3 Aggarwal, Ishani et al. "The Impact of Cognitive Style Diversity on Implicit Learning in Teams." *Frontiers in Psychology*, vol. 10, 2019, p. 112, doi:10.3389/fpsyg.2019.00112.

# 9

# SOCIAL PSYCHOLOGY

## Learning from Engaging and Empowering

### Key Social Psychology Learning Mindsets

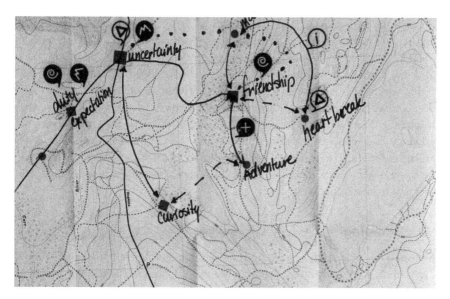

FIGURE 9.1 **Visualising (not)Belonging**: In this Belonging research workshop designed with colleague Gertrud Høgh Rasmussen, we were working with psychology researchers who had developed an online intervention for college students that revealed the value of normalising experiences of not-belonging. This pilot workshop explored if a co-creative space might amplify the sense of the shared experience. Students visually reflected through mapping how they navigated the challenges they had faced. The map legend, with metaphoric bridges, railway stops and cul-de-sacs, helped to retrospectively survey their lived experiences.

DOI: 10.4324/9780429429743-12

Reports and papers on school-based learner engagement often return to concepts around agency and autonomy, collaboration and belonging, motivation and relevance, authenticity and meaning, high expectations and relational connection, self-regulation and self-efficacy (1; 2; 3). These concepts live at the intersection of social and cognitive psychology and have been instrumental in shaping how WonderLab has constructed learning encounters. Evidence-based research in these fields offers designers and educators a different disciplinary perspective for understanding the social space and interior mindsets of the learner. However, it is important to note that the positivist nature of a lot of this evidence-based research must also be critiqued through a cultural lens.[1] For example, there can be sweeping intercultural differences with respect to religion or ethnicity; values like independence might be deeply embedded in countries like the United States, compared to Indigenous nations valuing interdependence and relationality. The case studies and practice vignettes in Part II make clear that cultural context is nuanced and complex.[2]

Hazel Markus and Alana Conner situate culture as the ideas, institutions and interactions that guide an individuals' thoughts, feelings and actions. Seeing culture as part of what shapes *institutions* (prisons, media and schools, etc.) and *ideas* (what is good and moral, etc.), is specifically relevant with respect to projects framed by structural challenges and mired in ethical questions. That said, the focus in this section is on the *interaction* level of Markus and Conner's framework. Specifically, we look at how an individual's exchanges with humans, non-humans and artefacts are shaped by and, in turn, shape the learning experience (5). The following sections on belonging, effort, agency and motivation connect to the field of learning mindsets and self-determination theory. There are mindsets, like self-efficacy or self-regulation, that are critical to learning; however, the focus on these four speaks to design's capacity to amplify the transformative potential of these core concepts.

## 9.1 Belonging

Seminal research studies into student belonging at universities and secondary schools have connected a student's sense of belonging with their academic

---

1   **Lisa**: With the dominant scientific paradigm privileging notions of replicability and scalability, some education researchers question whether integrity should be tied to principles of science over relationality of place, with some learning researchers cautioning how the design of studies unwittingly ignores the cultural and situation-specific nature of learning (4).

2   **Christopher**: In my design practice, I have witnessed directly the cost of ignoring cultural context. An unwillingness to confront the site-specific nuance and complexity amplified tensions between teachers in a Charter School who had been asked to run design thinking challenges and administrative staff who publicly lauded the success of these challenges. My (dis)ease with my complicity in that experience drove me to commit in my next job, at the central office of Detroit Public Schools Community District, to always foreground the socio-cultural context and the teachers' expertise.

performance (6; 7; 8). Greg Walton and Geoffrey Cohen's early research into belonging showed how a very brief online intervention could have a significant impact on student retention (9). First, there is the social dimension of a student asking themselves if they belong at this university, or in this majority white class, or in this predominantly male program. Yet, beyond asking the question, there is the cognitive overload that comes from a learner's attention being hijacked by thoughts around how, why and in what ways they do not belong. How much learning would you digest if you were also thinking, I didn't know we needed a laptop or am I the only one who does not know-how to take notes? Or where did they learn that skill – no one taught me! At the macro level, it is possible to consider how designing new approaches to orientation week is just one way that educational institutions might pay greater attention to fostering a sense of belonging. Yet, there are also micro-moves at the start and throughout learning encounters that can serve to deepen belonging.

Daniel Kahneman refers to how, in a state of cognitive ease, we get comfortable, we trust our intuition, believe what we hear and therefore our thinking can be more superficial. In contrast, if we are in a strained state, we are vigilant, suspicious and less comfortable (10, p. 60). The tension when it comes to designing learning encounters is how to wrestle with calls for a safe place of learning (a place where people can be vulnerable) and a challenging space (that promotes desirable difficulty). The notion of belonging can productively trouble a simplistic equating of being comfortable with being safe. Being pushed outside our comfort zone (some call this the 'stretch zone') promotes striving, learning and potentially fewer errors. The downside is, when in an unfamiliar place, we may also be less creative and trust our intuition less. In fostering belonging, is it possible for learner engagement to be simultaneously cognitively challenging yet psychologically safe? Beginning from a place of assuring people, they are in the right place does not work against the idea that they can be challenged. In fact, normalising that the experience should be creatively and critically challenging is a part of the process. Co-designer Kelly Ann McKercher identifies four key hospitality principles that offer a mindful approach to fostering less anxiety and more connection: you are appreciated, you are supported, you are welcome here, come as you are (11, p. 17). Without psychological safety, organisational psychologist Adam Grant, sees that people will protect themselves by hiding mistakes and withholding ideas.[3] To support learning, we need to avoid the harmonious homogeneity that masquerades as belonging, and instead create places where people feel supported to admit

---

3   **Sean**: When I think of working with people who have been historically marginalised the cost of feeling psychological unsafe is about a lot more than the environment created in that present-moment environment. Just as the experience of exclusion has oftentimes persisted for an extended duration, we too need to bring a temporal lens to participatory engagements. Design needs to shift its emphasis away from the tools that mediate and be more attentive to how we design spaces that bring a more durational notion to forging meaningful participation?

errors and challenge assumptions, and where they are empowered enough to learn from experimentation and to share diverse opinions (12).

Penny Hagen's Design Round activity seeded belonging from the outset with a simple embodied activity. The prompt was to position yourself on a continuum based on how novice or expert you were around the practice of co-design (not surprisingly, even the experts positioned themselves as learners). This could have corroded any sense of belonging if Penny had not followed up by asking everyone to look around and be grateful for the breadth of experience in the room. She assured the people new to co-design that their colleagues were there to answer their questions. She encouraged the experts to embrace the job of sharing their expertise by learning from the fresh questions a novice perspective can surface. In this move, Penny framed design as a relationship-building activity. This was a masterclass in establishing belonging, but also in the education adage to meet learner's where they are at. People walked away from this fleeting activity with a felt sense of why they were there – disarming any boredom or imposter syndrome that might have limited one's capacity to be present. Sonali's prompt to add the stone at the centre of the table affirmed people's right to be there and the importance of their voice.

In consultation with leading belonging researcher Greg Walton at Stanford, my design colleague Gertrud Høgh Rasmussen and I iterated on an activity to research student experiences around the challenges of belonging. We had second-year students label the emotions they felt in their first year by placing a pin on a map where the geography is named after emotions.[4] We then asked them to locate where they believed other students had spent their time. This *made visible* that most students saw their struggle as the exception, incorrectly imagining that everyone else felt a sense of belonging (Figure 9.1). Although the lived experiences people shared offered useful insights for the researchers, we sought to build reciprocity into the research design. For the room of first-in-family, Black, Queer and Latinx students who generously gave their time, we integrated into the activities what belonging research has revealed about the import of normalising feelings of not-belonging.

Recognising belonging as core to fair and inclusive societies has led to resources that work with the levers of design to create the space, rituals, roles and processes that deepen a sense of people seeing themselves in a socio-cultural context (14; 15). The social, convivial tools of design, the embodied, performative moves and the potential to translate lived experiences into shared stories are just some of the ways that design can support the critical work of promoting a felt sense of belonging.[5]

---

4   **Lisa**: For this activity, we printed out a large image of the World of Experience map. The students added pins to a topography that includes mountain ranges of work, peaks labelled drudgery, reluctance and perseverance, a cove called resignation, a peninsula of pleasure, a town called wonder and a region called adventure (13).

5   **Kelly**: Within participatory workshops, designers often frame participants as "experts in their experiences" (16, p. 12), while at the same time, co-design context places emphasis on the tools

## 9.2 Effort

Another area of educational research that design might be able to leverage is the research into effort. In her renowned research into mindsets, Carol Dweck identifies effort as one of the core components that shape a learners mindset (18). Her research observes that learners with a fixed mindset apply themselves differently than people with a growth mindset. If a learner believes they are terrible at math or excellent at track, this is a fixed mindset – the person's skill is already determined. Alternatively, a person who can see the potential to improve believes they are not good at life drawing *yet* or, with extra effort, that they can master algebra, have a growth mindset. The different mindsets do not just manifest in different approaches to putting in effort, they also affect how a learner addresses challenges and obstacles, as well as how they respond to the success of others and receive feedback. All of us have a fixed mindset about something (my story in the Preface depicts a fixed mindset around my public speaking abilities). I run mindset workshops that start from a place of the teacher identifying their own perceived limited capacity so they can empathise with students' fixed mindsets. Jennifer Garvey Berger would see this as a tactic for creating a different 'entry points', in turn designing psychologically spacious experiences that surface different perspectives and nudge people towards transformation (19). For Dweck, a core growth mindset strategy is to focus feedback on effort, not achievement. A learner then hears not that they are good or bad at a subject, but that the effort put in is worthy of praise. Angela Duckworth's research into grit further explores the relationship between effort and success (20). Duckworth's research suggests that grit is a greater determinant of success than IQ or talent. For Duckworth, grit is passion plus sustained persistence applied towards long-term achievement, with no particular concern for near-term rewards. My enthusiasm to surrender to the unfamiliar, embodied activities even though I felt uncomfortable paid off because my passion was paired with a belief that I would one day get better; the future reward felt clear. This is an example of a growth mindset and grit. Yet, clearly developing a growth mindset or being gritty does not simply translate to putting in mindless long hours. If I did not reflect through the debriefs on what I was cognitively and physiologically experiencing, and commit to work on the areas I found most challenging, I would not have learned from the hours I spent in the Play Gym (Narrative 2.1 and 12.1, Figure I.1). This is where Anders Ericsson's concept of deliberate practice comes in (18). A lot of education seems to work on a time-served model. For example, an academic degree equals a certain number of units, hours and assignments. Ericsson's theory prioritises the quality

---

used for expressing experience. My interest in de-centring the material affordances of design comes from wondering how other disciplines support a practice of story-making lived experience. Discourse analyst, Alexandra Georgakopoulou, for example, is focused on not the tools but the processes that can "stress the experiential, affective, and subjective ways in which people make sense of themselves over time" (17, p. 257).

of feedback and a focus on improving. We intuitively respect that someone being coached on the finer points of tennis by working on their fitness, serve and backhand will improve more than someone simply playing tennis for the same number of hours. The theory of deliberate practice suggests that expertise is acquired by incorporating a self-reflective feedback loop into the practice process, rather than simply performing a task repetitively.

It is not immediately clear how design can support certain kinds of deliberate practice, like the way a coach can directly improve a surgeon's performance. The exception is that we can consider how peers might coach each other to deliberately improve, say, equity-focused facilitation skills. Perhaps, it is through this conduit of feedback that design might leverage greater reflection to illuminate progress and sustain engagement through the boring parts.

The practice of the design critique could be creatively reimagined through the lens of growth mindset. How might the praising of effort over performance, or mapping progress over outcomes change the way we evaluate learning encounters? Formative feedback given throughout an ongoing project could focus on the fixed mindset, the 'backhand' as one company calls it, the person is seeking to improve. For decades, I have had students map the pitfalls and peaks of their motivation during the semester, the goal being to notice what happens in the moments that crush or inspire them. In paying attention to how they overcame the ups and downs of the semester, we can visualise how sustained effort is ultimately rewarded. This metacognitive insight helps internalise that failing and learning are synonymous. An alternative yet inverse of this exercise is found when we invite teams to create a transformation timeline. They playfully map where tensions will arise (with lightning bolt stickers and rain clouds), noting in advance how they will persevere in the face of multiple challenges. Myriam Diatta and I worked on a research project for Angela Duckworth on how to educate middle school students about grit. The standard deductive approach might begin with what scientific research tells us about grit. Our people-centred approach was informed by conversations with students who revealed how hard it was to *know* grit if you were unfamiliar with the experience. With a focus on ensuring the lesson resonated with the age group, we found amusing animal videos that light-heartedly captured perseverance over time so they might connect this back to their lived experience.

With respect to deliberate practice, amplifying engagement through visualising feedback can further focus the intention to develop mastery. Infinite games present a site that encourages ongoing practice through critique (through judging) and fun (through play). Similarly, story-making activities proffer a creative strategy akin to the replay in sports used to analyse previous games and generate future plays. Myriam Diatta's Master's thesis project at Parsons (21) worked with psychologists from the Child Mind Institute to improve parents' practice of a kind of family therapy. Myriam designed intentional yet intrusive objects to be installed throughout the home to support parents to integrate the therapy into their home life. These multi-modal strategies are some of the ways design capabilities can be applied to the research on effort, mindset and deliberate practice.

## 9.3 Agency

More familiar to design literature is the concept of agency. In participatory design, the connection to Freire's pedagogy of the oppressed and pedagogy of hope aligns with the role of liberating and empowering the learner (22; 23; 24). Indigenous concepts like relational agency (25) offer worldviews that connect the dots between unique life paths that support self-determination, variance and diversity (26, p. 498). For Karen Barad "agency is a matter of intra-acting; it is an enactment, not something that someone or something has" (27, p. 235). In education, the many dimensions of agency speak to the importance of self-advocacy, student voice and ultimately self-determination. More than student-centred approaches that promote student choice, learner agency integrates student voice with purposeful initiative to ensure that experiences are driven by their interests.

Research in this field positions agency as the opposite of helplessness, going some way towards offsetting the structural factors, such as social class, religion, gender, ethnicity, ability and customs that can influence academic performance. Intersecting with non-cognitive expertise, like growth mindset, grit and emotional regulation, agency catalyses these soft skills to boost academic success.[6] Amplifying agency in turn shifts a learner's orientation to mastery, effort and a growth mindset, fostering greater conscientiousness and drawing attention to future aspirations.

Core values of participatory design begin from a place of shifting power through participation, granting agency through empowering every stakeholder.[7] Similarly, the social dynamics of a learning community are disrupted when we blur distinction between who is the teacher, learner and researcher. Like in the narrative about the Transforming Mindset studio (Narrative 12.1), the social contract of learning is reimagined when we give learners a high degree of agency throughout a co-creative process (29, p. 34). This is evident in the sense of agency granted the teachers-as-experts in the *Edukata* case study and the youth-as-custodians in the *FutureBNE* project. Elliott's lessons for teaching high school students how to craft futures is founded in the belief that building the capacity to actively design the future you want to inherit increases agency. This is about more than student voice or advocacy, this is agency that comes from critical reflection, recognition and truth telling that is always situating in context. For

---

6  **Kelly**: About far more than academic success the notion of agency is entangled with concepts of individual ownership and self-determination. Natasha Jones notes that an affordance of the participatory possibilities of the design process lies with its potential "to enable people to engage in the activities necessary to achieve what they want, rather than to give them what they want" (28, p. 474).

7  **Sean**: I do not think we can talk about agency without talking about power. The politics of my research is concerned with undermining, redistributing and inverting authorities of power through participatory engagement. I would see designing for agency as a form of resistance. What does a design intervention into places where suppressive power is exercised and consolidated look like? Doing so as a way to amplify and centre the voices, actions and positions of those who are intentionally marginalized, exploited and under-considered. How do we design encounters that disproportionally privilege their contributions by designing engagements that enable different kinds of power – control, access and authority – over the outcomes of the engagement.

First Nations researchers Michael Dodson, Aileen Morten-Robinson and Marcia Langton change is inextricably tied to agency, accountability and awareness (30). The *Relative Creative* and *Design as Freedom* case studies illustrate how respecting Indigenous knowing and the lived expertise of co-learners can anchor an ethical, moral basis by which participation can elevate, not negate, a community's agency. In Sonali's Design Rounds workshop, compassionate listening to peoples' stories allows a place for emotions to be owned.[8] Linda Tuawhai Smith similarly links curiosity "at its core an activity of hope" (31, p. 257) with the emancipatory potential of imagination. Ruminating on the connection between wonder, anger and hope Sara Ahmed observes that

> wonder allows us to realise that what hurts, and what causes pain, and what we feel is wrong, is not necessary, and can be unmade as well as made. Wonder energises the hope of transformation, and the will for politics.
>
> *(32, p. nd)*

Ahmed and Tuawhai Smith theorise what Sonali's work demonstrated – for political projects to be effective, they must revel in wonder. Only then can we braid the capability to imagine and reimagine new worlds with the conscientisation of mindful agency to become a critical act of resistance.

By explicitly dismantling roles and subverting power, we can advance the mission to increase people's engagement with, and agency within, systems of education and learning (29, p. 34). A fleeting learning encounter cannot in itself change the structural, systemic and cultural challenges that might limit one's sense of agency.[9] Transformative learning does not happen in a vacuum, yet in design's capacity to *make space*, *make visible* and *make tangible*, there is an emancipatory gift. It is worth therefore noting the vitality, and indeed agency, that non-human actors bring to learning. Jane Bennet explains,

> no one materiality or type of material has sufficient competence to determine consistently the trajectory or impact of the group. The effects generated by an assemblage are, rather, emergent properties, emergent in that

---

8  **Sonali**: My work at Dreamcatcher's focused on how to give children who had often grown up on the streets of Mumbai a sense of agency over their future. Meaning-making and memory-making were at the heart of this emotionally centred work. Yet, for actionable agency to emerge, we needed to mess with some didactic idea of looking back to the past and forward to the future. We needed to own the deep reciprocity and charged potential that came with making meaning from old memories and making new memories meaningful.

9  **Lisa**: This particular tension is clear with a concept like imposter syndrome. I have students work on break-up letters to the overwhelming sense of not being worthy of belonging to help make sense of where the limiting belief comes from. While respecting the value of working on these internal scripts, it is important this feeling is also understood within the many structural, systemic and very real reasons why people may not feel welcomed and respected,

their ability to make something happen…is distinct from the sum of the vital force of each materiality considered alone.[10]

*(33, p. 24)*

If design moves and methods can help reveal the structures and systems people can and cannot change, there is, at least, an invitation to help citizens *make believe* what can be made possible. With this, a critical optimistic agency emerges, where one can give voice to the desired shift in mindset, actions and future they hope for. A sense of meaning emerges, purpose is defined and it becomes possible to enact the change one wants to be.

## 9.4 Motivation

In self-determination theory (SDT), studies into human motivation trace a direct connection back to agency. SDT research reveals how intrinsic motivation is more likely to drive change than extrinsic motivating factors. However, pure intrinsic motivation is rare. To be excellent learners, employees, managers, leaders, citizens, parents or even children, there is not a lot of behaviour we are driven to do solely for our own sake. In the absence of any societal constructs, would you be intrinsically motivated to be reading this book? Would I even be writing it?

To facilitate people's psychological need for autonomy, competence and relatedness, SDT prioritises identifying intrinsic motivation, internalising extrinsic motivations and emotionally regulating people's impulses (34). One way to channel intrinsic motivation is through a sense of purpose. William Damon identified only one-fifth of youth in the United States as highly engaged and focused on what they are doing with their lives. Damon's thesis connects thriving to motivation, specifically arguing that what sets engaged and disengaged youth apart is a developed sense of purpose (35). Purpose learning is a future-directed learning goal that is both personally meaningful and aimed at contributing to something larger than the self (36). Applying this research to the design of higher education, the Stanford 2025 speculative design project proposed reorienting the learning experience away from a disciplinary focus (my major is x) to a purpose orientation (my mission is y).[11] The second strategy of internalisation, calls for design encounters that facilitate the active, constructive, dynamic process of internalising motives external to us (37). With people preferring to be the *origin* of their own behaviour, we need to help learners feel like they are not being told what to learn but choosing to learn it for themselves (38). How might we

10  **Alli**: Bennet's point about material agency seems critical to include. To presume, we humans are alone agential in the assemblages of design encounters is arrogant. When I acknowledge as a facilitator that the material I have crafted with care help to steady my voice *and* to engage noisy humans so we might come together to learn, I can, by extension imagine the agency of the materials to grant the participant new ways of being present.

11  This video and summary introduce purpose learning: www.stanford2025.com/purpose-learning.

creatively scaffold for learners' activities that integrate a foreign motivation as if they were our own? In the case of this book, that would mean aligning my university's motivation to disseminate with my moral belief that I should share with others what I have had the privilege to research. If learning can bring into line the new lesson, the cultural context and the learner's personal values and needs, then the experience will feel more relevant. Like purpose learning, the goal here is to drive a learner's commitment by establishing the motivating factors and contextual support that will spark sustained commitment.[12]

Seeking to enhance the integration or identification of intrinsic motivation, I facilitated a professional learning workshop that had employees at a fake office party share stories about a fake project they had just finished. The party, set five years into the future, had people wholeheartedly and enthusiastically exclaiming how it felt to complete the most important project of their career to date. It was the opposite of a boardroom report; the affect-laced, purpose-defining chat uncovered what they valued about working on the project and the subsequent impact. Working in pairs, people rehearsed one-minute pitches that iteratively erased the extrinsic factors the company valued, to get closer each time to the driving purpose that would motivate the employee through the challenging times ahead. Again, using this book as an example, a first pitch might instinctively lean on institutional values like the quality of the publisher. Yet, by the third round I might attune to what I would learn from being in conversation with wise, informed people in this space. I actually did this exercise on myself, and this 15-minute future-me move seeded the idea of creating a learning encounter within the act of writing the book. This reframing led to the Design Rounds, elevating the experience from a solitary, intellectual exercise to a social and creative one. This activity, a playful twist on Motivational Interviewing, is informed by this clinical practice of psychology that takes a client-centred, facilitative approach to supporting clients to explore and resolve the kind of ambivalence that might forestall positive action (40). The story-making, co-realising, meaning-making practices of design present a breadth of tactics and methods for how design can deepen inquiry into the everyday, granular insights that can spark intrinsic motivation and allow the learner to frame investment, over-ride procrastination and catalyse future engagement.

Although the social and cultural concepts of belonging, effort, agency and motivation are called out here as distinct considerations, it is clear that they are entangled with each other. Design's impulse to create with interdependent

12 **Myf:** In 'The Location of Culture', the Indian critical theorist Homi Bhabha speaks about his experiences of enchantment sparked by a discovery of "off-centre" texts that he could identify with in ways that bridged the gap between intellectual fascination and genuine passion. Bhabha speaks of the need for emotional connections that may be bound up in individual or community identity and affirmation to enrich acquired knowledge or skills. Finding a 'subject of his own' that resonated with his lived experiences stimulated him in different ways than the standard intellectual curiosity he found in mainstream Western texts (39).

variables (Narrative 10.1) speaks to the integrative capacity to translate this social psychology research into meaning-making, purpose learning activities that establish relevance for the learner.

It is important to critically examine the systems and structures of a situated environment that might be antithetical to supporting these needs and goals. This might be as obvious as a system that negates autonomy or a transactional culture that devalues belonging. A mandatory online training module around cultural safety that includes multiple-choice questions does little to foster the learner's agency, mastery over the topic or sense of connection. In contrast, the need for autonomy, competence and relatedness could be met by a workshop designed to *make sense* of what cultural safety means for the individual, *make visible* how that shows up in an individual's daily practice and have them *make together* safety protocols that address their collective goals. The multiple-choice module does not create space for a learner's competence to grow, whereas the co-realising workshop designs for learner autonomy position learners as agents of change by inviting them to integrate what they are learning with what they already value. In creating space for reinforcing feedback and personal meaning-making, the learner's beliefs can be productively acknowledged or troubled. The reciprocal need of relatedness while learning from and making sense with others, serves to amplify the individual's potential (41).

The design moves that support the translation of this evidence-based research might be small, like the *ATLAS* design game that gives you the autonomy to address the component parts of a project in your chosen sequence. Or they might be grand, like the cultural and institutional changes required to embrace the mission-not-major proposition at Stanford. Elliott's futures wheel and Hannah's card game scaffold competence to introduce skills that grant greater agency over the future. Alli's change contraption drives motivation by inviting teachers to identify what drivers and levers for change they can control. Sean's paradoxical move to expose his brick-making incompetence in exchange for relatedness fosters belonging and respects the self-determination of his partners. Learning encounters that embrace a participatory orientation to co-creation enact this commitment to autonomy and relatedness.[13]

---

13  **Lisa**: In their research into creative collaboration, Chris Ertel and Lisa Solomon posit there are eight critical planks. A sense of shared purpose and a group identity align here to the emphasis on belonging and agency. A common understanding of the challenges and a shared sense of urgency are the planks that drive effort and motivation. Ertel and Solomon believe a shared language system and a base of information are prerequisites for inclusive participation. They highlight that without the final plank – the capacity to discuss complex, tough issues – it will be even harder for strategic moves to be undertaken (42).

---

## Narrative 9.1 Engaging: the Science of Memory-making

### 2017 – with Kevin Mattingly

*I am not at the centre of this story. I am an extra with a few lines. The perspective shift I am about to experience will forever change my mental model of how engagement works. I am transformed, even as I sit passively listening. We are a group of WonderLab design researchers sitting around a table with our PLUSSED+ partners. We have come together to critique a professional learning encounter we are designing for teachers. Analogous to a table read, this playtest is a place for rehearsing the design-led activities so we might see what needs to be iterated on further. However, instead of quickly running through the activities, our partner, Kevin Mattingly, invites us to grasp, in slow motion, the cognitive processes activated by our convivial methods. Passionately, yet humbly, Kevin draws on his science of learning expertise by getting curious about how the brain would navigate, in microseconds, the activities laid out before us.*

Let me first introduce what we thought we had designed from a design perspective. Kevin was reviewing a ten-minute photo-elicitation activity designed to prime the teachers to see their practice as evolutionary and adaptive (Figure 10.1). This first task was for teachers to choose an image from 20-plus photos on a table that spoke to a time they had experienced intentionally changing the way they do things. In connecting to a personal lived experience, we hoped to empower the teachers to see themselves as agents of change in the politicised education environment. For us, this activity was designed to engage teachers in the more difficult work of considering how to motivate transitions in practice when it feels like change is being imposed on them, not driven by them. For us, this was the opening scene before the title sequence.

*Kevin is now taking us inside the teachers' heads. Offering his perspective as a learning scientist and educator, he shares how the prompt to choose a photo aligned with a memory of change will trigger a real time recollection of a specific moment. Retrieving the memory – let's say of a teacher arranging furniture to facilitate more peer to peer discussion – will take no time at all. However, when the teacher scans for a photo of a classroom, there will be none. The photographs are of overgrown trails, misty mountains, bungee jumping and a bird in the sky. Kevin tells us that this dissonance will push the teacher to go back into his or her long-term memory and retrieve another moment they tried something new. Maybe this time they recall a curriculum change intended to customise student learning experiences. They scan the images and again no photo visually documents their memory. This cycle of retrieving, scanning, rejecting and retrieving again will happen, unconsciously, in a micro-second.*

*I am entranced. What Kevin is telling us about our pattern seeking brains is not so much disorienting as captivating. I lean in closer as he tells us that the* brain quickly assesses that meaning-making, with these metaphoric images, will not come from a descriptive representation of the memory. Flipping the retrieval source, the teacher would instead now start with the memories the evocative images uncover. Now the sequence is playing out in reverse. If the bungee jumping evokes risk to the teacher, the teacher tries to recall a change-memory associated with risk. I scan the images and I slow down to consciously flip the process. What change-memory comes to mind when I look at the low fog and the overgrown path? I connect with the sense of apprehension. I remember the times I have chosen the path less travelled. Several memories surface. I sense how different it feels when the retrieval request is wrapped up in affective cues. My practice knowing already affirms this activity works. I had not been looking for scientific evidence to legitimate my practice evidence. And yet, the resonance of the scientific translation seems wonderous. Kevin is explaining why these multi-sensorial memories are easier to recall. He tells us that memories interlaced with emotion are what you might call 'gold star' memories. In my own reverie I am hardly listening. I am wondering what the emotion is that is quickening my heart. How will I remember this luminous perspective shift?

Pulling back to the present, I see Kevin has transitioned from scientific translator into a space of rumination. He is quizzical about what else might bubble up due to how we have reversed the usual retrieval process. The cue for teachers to share with the other workshop participants is no longer framed by the specificity of a unique situation but by a metaphor of how it feels to lead change. The stories are now grounded in potentially shared emotional experiences, rather than defined by an individual's story. Kevin wonders whether some participants might be liberated by the self-distancing that comes with sharing an experience they are not at the centre of.[14] If teachers share a situation-specific experience – I moved the furniture around – a moment of connection might have been missed. Alternatively, the allegorical move – I embraced the uncertainty that came with reorganising the furniture – opens space for connection through mirroring, resonance and empathy. Kevin wonders whether a level of vulnerability, made possible by the this-is-me-but-not-me metaphor, paradoxically invites people to let their cognitive and emotional selves show up.

As I listen, I am flooded with wonder. I try to grasp how these microsecond interactions we were unaware of might deepen memory traces and in real time archive the teachers' memories differently in real time. I grapple with how these newfound insights ask me to see emotional responses and cognitive functions as more entangled. My own sense-making brain tries to reconcile this new knowing

---

14 **Lisa**: The research into self-distancing by Ethan Kross and colleagues at the Emotion and Self-control Lab at the University of Michigan explains why Kevin got to wondering if the metaphor might be another way to step outside yourself. This has me wondering if talking about yourself in metaphors is a creative way of doing a similar thing or if it scrambles the message? http://selfcontrol.psych.lsa.umich.edu/research/

*with my now faulty mental models of how emotions are made, experiences are remembered and memories are stored.*

In uncovering the teachers' memories of the risk, or the apprehension while recalling the curiosity or the giddiness, the elicitation activity makes it easier to talk about how hard, yet possible, change is. I now see how transformation is an extra-rational experience. This layering of an emotional recollection of the memory makes it stronger. Instinctively, I believed the encounters we designed to be memorable. Yet, this 20-minute revelation made clear how the extra processing required for this visually, emotionally grounded prompt further increased teachers' recall and in turn their perception of a practice that is always in evolution. The implications of this newfound know-how were about to similarly transform my own practice.

## Bibliography

1  Ferguson, Ronald et al. "The Influence of Teaching beyond Standardized Test Scores: Engagement, Mindsets, and Agency: A Study of 16,000 Sixth through Ninth Grade Classrooms." Achievement Gap Initiative at Harvard University, Report, 2015.
2  Deakin Crick, Ruth and Chris Goldspink. "Learner Dispositions, Self-Theories and Student Engagement." *British Journal of Educational Studies*, vol. 62, no. 1, 2014, pp. 19–35, doi:10.1080/00071005.2014.904038.
3  Elliot, Andrew J. et al. *Handbook of Competence and Motivation: Theory and Application.* 2nd ed., Guilford Publications, 2018.
4  Brady, Laura M et al. "The Importance of Cultural Context: Expanding Interpretive Power in Psychological Science." *Association for Psychological Science*, 27 February 2019.
5  Markus, Hazel R. and Alana Conner. *Clash!: How to Thrive in a Multicultural World.* Plume, 2014.
6  Yeager, David S. and Gregory M. Walton. "Social-Psychological Interventions in Education: They're Not Magic." *Review of Educational Research*, vol. 81, no. 2, 2011, pp. 267–301, doi:10.3102/0034654311405999.
7  Walton, Gregory M. and Priyanka B. Carr. "Social Belonging and the Motivation and Intellectual Achievement of Negatively Stereotyped Students." *Stereotype Threat: Theory, Process, and Application*, edited by Michael Inzlicht and Toni Schmader, Oxford University Press, 2012, pp. 89–106.
8  Farrington, Camille A. "Academic Mindsets as a Critical Component of Deeper Learning." William and Flora Hewlett Foundation, White Paper, April 2013, www.hewlett. org/wp-content/uploads/2016/08/Academic_Mindsets_as_a_Critical_Component_ of_Deeper_Learning_CAMILLE_FARRINGTON_April_20_2013.pdf.
9  Walton, Gregory M. and Geoffrey L Cohen. "A Brief Social-Belonging Intervention Improves Academic and Health Outcomes of Minority Students." *Science*, vol. 331, no. 6023, 2011, pp. 1447–51, doi:10.1126/science.1198364.
10  Kahneman, Daniel. *Thinking, Fast and Slow.* Kindle ed., Penguin, 2011.
11  McKercher, Kelly Ann. *Beyond Sticky Notes – Co-Design for Real: Mindsets, Methods and Movements.* Beyond Sticky Notes, 2020.
12  Grant, Adam. "Building a Culture of Learning at Work: How Leaders Can Create the Psychological Safety for People to Constantly Rethink What's Possible." *strategy+business*, 3 February 2021, www.strategy-business.com/article/Building-a-culture-of-learning-at-work.

13  Klare, Jean and Louise van Swaaij. *The Atlas of Experience.* translated by David Winner, Bloomsbury Publishing, 2000.

14  Raz, Ariel et al. "Design for Belonging." *Stanford D.School*, 2021, www.dschool. stanford.edu/resources/design-for-belonging.

15  Wise, Susie. "Home." *#DesignForBelonging*, nd, www.designforbelonging.com.

16  Sanders, Elizabeth B-N and Pieter Jan Stappers. "Co-Creation and the New Landscapes of Design." *CoDesign*, vol. 4, no. 1, 2008, pp. 5–18, doi:10.1080/15710880701875068.

17  Georgakopoulou, Alexandra. "Small Stories Research: Methods-Analysis-Outreach." *The Handbook of Narrative Analysis*, edited by Anna De Fina and Alexandra Georgakopoulou, Somerset: John Wiley & Sons, Inc., 2015, pp. 255–71. /z-wcorg/.

18  Dweck, Carol. *Mindset: The New Psychology of Success.* Ballantine Books, 2006.

19  Garvey Berger, Jennifer. "Changing on the Job Developing Leaders for a Complex World." 2012.

20  Duckworth, Angela. *Grit: The Power of Passion and Perseverance.* Scribner, 2016.

21  Diatta, Doremy. "Material Communications." *JAWS: Journal of Arts Writing by Students*, vol. 1, no. 1, 2015, pp. 63–75, doi:10.1386/jaws.1.1.63_1.

22  Freire, Paulo. *Pedagogy of the Oppressed.* Continuum, 1989.

23  Freire, Paulo. *Pedagogy of Hope: Reliving Pedagogy of the Oppressed.* Bloomsbury Academic, 2014.

24  Ehn, Pelle. "Learning in Participatory Design as I Found It (1970 to 2015)." *Participatory Design for Learning: Perspectives from Practice and Research*, edited by Betsy DiSalvo et al., Routledge, 2017, pp. 7–21.

25  Martin, Brian. "Methodology Is Content: Indigenous Approaches to Research and Knowledge." *Educational Philosophy and Theory*, vol. 49, no. 14, 2017, pp. 1392–400, doi:10.1080/00131857.2017.1298034.

26  Simpson, Leanne Betasamosake. *As We Have Always Done: Indigenous Freedom through Radical Resistance.* Kindle ed., University of Minnesota Press, 2017.

27  Barad, Karen Michelle and Duke University Press. *Meeting the Universe Halfway Quantum Physics and the Entanglement of Matter and Meaning.* Duke University Press, 2007. https://ezproxy.lib.monash.edu.au/login?url=http://dx.doi.org/10.1215/9780822388128.

28  Jones, Natasha N. "Narrative Inquiry in Human-Centered Design: Examining Silence and Voice to Promote Social Justice in Design Scenarios." *Journal of Technical Writing and Communication*, vol. 46, no. 4, 2016, pp. 471–92, doi:10.1177/0047281616653489.

29  Bonsignore, Elizabeth et al., editors. *Participatory Design for Learning: Perspectives from Practice and Research*, Kindle ed. Routledge, 2017.

30  Grossman, Michele, editor. *Blacklines: Contemporary Critical Writing by Indigenous Australians/Michele Grossman, Coordinating Editor.* Melbourne University Press, 2003.

31  Smith, Linda Tuhiwai. *Decolonizing Methodologies: Research and Indigenous Peoples.* 2nd ed., Zed Books, 2012.

32  Ahmed, Sara. "Feminist Wonder." *Feminist Killjoys*, vol. 2021, 2014. https://feministkilljoys.com/2014/07/28/feminist-wonder/.

33  Bennett, Jane. *Vibrant Matter a Political Ecology of Things.* Duke University Press, 2010.

34  Deci, Edward L. *Intrinsic Motivation and Self-Determination in Human Behavior.* Plenum, 1985.

35  Damon, William. *The Path to Purpose: How Young People Find Their Calling in Life.* Free Press, 2009.

36  Malin, Heather. *Teaching for Purpose: Preparing Students for Lives of Meaning.* Harvard Education Press, 2018.

37  Ryan, Richard M. "Psychological Needs and the Facilitation of Integrative Processes." *Journal of Personality*, vol. 63, no. 3, 1995, pp. 397–427, doi:10.1111/j.1467–6494.1995. tb00501.x.

38  de Charms, Richard. *Personal Causation: The Internal Affective Determinants of Behavior.* Academic Press, 1968.

39 Bhabha, Homi K. *The Location of Culture*. Routledge, 2004.
40 Rollnick, Stephen and William R. Miller. "What Is Motivational Interviewing?" *Behavioural and Cognitive Psychotherapy*, vol. 23, no. 4, 1995, pp. 325–34, doi:10.1017/S135246580001643X.
41 Deci, Edward L. and Maarten Vansteenkiste. "Self-Determination Theory and Basic Need Satisfaction: Understanding Human Development in Positive Psychology." *Ricerche di Psicologia*, vol. 27, no. 1, 2004, pp. 23–40.
42 Ertel, Chris and Lisa K. Solomon. *Moments of Impact: How to Design Strategic Conversations That Accelerate Change*. Simon & Schuster, 2014.

# 10

# COGNITIVE PSYCHOLOGY

## Learning from Remembering and Integrating

**Key Learning Science Practices**

FIGURE 10.1 **Building and Retrieving Memories**: A series of teacher professional learning activities designed to introduce the RISE science of learning principles introduced in this chapter came from our partnership with PLUSSED+. This pilot, designed by Sarah Naarden and Hannah Korsmeyer, is an evolution of the photo-elicitation activity described in the previous chapter (Narrative 9.1). We set out to see if asking teachers to rapid-fire retrieve multiple memories of shifts in their practice, encoded by experiential metaphors, could modify their memories and potentially reframe how they see themselves as agents of change.

DOI: 10.4324/9780429429743-13

In addition to attending to the psychological needs a supportive learning environment might foster, we can design in ways that support cognitive function. The science of how we learn is another field that can inform how we design to maximise memory-making, so learners can retrieve and apply those memories in the future. Scientific researchers often study the component parts of how we learn independently, but as designers our role is to recognise the virtuous circle animated by activating any one as a lever that deepens learning. This chapter identifies four specific areas that design can influence: retrieval practice, interleaving, spaced practice and encoding. Although introduced here as separate principles, like the previous chapter, they are interconnected and can be leveraged simultaneously through multi-modal activities. The entanglement of these science of learning principles, together with the social principles of belonging, effort, agency and motivation, drive learner engagement and the potential for sustained, meaningful shifts in thinking, doing and being.

My collaborator and Design Rounds participant, Kevin Mattingly, is also the designer of Columbia University Teacher College's massive open online course (MOOC): The Science of Learning – What Every Teacher Should Know (1). In introducing me to this research, Kevin profoundly shifted my understanding of what design already does well and my perspective on what we could do better (Narrative 9.1). Designing learning encounters in collaboration with Kevin was the ultimate learning-through-doing way to internalise his scientific understanding of how to create learning experiences that stick. There are many key science of learning principles correlated to increased academic performance; however, the four highlighted here are chosen for their relevance to transformative learning and design practice. The research-informed resources found at The Learning Scientists (2) and the visual guide to understanding how we learn (3) offer a deeper introduction to these core principles. Neuroscience and cognitive psychology are not the focus here. Instead, the chapter traces the connection between the well-articulated principles and the attributes of design.

## 10.1 Retrieval Practice

Retrieval practice is a learning strategy that enhances someone's capacity to later recall information by having the learner intentionally, without reference to notes, practice bringing information to mind. This sounds logical. Yet, many of us can acknowledge that we spend a disproportionate amount of time designing videos, slides and activities around how to get content into people's minds, compared to supporting how to get information out. A commitment to transformative learning is synonymous with durable learning. We need to be attentive to how we draw on new concepts in the months and years ahead. Our habits might suggest that taking and re-reading notes serves this purpose, yet what retrieval practice shows is that deliberately doing the hard work of recalling (not re-reading) ideas does more to ensure that the information will be accessible later.

The diverse moves design has for creating sticky memories can aid retrieval. When we design for embodied and emotional engagement, we indirectly create higher order memory.[1] Trying to remember what someone said is a lot harder than recalling how we felt. The key point is that the brain remembers the emotional components of an experience better than any other aspect (5). Design experiences that unsettle, create suspense, invite risk, spark hope, identify worries, make us laugh, ask us to be vulnerable, rely on touch, elicit co-realising, initiate play, move our bodies or foster belonging, work to effectively activate multiple senses and make retrieval significantly easier. Even though retrieval practice is a strategy deployed after being introduced to the new lesson, throughout a lesson, you can incrementally include moments for recalling what has been learned. This will strengthen the neural pathways for later retrieval.

At WonderLab, we often use prompts like, "Think of a time you have changed your practice in the past…" as a priming activity that invites participants to see themselves as agents of change (Narrative 9.1). Alternatively, we might focus on retrieving the feeling of learning with prompts like, "Remember a time you learned through play. Recall what you were doing, what it felt like, who else was there…" To understand this move as a retrieval practice activity is to see the prompt as doing something more than working with a learner's already-identity. How might this form of recalling from the past support the archiving of the new memory for future retrieval? How might the new memories evolve and reconfigure old memories? A move we often use to conclude an encounter is to reflect on the *one* lesson or insight you wish to act on in the future. This works simply as a commitment device that animates future action, but I wonder how we could mobilise the science of retrieval practice to increase the traction? What if people were instructed to recall, without checking notes, the key affective moments from the experience – could people then diagram how these moments intersect with their current practice? What would meaningfully happen next to help integrate the new knowing with the current habits? The design challenge is to play with how we might consolidate ideas retrieved from short-term memory, so they can become anchored into long-term memory (6, p. 75). The ultimate practice would be to build goals into the encounter to retrieve these ideas in a future context.

Counter-intuitively, easy retrieval does not have the desirable difficulty to make a memory more robust. The act of retrieval is more powerful, if slightly challenging. Bjork's Learning and Forgetting Lab research into retrieval as a

---

1   **Kelly**: We can use embodiment to design memorable encounters for future retrieval, but we can also design experiences to make retrieval of lived experience easier. If we want people to be able to express their lived experience, we can draw on sensory information that supports remembering the past. In her work on cultural and social effects and affects, sociologist Joanna Latimer contends there is a phenomenological "labour of investigation". Disinterested in the chronological accuracy of the experience, Latimer notes how the act of affective recall can "restore a sense of the past, not as history, but as vitally present in the bodies of actors in the present" (4, p. 14).

memory modifier builds on their research into desirable difficulty (7). The salient point is that, just as using a muscle builds muscle, the act of retrieving memories in turn modifies our memory archives. Memory retrieval changes how we connect memories, and makes the memory trace stronger and more easily accessed. Beyond simply making knowledge easier to recall, as designers we might think of how retrieving memories from lived experiences might change how people see themselves (3.1a).

To use these ideas in class, I often conclude the semester not with a review of final projects but with a collective act of retrieval. Framing the 'why' of retrieval through the lens of future practice, the students write an individual post-it for each key concept they learned during the class. Sometimes the activity is framed as a race (first person to 20), sometimes it is pitched as a collective effort (when we have filled 200). Either way, there is no cheating by looking at notebooks. And, every time people struggle to recall lessons learned until they don't. In this social context, a peer's retrieved memory sparks adjacent personal memories to reveal a diverse range of explicit and implicit lessons. To make the memories more robust, we might vote on the top lessons they do not want to forget years from now.

Neurobiologist John Medina explains that ideas that "grab our attention are connected to memory, interest, and awareness" (5, p. 75). Sticky learning encounters would use the concepts of purpose and motivation (9.4) with ideas of relevance and resonance (12.2) to elevate future retrieval and ultimately create durable learning that translates to transformed practice.[2]

## 10.2 Interleaving

Interleaving is the cognitive science word for a studying practice that mixes up related but distinct content. We might all remember experiences where intensive, repetitive practice led to improved competence (rote learning multiplication tables, practicing roller-skating for hours), so it can seem counterintuitive to accept that mixing things up is a better way to study. Yet, take a moment to reflect on how you might learn a sport. It is unlikely a coaching session would include shooting goals for 60 minutes. Instead, you might expect to alternate between endurance, strength and drill exercises with some strategy or a practice game in the mix.

The pedagogical orientation of a design studio inherently practices interleaving. In one class, you might interleave concept development with critique, drawing sketches with 3-D prototyping. At a different scale, interleaving can be compared to block learning. I studied design at a time where I learned everything

---

2 **Alli**: Alternatively new materialist's present stickiness as a cultural concept, affective condition *and* performative practice. As a designer, I am specifically curious about how materials enact and broker the stickiness of these affective engagements. Cala Coats uses 'stickiness' to describe a sort of methodological conditioning that enables people to break free of complicity, becoming able to stick with and be open to a kind of vulnerability grounded in precarity (8).

in blocks. I would study publication design every day for a semester, then corporate identity the next semester. To this day, against all evidence, my lived experience has me believe that block learning is a better learning experience. It is not. In *How We Learn* Benedict Carey shares the research on how interleaving is significantly more effective for learning than block learning, but even after tests people sense the block learning served them better.

> This much is clear: The mixing of items, skills, or concepts during practice, over the longer term, seems to help us not only see the distinctions between them but also to achieve a clearer grasp of each one individually. The hardest part is abandoning our primal faith in repetition.
>
> *(9, p. 2407)*

Contemporary design students who interleave multiple courses a semester learn from the adjacent integration. The connections seen between subjects, like prototyping in different modes across multiple subjects, play to the brain's impulse to heighten engagement when patterns are not easily traced. Research evidence confirms that interleaving works better whether applied to maths (trying out different kinds of problem sets) or to basketball (throwing not just from the free throw line but somewhere in that vicinity) (9, p. 2482).

Beyond reconsidering design curriculum and instruction, we can consider what creative practice might bring to interleaving. The hypothesis for why our brains respond to interleaving is due to the additional work required to make sense of emerging patterns and the engagement that is activated by the unexpected. In the context of transformative learning, our brains' receptivity to delight at what is novel (12.4) to be challenged by the not-yet-explained, and drawn to the unfamiliar offers potential applications for interleaving. As the nudge to wake up and pay attention, interleaving feels akin to the creative acts of synthesising, sense-making and meaning-making. Beyond serving our capacity to remember, the tactic of interleaving might work to support the ways design troubles expectations so we might attune to what is ambiguous, notice what is missing and imagine what is possible.

The *Relative Creative* water security challenge (7.2) works back and forth, through knowledge cards, peer-to-peer discussions, design fictions and creating a model. At the level of the day's program, the creative and dialogic engagement is interleaved with the theorising and designing. Yet, there is also a meta level of temporal interleaving. Through the conceptualising of a different future, the students' become more aware of the present. This interleaving of different conceptions of time draws students' whole selves into considering the consequences of their actions from multiple perspectives.

The *Transforming Mindsets* studio at Parsons (Narrative 12.1) often seemed to be at risk of pulling the students in too many directions. The students were working on a project with an external partner around shifting mindsets and practices, while simultaneously working on a project aimed at shifting a learning mindset of their own. We began each six-hour studio with a dedicated two hours of embodied exercises framed as play to intentionally uncouple the 'Play Gym' work from the project work (10). In addition, there was the rapid interleaving that comes with routine studio learning experiences like peer evaluations, self-reflection activities, vulnerable debrief sessions, reading design theory and learning through designing. All this interleaving activity was anchored by ensuring that new knowledge was always in conversation with old knowing. In the *Transforming Mindset* studio, new experiences were given space to be made sense of through well-established studio practices. The interplay between translating mindset lessons from their partner projects and to their own lives had students' constantly evaluating the relevance of the learning. The Play Gym teacher, Roger Manix (1.1a), shared idioms each week that made it clear that these seemingly unrelated activities were amplifying each other (Figure I.1). At the end of the semester, students expressed their primary frustration as dedicating 30% of studio time to play and reflection. They felt that this took away from time to work on their external projects. Paradoxically, when asked what the greatest surprise from the studio was, the students conceded they had produced their best work yet. Beyond their pride at the designed outcomes, they acknowledged they had learned more about themselves, had clearer self-awareness of their strengths and weaknesses, expressed a deeper sense of belonging and felt safer to take risks (11).

I have intentionally considered how to apply interleaving to this book. In weaving the personal narratives throughout the book, in letting the *Making Design* constellation echo throughout the sections (Figures 4.1 and 13.2) and juxtaposing project case studies with up-close practice vignettes, different voices and perspectives sit adjacent to each other. In threading lessons from practice betwixt and between the design theory, learning sciences and critical theory, I seek to juxtapose epistemological and ontological perspectives that tease the brain into making patterns. My hope is that the work of cognitively making connections between concepts that at first seem incongruous will deepen your ability to not just retain these ideas but walk away with a more critical position of your own experiences in relation to what you are reading.

## 10.3 Spaced Practice

These heralded cognitive learning strategies are linked to academic performance. In other words, they often help students get good grades. The comprehension and memory skills needed to ace exams, however, is not necessarily connected to the work of shifting mindsets or adopting new habits. Spaced practice – also known as deliberate practice – most strongly illustrates this point. This learning strategy is the scientific argument against cramming. Like retrieval practice, the strategy works with a forgetting-to-remember logic that has students learn material over a protracted period of time to intentionally increase the cognitive effort of recalling old material (6). In contrast to massed practice, for example, spending 4 hours studying the night before a test, spaced practice might propose eight, 30-minute sessions over a month. Peter Brown argues we are drawn to cramming (or in design why we might valorise the design sprint) because: "The rapid gains produced by massed practice are often evident, but the rapid forgetting that follows is not" (6, p. 49). If we want to get beyond learners simply performing well to learners deeply understanding material, then spaced practice shows how we might design learning encounters that do not ignore the research on forgetting.

Science explains how neural processes allow material to become stabilised in ways that result in the storage of enduring memories. I do not claim to understand a small percent of the scientific papers on these subjects, however this process of memory consolidation asks us to re-examine the high-energy, short-burst events we often design. As satisfying as the design sprint or fast-paced workshop feels, this massed practice approach leans on short-term memory when we often hope to create durable memories. Spaced practice research identifies that strengthening representations of new knowing for transfer to long-term memory comes with giving our brains time for mental rehearsal (6, p. 49). This idea of rehearsing creates stronger synaptic connections, in turn hinting at ways that design might play with integrative, creative and temporal strategies for maximising the benefits of spaced practice.

The promise of spaced practice is not selected here because it is something design does well, as much as it is an area we need to be more mindful of. How might we understand this move of rehearsing, as an iterative run-through that plays out when we story, prototype and imagine? How might an integrative approach to meaning-making return to refrains that question the purpose, the motivation and the relevance of a lesson? In designing encounters that work with a chorus and a verse, a call and a response, we can merge new memories with old and increase the likelihood that new material will be accessible for future use.

Knowing that massed practice leads to short-term satisfaction and spaced practice leads to long-term understanding, we need to consider how enthusiasm for brief, blocked workshops is balanced with the efficacy of more deliberate, staged introductions to content. Kevin Mattingly's critique of design-led encounters as learning experiences lies in a lack of follow through and experimental rehearsal space to integrate the insights into future practice. When designing a one-off event, Kevin's nudge was always to ask: 'Then What?' He knew the science and he knew that what happened when the event was over could not be ignored. Scheduled future prompts, ongoing feedback, informal interactions and moments of applied experimentation are all critical to supporting the consolidation practices that drive memory retrieval. Similarly, like the flipped classroom concept, we need to consider the learning that can meaningfully happen before people come together. A range of online, asynchronous or independent priming activities or intention setting prompts can supplement the participatory encounter. Strategies can stoke commitment in advance by having participants engage with information beforehand to frame priorities, identify shared lines of inquiry or fuel a sense of urgency. Concluding workshops with spaced-out instalments can anchor future action to a specific place or situation to which participants plan to apply the new lessons. Consider prompts that trigger a small move, like scheduling a meeting with a colleague to share what has been learned, or a prompt to tell a manager the one thing you hope to put into place so the tasks ahead feel achievable and factor in revisiting memories. Future framing activities, like break-up letters to an old mindset or fast forward emails to your future self, all work as strategies to bridge lessons learned with what you want to do, remember or hold dear in one week, three months or five years. Similarly, the spaced-out application of commitment devices can minimise the gap between intentions and behaviour. To weave multiple concepts together, how might an affect-driven approach to closing the gap increase the chances that a commitment device could remind someone of how they hope to feel if they successfully integrate the new knowing into future practice? Or could gazing at a souvenir placed strategically in the workplace trigger recollections of the experience over weeks in support of long-term memory consolidation.

Spaced practice can also be a logistical consideration. The *Edukata* case study worked with the assumption that a fly-in fly-out approach would ultimately not lead to sustained shifts in teacher practice. They made a strategic decision to appoint individual champions within the school charged with leading the activity once the researchers left. The assigning of the spaced practice work to be the responsibility of the personalised learning communities, project ambassadors or in-house coaches can be simultaneously efficient and empowering.

Adopting spaced practice in the context of formal education is comparably easy. However, revisiting and spacing content over years can be harder to operationalise. The *Transforming Mindset* students noted that much of what they internalised about mindsets and collaborating was undone when subsequent studios reverted to collaborations that privileged project outcomes over learning outcomes. Together, the students had come to value a learning environment that emphasised reflection, vulnerability and risk-taking. Yet, in studios with peers unfamiliar with this ethos, they defaulted to delegating tasks instead of building relationships. This more transactional approach allowed them to minimise the need for trust, belonging or shared purpose (11).

The weekly practice of the *Transforming Mindsets* Play Gym provided a point of comparison from one-off, half-day workshops. Previously, I had engaged Roger to run one-off sessions for classes that had, at the time, seemed profound. However, once spaced throughout a semester, the sessions moved from playfully disorienting to constructively transformative. Long-term memory consolidation relies on revisiting old material alongside new material. The weekly practice became an embodied reference point for how these encounters were changing all of us. The teachers engaged in the Play Gym, alongside the students. I came to notice the moments I less fearlessly engaged in games that once paralysed me, or the time I stepped into the unknown not needing to control what came next. The spaced practice did more than strengthen my memory; it also allowed me to witness my own growth. Also of note is the reflective debriefs at the end of each play session. Here, Roger expertly and generously invited each individual to pay attention to whatever had come up for them next time. With spaced practice came the promise of another chance to explore, rehearse and integrate. If we reframe this iterative orientation of design as a kind of spaced practice, it becomes possible to consider how the feedback loops of sacrificial moves might scaffold how we design experiences that reinforce, reframe and reimagine over time.

## 10.4 Encoding

If spaced practice is an area design needs to work on, encoding memories is the area where creativity already shines. Psychologists understand the learning and memory process in three stages: encoding, storage and retrieval. The choice to end this chapter on the first stage of the process is to conclude by asserting (12) the greatest contribution of design to memory-making is in how learning is encoded from the outset. We can work on spacing and interleaving to ensure knowing is storied for better retrieval, but the heavy lifting design brings lies in the ways that a material, multi-modal, performative practice codes and recodes insights, lessons, events, moments and experiences. Encoding refers to the initial learning of information. If the encoding process is powerful enough, then the ability to access the information later is easier. In *Make it Stick*, Peter Brown describes creating durable, robust learning as a two-part process (6, p. 75). First, we must recode and consolidate new information to ensure ideas that move from short-term to long-term memory are securely anchored. Second, we build associations between the material and a range of cues to make the encoded memory easily accessible at a later date. Design practices that draw on imagination and imagery inherently support this work of meaning-making and association building, just as unfamiliar, unexpected and uncertain experiences and interactions create a distinct and novel atmosphere.

Design brings new strategies into how, as facilitators of learning, we might imagine converting sensory perceptions into meaningful representations in the brain. These encoded representations are called memory traces. Research into memory traces reveals what intuitively any tourist knows – novel moments are more memorable than routine. Psychologists recognise the distinctiveness of a moment that is novel, unexpected or bewildering (13; 14). My vivid memory of Sonali's encounter (7.3) comes from the emotional response I had to the novel prompt to look at my hands for a full three minutes. My inability to recall professional learning encounters that bring out the ubiquitous post-its lies in the predictable familiarity of those encounters. Learning and memory research considers how and why our memories are more vividly encoded and easier to recall when emotional arousal and/or valence are present.[3] Like the teacher's

---

3   **Lisa**: There is a breadth of theories from biobehavioural psychology on how emotional arousal is connected to activation of the amygdala, neurobiological processing and increased memory strength to social psychology theories on how interrelated dimensions of affect are (15; 16; 17; 18; 19).

photo-elicitation activity (Narrative 9.1 and Figure 10.1), designer's affective prompts build associations by linking back to previous emotions or experiential memories and they can powerfully draw on previously encoded experiences. Similarly, using imagination to make events vivid in one's mind can be done by elaborating on sensory details, like what can be seen, what it might smell like and what might the atmosphere looks and sounds like.[4] If one was teaching history, it is easy to see how creating imagery might be limited to a mental exercise (what was the smell on the battlefield?). But in design, the options to enrich encoding through mapping, making, storying or performing these questions seem infinite.

The practice of drawing on different multiple hooks for strengthening memory is a cognition theory known as dual coding (22). In education research, the benefits of coding new content in two modes largely comes from studies where subjects visualise and write. Not so much mind-mapping, but separately writing the material and then thinking of how to give it visual form. The extra layer of visually coding with a symbol, timeline, diagram or photo leads to more associations at the point of retrieval and more time considering how to make sense of the content (Figures 3.1, 4.0, 12.1). Extrapolating that each additional layer of coding can make memories more readily accessible at a later date helps to explain why an interactive design encounter can be highly memorable. Beyond the duality of visual and written is the potential for the learner to code for emotion, embodied memories, social interactions and haptic making. Mapping a timeline of one's emotional, material and conceptual learning journey through a tough project supports multi-coding. This exercise normalises the productive struggle inherent to transformative learning and builds memory traces that holistically connect different felt, physical and cognitive dimensions of the learning experience.

The diagram that surfaces, the peer discussion that reframes and the commitment device that internalises can all be understood as creative forms of elaboration. Elaborative interrogation is a questioning strategy that brings a curious line of inquiry to new material (23). The rhetorical wondering questions throughout the book are a kind of elaborative practice, just as the graphic diagrams offer a form of dual coding. This mindset of wondering is to ask why, to question how, to talk with others in a process that has the learner always checking in. As a curiosity-led encoding strategy, elaborative interrogation has people wondering in bigger circles and from multiple perspectives. In designing for transformation, elaborative interrogation, like abductive sense-making, can help situate the relevance and purpose of new material. To strengthen memory traces, elaboration is often grounded in comparison to known material. Creative strategies for questioning how things are the same but different can help shift perspectives. Am I procrastinating making a change because I believe I will fail or because I believe I have more time? How might my past self feel about meeting my future self?

---

4   These papers introduce ways imagination and imagery connect to memory research (20; 21).

Whether questioning assumptions, establishing urgency or getting vulnerable, an elaborative line of inquiry makes robust memories by tracing connections to previous memories. The one caution here is that your memory will store the elaboration and that will be remembered as accurate. This is potentially not a useful process if working with ideas still in formation.

This is where the idea of the concrete example can be useful. It can be hard to reliably store abstract ideas. When a teacher uses a concrete example, a case study or a personal reference, the theory or principle being taught becomes stored alongside what we already know or by association with references we can make sense of. Later chapters in this Part reference the ways designers use fiction, allegory and analogies to think through metaphors, situations and narratives in ways that use concrete, if fictitious, examples. Encoding, elaboration and examples in design can bring a specificity to analogous questioning. For example, someone can wonder whether achieving a goal might metaphorically compare to crossing the line of a marathon or diving off a high platform. Or the elaboration might come from concrete examples of plurality. How is my everyday experience of privilege distinct from that of my colleague, childhood friend or sister-in-law? In more transmission-based learning, we might use a mnemonic to recode and recall the colours of a rainbow. But in transformative learning, we draw on all of the above to engage the whole self. The affordances of designing allow encoding to be a sensorial, creative act that does more than support cognitive recall by also storing felt and embodied memories that remind us what future state is needed, possible and desirable.

The haptic crafting of commitment devices (Figure 13.0), the physical digging in Sean's brick-making activity (8.3.2), the bodily play of *BudgetBall* (7.1.1) and the somatic slow processional walk in Sonali's (8.3.1) all speak to not just a dual coding, but to multiple layers of coding that come with an embodied, creative, reflective experience. Hannah's ruminating futures game (6.3.1), the viewing from multiple perspectives of Kelly's embodied workshop (7.3.2) and the deliberate experimenting with various levers in Alli's magical contraption (5.3.2) show how elaborative inquiry need not be a dialogic exercise alone. These creative and cognitive activities can lead to stronger learning by retrieving previous lessons from old memories, connecting these to new experiences and visualising and mentally rehearsing what you might do differently next time. This is how new ways forward begin to emerge.

In reviewing the ideas introduced in this chapter on key theories or practices from the learning sciences, it is possible to see *Particle in a Box* (7.2.1) as a project that integrates all of this knowing. The game is conceived to build on knowledge the students already have and be interleaved with the theoretical introduction to quantum physics. The playful, concrete experience encodes in different ways students' perception and understanding of abstract theory that is otherwise hard to comprehend. The gameplay invites spaced interaction with the material, supporting learners to repeatedly engage with the content. Given that new learning is labile and not fully formed until consolidated, repeat engagement does more than provide feedback or retrieval practice; it stabilises and organises for future application.

For encounters to be transformative, we rely on synaptic plasticity – the biological capacity of the brain to change with learning. You have probably heard of this as the formation of new neural pathways, new connections reinforced through repetition, retrieval and distinctive experiences. There is still so much unknown about how this plasticity might be enacted, how sequences are activated and how memory traces are strengthened. Research suggests there is no simple sequential process but instead a complex, integrated interplay of stimuli. Kevin would reduce all this unknowingness and promise to the simple statement that memory is the residue of thought. I resisted this cognitive framing because instinctively I felt memory could be the residue of more things than thought. Over time, I came to understand that we remember what we wrestle with, what we spend time making sense of and what we dedicate hours to processing. The term productive struggle is an umbrella way to explain what it means to retrieve ideas instead of looking at notes, to mix up content so we have to more actively make connections, to space material out so we have to try harder to remember or to elaborate on what we do not know so we might better know (24). With the hard struggle comes additional time spent, which inevitably leads to more thought and more robust memories. When we see the figuring, negotiating, reconciling, making, touching, critiquing, moving, creating and experiencing of the verb designing as moves that amplify cognitive processing, then we begin to see the potential of design to use these cognitive principles to deepen learning. Our goal is to design confounding and profound experiences that create a lot of internal wondering. The residue of thought prompted by the wondering will greatly increase the chance a transient experience might lead to deep, persistent memory traces.

Before we transition away from the social sciences into the design-based chapters, I am left wondering how to connect these cognitive strategies focused on an individual's memories and mindsets, and the socio-cultural motivation to design new habits and new worlds into being. What happens if we interleave feminist biologist Donna Haraway's term "staying with the trouble" with this cognitive and social psychology perspective? Might these very different perspectives on struggling, unsettling and troubling offer some new way to make sense of what it is being asked of us? In seeking new ways of making with and thinking through the critical act of building more liveable futures, Haraway asserts the need to stay with what is complex and hard (25). For Haraway, staying with the trouble is far more than a cognitive process. It is a feminist, ethical and ecological provocation. Whether we want to build stronger memories, better connections or bolder futures, we need to create learning experiences that one can hold on to, return to and act upon. Yet Haraway reminds us not to lose sight of the complexity. In negotiating incommensurable positions, in trying to see the whole person, in figuring what is not-yet-known or in seeking to sense what is ineffable, we must resist reductive methods, homogeneous narratives and oppressive characterisations. To stay with the trouble, we must engage with the complexity and the plurality, the urgency and the irreconcilability. This reframing of struggle will create strong memory traces if not easy answers. In scaffolding retrieval, we also productively make it easier for the lessons from a specific encounter to be remembered. These types of lessons are not easily transferable, and yet internalising the core ideas and recalling the key principles will allow for new knowing to be reconfigured and contextualised anew. This is why we need to reframe the experience of struggling as difficult yet desirable. We need to normalise getting uncomfortable to get curious, because it helps to be a little bit lost if we want to learn.

---

## Narrative 10.1 Researching: the Humility of Interdisciplinary Perspective-taking

### 2014 – with Myriam Diatta

*I am at a Character Lab meeting, a non-profit organisation that connects researchers with educators to create greater knowledge about the conditions that lead to social, emotional, academic, and physical well-being for young people throughout the country. It is late spring, the sun streams into the room full of social science researchers. I am the only design researcher. I try not to smirk as Dominic Randolph, co-founder of Character Lab and Head of School at Riverdale Country School, implores the community to consider how their vital research translates to the practice of teaching. It is true that so far, I cannot (or choose not?) to follow the inside-baseball conversation on research integrity. He is telling them how the day before, my design lab had run a growth mindset session for the teachers. I did not know he was going to mention my humble workshop. It hardly seems noteworthy in a room with world renowned researchers who bring in millions in funding. Dominic's provocation to the scientists is that he believes the co-design workshop made the idea of growth mindset more sticky in three hours than eight years of research presentations he had attended. I leave the meeting that day with three new collaborations for the summer ahead. I remember the intense optimism I felt as I rode the subway back to Brooklyn. I was completely assured, cocky you might say, that the opportunity to work with some of the country's leading researchers would translate to them seeing how design was central to the goal of amplifying the impact of their research.*

*I was so wrong.*

*Months later, I am on an Amtrak train back to Brooklyn. It is late summer the sun is low, and I no longer carry with me the optimism I had that afternoon. I am traveling back from a meeting at Cambridge with one of our collaborators. Over the last three months my lab has worked on education research projects into deep practice, belonging and reflections on homework. Although each collaboration failed to translate to the game-changing respect for design I had hoped for, I am not capable of bringing any perspective to my reflections. I am consumed in the present with my inability to process what happened in the day's meeting. I am feeling incredulous, bemused, defensive and somewhat defeated.*

*We had been bought in to redesign the booklet used in a large-scale school-based intervention. An earlier intervention had failed to produce any significant data and we were optimistic that out new design would turn things around. The old booklet had students filling out the same text-based worksheet every day for six weeks. The booklet Myriam has redesigned[5] is founded in the principle of reciprocity, which aims to make the onus of participating in the research more engaging for the students. Each day's reflective activity sought to creatively draw students into reflecting on what constrained or facilitated the of meeting their homework goals.*

*This afternoon our project partner held the prototype in his hands, he smiled encouragingly, he then looked uncertain, then he put the booklet down. Looking dismayed, he announces that our strategy is "so good, I am worried we won't be able to get it published." We talk for hours that day. Yet it is this nonsensical sentence that is playing on loop as we head south.*

There was a disorienting logic to our collaborator's wariness that confounded my disciplinary perspective. Earlier that afternoon, he had patiently explained the conundrum at the core of his position. His concern was not about whether our booklet could engage students in active reflection in ways that improved homework performance and academic performance. Rather, his concern was that the booklet might succeed in elevating the performance too much. A peer reviewer would be familiar with the statistical bump that a planning intervention and a reflection intervention might generate. If our booklet produced an effect size that was significantly greater with no logical explanation, the research could simply be dismissed. Our counter, that the contribution of design was the explanation for the bump, was not useful since it was not an intervention about design or engagement for that matter.

That afternoon, I got introduced to the concept of independent variables. It was explained that the visual design, engagement strategy and playful reciprocity problematically introduced a flood of new variables that might potentially increase the outcome but in turn contaminate the integrity of the results. This is how 'too good' becomes 'unpublishable'. Over time I came to understand (if not value) that independent variables are key to knowing why

5  **Myriam**: In general, my memory is spotty. This happened so long ago. I don't think I had the self-assurance to strongly critique or distance myself from the collaborators' science-based approach when there was so much for me to critique in myself as a relatively new member of Lisa's research team. Looking back in the self-critical way of reflecting that I defer to, it is not mapping process but naming assumptions about the driving forces, inevitable politics of a research project and more direct and honest attitudes about each of our fields that might make for a stronger start in another collaboration of this kind.

certain social science interventions work. I did come to understand (and begrudgingly respect) that this is the data that informs educational policy. Still, our weeks spent designing an intervention with thoughtful consideration for the person filling out the booklet seemed upended by our collaborators essentially designing an intervention for their peers to review. We had been focused on the school-based application of our research, imagining our booklet could become a classroom resource. In contrast, our collaborators had been focused on getting the evidence that could shape policy and direct funding into interventions that create meaningful impact.

We had designed with care an encounter that could help students learn about themselves while gathering data for the researchers. Had we completely missed the point? Already disinterested in designing interventions that ignore the entangled, interdependencies design engages with, I am conflicted about what the implications of independent variables might mean for design research.

*I am now in the Southern Hemisphere. Six months have passed and it is late summer again. I am in a hotel room working at a desk that's too small on a presentation of my research for the University of Melbourne Graduate School of Education. I keep readjusting myself thinking I can make my workspace more comfortable. But I can't because the discomfort is more than physical. I want to win over the researchers with a highly visual presentation of our research: the belonging maps, the deep practice gifs and the homework obstacle course booklet. But I have to remind myself they are not designers. I have to let go of the idea that the failed collaborations of the North American summer were somehow idiosyncratic. I begin with the afternoon in the office in Cambridge. I am still resisting the work I will do late into the night. At some point I will swap discomfort for curiosity. I will humbly attempt to see design research through the lens of an education researcher. I will find a generous way in to understanding the ontological and epistemic disciplinary orientations my collaborators bought to their research. Through this perspective-taking exercise, I will once again make sense of what design can offer other disciplines.*

*The next morning, I again step into a room of interdisciplinary researchers. This time I empathically, confidently and candidly breakdown my perspective on how and why the recent collaborations failed. In trying to connect with a new group of potential researchers I learn more from the exercise of considering how my collaborators might, in turn, experience our biases and assumptions.*

I do not pretend to know how my collaborators might remember that summer. What I do know is that the intentional act of being reflexive about my own praxis, disciplinary orientations and my own epistemic beliefs are what forever shifted my belief in and critique of design research. This is not a trite testament to how we learn from failure, but more a story of how interdisciplinary collaborations rest on bringing a humility, generosity and reciprocity to what we can learn from disciplinary perspectives so different to our own.

## Bibliography

1 "The Science of Learning – What Every Teacher Should Know." *edX*. 2021. www. edx.org/course/the-science-of-learning-what-every-teacher-should.

2 "About Us." *The Learning Scientists*. nd. www.learningscientists.org.

3 Weinstein, Yana and Megan Sumeracki. *Understanding How We Learn: A Visual Guide*. Routledge, 2019.

4 Latimer, Joanna. "Introduction: Body, Knowledge, Worlds." *The Sociological Review*, vol. 56, no. 2_suppl, 2008, pp. 1–22, doi:10.1111/j.1467–954X.2009.00813.x.

5 Medina, John. *Brain Rules: 12 Principles for Surviving and Thriving at Work, Home and School*. Pear Press, 2014.

6 Brown, Peter C. *Make It Stick: The Science of Successful Learning*. Kindle ed., Belknap Press, 2014.

7 Bjork Learning and Forgetting Lab. "Applying Cognitive Psychology to Enhance Educational Practice." *UCLA*. nd. www.bjorklab.psych.ucla.edu/research/#itemI.

8 Coats, Cala. "Stickiness as Methodological Condition." *Journal of Social Theory in Art Education*, vol. 40, 2020, pp. 17–28.

9 Carey, Benedict. *How We Learn: The Surprising Truth About When, Where, and Why It Happens*. Kindle ed., Random House, 2014.

10 Grocott, Lisa et al. "The Becoming of a Designer: An Affective Pedagogical Approach to Modelling and Scaffolding Risk-Taking." *Art, Design & Communication in Higher Education*, vol. 18, no. 1, 2019, pp. 99–112, doi:10.1386/adch.18.1.99_1.

11 Grocott, Lisa and Kate McEntee. "Teaching Intrapersonal Development, Improving Interpersonal and Intercultural Skill Sets: The Transforming Mindsets Studio." *Public Interest Design Education Guidebook: Curricula, Strategies, and Seed Academic Case Studies*, edited by Lisa M. Abendroth and Bryan Bell, Routledge, 2019, pp. 141–46.

12 Melton, Arthur W. "Implications of Short-Term Memory for a General Theory of Memory." *Journal of verbal learning and verbal behavior*, vol. 2, no. 1, 1963, pp. 1–21, doi:10.1016/S0022-5371(63)80063-8.

13 Roesler, R. and J.L. McGaugh. "Memory Consolidation." *Reference Module in Neuroscience and Biobehavioral Psychology*, Elsevier, 2019.

14 Posner, Jonathan et al. "The Circumplex Model of Affect: An Integrative Approach to Affective Neuroscience, Cognitive Development, and Psychopathology." *Development and Psychopathology*, vol. 17, no. 3, 2005, pp. 715–34, doi:10.1017/S0954579405050340.

15 Bradley, Margaret M. et al. "Remembering Pictures: Pleasure and Arousal in Memory." *Journal of Experimental Psychology*, vol. 18, no. 2, 1992, pp. 379–90, doi:10.1037/0278–7393.18.2.379.

16 Conway, Martin A. et al. "The Formation of Flashbulb Memories." *Memory & Cognition*, vol. 22, no. 3, 1994, pp. 326–43, doi:10.3758/BF03200860.

17 Kensinger, Elizabeth A. "Remembering Emotional Experiences: The Contribution of Valence and Arousal." *Reviews in the Neurosciences*, vol. 15, no. 4, 2004, pp. 241–52, doi:10.1515/REVNEURO.2004.15.4.241.

18 Kensinger, Elizabeth A. and Suzanne Corkin. "Memory Enhancement for Emotional Words: Are Emotional Words More Vividly Remembered Than Neutral Words?" *Memory & Cognition*, vol. 31, no. 8, 2003, pp. 1169–80, doi:10.3758/BF03195800.

19 Mather, Mara. "Emotional Arousal and Memory Binding: An Object-Based Framework." *Perspectives on Psychological Science*, vol. 2, no. 1, 2007, pp. 33–52, doi:10.1111/j.1745–6916.2007.00028.x.

20 Craik, Fergus I.M. and Robert S. Lockhart. "Levels of Processing: A Framework for Memory Research." *Journal of Verbal Learning and Verbal Behavior*, vol. 11, no. 6, 1972, pp. 671–84, doi:10.1016/S0022–5371(72)80001-X.

21 Bower, Gordon H. and Judith S. Reitman. "Mnemonic Elaboration in Multilist Learning." *Journal of Verbal Learning and Verbal Behavior*, vol. 11, no. 4, 1972, pp. 478–85, doi:10.1016/S0022-5371(72)80030-6.

22  Clark, James M. and Allan Paivio. "Dual Coding Theory and Education." *Educational Psychology Review*, vol. 3, no. 3, 1991, pp. 149–210, doi:10.1007/BF01320076.

23  Dunlosky, John et al. "Improving Students' Learning with Effective Learning Techniques: Promising Directions from Cognitive and Educational Psychology." *Psychological Science in the Public Interest*, vol. 14, no. 1, 2013, pp. 4–58, doi:10.1177/1529100612453266.

24  Sriram, Rishi. "The Neuroscience behind Productive Struggle." *Edutopia*. 13 April 2020, www.edutopia.org/article/neuroscience-behind-productive-struggle.

25  Haraway, Donna J. *Staying with the Trouble: Making Kin in the Chthulucene*. Duke University Press, 2016.

# 11

# CREATIVE IMAGINING

## Learning from Sensing and Wondering

**Resonant Design Sense-making Skills**

FIGURE 11.1 **Alibis for Play**: This is a sequence of stills from a video created by Christopher Patten and Maggie Ollove to introduce the Playmobil video activity described in the introduction to this chapter as an invitation to play. The fictional video narrative is presented here as a tactic for priming the learners' curiosity and driving engagement. To mistake the Playmobil video as the solution or the outcome is to misunderstand the catalytic role the rushed script-writing and embodied enacting also play in fictional scenarios conceived to reveal inner worlds.

DOI: 10.4324/9780429429743-14

With the advent of the fourth industrial revolution, we bear witness to accelerating automation and the urgent implications for future skillsets. Ranking the top ten job skills in the future The World Economic Forum bumped 'creativity' from number ten in 2015 to number three in 2020. Given the interconnectedness that comes with complexity, it is worth noting that abductive mode of design inquiry (1) further supports the top two skills as well, with complex problem solving defined as "crafting creative solutions" and critical thinking described as the translation of data into "insightful interpretations" (2).

Following neither a bottom up- nor top-down logic, the process of abductive reasoning can be generally understood as working from an incomplete set of observations to sense-make from the data at hand. The designer brings this orientation to the synthesising of different kinds of data in a distinctly creative and generative direction. Consider, for example, how a private investigator might work with gaps in information compared to a designer. Whereas the investigator seeks to disclose something unseen, the designer iteratively engages with information to see something anew. The practice of sensing and wondering in design is more than simply abductive; it is performative. It is grounded in a creative practice that embraces the ambiguity of not-knowing (3) and explores hunches through making a move (4). The relevance of design abduction in a world of multifaceted, interdependent problems lies in simultaneously proposing problems and solutions by co-creating the *what* and *how* of a situation (5).

Other discipline orientations to critical thinking may seek to be objective, evaluative and leading to an informed judgement. Yet in design, critical thought and action come together in a performative quest to reconcile incommensurable conditions. The methods of this chapter seek to invite critical wonderment by resisting the oftentimes affirmative manifestation of design fixation (6). These methods present tactics and moves for disarming the optimistic and blinkered desire to seek self-confirming evidence, bringing a critical rigour to a generative and subjective practice. The emphasis here is on preparing the soil conditions for a practice grounded by the critico-creative act of designing. This section specifically renders the creative capacity to imagine, critique and pivot 'what could be' during the act of learning.

Complementing the two previous chapters' focus on social and cognitive psychology, this chapter attends to the contribution of the generative, imaginative grammar of design when it comes to creating learning encounters. Beginning with situating designing as a reflective practice, the first section addresses the discipline of attuning to the self and the learner. The second picks up the allegorical methods that can spark abductive reasoning and structure creative sense-making. Kaleidoscopic moves enact the third keyword, linking the designer's commitment to see situations from new perspectives with the capacity to generate unforeseen possibilities. The connection between emotions and the affective domain closes out the chapter.

The chapter opens with a practice vignette, a narrative that offers a glimpse into a design studio end of semester class. I am the teacher and designer of the learning experience, and *Riverdale Country School* sponsored the studio. Yet, this story is of two Masters of Transdisciplinary Design students from Parsons – Christopher Patton and Maggie Ollove. They have spent the semester working on the professional learning challenge of getting educators excited about team teaching. To understand the challenges, they had interviewed and shadowed teachers in class and subsequently heard all the reasons why teachers often resist the extra work that comes with establishing a strong team-teaching alliance. In the final class of the studio, I resisted the convention of students' presenting their tidy solutions of what had been learned from the semester projects and alternatively invited the Riverdale educators to sense-check what had been made of the ethnographic research insights. Instead of being a moment for assessing what had been done, the day provided a communal space for reciprocal learning between the Riverdale teachers and the Parsons graduate students.

The design challenge, only disclosed at the beginning of the workshop, was to create and produce a three-act narrative of the situation, the tension and a way forward. Adapting the video-based scenario method (an evolution of the method introduced in Narrative 5.1), the participants had two hours, some Playmobil characters and a blank backdrop (Figure 11.1). Providing the toy characters was an explicit invitation to see the Playmobil as an alibi for play, design here granting permission to act against convention. The task was to furiously create a story arc and script, design a set, then shoot the narrative to video. The video that Christopher and Maggie's team produced was as hilariously makeshift and unresolved as any of the others that day. Yet, beyond the unremarkable final product, evidence emerged that revealed how the rushed, untidy, spontaneous creative process of co-creating something together was the more meaningful outcome.

A divide and conquer approach to rushing through the deadline had Maggie and Christopher working on a script. When they shared the script with their teacher-collaborators, there was no time for sugar-coating the feedback – one teacher laughed at the sketch of a scenario and bluntly exclaimed, "That would never happen!" The group, which was curious to better understand what was behind the impulsive confession, paused the frenetic action to go deeper. The teacher explained that the script would never play out because no teacher would let themselves be that exposed. In that one blurted out comment, the connection between relational design, generative co-creation, affective learning and social co-realising was made visible. Taking a broader view, this chapter pulls out to illuminate some of the conditions, orientations and dispositions that helped create this moment of learning that shifted the direction of the whole project.

## 11.1 Reflective Practice

The emphasis in design on the prototype, artefact and materials can minimise the contention that the learning these things animate comes from bumping up against people. However, a participatory orientation and commitment to learner engagement can be mediated through the inter- and intra-personal conversation between the co-learners, co-facilitators and the materials of the situation.

Donald Schön's seminal books on the reflective practitioner offer a counter argument to the techno-rationalists who position design in sweeping methodological terms (7; 8). Curious about the situated practice of design, Schön paid attention to the small, critical conversations between the materials and the designer, between the 'universe of one' situation and the design process. Schön's theories on how designers work with reflection-in-action to navigate the oftentimes implicit knowing-in-action have offered potential frameworks for understanding, amplifying and describing the situated, reflective practice of design (9; 10). Yet what is the role of reflective practice in both designing and experiencing learning encounters? Schön sees design activities as driving action, and design expertise as making informed decisions based on what those actions teach us. While prototypical activity enacts the move-testing, the real lesson comes from the designer's scrutiny of the state that emerges. The relevance of this for transformative learning is two-fold. There is the reflective acumen of the designer/researcher/ facilitator of learning, and the potential to design materials and embodied encounters that prompt the learner to be in reflective conversation.

To get past surface reflections, we need to ask learners to do move beyond simple descriptions of action like 'I did X' and or even straightforward correlations of 'I did X because of Z'. To surface quality reflection, we need sophisticated critical interrogations, like: 'In wondering why I keep getting stuck on Z, I first tried Y before X'. Better still we can look to John Mason's advice in *Researching your own Practice: the discipline of noticing,* to attune to things we might not be trained to notice (11). As facilitators of learning might be cognisant that people are listening closely to what we are saying, yet less attentive to how hard it might be to pull attention back after a breakout activity. A noticing practice asks us to be awake to possibilities as they emerge in complex dynamic of learning encounters, just as it asks the learner to stay rigorously attuned to their inner world of action and decisions.[1]

Design materials and convivial activities can be generative co-facilitators of in-the-moment reflective inquiry, scaffolding for learners how they might attune to their bodies, beliefs and internal back-talk more deeply (Figures 2.1, 3.1, II.1, 6.1, 7.1, 8.1). Just as a designer learns about typography through attentive comparison with different types, the designer of learning attends to the atmosphere and the non-verbal body language.[2] As the designer of learning, we need to be

---

1    **Shanti:** The term attuning can help the facilitator-researcher pay attention to more than what the workshop participants are doing, as if they are somehow outside these happenings. Rather it is a way of participating by being with the ebbs and flows of energy, attention and feelings as they emerge. Attunement could be thought of as a way of being with others, with materials, with ideas and more.

2    **Shanti:** Attuning to the workshop atmosphere offers another form of relationality, a sort of bridge that recognises the co-presence of all the different people and things in the workshop setting. The value of thinking like this is that the facilitator isn't set apart from the workshop, but rather is participating in, and indeed making it ongoingly, along with everything and everyone else.

sense-making on multiple levels to evaluate what is working. This can be the difference between activities that stall engagement or ignite curiosity. Furthermore, in a social learning context, the reflective conversation with the situation is informed not just by the back-talk between the materials and the learner, but by how the move-testing experiments in a social context can illuminate our different tacit assumptions or normalise our shared mental models (12).

When we move into more reflexive vulnerable spaces of learning, we need to paradoxically consider the more mundane aspects of designing learning encounters. If we want learners to engage in introspection we need to meet their anticipated needs. With this shift, our orientation needs to transition from a functionalist perspective to a care perspective, towards mutual responsibility and interdependency. By 'mundane' my colleagues and I are talking about:

> the opening exercise that makes you feel like you are meant to be here, the playful priming activity that gives you an alibi to perform another side of yourself, the material choices that signal inclusivity or a seating plan that intentionally provokes debate. Each of these examples involves careful decisions essential to creating spaces that seek to facilitate belonging yet have a tolerance for turbulence, or to invite vulnerability yet embrace conflicting ambitions.
>
> *(12, p. nd)*

The relational orientation of these gestures cannot be ignored when it comes to engaging in the difficult labour of imagining futures that do not reproduce the everyday inequalities we have become used to.

## 11.2 Allegory and Metaphor

As a situation-specific practice, Design is grounded in the complexity and specificity of a community, system, context and oftentimes a designated site. This presents the challenges of how a designer applies previously learned lessons to a seemingly always-unique situation. Many designers draw on storytelling and symbolism methods to bridge between the repertoire of a designer's lived experiences and the knowing a stakeholder or community brings as expert of their own experience. Allegory is broadly understood as a creative work (for example, a story, artwork, or poem) that serves to reveal hidden meanings.

The designer is less interested in the moral lesson behind traditional allegorical stories and uses the power of investigative imagination to reveal hidden possibilities or pitfalls within a potential solution. The play alibi video vignette is one example of how a designer might use storytelling and use-case scenarios to engage participants in authentic learning. Alternatively, graphic storyboards, speculative fiction, metaphors and analogous situations offer detached tools for shaping and evaluating a proposition by way of the new perspective the now-but-not-now, or the this-but-not-this lens offers.

What is the power of storytelling when it comes to grafting new imaginaries, new ways of seeing, doing and becoming in the world? Jonathan Gottschall makes the case that we humans are storytelling animals, unable to resist the pull of alternate worlds (13). Creating fictional scenarios using allegory and storytelling are therefore sticky tools for amplifying learner engagement. Although the playfully imagined team-teaching scenario is not presented as a world we cannot imagine, or a dystopian future to reckon with, the mode of speculation still hints at the value of constructing futures that invite debate, reflection, provocation and inspiration (14). In acknowledging that plural alternate-present worlds can exist the not-pretending-to-be-real video narrative suspends the pretence there is a defined problem to solve. In dismissing the reductive nature of solutioning, an invitation to plural interpretations of a situation is afforded. The potential of fiction to invite one interpretation while setting the stage for future action is of particular relevance to the shift work of transformation.

The act of story-making fictional narratives has tangible props and learners coming together to rehearse potential futures (14).[3] Even if the quick-and-dirty Playmobil example (Figure 11.1), with its ready-made figures and slapped together sets, is far from the highly crafted materiality of Dunne and Raby's speculative design, the grounded yet emergent situation offers a social learning, co-creative platform for exploring an alternate present. The teacher's verbalised emotional resistance, "that would never happen" and the researcher's noticing of the blurted reaction allowed the synecdoche of the implausible script to reveal a greater insight about trust, vulnerability and teamwork in the classroom.

Analogous thinking is a similarly imaginative tactic for scaffolding inquiry by way of a calculated redirect. For the designer trying to better understand a context or looking for a source of inspiration, the Analogous Situations method invites a new perspective by way of a same-but-different situation (16, p. 161). In the context of education, there are many non-educational spaces that offer different services, experiences or artefacts that enable learning. In choosing a reframing site, the skill is in selecting a situation that is more tangential than parallel. In looking at alternative modes for learning, we did not visit a library (too close), but instead I took a studio on an outing to beauty store Sephora, where the students observed the shop through the lens of how learning happens. This trip offered a quick, accessible study in blended learning (how-to-videos), just-in-time mentors (associates teaching through a makeover) and hands-on learning (encouraged through samples and testers).

---

3   **Kelly**: This underscores my perception that the artefact alone has no meaning. It is only "through stories told about it, and the scenes in which it plays a role" that it generates "opportunities for creativity, expression, and discussion" (15, p. 7). Coming from an industrial design background a lot of unlearning had to happen for me to not see centre the objects in the participant's experience, but rather to see them as an avenue for interpreting and discussing experiences.

The power of metaphors to harness imagination, focus discussion, surface beliefs and generate ideas runs through design practice. In a social learning context, a familiar metaphor offers a shared way into grasping something simple yet exploring the complexity. The exploratory value of the metaphor lies not in how perfect it is but in getting curious about where the metaphor falls apart. In contrast, the explanatory metaphor offers a way into understanding how something is or could be. This twin-capacity of the metaphor to be divergent and convergent can play a critical role in moving mindsets and supporting transformative learning. Metaphors show up everywhere in our research lab; as word cards, as experiential prompts (12.2, Figures 3.1 and 7.1) and as photographic elicitation tools (Narrative 9.1, Figure 10.1). We use metaphors for quick check-ins on how people are feeling, or as a playful introduction move that can reveal different aspects of themselves than a name and title. The next section even uses the kaleidoscope as an exploratory metaphor for interrogating the reframing, iterative moves of a designer.

Allegory, analogy and metaphor are just some of the tools familiar to a designer that can be used to wonder new ways learners can compassionately, playfully, vulnerably, assertively, poetically or humorously construct an alternate here-and-now response to a situation. The power of the imaginary to graft never-before-seen ideas lies in this improvisational capacity to drive a learner's motivation, the participants' shared curiosity and an emotional engagement. The conceit of allegorical inquiry lies in how, with just a few sketched outlines, the learner can be tricked into doing the imaginative work of colouring in the scene (13).

## 11.3 Kaleidoscopic Moves

The generative orientation of a designer's mindset is committed to iteratively pausing and holding space for sacrificial prototypes, candid feedback, serendipitous openings and other design moves that subtly nudge one's design in a new direction or propose a dramatic pivot. The reflective commitment to attune to what is being revealed, to sense the merits of potential pathways and to be responsive to where the process might take you is anchored by the quest for to a more 'right' future.[4] Yet this capacity to attend to possibilities that are always in flux is not achieved by holding this breadth of conflicts, conditions and potential in one's head. The ability to get comfortable with infinite possibilities and the not-knowingness of what comes next is supported by a full range of visual, material and discursive moves that give shape to what is emerging.

---

4   **Hannah**: Sara Ahmed refers to feminism as 'sensational', stressing that feminist understanding can *begin* with an embodied sense that things are not right. I am less interested in applying feminist theory to design and instead am left wondering if design practice can shift our personal understanding of feminism. How do the obstacles and challenges that we 'come up against' while designing in unequal worlds sharpen and inform our feminist commitments?

The kaleidoscope as metaphor offers a way into considering what it means to act in the face of an entangled, composite and complex mosaic of problems and challenges, opportunities and potential solutions. The toy kaleidoscope playfully invites you to open the aperture wide to see a universe of possibilities or narrow the focus to the magic of a few pixels of colour. More than just capturing divergent and convergent moves, the infinite configurations model the challenges of what to pay attention to and the interdependencies inherent in each move we make. The kaleidoscope manifests the potential paralysis a designer (or learner) can feel faced with an avalanche of data, contradictory perspectives, systemic barriers, cultural inequities and unlimited technological affordances. Yet, the kaleidoscope also asks us to resist the narrative of problems as solvable or solutions as answers, to instead accept the wonder that comes with staying curious and critical. The kaleidoscope speaks to the capacity of a dextrous design practice that can make a move even in the knottiest of situations. The ability of design to negotiate the incommensurable, to reckon with information and observations that are not comparable and cannot be isolated is key here. The positioning of design as a future-oriented practice is grounded in this ability to find a way forward. In theory, the designer negotiates the incommensurable by (1) mentally, accepting the complexity of the situation; (2) literally, engaging in a conversation with the people, artefacts and environment of the situation; (3) configuratively, by tentatively fixing the incommensurable factors in a proposition that offers a way forward (17).

It is possible to understand the kaleidoscopic potential of design in contrast to other disciplinary orientations. I find the psychologist's impulse to identify the one independent variable essential in a research study to be disarming (Narrative 10.1), just as our desire to work with many interdependent variables can confound other disciplines' notions of rigour. If you seek to isolate the individual pixel in the kaleidoscope, you are not curious to turn things left or right. However, the deductive reasoning of the scientists led us to introduce more A/B testing while holding on to the abductive reframes. Similarly, working with ethnographers mindful of interventions led us to be more wary of the designers' bias to action. In ethically owning the diffracted ripple effect of grand interventions, there is a call to take more time to attune to place and gather feedback before acting. This is an invitation to pause the kaleidoscope long enough to evaluate our moves more intentionally (18). In a paper on the affordances of design for the learning sciences, Mai Kobori and I developed the Potential for Intervention Framework, which proposed the idea of scrappy experiments early in the framing of research projects. The idea was to intentionally turn the kaleidoscope to engage with new frames, to look at potential future interventions through the lenses of: People, Place, Prototypes and Participation (19).

Design has the agitating capacity to use design moves, methods and materials to reconcile incommensurate conditions (20). Elliott's use of the STEEP framework (5.3) is one approach to proposing lenses by which to pause and consider what is prioritised or ignored. Framing can isolate a particular focus while not permanently dismissing the existing and competing conditions at play. The acrobatic process of reframing intentionally pulls the prismatic possibilities of different viewpoints into focus.[5] This agility requires breaking apart ideas that seem fused, making connections that seem implausible and being open to a frame that seems opposable to your intent. The act of *figuring* what we are wondering about can be understood as a kaleidoscopic method designed to diffract the back-talk that comes from the designer rifling through different visual framings of the ideas being explored (5.4), (9; 21).

This is how the designer makes inferences, sees patterns and proposes insights so we might generate new ways of seeing.[6] It is in this ability to reframe, to make sense of and see anew that is relevant to the design of learning encounters. Embodied and material acts of kaleidoscopic synthesis within a learning encounter help the learner forge connections between seemingly incommensurate data points. The act of making ideas visible can precede the cognitive making sense of something tacit or complex.[7] The design goal is not to deduce or induce the truth but to reveal connections that prompt a reframing or new perspective. In this way, the wondrous, infinite possibilities of the kaleidoscope propose ways into considering how creative acts of freezing, framing and figuring can be used to reckon with the design impulse to make a move in the face of complexity and uncertainty. The co-creative act of framing the play alibi video around a very specific scene in a classroom and the social encounter of figuring it out together is what allowed the single, critical insight to emerge. Turning the kaleidoscope one degree to the left, three degrees to the right, is sometimes all that it takes.

---

5   **Sean:** I understand my practice-based research methodology in a similar way – a cluster of lenses that shift, grow and change depending on the situation and context. Design has to be at the core because it is very much how I see, understand and synthesise the word around me. Yet, the multidisciplinary selection of theories, practices and worldviews that orbit the core is how the framing becomes generative. The kaleidoscopic moves allow my research into power, participation and social justice to always be simultaneously challenging a series of normativities within design.

6   **Dion:** If we appreciate learning as a process facilitated through language, it follows that our perceptions are limited by the language we have available to us to scaffold the expression and communication of our learning. And, if we see the actions of sense-making to make the sensate intelligible – to join our past experiences with the present – then to 'see', and to 'make-sense' of what is unfolding in practice requires the giving of attention to the present moment and the unfolding events in front of us. What form might this attention take? Is there a language of designing that makes visible – and possible – the language we need to make sense of our world as it emerges through learning?

7   **Ricardo:** I see becoming aware of what we have-no-words-for as a critical step in the context of transformative learning. We know design to be good at giving tangible form to outcomes, what I am curious about in my Ph.D. is how, through embodied gesture, we can engage with non-verbal knowing (or should I say pre-contemplative or pre-reflective knowing?) What might the body bring to the translational act of giving form, to surface awareness. Not assuming we need to make *evident* or make *explicit*, the research does still seek to make *visible*, to make *aware*. Sonali's and my work with teachers in India showed how embodied activities scaffolded access to one's ineffable knowing, allowing the teachers to engage with their inner world of mindsets, emotions and beliefs and in turn seeding different responses to future action.

## 11.4 Emotions and Affect

If widening the aperture of a kaleidoscope allows us to parse the whole system, then zooming in opens up a portal into the interior worlds of learners. Seeing beyond empathy (the emotion most widely associated with a human-centred approach to designing), (22; 23; 24) we look passed shadowing practices and empathy maps to consider the kind of emotional landscape that allows learners to be curious, open and present. The question becomes how design methods might work with emotions and affect to foster the kind of self-awareness, trust and engagement evident in the play alibi narrative. Somehow, the combination of established relationships, creative serendipity and shared inquiry fostered a space for the actors to be vulnerable and courageous, uncertain yet decisive, respectful and humble. Paradoxically, against pressure to not equivocate and to make rapid decisions, in just two hours the team revealed a significant, felt insight. This stands in contrast to the ethnographic insights gathered over 12 weeks.

The psycho-social themes of belonging, agency and motivation introduced earlier (9.1, Figures 3.1 and 9.1), outlined the connection between learning and one's emotional landscape. This claim is confirmed by brain imaging research – we are not thinking machines that feel, but feeling machines that think (25). This places the importance of rescripting the stories we tell about ourselves and our worlds as a central challenge of transformative learning. In psychiatry, this can be translated to a learner's capacity to be flexible and adaptive; the motivation to develop coherent narratives of our worlds; the vitality that drives engagement and the self-regulation that anchors stability computes with the insight that our ability to learn is deeply affected by our learning relationships. An expansive understanding of the brain as an extended nervous system that is distributed throughout our bodies further highlights the importance of *integration* (26, p. 255). The potential to sustain new ways of being and acting in the world comes with our capacity to not just change the stories we tell ourselves but to holistically internalise those stories.[8]

Earlier chapters highlight the value of curating affective responses that encode memories for retrieval or encounters that motivate. But can working in the affective realm help learners be more than engaged? Might teaching to emotions help learners act differently in the future? (30; 31) Lisa Feldman Barrett, the director of Interdisciplinary Affective Science Laboratory, is interested in people's capacity to differentiate and give words to specific emotions. Feldman Barrett interest in 'emotional granularity' has her curious about the connection between naming our emotions and the subsequent capacity to act on them. Imagine you

---

8  **Lisa**: Social work, the humanities and queer scholarship also see, without the need for scientific imaging, the intersection between our stories and our potential transformation. From Brené Brown's belief that it is only in owning our stories that we can write brave new endings, to Rebecca Solnit's invocation that to hope is to give yourself to the future so the present can be inhabitable, to Sara Ahmed's call to tell each other stories, there is an emancipatory force that comes with entwining our stories, our emotions and our agency (27; 28; 29).

are a student. It is Monday morning and you simply feel 'sad' that the school week has started. Feldman Barrett would argue that if you could differentiate beyond a generalised description of sad then possibilities for future action open up. Imagine you had the emotional agility to express to a teacher or parent that you feel threatened, bored or excluded (Figure 15.1). Feldman Barrett's hypothesis is that the specificity of naming these emotions helps to consolidate future action. Brian Massumi brings a different philosophical lens to the idea of the potential. For Massumi, we encounter the creative force of affect in noticing the role of embodied microperceptual shifts. The capacity then to affect, or be affected, is linked to opening up space for new propensities to be felt.[9] (32, p. 64) Even across these vastly different disciplinary orientations, Feldman Barrett and Massumi both trace a connection between attuning to affect, self-awareness and a sense of agency[10] (Figure 15.1).

In designing encounters with affect, we have to consider how learning environments might work with a full spectrum of emotions (except perhaps shame). Highly charged negative emotions (like frustration or rage) can be used for activism or debating, just as low energy high pleasantness (like relaxed or grateful) can be useful for reflective activities. One emotion-led activity we have used at WonderLab is to craft emotion equations that underly our research questions. With a worksheet of mathematical symbols, we designed emotion equations for motivation, engagement, openness and agency. Not seeking to be empirically true, playing with equations helps us wonder how the construction of emotions might serve the outcome one is designing for. The internal back-talk of 'is it the equals sign or the equivalent to, the less than or not equal to?' being in conversation with a felt experience was revealing. The motivation equation had us seeking to amplify the learning experience as meaning-making. We questioned whether engagement was equal parts wonder and enthusiasm, or if openness needed a level of comfort with uncertainty. How might we design for empowerment? How might our activities grant hope while not gaslighting inequities? Playing with emotions as formulas opened up more questions than answers, but

9    **Ricardo**: Engaging with embodiment and emotions Sonali and I, in our work in India, helped teachers make this connection between affect, emergence and potential. We saw our workshop as a place to learn how attuning to and sensing where students are at, would help to reveal what *new* is possible, what is unvoiced that is seeking voice. In this way, the capacity to sense emergence can help define pathways for learning. **Sonali:** I am always paying attention to what is invisible that is seeking to be made visible.

10   **Shanti:** As Ricardo says, affect and potential come together in the work of Massumi and others – this refers to the possibilities that exist in any given moment for things to shift one way or another, of unknown next steps that follow from the distinct relationalities of people, things, environments and more. For me, this connects to design in the ways that purposeful artefacts, systems, workshops and other examples of designed 'things' configure into the world and its ongoing potential. Importantly, these affects are *specific* to the worldly configurations they emerge from them – so in the WonderLab example, feelings like motivation, engagement, openness and agency are always contingent and emerge from *particular* constellations of design and designing. They are *always* somehow attached to things, rather than abstracted.

in the process, it nudged us to be more granular with our emotional vocabulary and consider the affective, aesthetic force of designed experiences.

---

## Narrative 11.1 Speculating: a Prop for Sense-checking

### 2015 – with Helen Chen and Kelly Schmutte

Recently, I came to fully understand something that happened years back while on a residency at Stanford's d.school. Half a sentence – three words in fact – was all it took to illuminate the affordance of a design move I made six years ago. Sometimes I bear witness to an opening, yet I am unsure why. That design move, at that moment in time, created a shift.

It was 2015 and my d.school host was Kelly Schmutte. I was drawn here as a big fan of the speculative propositions that emerged from a project Kelly and colleagues worked on to reimagine undergraduate education. Stanford 2025 was a year-long project that involved researchers consulting with faculty, students, administrators and designers to explore how the education model, which had hardly changed in the past 100 years, might meaningfully and purposefully evolve to align with the emerging future. Disrupting any linear notion of time, the launch event staged an experiential time-travel journey where participants land in the year 2100 to retrospectively look at the paradigm shifts that 'happened' around 2025 to transform the structures, services and systems of Stanford (33).

*Learning from the 2025 provocative artefacts and videos, I am here to design a prop from the future to see how it might shift conversations in the present. My intent is to reimagine the academic transcript. My hunch is that this piece of paper, with its own arcane history, could do a lot more than be a record of course titles and grades. I have spent no time thinking about university transcripts and I am not invested in designing a model for Stanford to adopt – this nonchalance works to my advantage. I am clear that my motivation is to explore the affordances of making learning visible. How might a student see the transcript as a map of where they have come from and where they need to go? For an employer, how might we capture a graduate's potential for future learning? At a more systemic level, could a new record of learning devalue the weight placed on grades and instead prompt reflection on how to proactively learn how to learn? The idea that this is a prop, a stand-in artefact that signals not just where we are but where we might go, is one I hold close.*

*I begin with a meeting with the (then) Stanford Registrar Tom Black, and his colleague Helen Chen from the Designing Education Lab. Together they lay out a critique of the outmoded current system and propose how an alternative record of learning could be designed to be student-facing in meaningful and transformative ways. The caveat they offer is for me to avoid the word 'transcript', to distance the project from a system invested in not changing a century old practice. The following day, I meet with university advisors. I enter the room giddy with potential from the previous day's conversation and optimistic about what I expect will be enthusiasm for my great ideas. Lack of humility aside, my assumption is that my suggestions will make life easier for the student advisors (the people in the United States most directly connected to guiding students through their academic experience). An hour later I walk out of the room defeated by the chorus of dissent and the echoed refrain that these ideas are not realistic or attainable.*

It will be years before I truly unlearn the designer's impulse to affirmatively pitch my thinking, years before I become a co-designer interested in learning alongside others instead. But tonight, in my cramped Airbnb studio, I can see how going in armed with nothing more than ideas and enthusiasm did little to create a space for expansive thinking. When a system like the university transcript has been in place for centuries, with services and values built around it, the idea of upending how we currently communicate student learning is going to be perceived as a threat to more than just the piece of paper.

*It is clearer to me now that a sacrificial prototype could be easily dismissed simply because it cannot be imagined. If my goal is to emotionally engage people so we can see beyond our internalised cultural practices, I need to resist cognitively addressing each rational reservation. Again, I circle back to the promise of the prop. I need to reframe the prop as not asking how things could be, but instead position the prop as from an alternate, deviant present. This is how a prop can unseed established thinking and represent the courage that comes with stepping away from the accepted known toward a not-yet-anticipated tomorrow.*

*Through the night I design my prop. At 3:37am I am questioning how machine learning might allow the feedback loop of the learning record to be customised for the individual. As the sun rises, I try different fonts on for size, I play with the corner radius of my boxes. I repeatedly remind myself this is not a prototype, but a prop. The functional perfectionism of design does not apply here. It does not have to work, yet it has to simulate a finished thing. In the morning, I will show my alternative record of learning to the advisors. This time they will smile knowingly, as if they had seen this artefact before, assured that they too can see how this can work.*

Yet, to reduce this tale to one of moving the advisors from 'this will never happen' to 'I get it now' is to gloss over the affordance of the superficial, non-functioning prop. When I first arrived at the d.school I thought of the prop as a time capsule, the promise of potential from another time. Yet, the half sentence I read in 2021 was the academic insight that design, in this scenario, succeeded in 'puncturing the present' (34). The real contribution of the prop lies not in a suspension of disbelief, but in a suspension of what we believe unquestioningly. The prop from the future, a provocative representation of alternative ways, creatively and constructively takes the air out of the stories we hold too tightly in the present.

This was no high-fidelity work of speculative design on show in a gallery, but a sense-checking prop sent out into the wild to plant seeds of change. This unresolved, idealised prop did not solve anything, nor radically change anything, and yet it did imagine anew how institutions might codify how we account for learning.

## Bibliography

1　Martin, Brian. "Methodology Is Content: Indigenous Approaches to Research and Knowledge." *Educational philosophy and theory*, vol. 49, no. 14, 2017, pp. 1392–400, doi:10.1080/00131857.2017.1298034.

2　"The Future of Jobs Report 2020." World Economic Forum, Report, 20 October 2020, www.weforum.org/reports/the-future-of-jobs-report-2020.

3　Gaver, William et al. "Cultural Probes and the Value of Uncertainty." *Interactions*, vol. XI, no. 5, 2004, pp. 53–56.

4　Haseman, Brad. "A Manifesto for Performative Research." *Media International Australia*, vol. 118, no. 1, 2006, pp. 98–106, doi:10.1177/1329878X0611800113.

5　Dorst, Kees and Nigel Cross. "Creativity in the Design Process: Co-Evolution of Problem–Solution." *Design Studies*, vol. 22, no. 5, 2001, pp. 425–37, doi:10.1016/S0142–694X(01)00009-6.

6　Cross, Nigel. *Designerly Ways of Knowing*. Birkhäuser, 2007.

7　Schön, Donald. *The Reflective Practitioner: How Professionals Think in Action*. Basic Books, 1983.

8　Schön, Donald A. "Designing as Reflective Conversation with the Materials of a Design Situation." *Knowledge-Based Systems*, vol. 5, no. 1, 1992, pp. 3–14.

9　Grocott, Lisa. *Design Research & Reflective Practice: The Facility of Design-Oriented Research to Translate Practitioner Insights into New Understandings of Design*, 2010. RMIT University, PhD Thesis.

10　Roozenburg, Norbert F. M. and Kees Dorst. Eckart Frankenberger et al., editors. *Describing Design as a Reflective Practice: Observations on Schön's Theory of Practice*, Designers, 1998, London, Springer.

11　Mason, John. *Researching Your Own Practice: The Discipline of Noticing*. Routledge/Falmer, 2006.

12　Korsmeyer, Hannah et al. "Understanding Feminist Anticipation through 'Back-talk': 3 Narratives of Willful, Deviant, and Care-full Co-Design Practices." *Futures*, 2021, In Press, https://doi.org/10.1016/j.futures.2021.102874.

13　Gottschall, Jonathan. *Storytelling Animal: How Stories Make Us Human*. Houghton Mifflin Harcourt, 2012.

14　Dunne, Anthony and Fiona Raby. *Speculative Everything: Design, Fiction, and Social Dreaming*. The MIT Press, 2013.

15　Sanders, Elizabeth B-N and Pieter Jan Stappers. "Co-Creation and the New Landscapes of Design." *CoDesign*, vol. 4, no. 1, 2008, pp. 5–18, doi:10.1080/15710880701875068.

16　Boeijen, Annemiek van. et al. *Delft Design Guide: Perspectives, Models, Approaches, Methods*. BIS, 2020.

17　Fry, Tony et al. *Design and the Question of History*. Bloomsbury Academic, 2015.

18　Akama, Yoko and Shana Agid. *Dance of Designing: Rethinking Position, Relation and Movement in Service Design*, ServDes2018 – Service Design Proof of Concept Conference, 2018, Linköping University Electronic Press, 2018.

19  Grocott, Lisa and Mai Kobori. *The Affordances of Designing for the Learning Sciences*, LearnxDesign, 2015, Aalto University, Finland.

20  Sargent, Philip. "Design Science or Nonscience." *Design Studies*, vol. 15, no. 4, 1994, pp. 389–402, doi:10.1016/0142–694X(94)90003-5.

21  Grocott, Lisa. "The Discursive Practice of Figuring Diagrams." *TRACEY Journal: Drawing Knowledge*, 2012, pp. 1–15, www.lboro.ac.uk/microsites/sota/tracey/journal/edu/2012/PDF/Lisa_Grocott-TRACEY-Journal-DK-2012.pdf.

22  Mattelmäki, Tuuli et al. "What Happened to Empathic Design?" *Design Issues*, vol. 30, no. 1, 2014, pp. 67–77.

23  Chapman, Jonathan. *Emotionally Durable Design: Objects, Experiences and Empathy*. 2nd ed., Routledge, 2015.

24  Chase, Caitlin. "Beyond Empathy in Design." *UX Collective*, Blog Post, August 2020, 2020, www.uxdesign.cc/beyond-empathy-in-design-f0f294c977b6.

25  Damasio, Antonio. *Descartes' Error: Emotion, Reason and the Human Brain*. Random House, 2008.

26  Siegel, Daniel. *Mindsight: Transform Your Brain with the New Science of Kindness*. Oneworld Publications, 2010.

27  Brown, Brené. "Sonya Renee Taylor on 'the Body Is Not an Apology'." *Unlocking Us*, Podcast, 16 September 2020, www.brenebrown.com/podcast/brene-with-sonya-renee-taylor-on-the-body-is-not-an-apology.

28  Solnit, Rebecca. *Hope in the Dark: Untold Histories, Wild Possibilities*. 3rd ed., Haymarket Books, 2016.

29  Ahmed, Sara. *What's the Use?: On the Uses of Use*. Duke University Press, 2019.

30  Picard, Rosalind W. et al. "Affective Learning – A Manifesto." *BT Technology Journal*, vol. 22, no. 4, 2004, pp. 253–69, doi:10.1023/B:BTTJ.0000047603.37042.33.

31  Shephard, Kerry. "Higher Education for Sustainability: Seeking Affective Learning Outcomes." *International Journal of Sustainability in Higher Education*, vol. 9, no. 1, 2008, pp. 87–98.

32  Massumi, Brian. *Politics of Affect*. Polity Press, 2015.

33  Stanford2025. "Learning and Living at Stanford." 2016, http://www.stanford2025.com/.

34  Akama, Yoko and Ann Light. "Readiness for Contingency: Punctuation, Poise, and Co-Design." *CoDesign*, vol. 16, no. 1, 2020, pp. 17–28, doi:10.1080/15710882.2020.1722177.

# 12

# DESIGNING EXPERIENCES

## Learning from Making and Interacting

## Core Designing Engagement Moves

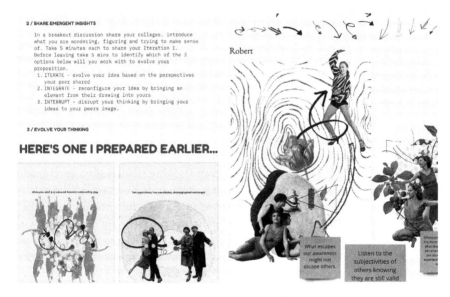

FIGURE 12.1 **An Online Playdate**: When the pandemic opened up new ways to work with international partners we began with online playdates, an informal space designed to amplify adjacent co-learning. After testing online playdates online within WonderLab, we extended who we invited over to play and learn with us. This Miro screenshot, from a collage workshop designed with Shanti Sumartojo, had us envisaging with interdisciplinary colleagues at Newcastle University how we might create a learning exchange between Ph.D. candidates.

DOI: 10.4324/9780429429743-15

It is easy to grasp why creativity is identified as a timely, relevant expertise given the skills that will be resilient in the face of workforces redefined by everyday automation and deep machine learning. This chapter explores another not-at-all surprising expertise newly identified in the latest Future of Jobs Report that outlines the top skills projected for 2025 (1). Active Learning and Learning Strategies debuted at number 2, underscoring that it is not just a question of the type of knowing (bringing creativity to complex problem solving) but also an orientation to how we navigate rapidly changing workplaces, technologies and socio-cultural contexts. This chapter entwines these skills by considering the experiential ways the creative act of generating novel ideas and prototyping for feedback sits alongside embodied strategies for troubling, unsettling, forgetting and learning.

Specifically, this chapter explores how to design experiences that allow long-held, obsolete internal scripts to evolve into something altogether new. Here, I use the term 'internal scripts' to reference a diverse range of inner narratives that shape how we act, engage, show up, regulate, make, intellectualise, hope, resist, discern and empathise. Our inner worlds are made up of stories we tell ourselves based on what we have experienced, witnessed, imagined and learned. Whether they are explicit, easy-to-articulate convictions or tacit hard-to-access internalised stories they are still shaping our actions. These polyvocal, often-times competing, cognitive, emotional and behavioural internal scripts shape the contours of our lives. They might hold us accountable or no longer serve us, might be faulty or cherished, might need to be honoured or critiqued, evolved or discarded. Either way, unlike transmissive learning, the work of transformative learning asks us to examine the stories we tell ourselves. To help do this work, this chapter explores the conditions by which we can design experiences that reconfigure how a learner thinks, acts and feels.

First, let us make the distinction between learning that leads to good grades and learning that leads to new ways of being. A study of a university science class shows how possible it is for students to excel in exams while holding on to misconceptions of the subject (2). In the research, top students were confronted with physical models that aligned with the answers they had given in exam papers, yet contested their long-held understanding of how motion works in physics. What the study reveals is that it was easier for the students to keep their early mental model of motion than it was to internalise the new models of physics presented in the course they had just excelled at. The students chose to believe the model was the exception to the rule rather than to challenge and rethink their constructed understanding of physics in the world. The short documentary 'A Private Universe' shows students in real time resisting letting go of their misconceptions when confronted with theories that contest their understanding (3). This cautions us to see how easily transmissive learning encounters might look effective and yet fail to shift a learner's internalised script – be that a belief, mental model, mindset or bias.

The playdate as a learning workshop is the practice vignette that underpins the sections of the chapter. The design workshop as playdate is more analogous to a humble weekend hanging out with friends than a highly anticipated birthday. In WonderLab, we developed the playdate as a format whereby communities of practice could learn from each other (4). Our regular playdates are more parallel play than a competitive game. Think of two young children building Lego towers alongside each other. We are working on something independently while being influenced by the adjacency of another. The playdate host is in charge of framing an experience that offers different lines of inquiry, so people can draw on their own internal motivation to participate. Yet, the social interactions between players are central to an experiential inquiry that asks that ideas are willingly surrendered, contested and iterated on. This relational orientation embraces improvisational and unpredictable moves that come with people being in a trusting, playful space with each other and the design materials. With the play constructed around the principle of reciprocity, it is critical that all players can bring what resonates with them to the shared learning space. In this way, the playdate scaffolds interactions for formative feedback, whereby the host and players learn side-by-side how to surface assumptions, unsettle mental models and evolve future practice. You can find WonderLab Miro board templates for playdates at the book website: www.designingtransformativelearning.com.

The playdate introduced here is an online template that considers how to begin co-designing a learning exchange with a community. Specifically, this vignette introduces a figuring playdate between two communities meeting for the first time, conceived to generate some guiding principles that will inform how they will collaborate on the design of future learning encounters. Although experienced on a Miro board across hemispheres and during a pandemic, the convivial and haptic nature of playdates lends itself to face-to-face encounters and different modes of engaging beyond the practice of figuring.

The two-hour workshop begins with an acknowledgement of the country we are on and an honouring of the Indigenous peoples of the land. This performative move immediately introduces a different relational understanding of place and people, laying bare contested notions of history and priming an audience to be open to alternate worldviews. This political, ethical move sits alongside the highly visual board in ways that simultaneously unsettles and invites the participant in. The first collective activity is to share a quote or artefact that positions the learner within the conversation. Second, we choose from pre-selected metaphoric images what we hope the future learning exchange will 'feel like'.[1] In ruminating on the affective potential, each person declares an embodied, felt value they would like to hold on to before we discuss the pragmatics of hosting the exchange. The transition from 'feels like' to 'looks like' takes us into the figuring phase of the playdate. The collaging activity invites players into an adjacent practice of co-figuring (Narrative 6.1). Amplifying the iterative orientation of

---

1   **Lisa**: This language is an iteration of a workshop activity I was introduced to by Adam Royalty and Rich Crandall at the K12 Lab at Stanford's d.school (www.dschool.stanford.edu).

design, the figuring activity intentionally pauses for feedback half-way through, with small breakout discussions offering novel interpretations and productive mis-readings (Figure 12.1). It is in this convivial space that one's individual visual reverie collides with another. Distinct from a co-creative exercise, this fleeting moment of intersection is not constructed to collaborate on the next move but to reveal, refract or reframe the participant's ideas. Each person then uses the feedback to iterate on or interrupt their own thinking in a second collage. The last moves involve annotating what could be, what was surfaced by the act of pro-totyping alongside each other and identifying the salient points for future design and implementation. The following five sections will elaborate on aspects present in the design of this experience that we repeatedly return to.

## 12.1 Participatory Prototyping

Let's start with what it means to iterate on ideas in real time, alongside and in conversation with others. A practice that values engaging end users in the de-sign process might fall under terms like human-centred design, co-design or participatory design. Although the practices have different histories, they share a commitment to create space in the process for creative partners or a range of stakeholders to be consulted in the process. This commitment to designing *with* is towards the goal of designing outcomes that are more likely to meet the needs across the whole system. The strategies deployed to do this work can range from a focus on ethnographic practices in the research stage to surface unmet needs and potential opportunities, to facilitating the design process so others might design alongside you, or spaced consultation throughout to ensure participant's voices are heard (5; 6; 7; 8; 9).

As participatory design was grounded in the politics of giving voice to the marginalised (10), then the call for student-centred learning can be understood as granting the learner greater agency (11). Encounters that invite the student to be the director of their own learning all require a level of active participation and thus investment. For us, participation and agency operate as twin catalysts for learner engagement.[2]

How might we make sense of the term 'participatory' at the intersection of designing and learning? One guiding principle of participatory design is that the coming together of people creates a platform for mutual learning. Tone Brat-teteig and colleagues define this mutual learning as two-way learning between

---

2  **Sean**: I have always struggled with this simplistic equation that with participation comes greater agency. I reject the presumption that democratising the materials of design and conceding the modes of design production to participants somehow, in and of itself, creates equitable oppor-tunities for engagement. I want to keep questioning how designers negotiate the politics of par-ticipation. Particularly, the dynamics exercised between institutions, community, people and place. I think that then becomes interesting with respect to learning. How different would these learning encounters look if the participatory spaces and activates are designed to undermine, redistribute and invert authorities of power in efforts of redress?

the users and the designers. This conceptualisation has users sharing new insights with designers about the use context and designers revealing new possibilities for the situation (12, p. 139). I would argue that the peer-to-peer interaction is as substantively important. This might be people learning from the diversity of perspectives in the room or from having their lived experiences normalised or challenged. Either way, the mutuality of encounters is more than bi-directional. Within educational psychology, Russian psychologist Vygotsky's theories around the 'zone of proximal development' (ZPD) social interactions and communication are at the centre of how learning is scaffolded (13). Vygotsky's theory is anchored by the role of the 'more knowledgeable other' (the MKO) (14). If participatory design's position on mutual learning emphasises the exchange between the designers and the user/participants, then Vygotsky's emphasis on social interactions potentially illuminates how an object (not a parent or teacher) could be the MKO (15). The relevance of Vygotsky at the intersection of design and learning lies in the role materials and participatory moves can play in scaffolding social interactions to amplify mutual learning.[3]

Defining how the term 'prototyping' can help us better understand how 'participatory prototyping' (16; 17, p. 153) sits with learning. Staged evolutions from sketch to refined prototype are a staple of designing artefacts. From architectural models to fashion samples, there is at the heart of design practice a commitment to test the functionality, interrogate the use-case scenario or experiment with different materials by putting not-resolved ideas out into the world. We use the term prototyping as a catch-all term for a range of evaluative activities that evolve the development of an idea. Given the domain of the book, we wonder what a people-centred practice that performs iterative, experiential testing of not fully realised ideas might look like.

A design practice focused on services, experiences and behaviour invites more nuanced terms for the evaluative act of prototyping. To follow are just some of the ways proof of concept experiments, play-testing, props and pilot programs introduce complementary conditions for proposing, experiencing and evaluating the not-yet-known.[4]

---

3  **Alli**: Through a new materialist lens, I understand my role as a facilitator of learning within a given assemblage. My agency is enhanced or diminished by the factors in the assemblage, and by the vitality of the materials available to think with, to inspire others and to become facilitator with. In this assemblage, my materials and I become co-facilitators. Just as my framing of expectations in a workshop catalyses the tools and toys into an action, the willingness of people to engage is how the artefact becomes imbued with meaning.

4  **Hannah:** My reframing of our interactions with materials came from Sara Ahmed's understanding that we learn about worlds through trying to transform them. What I like is how her feminist practical phenomenology accounts for the *difficulty* of transformation. It seeks to notice and describe the micro-efforts and strategies that a designer might employ when navigating the blockages and restrictions within institutional worlds. It attends to how designers come to understand transformation in practice: through worldly impressions and embodied actions. The practical experience of 'coming up against something' while trying to transform it is what can allow an injustice to be perceived (18).

### 12.1.1 Proof of Concept – Make Do

A proof of concept is an early-in-the-process strategy for testing the potential of an idea (Figure 14.2) – think of whether temporary tattoos could be used with middle school children to make the practice of grit seem more desirable than dorky. The lessons observed in these 'scrappy experiments' of students interacting with tattoos would help inform the 'potential of the intervention' (19). If a proof of concept confirmed that an idea *could* move forward, then the prototype would be used to explore *how* it might work.

### 12.1.2 Prototypes and Props – Make Again

The prototype offers a tangible representation of iterating on ideas in development (Figure 14.1) – think of people pretending to be students who are taking photos of their grit tattoos and sharing them on Instagram. The prototype of people role-playing how students and social media might interact could directly inform the look and feel of the next iteration of the tattoo. Perhaps, add design props to this scene that operate as stand-ins for how interactions might unfold, like the introduction of a cardboard photo booth. In this scenario, the cardboard photo booth is not a prototype intended to evaluate the look of the final program, but more to inform how it might work.

### 12.1.3 Playtests and Pilots – Make Happen

Similarly, a play test serves a similar function with participants experiencing iterations of the game play (Figure 10.1) – think of students tagging evidence of gritty behaviour to peers' initial tattoo photos. Here, the playtest gives the designer (as observer) a sense of what motivates the students. Once a game's quest and goals have been defined through iterative playtests, the last phase might be to pilot. The pilot offers a small scale 'live' roll out to learn from the early stages of implementation, such as a fully realised tattoo/grit game-based program being piloted in one classroom before being introduced to the whole school. The pilot grants the designer a disciplined space to evaluate how the program might be refined in support of successful implementation.[5]

---

5  **Shanti:** I think there is an important link here to the discussion in 3.0 on the feasibility of how design might be taken up, in the example of teachers not wanting to make themselves vulnerable via a particular classroom activity. Prototypes are not just about the design artefact itself but also about the social, cultural and political contexts that they intervene in, and they can foreground these aspects in ways that may not have been considered before. Also, putting prototypes into the world allows new possibilities to open up, new questions and tensions to become visible and new ways of framing a complex problem to emerge. For example, Christian Nold has used prototypes to explore the problem of noise pollution, providing research participants with several iterations of a computerised noise sensor to enable simultaneous multiple perspectives on the issue. He argues that such devices allow for the stacking of multiple ontologies. This

In the playdate learning exchange, the act of participatory prototyping through figuring intentionally moves betwixt and between these modes (Figure 12.1). The aim of the playful inquiry is not to 'figure out'. The invitation is not to prototype towards a fixed diagram of 'what is' (Narrative 6.1). Instead, to be figuring is to speculate and reflect through ambiguous mark-making of what might become (21). Figuring is a sense-making activity that asks everyone to explore the known unknowns together. In the playdate, the adjacent practice of co-figuring alongside each other aligned with participants expressed desire, by way of the metaphors, for the learning exchange to embrace the messiness of playing in the mud (an experience that is simultaneously uncomfortable and joyful) and for the exchange to emerge from what everyone brings (analogous to the potluck dinner party).

In this way, we use prototyping as a broad term for the iterative, evaluative mindset contemporary design uses in the creative process. The people-centred modes of prototyping described here exemplify the tangible ways the designer learns from doing that go beyond notions of mutual learning. Whether designers are role playing being students, students play-testing a game or learners test driving a pilot program, this improvisational approach to co-creation respects how the material tools of participatory design and the prototyping mindset of experiential evaluation can scaffold learning-through-doing in a social context.[6]

## 12.2 Resonance and Relevance

In considering the positive conditions for learning, we need to consider the designer and learner's connection to the material. If the ideas at the core of an experience are outside the learner's mental model of the world, then they can lose them before they've even started. If a designer is creating experiences that reflect or react to their lived experiences of education, they might not be meeting people where they are at. A designer's own learning orientation is likely to be distinctly different from that of the social worker or data analyst, just as a person with intellectual, emotional or class privilege will likely have different memories of schooling. Whether motivating a teacher who believes her 20 years

---

capacity to draw together different perspectives, and thereby open up new ways to think about and address problems, is a powerful quality of prototypes (20).

6 **Sean**: I am unsure what to make of this expansive framing of participatory prototyping. My focus on global issues and social justice in a local context has me reckoning with the Bauhausian and Constructivist form vocabularies and processes as never neutral actors in the design endeavour. On the one hand, I question how design is reconciling (or not) their use of these languages in participatory endeavours whose values preach inclusion while ignoring what these formal languages have erased. On the other hand, I see in this broad positioning of prototyping (the embodied moves and improvised gestures) an opportunity to move past some of the normativities embedded in Design's Western Formalist Vocabularies and Western Worldviews. In my work with the historically excluded it seems critical that we attend not to the design of participatory activities but to the design of safe spaces that enable full engagement with the activities.

of classroom experience is all she needs, or engaging a high school student who believes peer-feedback is a waste of time, we need to consider how to establish relevance of what is about to be learned and how we need to find hooks that resonate with a learner's lived experiences.

The story of principal Dominic Randolph (5.2.1) shadowing his students is one example of creating multiple points of resonance for himself, the students and parents. Another way to establish relevance for the learner is to draw on affective memories to bring awareness to one's own perspectives on learning. In another collaboration with Helen Chen (Narrative 11.1), we ran a workshop with university administrators to explore experiential metaphors as a tool for finding resonance with a learner. Participants were invited to connect a personal recent airport travel experience as analogous to how a student on their campus might experience the learning journey. One participant reflected on how disempowered he felt when he was repeatedly bumped to the end of a waitlist. The participant was humbled to own how aggrieved he felt when the previously backgrounded reality of airline status points was bought to the foreground. The exercise helped *make aware* that there was no level playing field, in turn leading him to critically examine the ways administrative touchpoints with students, who have significantly less privilege than him, are unconsciously messaging who has status. Another participant simply sat with the impotence and uncertainty that comes with a seatbelt sign left on for so long you wonder if the pilot has forgotten. This resonated with the educator who came to question how a teacher's interactions constantly signal to the students in the room that they are being heard. This analogous frame opened up an affective strategy into considering the student perspective; however, the complementary work of considering where students are at, what they need and why they would care involves a lot of active listening, repeated checking in and relationship building.

The playdate format is explicitly grounded in a principle of reciprocity and resonance. Just as the host of a child playdate seeks to ask their guest what they would like to play, the host of a learning exchange playdate is compelled to begin with a prompt that motivates all participants. Framing the encounter around 'play' helps signal a pulling away from planned problem solving and towards emergence and plural perspectives. The 'date' nomenclature asserts the relational dimension and the importance of the host creating a social encounter that resonates with everyone. Sometimes, we have to talk to find the shared hook that ensures everyone is engaged by the line of inquiry. Taking the time to situate each learner is how the playdate establishes communal belonging, respects resonance and drives meaning-making for all.

## 12.3 Unsettling Scripts

The call to unsettle dominant socio-cultural scripts is grounded in the moral imperative to create encounters that reduce barriers to engaging, understanding and expressing so all learners might flourish. These scripts might be personal, bound to our lived-in experiences or political, shaped by hidden social structures. Most likely they are both. Oftentimes, they are only tacitly understood. Already we have established the need to uphold a learner-centred practice that promotes agency (9.3). The participatory orientation described above underscores the question of how to get people to inform the design, but attends less to who has a voice, who is listened to, what stories we tell ourselves and what narratives we must leave behind. This section considers the importance of seeing beyond everyday stories by considering critical theory from disability, feminist, queer, de-colonial and Indigenous studies. Design can help us move beyond a discussion of which dominant norms we want to unsettle, to creating materially-mediated and situation-specific places for practicing having these discussions.[7] The goal here is to take a pluriversal position that invites new ways for wondering with people, that do not fall back on social structures and education systems designed in another time and place. As a means for unsettling what to expect the learning encounters can become places for exposing obsolete, inequitable or limiting scripts by enabling participants a safe space to "experience the clash of epistemologies" (23, p. 31).

The term 'universal design' was first introduced by architect Ronald Mace with respect to creating accessibility legislation for the built environment back in the 1970s. Yet, even before that, there was broader recognition that systems designed around some notion of the average person would be destined to fail (24).[8] There is a plethora of ever-changing terms that signal an ethical commitment to designing for the full range of human diversity: inclusive design, liberatory design, (25) public interest design, (26) feminist design, (27) emancipatory design thinking and Afrofuturism design (28). There is an Indigenous Design Charter (29) and there are design card decks that define terms from critical theory (30) to trauma-informed models of care (31). With reference to Arturo Escobar's

---

7   **Hannah.** It seems important here to consider what happens if the unsettling is directed toward design. Designers likes to position themselves as the creative disruptors, comfortable with uncertainty, open to possibilities. It is therefore telling that literature emerging from the design and public sector space reveals that many designers feel that the unsettling is for participants involved in the process (22). I argue, that designers should not avoid our own unsettling while resisting structural forms of oppression, such as heteropatriarchy, colonialism and/or white supremacy. Just because we are using creative methods does not somehow remove our implication within these entangled and complex contexts.

8   **Sean:** What seems critical here is to acknowledge are the scripts of a Western design education. I reject the default privileging of Eurocentric Worldviews in design practice that are still pervasively located in Modernist notions of universality. I question the extent to which the perpetuation of these rhetoric's gaslight designs' understanding of the world. Specifically, those exercised through 'good work' in the name of social justice, as typified in humanitarian design. The term 'rhetorics of good' characterises the trifecta of influences – Victorian notions of philanthropy, Christian missioning and the unquestioned assumptions that community is a singularly affirmative state of relationship – that fundamentally shape design for international development.

pluriverse, Mia Perry recognises we have to trouble any notion of a universal as an onto-ethico-epistemological concept. Perry notes:

> what is understood as common across the universe depends on where you stand (figuratively and literally) and how you see and experience this universe. We might then imagine that there are many universals depending on where the teller is positioned.
>
> *(32, p. 296)*

In respecting infinite positions, co-existing narratives and different orientations to designing, we move the conversation away from a universal framing to a pluriversal understanding (33; 34). The social model of disability (35) provides a productive conceptual frame that asks us to see beyond an individual, medical model of disability by arguing that it is society that dis/ables the person with the impairment from full participation. In designing for learning, this social model implores the system, service or experience to adapt to and meet the needs of all people it serves. Yet, the work needed to unsettle dominant education and societal narratives calls on recognising multi-variate socio-cultural and economic barriers to full participation.

From a critical perspective, we must extend this logic to consider how learning encounters resist defaulting to heteronormative future scenarios, to respectfully engage the workshop participant with dyslexia, or learn from the Indigenous woman who might wholeheartedly share in the collective space of the yarning circle yet resist an individual activity. To enact this critical work, the unsettling has to happen on multiple levels. At an epistemic level, we need to design experiences that support colonial de-linking from the scripts of modernity, (36) just as we need to turn an epistemological lens (37) towards the learning designer to note how one's justified belief or bias might contribute to disabling a learner's chance to succeed. Bringing a relational lens to a reflexive praxis of unsettling potentially allows for a critical examination of mental models and worldviews, habits and practices. Whether interrogating macro dimensions on a cultural and structural level or operating at the level of a sensorial or psychological microverses, to see unsettling as brokering new systemic and social relationships can help challenge pervasive assumptions we have around normative and difference.

Feminist critic of design thinking, Daniela K. Rosner, generously reframes dominant narratives of design to help do the work of unsettling (38, pp. 3202–03). *Alliances* is introduced to highlight the relational aspect of design as a critique of *individualism*. To counter the pretence of *objectivism*, Rosner proposes *Recuperations* to shine a light on the absent narratives silenced or erased in a design setting. As I do here, Rosner critiques the notion of *universalism* with the term *Interferences* to get at what it means to deviate from, disrupt and unsettle. Lastly, *Extensions* seeks to present a more ethically accountable, staying-with approach to implementation that extends beyond the moment a *solution* is launched, released or shipped.

The book *Unsettling Education*, (39) reminds us that much of the work of school is about settling (through grades, curriculum and policy) while paradoxically owning that learning happens when we are disoriented, grappling to understand and untethered.[9] The book's references to learning through play, fostering empowerment and understanding misrecognition flag the unsettling potential of design's ways of knowing and being that are made manifest in the playdate practice vignette. The decision to call the learning exchange a playdate is in itself an intentional move to telegraph, even before people engage to participate, that this will not be a normative experience. The choice of a not-yet-fixed, interpretative visual grammar channels uncertainty. Baked into the adjacencies and the ambiguities a space for parallel play opens up and wonder walks in. When wondering meets figuring in the social space of a playdate, misrecognitions are surfaced, lines of inquiry are disrupted, faulty beliefs are challenges and peer learning happens.

For Sara Ahmed, the "critical wonder" of feminism offers the "troubling effect of certain questions" (42, p. nd). In a playdate, the verb 'wonder' is as much about being in a state of doubt, to wonder 'how did this come to be' as it is to be dreaming 'how could this be different?' This is how wonder can catalyse transformation. Yet, we must not be complacent of our own roles as facilitators of learning, we must recognise our own imbrication in what is being unsettled. Owning the ways in which we are entangled in the learning situations, we are designing opens space for self-reflexive interrogation and opportunities for us to intentionally plan for how design can *unmake* how hard it is to deviate from what is accepted and expected (43).

## 12.4 Novel Imagining

The magic circle created by the playdate embraces the liminal space opened up by the social contract the new space invites the players into (44). There is a novelty that comes with the suspension of some rules and the permission to act otherwise. This is a design practice grounded in exploring the unknown, motivated towards a goal of producing something unfamiliar – what proponents of design-based learning could call the never-before-seen (45). Sara Ahmed continues to explore this never-before unfamiliarity through the gaze of wonder. "Wonder is an encounter with an object that one does not recognise; or wonder works to transform the ordinary, which is already recognised, into the extraordinary...we wonder when we are moved by that which we face" (42, p. nd).

---

9  **Kathryn**: I have been teaching, troubling and w/riting with colleagues Sarah Healy and Susan Wright about this. We have written: "There is a break, a rupture and loss in the first few weeks of Capstone, when you come unstuck. Things you thought you knew have slipped, and things you felt the affect of before, have turned. It is a moment when something snaps, producing a tangible shift: 'you can no longer stand what you put up with before, even yesterday; the distribution of desires has changed in us' (40, p. 126; 41).

In everyday use, the term 'novelty' – think unique, quirky and silly – is associated with funny yet useless gifts. However, in research, the case for novelty – think rare, ingenious and imaginative – is associated with the idea of creativity (46). Yet, when it comes to transforming perspectives, the most useful part of novelty might come from wondering with the unfamiliar. Paradoxically, the learning that comes from engaging with the unfamiliar and unknown simultaneously sharpens our perceptions of the familiar and known.

In theorising on wonder as pedagogy, Ramos and Roberts they speak to the movement of wonder as making space for something new to emerge (47). Their interest in nurturing de-colonial feminist ways of knowing-doing-being has them valuing the affective dimension of wonder that requires the learner to *feel* their partial standpoints and the limits of their knowledge. Interested in bell hooks ideas that with wonder comes mystery they see wonder's potential for "instigating passion for learning that disrupts taken-for-granted truisms…in favour of knowledge as a relationship that is multiple, dynamic and never complete" (47, p. 36).

I am interested in the role of novelty for navigating the space between ideas that resonate (12.2) and ideas that unsettle (12.3). In designing for transformative learning, we need to think of how the disruption of the taken-for-granted truisms stick. For the learner re-evaluating a knowledge position in the midst of a playdate, the hope is that the new insight sticks. Although coming from an epistemically different perspective, information systems researcher Douglas Dean and colleagues, offer the idea that the creative potential of novelty lies with the idea of 'paradigm relatedness'. Ramos and Roberts talk about how if a space for learning is too uncomfortable wonder can be shut down, the learner disengages (47, p. 39). For Dean et al. the reason a disruption of perspective might stick comes down to the distinction between ideas that are either paradigm preserving (no real change) or paradigm modifying (a shift in reality) (48). The novel encounter promotes a kind of imagining that resonates *because* the idea is located within a specific paradigm yet has the potential to radically reframe our thinking in relation to the paradigm. The agency of novelty comes from the transformational property of ideas to radically revolutionise our thinking (49).

Bringing paradigm-shifting imagining into learning encounters can clash against the argument for real-world learning experiences. In his critique of contemporary design education, Anthony Dunne laments the narrow and affirming narratives of design briefs that celebrate consumption and technological progress (50). Believing in foregrounding the imagination as the path to crafting counter narratives, Dunne cautions that design education's current emphasis on solving real-world problems or detached idealised future scenarios adversely obstructs the potential of design to imagine alternate possible futures. James Auger and Julian Hanna further argue that many of the taught internal scripts they refer to as 'myths' of design education narrow the impact of design by leading to a "paucity of original thinking and a chronic neglect of responsibility" (51, p. 93). How can our learning encounters not fall for preserving the current paradigm, nor ignore the modifications to our paradigm that the climate crisis calls for?

Film-makers, writers, performers and artists can all teach design something about how we might create whole new worlds. In designing transformative learning, how might design's potential to craft affective learning experiences (like being blindfolded) engage different senses, and shift one's perceptual capacity? The deprivation of sight in turn heightens other senses, and draws on the imagination to create alternate mental representations and deepen the memory trace. However, if students are routinely blindfolded, the experience would become familiar, the memory diluted and the lessons harder to retrieve. This is why in my quest to deviate from the instructor-as-expert mode of critique in design, I had students engage in a range of novel reflexive activities at the end of semester. Whether throwing eggs from a tower of chairs to reflect on what they held dear, or data-visualising how they navigated the learning process, or scripting a hero journey story about how the semester had changed them, each intentionally novel experience had the learner reflecting on not what had been *made* but what had been *learned*.

Drawing on productive ambiguity and subsequent disorientation, the design of transformative encounters can intentionally heighten sensorial engagement by creating unfamiliar environments. Reflective, emancipatory, embodied encounters allow us to see novelty as more than the never-before-seen but also the never-before-felt, or the never-before-imagined.

## 12.5 Embodied Learning

This holistic approach to learning is often understood as experiential. David Kolb (52) explains experiential learning as travelling through a learning cycle that moves through four stages: doing an experience, reflecting on it, learning from it, then trying out what has been learned. In education, more specific terms like problem-based or project-based learning might more specifically align with the types of applied inquiry we associate with studio learning in design education. Whereas Kolb's notion of the experiential could be applied to learning to drive a car or creating a science fair experiment, here we are specifically referencing embodied encounters that draw on a whole-self, creative inquiry that design can enable. In the transformative context, there is a running thread that more specifically elevates a mode of inquiry that respects the affective and liberatory orientation of embodied learning. Feminist scholar Donna Haraway (53) frames this around the importance of acknowledging embodied knowledges that get us out of only seeing the "view from above, from nowhere" (p. 589), so we might attend to the "connections and unexpected openings situated knowledges make possible" situated and embodied knowledges (p. 590). Given the sensorial act of making activates embodied ways of knowing for the learner, (54) we are definitely concerned with engaging multiple sensory modalities.[10] The plural

---

10  **Ricardo**: In Sonali and my work with teachers, we wanted to help them see how they could enhance one's embodied perception by being present in the moment-to-moment unfolding of things (55). Our body, in that way, is like a sensing organ that can attune to individual and/or

interactions that came from learning Māori language using blocks (Narrarive 1.1) are one example of an integrative, embodied experience that draws on touch, sight and sound as it did place, culture and community. The key point here is for the embodied activity to be meaningfully integrated, not incidental to, the task and content (56).

For Kamil Michlewski, a designer's capacity to tune into the sensory possibilities of near and far senses prepares them for designing sensorial learning experiences (57). For Mattelmäki and colleagues, it is at the intersection between empathy and imagination that the learning potential of world-making is revealed, with co-designers observing, experiencing and sensing what and how people say, do and make in these worlds (58). For Dan Lockton and Stuart Candy, experiential futures present a learning paradox that works with the friction of having a sensorial experience of the yet-to-be (59). In positing a tangible 'what if', the imagined future allows the participant to materially or performatively trick the body into taking the experience seriously. For my colleagues and I, affective pedagogies call for an entwining of embodied and studio learning, so a new generation of designers can learn the requisite intra-personal skills to ethically work with people in complex socio-cultural contexts (60). Whatever the perspective the different design researcher brings, there is a value placed on embodied activities that ask the learner to build, tinker, create woven into this learning-through-doing orientation.

Another way to make sense of the embodied in the context of learning is to return to the notion of integration. Beyond the psychological understanding of integrating parts of ourselves into a coherent narrative, there is the feminist critique that resists some Descartian split and instead recognises the thinking body as the messy yet intelligent instrument that sense-makes for the conscious mind (61). For education research David Perkins, we must seek to create fully realised worlds of learning that widen the circle beyond the teacher, student, problem and designing (62, p. 7). In designing learning, we need to go beyond ensuring the jigsaw pieces are all available and create opportunities to fit them together. To design transformative learning, perhaps we need to further ask what is not made visible and what lies beyond the frame? We need to consider the lost opportunity for deeper understanding that comes from a learner being handed a completed jigsaw with no chance to figure out how the pieces fit together. We need to own the engagement loss that comes with completing a jigsaw alone. We can embrace the delight of discovering the corners and the despair that comes with realising there are missing pieces.

---

collective experiences in the classroom. The emphasis on embodiment is understood here as a portal into sensing emergence and questioning what is becoming. In this way, we were helping teachers to see that sensing emergence is a skill in itself that could change how they attune to the learners, space and potentialities.

## Narrative 12.1 Integrating: a Scaffold for Risk-taking

### 2015 – With the *Transforming Mindsets* studio

*I am staring out the window, with my back to the class. I can hardly breathe. The breathlessness is neither overwhelming anxiety nor pure elation but some intoxicating cocktail of vulnerability. As if outside my body I see myself — chest cleaved open, my beating heart exposed, an irrepressible grin on my face. The tender, frightening, giddy, riskiness of that moment captured in this visceral memory.*

This was the first day of semester and I was part-way through an exercise with my studio class at Parsons. The course is called *Transforming Mindsets* and the studio is in the Masters of Transdisciplinary Design. A few hours earlier I declared to the class my hunch that it would be ethically wrong to try and teach designers how to work with people to shift their beliefs and habits without us navigating a similar challenge. This is why the studio requires us all to experience first-hand the hard work of shifting personal long-held beliefs and internal scripts. Come the end of semester students will reflect on how they learned as much from this parallel assignment as the studio assignment with external partners, but on day one they looked as apprehensive as I felt.[11] I say 'all', because I want this studio to be a learning environment for myself and my colleague Roger (the actor from Narrative 2.1).

To begin the semester from this extremely vulnerable position, I need some scaffolding, a script to structure this conversation. I adapted the Presencing Institute's leadership activity, the Case Clinic,[12] for this learning context. The person presenting 'the case' shares the challenge they are wrestling with by outlining how the situation affects others (in this situation, the students) and what I might need to let go of (in my case, an old belief that no longer served me). I recall the emphasis on positioning the people listening as my 'coaches' and the value placed in clearly articulating to them how I had reached my 'learning edge'.

*The room is silent as I stare out the window. The exquisite emotional state I feel looking at the window comes from the risk I took fifteen minutes earlier. I have just asked a group of students (my coaches), to guide me toward the learning threshold that will help me become unstuck. My whole body is pulsing as I feel liberated*

11  **Lisa**: As part of a research study, the students were interviewed 6 months after the studio concluded. When asked to identify what component part of the studio lead to different outcomes the most consistently mentioned move was the act of the teacher centring herself as a learner alongside the students on day (63).

12  The original activity is here: www.presencing.org/files/tools/PI_Tool_CaseClinic.pdf.

*and muted by the decision to stand, on Day 1, and tell a group of students that didn't know me that I am not sure I know how to teach.*

*Traditionally this activity is to be done with peers. You are not supposed to do this with people who you have an unequal power relationship with. Makes sense. It's not like the students can sit here and tell me how to step up. Or might they? We are supposed to be sitting in contemplative silence for three minutes following the presentation of my case. Some students sit contemplatively, eyes closed. I am standing, alert, eyes wide open.*

The internal struggle I laid out for the students came from my early adoption of a student-led pedagogical approach to teaching. I confessed that when students complained about not being 'taught' by me I critiqued their feedback from my position that they were looking for easy, passive learning experiences. The challenge to my teaching identity came from recently reading research that proclaimed student-led teaching only works best for the students the system privileges. I had unwittingly been teaching from the position of what had worked for me. I told them the story of Tama (Narrative 1.1) and how I had walked away from the *Te Ataarangi* class focused on my experience – that when we came together as peers our learning collectively amplified. I acknowledged that my love of this peer-led approach was no doubt shaped by my harsh critique of the very teacher-led experience of my undergraduate years (Narrative 3.1). In preparing the 'case' I saw, for the first time, that my wholesale adoption of student-centred learning had ignored the other *Te Ataarangi* lesson that had been hiding in plain sight. Tama's sense of not-belonging in school had come from living every day with the feeling of being left behind. The research I had just read, backed up his story, I could not ignore that student-centred learning does not work for learners already struggling. My hands were shaking as I read from my notes. But my throat constricted, tears welled as I paused to own the fact that in ignoring the feedback the student evaluations telegraphed, I had quelled the voice of two decades of struggling students. I had used the students succeeding in my class as anecdotal evidence my teaching practices worked. I confessed that armed with this quantitative research data I still chose to not investigate the long-held belief, the internalised script, that took hold in that Māori classroom decades earlier.

*It was six months ago that I read that research paper. With the class silent behind me I find myself recalling a felt memory of the days after, walking around with this tugging dis-ease that something bad had happened. I look back and remember that within a week I succeeded in suppressing the niggling doubt. The gift of disorientation the paper offered had been squandered. I continued to teach as I always had. Until today.*

*I have been vulnerable with students before. I have granted agency to students before. I have positioned myself as a learner before. I stand here unmoored and ashamed because this is what it feels like to let go of, to truly question, to be held*

*accountable, to own the ways the position I have taken has caused harm to oth-*
*ers. I stand here grinning and alive because this is what it feels like to take the risk*
*to question, to imagine anew, to ask for help, to be unstuck. This is what it feels*
*like to begin the semester with the humble declaration that after decades I don't*
*know how to teach anymore.*

*I calm my beating heart. I turn toward the class as we gather in a circle to*
*move into the next phase.*

I have pitched this activity to the students as me enacting what it looks like
to do something deeply uncomfortable and me sharing that hard facts alone
are often not enough to drive change. My message is we will be learning
together. I have over the years got comfortable-ish with play and more open
to risk-taking. Still. This is the biggest risk I have taken in a class. The stakes
seem enormous.

Up next were three rounds of 'mirroring images'. The first, to 'open our
minds', was tolerable. People shared *images* of what came up for them listening to my case. One person talked of the studio we were in growing wings,
another of a tree that had a decade old root system. As the woman described
how her attention moving away from the rotting parts of the tree towards
the sapling branches with their new leaves, I found my grin widening and my
pulse quietening. The second round, to 'open our hearts' was more unsettling, the students were to describe the *feelings* that surfaced. Yet, as a student
relayed how it felt like when she heard her parents were Santa, I was drawn
into her non-verbal facial enactment of her initial shock, disappointment,
then delight as she processed this new insight. Lastly, to open 'our collective
will', my coaches posed in a *gesture* to reflect back what they sensed when
I spoke. At this point, embodiment and affect were not in my vocabulary, I
needed Roger to even help show what that might look like. He silently stood,
lay across the table and reached down to the floor in a gesture of help and
support. My dread was allayed. I could see now, from experience, how it was
the newness that was so disabling. Introducing into my teaching pre-verbal
ways of sensing and accessing knowing felt uncharted and transgressive. Yet,
I had already conceded that cognitive reflection alone was not going to reframe my perspective enough to shift future behaviour. On the outside the
students seemed more comfortable than me. Later, one confessed that the
first-day move made her want to drop the class, for those more culturally
familiar with contemplative practices the change was welcomed.

*Six hours later the class is over. I look around as everyone packs up to leave. I feel*
*curious, shy, buzzing, insecure and grounded. I wonder what they are thinking. I*
*wonder if this class feels as novel for them as it did for me. Ricardo walks towards*
*me. He too is lost for words. Still, in one sentence he unlocks the struggle the case*
*clinic highlighted. "I do not know how this happened I just know that somehow*
*you changed the social contract of the class."*

## In Conclusion

There is an ecosystem heuristic hidden in these chapters that helps me recall the conditions knitted together within a chapter and the dimensions gathered together across the section. I remember the different keywords by the role they play in holding up, nurturing, fertilising and maintaining growth. Picturing a garden trellis, I think of Chapter 9 as the beams that lay the foundation: Belonging, Effort, Agency and Motivation. Chapter 10 reminds me of the cognitive psychology research that scaffolds learning to rise up the trellis: Retrieval, Interleaving, Spaced and Encoding practices. The generative sense-making of Chapter 11 is about how design can rake the soil and prepare the conditions by which creative ideas can come into being: Reflective practice, Allegory, Kaleidoscopic moves and Emotions. Lastly, the divergent/convergent rhythm of learning from doing in Chapter 12 speaks to pruning back, sacrificing and forgetting, as it does about imagining and experiencing anew: Prototyping, Resonance, Unsettling, Novelty and Embodiment.

There is something antithetic, clunky and too precise in this learning trellis heuristic, an idea easy to disregard for its inability to capture in capitalised words how interdependent and entwined these concepts and conditions are. Yet, I find myself bringing to mind an image of an overgrown trellis – with its crisscrossed beams, rising ivy, oxygenated soil and maintained growth – I need no longer critique the component parts. Instead, I see how the belonging scaffolds the metaphoric thinking and I wonder how the interleaving practice might feed the unsettling. I have held on to this inelegant heuristic because this visual encoding of the learning metaphor allows me to reframe, retrieve and remember what this section was about.

You will decide for yourself if the BEAM, RISE, RAKE, PRUNE heuristic is useful. Either way, Chapter 14 revisits the garden metaphor by reconfiguring the themes introduced in the preceding chapters into a set of four commitments that summarise the transformative capacity of designing learning to SEED unfamiliar ways of seeing and being.

---

## Part III Wonderings

Looking back over this section, I am curious about how my auto-ethnographic practice has evolved into an unusual application of retrieval practice, a move by which I could go back to stories in my long-term memory and analyse them anew. Just as the teachers' pattern-sensing brains had to rifle through an array of experiences of when they had made changes in the classroom, I had to mine my lived experiences to identify which practice stories shifted my internal scripts of design, along with which might resonate with you, the reader.

I came to see how easy it was to retrieve affective memories of my first co-design workshop (Narrative 5.1), learning clinic (Narrative 12.1) or Play Gym class (Narrative 2.1), in part because of how foreign and disorienting each experience was before it became a part of my everyday practice. I came to see that perspective shifts (Narrative 9.1) could come from interdisciplinary tensions (Narrative 10.1). Taking the time to interrogate the oftentimes competing disciplinary orientations granted me humility and clarity. Seeing the conflicting disciplinary positions allowed me to reframe the projects I had seen as failures into experiences that revealed core assumptions and principles. In the presentation, I gave to the education researchers months later, I openly wondered how evidence-based research might be complemented by the situational, people-centred approach of design. I questioned how a speculation-driven, futures orientation might ensure the initial hypothesis starts with a practice-based problem. I proposed an exploration of how the solution-seeking moves of design might focus on classroom impact and the translational potential of design research. It was at this presentation I met the people I went on to collaborate with on the ILETC project (6.2.1). I might always reckon with reconciling the importance of gathering policy-setting quantitative data with a creative practice that embraces the messiness of interdependent variables colliding against each other. But I recognise the gift of the practice lessons that summer was that my future collaborations created space for candid and generous discussion of this ongoing research tension.

The auto-ethnographic stories have also made clear the extent to which transformation happens over episodes. Is it possible Kevin's meaning-making of what design brings to retrieval practice and long-term memory would have stayed with me simply because he is an excellent teacher? Or did the collaborations with the cognitive psychologists prime me to be open to challenging my epistemic belief system? Furthermore, follow-up conversations with Kevin gave space for the formation of deeper memory traces and the integration new ways of understanding design.

The conviction to position myself as a learner is made visible in stories that are framed around narrating what shift has happened and what lesson has been learned. In *Transforming Mindsets*, I questioned the morality of a studio that educated designers about transforming others' mindsets without asking the students to turn the lens on themselves. The studio had one assignment where the students worked for an external partner on learning mindsets, complemented by a personal assignment that had them accountable to themselves. I wanted them to experience first-hand how hard it is to change our own internal scripts, so that we might compassionately respect how layered and entangled this work can be. There is a direct line to be traced from the peer-to-peer values internalised in my Māori language class decades earlier (Narrative 1.1) and my expressed impulse to ignore the evidence against student-centred learning (Narrative 12.1). I had long held on to the lesson from that formative Indigenous experience that the authority of the teacher should be subjugated for the collective agency of the community. Yet somehow, I had not attended to all the ways the Māori class had also ensured no learner was left behind. The interleaving of these narratives, seeing them in conversation with each other, revealed the value of re-watching old episodes to (re)make sense of the current season.

Just as my interpretation of the stories will always be in flux, the affective recollection of these snapshots in time revealed not just what had been overlooked, but also what has forever changed. Even though I had, over the years, become comfortable-ish with play, the quiet contemplation introduced that day in the learning clinic terrified me (Narrative 12.1). It was uncharted territory for me to trade in pre-reflective ways of sensing and expressing of emotions for this new way of accessing knowing. I wanted to run from this landscape, not make it a home. Yet, if emotions are signposts for future action, I came to see beyond my initial vulnerability by attuning to the transformative force these affective encounters had on me. The giddy, liberating disconfirming evidence made clear that learning would come faster if I could walk away from the well-worn cognitive maps of my past and set up camp on this seemingly hostile, yet exquisitely curious land.

When you think of how your ideas about designing have been unsettled, how your practice has evolved, what memories do you retrieve? What stories are you left telling yourself about designing and learning? What are you left wondering…?

## Bibliography

1 "The Future of Jobs Report 2020." World Economic Forum, Report, 20 October 2020, www.weforum.org/reports/the-future-of-jobs-report-2020.
2 Halloun, Ibrahim Abou and David Hestenes. "The Initial Knowledge State of College Physics Students." *American Journal of Physics*, vol. 53, no. 11, 1985, pp. 1043–55.
3 Schneps, Matthew. "A Private Universe." 1987, p. 20 minutes. general editor, Harvard-Smithsonian Center for Astrophysics, https://www.learner.org/series/a-private-universe/1-a-private-universe/.
4 Grocott, Lisa and Ilya Fridman. *The Playdate: Exploring How to Host a Learning Exchange*, ServDes 2020: Tensions Paradoxes Plurality Conference, Linköping University Electronic Press, 2020.
5 Akama, Yoko and Ann Light. "Readiness for Contingency: Punctuation, Poise, and Co-Design." *CoDesign*, vol. 16, no. 1, 2020, pp. 17–28, doi:10.1080/15710882.2020.1722177.
6 Botero, Andrea et al. "Getting Participatory Design Done: From Methods and Choices to Translation Work across Constituent Domains." *International Journal of Design*, vol. 14, no. 2, 2020, pp. 17–34.
7 Hyysalo, S. and J. Lehenkari. *Contextualizing Power in a Collaborative Design*, PDC Conference Proceedings, 2002.

8 Avram, Gabriela et al. "Repositioning Codesign in the Age of Platform Capitalism: From Sharing to Caring." *CoDesign*, vol. 15, no. 3, 2019, pp. 185–91, doi:10.1080/15 710882.2019.1638063.

9 Sanders, Elizabeth B-N and Pieter Jan Stappers. "Co-Creation and the New Landscapes of Design." *CoDesign*, vol. 4, no. 1, 2008, pp. 5–18, doi:10.1080/15710880 701875068.

10 Ehn, Pelle. "Learning in Participatory Design as I Found It (1970 to 2015)." *Participatory Design for Learning: Perspectives from Practice and Research*, edited by Betsy DiSalvo et al., Routledge, 2017, pp. 7–21.

11 "Student-Centered Learning: Building Agency and Engagement." *Edutopia*, Video, 3 May 2017, www.edutopia.org/video/student-centered-learning-building-agency-and-engagement.

12 Bratteteig, Tone et al. "Methods: Organising Principles and General Guidelines for Participatory Design Projects." *Routledge International Handbook of Participatory Design*, edited by Toni Robertson and Jesper Simonsen, 2012, pp. 117–44.

13 Fani, Tayebeh and Farid Ghaemi. "Implications of Vygotsky's Zone of Proximal Development (Zpd) in Teacher Education: ZPTD and Self-Scaffolding." *The 2nd International Conference on Education and Educational Psychology, Istanbul, Turkey*, vol. 29, 2011, pp. 1549–54. doi:10.1016/j.sbspro.2011.11.396.

14 Stuyf, Rachel R. Van Der. "Scaffolding as a Teaching Strategy." Unpublished Work, Academia, 2002, pileidou.files.wordpress.com/2013/11/scaffolding-as-a-teaching-strategy.pdf.

15 Rogoff, Barbara. *Apprenticeship in Thinking: Cognitive Development in Social Context.* Oxford University Press, 1992.

16 Halse, Joachim et al., editors. *Rehearsing the Future.* The Danish Design School Press, 2010.

17 Brandt, Eva and Thomas Binder. "Tools and Techniques: Ways to Engage Telling, Making and Enacting." *Routledge International Handbook of Participatory Design*, edited by Toni Robertson and Jesper Simonsen, Kindle ed., Taylor and Francis, 2013, pp. 145–72.

18 Korsmeyer, Hannah. *Feminist Tendencies, Tensions, and 'Co-Design' Practice*, 2022. Monash.

19 Grocott, Lisa and Mai Kobori. *The Affordances of Designing for the Learning Sciences*, LearnxDesign, 2015, Aalto University, Finland.

20 Nold, Christian. "Turning Controversies into Questions of Design: Prototyping Alternative Metrics for Heathrow Airport." *Inventing the Social*, edited by Noortje Marres et al., Mattering Press, 2018, pp. 94–124.

21 Grocott, Lisa. "The Discursive Practice of Figuring Diagrams." *TRACEY Journal: Drawing Knowledge*, 2012, pp. 1–15, www.lboro.ac.uk/microsites/sota/tracey/journal/edu/2012/PDF/Lisa_Grocott-TRACEY-Journal-DK-2012.pdf.

22 Blomkamp, Emma. "The Promise of Co-Design for Public Policy." *Australian Journal of Public Administration*, vol. 77, no. 4, 2018, pp. 729–43, doi: 10.1111/1467-8500.12310.

23 Boehner, Kirsten. "Reflections on Representation as Response." *Interactions*, vol. 16, no. 6, 2009, pp. 28–32, doi:10.1145/1620693.1620700.

24 Rose, Todd. *The End of Average: How We Succeed in a World That Values Sameness.* HarperCollins, 2015.

25 "What We Do." *National Equity Project*, nd, www.nationalequityproject.org.

26 Abendroth, Lisa M. and Bryan Bell, editors. *Public Interest Design Practice Guidebook: Seed Methodology, Case Studies, and Critical Issues.* Routledge, 2015.

27 Chivukula, Sai Shruthi. "Feminisms through Design: A Practical Guide to Implement and Extend Feminism." *Interactions*, vol. 27, no. 6, 2020, pp. 36–39, doi:10.1145/3427338.

28 Winchester, Woodrow W. "Afrofuturism, Inclusion, and the Design Imagination." *Interactions*, vol. 25, no. 2, 2018, pp. 41–45, doi:10.1145/3182655.

29 "International Indigenous Design Charter." *International Council of Design*, 2015, www.ico-d.org/resources/indigo.

30 "A Designer's Critical Alphabet." *Etsy*, 2021, www.etsy.com/listing/725094845/a-designers-critical-alphabet.

31 "Bulk Order the Model of Care Practice Cards." *Beyond Sticky Notes*, 2021, www.etsy.com/listing/725094845/a-designers-critical-alphabet.

32 Perry, M. "Pluriversal Literacies: Affect and Relationality in Vulnerable Times." *Reading Research Quarterly*, vol. 56, no. 2, 2021, pp. 293–309, doi: 10.1002/rrq.312.

33 Escobar, Arturo. *Designs for the Pluriverse: Radical Interdependence, Autonomy, and the Making of Worlds*. Duke University Press, 2018.

34 Noel, Lesley-Ann. R Leitão et al., editors. *Envisioning a Pluriversal Design Education*, DRS Pluriversal Design SIG Conference, 4 June 2020.

35 Oliver, Michael. *Social Work with Disabled People*. 4th ed., Palgrave Macmillan, 2012. Bob Sapey and Pam Thomas.

36 Mignolo, Walter D. "Delinking." *Cultural Studies*, vol. 21, no. 2–3, 2007, pp. 449–514, doi:10.1080/09502380601162647.

37 Goodley, Dan. "'Learning Difficulties', the Social Model of Disability and Impairment: Challenging Epistemologies." *Disability & Society*, vol. 16, no. 2, 2001, pp. 207–31, doi:10.1080/09687590120035816.

38 Rosner, Daniela. *Critical Fabulations: Reworking the Methods and Margins of Design*. The MIT Press, 2018.

39 Charset, Brian and Kate Sjostrom, editors. *Unsettling Education: Searching for Ethical Footing in a Time of Reform*. Peter Lang, 2019.

40 Deleuze, Gilles and Claire Parnet. *Dialogues Ii*. Columbia University Press, 2002.

41 Coleman, Kathryn et al. "Activating Teacher Education through a/R/Tographic Practice in Space." *Visual Methods, a/R/Tography and Walking*, edited by J Roldan et al., Tirant Lo Blanch, in press.

42 Ahmed, Sara. "Feminist Wonder." *Feminist Killjoys*, vol. 2021, 2014. https://feminist-killjoys.com/2014/07/28/feminist-wonder/.

43 Korsmeyer, Hannah et al. "Understanding Feminist Anticipation through 'Backtalk': 3 Narratives of Willful, Deviant, and Care-full Co-Design Practices." *Futures*, 2021, In Press, https://doi.org/10.1016/j.futures.2021.102874.

44 Petry, Arlete dos sAntos. "The Concept of Magic Circle: A Critical Reading." *Interactividad y Videojuegos*, vol. 5, 2013, doi:10.25029/OD.2013.30.5.

45 "What Is Design Based Learning?" *Design Based Learning*, nd, www.dblresources.org.

46 Dean, Douglas et al. "Identifying Quality, Novel, and Creative Ideas: Constructs and Scales for Idea Evaluation." *Journal of the Association for Information Systems*, vol. 7, no. 10, 2006, pp. 646–99, doi:10.17705/1jais.00106.

47 Ramos, Fabiane and Laura Roberts. "Wonder as Feminist Pedagogy: Disrupting Feminist Complicity with Coloniality." *Feminist Review*, vol. 128, no. 1, 2021, pp. 28–43, doi:10.1177/01417789211013702.

48 Nagasundaram, Murli and Robert P. Bostrom. "The Structuring of Creative Processes Using GSS: A Framework for Research." *Journal of Management Information Systems*, vol. 11, no. 3, 1994, pp. 87–114, doi:10.1080/07421222.1994.11518051.

49 Besemer, Susan P. and Donald J. Treffinger. "Analysis of Creative Products: Review and Synthesis." *The Journal of Creative Behavior*, vol. 15, no. 3, 1981, pp. 158–78, doi:10.1002/j.2162-6057.1981.tb00287.x.

50 Dunne, Anthony. "A Larger Reality," *Fitness for What Purpose?*, edited by Mary V Mullin and Christopher Frayling, Eyewear Publishing, 2018, pp. 116–17. www.readingdesign.org/a-larger-reality.

51 Auger, James and Julian Hanna. "How the Future Happens." *Journal of Future Studies*, vol. 23, no. 3, 2019, pp. 93–98, doi:10.6531/JFS.201903_23(3).0007.

52 Kolb, David. *Experiential Learning: Experience as a Source of Learning and Development*. Prentice Hall, 1984.

53 Haraway, Donna. "Situated Knowledges: The Science Question in Feminism and the Privilege of Partial Perspective." *Feminist Studies*, vol. 14, no. 3, 1988, pp. 575–99.

54 Woodward, Sophie. *Material Methods Researching and Thinking with Things.* Sage, 2020.

55 Hayashi, Arawana and Ricardo Dutra. "Social Presencing Theater the Art of Making a True Move." 2021, http://public.eblib.com/choice/PublicFullRecord.aspx?p=6514862.

56 Skulmowski, Alexander and Günter Daniel Rey. "Embodied Learning: Introducing a Taxonomy Based on Bodily Engagement and Task Integration." *Cognitive Research: Principles and Implications*, vol. 3, no. 1, 2018, p. 6, doi:10.1186/s41235-018-0092-9.

57 Michlewski, Kamil. *Design Attitude.* Kindle ed., Farnham Ashgate, 2015.

58 Mattelmäki, Tuuli et al. "What Happened to Empathic Design?" *Design Issues*, vol. 30, no. 1, 2014, pp. 67–77.

59 Lockton, Dan and Stuart Candy. "A Vocabulary for Visions in Designing for Transitions." *Design Research Society (DRS) 2018*, 2018.

60 Grocott, Lisa et al. "The Becoming of a Designer: An Affective Pedagogical Approach to Modelling and Scaffolding Risk-Taking." *Art, Design & Communication in Higher Education*, vol. 18, no. 1, 2019, pp. 99–112, doi:10.1386/adch.18.1.99_1.

61 Davies, Sally. "Women's Minds Matter." *Aeon*, 30 May 2019, aeon.co/essays/feminists-never-bought-the-idea-of-a-mind-set-free-from-its-body.

62 Perkins, David. *Making Learning Whole: How Seven Principles of Teaching Can Transform Education.* Kindle ed., Jossey-Bass, 2013.

63 Grocott, Lisa and Kate McEntee. "Teaching Intrapersonal Development, Improving Interpersonal and Intercultural Skill Sets: The Transforming Mindsets Studio." *Public Interest Design Education Guidebook: Curricula, Strategies, and Seed Academic Case Studies*, edited by Lisa M. Abendroth and Bryan Bell, Routledge, 2019, pp. 141–46.

# PART IV

# Transformative Learning

## A Matrix, a Constellation, a Framework and More Questions

FIGURE 13.0  **A Commitment Device**: present-moment wondering to channel near-future action, in a *Making Space* workshop.

DOI: 10.4324/9780429429743-16

## An Introduction

The previous sections explicitly reveal the extent to which transformative work is not about some singular cognitive 'aha' moment any more than it is about simply being motivated or putting in thousands of hours of practice. The work of shifting how we respond to situations, navigate change and evolve our own thinking and practice in unfamiliar ways is never a binary cause-and-effect relationship, but a series of inter-related moves flowing together. This interplay between what we know intellectually to be true, what we know practically from doing, what we know in ourselves from experience and what we come to know from experimenting with new ways of being come together to inform all that has come in the preceding sections. These final chapters reconfigure the earlier material in new ways, in part to recontextualise, in part to clarify and in part to continue questioning.

The first chapter examines the idea of learner engagement beyond the narrow lens of the person we are designing for. This broader frame allows us to see how we might position our own personal evolution, as well as engaging with broader shifts within the practice of design. Building on the story in this section's only practice narrative, the first part considers what it takes to engage ourselves, the designer, educator and/or researcher in a practice of constant evolution. The theorising from stories loops back to earlier mentions of purpose, motivation and curiosity, and stems from an exploration of the pedagogical conditions that helped three designer-researchers and myself to continuously learn from our design research practices. The next section revisits the *Making Design* constellation introduced in Part II (Figure 4.1). In it, I propose an additional 12 *makes* (Figure 13.2). In doing so, I demonstrate the extent to which I am changed by engaging not just with my own narratives but also the practice, interdisciplinary and experiential knowing from the case studies and practice vignettes. Aligned with Escobar, this revised framework speaks to the shift required for design to be in the service of the social – as opposed to falling back on the script that casts design in the role of service provider to industry (1, p. 34). More directly, the additional *makes* offer a way into wondering how design can express social ideas in the context of designing learning. The third and final part considers the power of engaging with worlds other than our own. The section considers personal, private, possible and potential worlds through the lens of the inquisitive power of the paradox. It introduces the notion that each of us can only have a limited understanding of the worlds around us.

The second chapter begins by briefly elaborating on the ways the work of designing for transformative learning intersects with and departs from literature on behaviour change and theories of change. However, the substance of the chapter is centred on the synthesis, summary and distillation of the design insights surfaced in Parts II and III. The heuristic SEED proposes the pedagogical lessons and moves of this research into four memorable, retrievable component parts. At the core of this framework is the conviction to be curious and mindful of the shift work required for seeds of change to break through the soil and transform into new habits and mindsets. Stories from practice and design literature come together to propose the specific way that design contributes to creating learning encounters that lead to sustained shifts in practice.

In navigating my own transformation through the writing of this text, I accept that not all ideas have settled. With the ideas I present unashamedly in perpetual evolution, the concluding chapters speculate and reflect on what might come next. The first part locates Mezirow's ten-phase process within SEED and takes a prismatic view of what this research has to offer in the field of Transformative Learning. The second part extrapolates from the lessons revealed from my past practice to dismantle the assumption that new practices are to be found in the future, not restoring from the past. I own that the reclaiming of old knowing, in my case the Indigenous lessons of my past, might offer fertile ground for activating new ways of being. Lastly, I sit with the nuanced, multi-dimensional nature of shift work. As the book ends, I reckon with the irrefutable, felt understanding of the importance of a more relational approach. I respect the relational dimensions I centred, yet I own what I let sit in the margins. I speculate on what a truly relational design practice might look like, not just for the designing of transformative learning, but for all of us engaged in transformative work.

## References

1 Escobar, Arturo. Designs for the Pluriverse: Radical Interdependence, Autonomy, and the Making of Worlds. Duke University Press, 2018.

# 13

# TRANSFORMATIVE ENGAGEMENT

## Curiosity, Paradoxes and Making Reconfigured

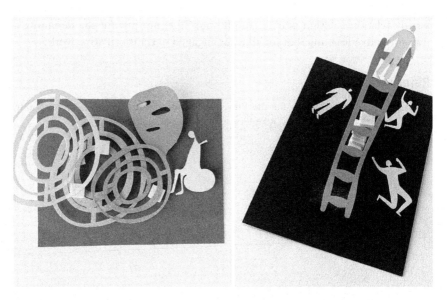

FIGURE 13.1 **The Worlds We Learn in**: This workshop (13.3) co-evolved as a learning community, with each new researcher posing new questions. One researcher's focus might have be on the affordances of the materials, another's on owning what we do not know about someone else's world. As a learning community, WonderLab was conceived to maximise research intersections over collaborations. Metaphorically, we saw this as people researching on their own planets while honouring the solar system we shared. The iterations of this workshop became a space station for individual-collective wondering.

DOI: 10.4324/9780429429743-17

The visualisations, diagrams and tables of this chapter consider the role of engagement when it comes to transformation. Each part brings a new orientation to the question of engaging with whom, in what ways and towards what end. The first section pulls back from the focus on designing of learning encounters where other people's learning is prioritised. It proposes how, as designers or educators, we might engage with researching our own practice. Redrawing the *Making Design* constellation from Part II (Chapter 4, Figure 4.1), the next section explores how designers engage with transforming design practice itself. The aperture widens in the following section to consider the interior and exterior, known and unknown worlds learners engage with when designing for learning. In the conclusion, ideas from throughout the book are summarised into a table about how transformative engagement aims and objectives can be realised with various design moves and methods.

## 13.1 Engage to Shift Design Practice

A paper on 'chasing curiosity' was the outcome of the collaboration with the peers who had successfully navigated their own transformation from graphic designers to transdisciplinary researchers (1). It was this research-wondering study (p. XX) that propelled my own curiosity to explicitly reframe (re)searching as learning. Those embryonic conversations are the seed planted years ago that grew into the body of practice-led inquiry captured in this publication.[1] The concluding framework of the paper presented a way to consider our own learning evolution. Pulling back from how we might design encounters for others, I proposed three cornerstones for supporting our own transformation as designers, researchers and life-long learners. The focus on chasing curiosity came from knitting together a meaning-making, world-making, sense-making practice. This paper was to be my earliest experimentation with the word play of making.

A *meaning-making* practice addresses the importance of orienting and owning our internal motivations. This is in part about, intentionality, reciprocity and ensuring the transcendence of the work beyond the here-and-now (2). This is to strengthen the connection between meaning-making and purpose. Return regularly to ask why you are invested in a particular project by considering the impact you are hoping to achieve. This should help ensure that the more instrumental and transactional reasons for doing something do not undercut a more internal motivation. The second cornerstone is for that purpose to be acted upon

1  **Sean**: It is interesting to reflect on a 20-year practice through a learning/research space. Back when you interviewed me my investment in directing the lens of design towards global issues of social justice had led to example after example of situations where design, and thereby I, were ill prepared to own or be held accountable for the erasures and violence of my discipline. I was drawn to doing a PhD so I might better recognize the power dynamics of participation and potentially critically navigate designs embedded privileges. While simultaneously understanding these series of entanglements also signals the interior work I will always have to do.

through *world-making* projects (3; 4). The project-grounded, future-oriented nature of design practice affords a place for an interventional practice that can amplify impact and seed transformation. This is an invitation to expand the field of design beyond the limiting scope of problem solving. The invitation is to see our work as context-setting and world-building – thoughtful, ethical practice that requires attuning to what you do not know, rather than aggrandising ego-led practice. In this way, the third cornerstone of *sense-making* becomes critical. This is not sense-making the activity when designing, but a commitment to engage in making sense of design the discipline. It is about wondering the contribution of design, about being curious and critical about design's blind spots, about translating the lessons of one project to another situation. The interrogative act of taking a more distant view with each individual project so we might make sense of the affordances and limitations of design is central to how we sustain inquiry and consequently transform our own practice.

Personally, my meaning-making, world-making and sense-making in the context of this text has been to chase my own curiosity to interrogate, through pilots and prototypes, ways design can deepen learning and support transformative change. However, this publication is about more than my practice and perspective. The case studies, practice narratives, research studies and interdisciplinary theories allow the potential of designing transformative learning to be viewed through a lens of intellectual humility.[2] For another way to stay curious is to engage with different epistemic beliefs, question your own viewpoint and be prepared to consider alternative explanations. We can more easily surface and interrogate our own beliefs if we view them in relation to the stories of disciplines, cultures and contexts other to our own lived experiences.

## 13.2 Engage to Transform Design Practice

I began this book seeing the *Making Design* constellation (2.0, Figure 4.1) as a move towards an expansive understanding of design. I came to see the naming of the different makes as a way to capture possible wondering moves in the service of designing learning. Understanding this exercise to be always a work in progress and perpetually in a state of becoming, I today see the mutable terms as a set of contingent ideas always meaningfully in negotiation. Here, I critique my yesterday-self in the spirit of chasing curiosity. I pause the kaleidoscopic crystals

---

2   **Lisa:** The psychological concept of 'intellectual humility' is like the sibling of curiosity. If curiosity is a propelling outward facing force, inviting you to go out and explore what you do not know, then intellectual humility is a more interior stance that has you questioning what you know and believe. Shane Snow, (5) characterises intellectual humility as (a) Respect for Other Viewpoints; (b) Lack of Intellectual Overconfidence; (c) Separation of Ego from Intellect; (d) Willingness to Revise Viewpoints. This animation is a compelling visual argument for why intellectual humility is a critical skill to nurture in time of polarising perspectives: https://www.templeton.org/discoveries/intellectual-humility.

of making to ruminate over what I have learned about designing, making and learning in the writing of these stories.

The case studies and practice vignettes highlight a commitment to *make sense, make possible, make visible, make believe, make fun, make tangible* and *make together* so we might *make change*. The expertise of making and mastery taught to design students for decades are foundational to these moves. There is the design commitment to *make do*. In making do, a belief is instilled in the designer to work with what you have, to see constraints as positive, to know that with doing comes insights. Closely aligned to the practice of learning from prototyping, there is an acknowledgement that to iterate, to *make again*, is core to the feedback loop. Yet, the impulse to make, even in the face of no clear way forward is about more than seeking insights. There is a hubris that comes with making when one knows that no single solution will be enough, that many problems are intractable and that every action triggers unintended consequences. Yet to *make anyway* is to not give into the paralysis that comes with a detached analysis. To design is to go beyond a theoretical position or even a cognitive shift, but to take action. At its core, design is an interventionist practice propelled to *make things happen*.

Aligned with Escobar, this revised constellation speaks to the shift required for design to be in the service of the social – as opposed to falling back on the script that casts design in the role of service provider to industry (6, p. 34). More directly, the additional *makes* offer a way into wondering how design can express social ideas in the context of designing learning.

In exploring transformative learning, a circular process of making lies in the invitation to be forever learning. To *make waves* begins the process of unsettling one's position and troubling the present so we might critique fiercely held beliefs or deep structural narratives. To *make connections* further amplifies the design expertise of synthesis and sense-making. Tracing connections might come from a systems awareness perspective, or from identifying leverage points for change, or by grasping the relational dimensions of change, or recognising the integrative value of a whole-person approach to shifting hearts and minds. Bringing the pragmatism of design to the psychology of motivation helps convert mindset shifts into sustained change. To *make plans* is to recognise the importance of the final push, what mobility designers call the last mile challenge. Analogous to the challenge of getting people from public transport to their front door safely, the question here is to remember that we are designing for learning that finds its way home. For the process of transformation invites the learner to make waves then to *make peace*. However, this settling in and getting comfortable with ideas that were once disorienting and confusing is not a permanent state. A commitment to life-long learning focuses instead on becoming familiar with the cyclical tension of settling and unsettling so that the next time your assumptions are challenged, you can find the intellectual humility to engage in the process of making waves again.

There is a significant unmaking that the designer must attend to as well. The modernity narrative runs deep in design, bringing with it a bias to action and an oftentimes unwarranted belief in the interventionist agenda of progress. To ensure a critical, reflexivity is brought to the foundational orientations to make anyway and to make happen, design must reframe some mental models of making. Early versions of the *Making Design* constellation problematically emphasised the term *make right*, begging the question: right for whom? What if to *make right* did not ascribe to the modernity script of designer as problem solver? Could this alternatively not be about being right, but instead about asking better questions? Hannah's footnote (11.3) unspools this framing again, asking whether an embodied attuning allows us to sense what is not-right so things can be made more-right. Similarly, *make good* appeared in earlier versions before troubled by Sean's 'design for good' footnote critique (12.2) of the inherent hubris that comes with the imperialist, modernist, universal design script. I wonder whether Sean would think *make amends* a more appropriate commitment to owning our complicity in dominant oppressive systems? An expansive reconceptualising of not just how but why we *make together* calls for designing not simply for inclusion, but pluriversal encounters that welcome multiple perspectives. Design can build on what we know about convivial tools, analogous situations, fictional stories to *make space* for dissenting voices and courageous conversations so learners might reckon with conflict yet feel belonging, so participants might normalise sharing emotions yet be respectful of difference. These small shifts signal the ever-emergent relational ways of being with ourselves and each other. Potentially, the mindset shifts, the incremental moves, the attuning to affect reframes how the designer might think of the work of making shifts. The apologetic form of a makeshift work-in-progress that is yet to come together is replaced in learning by the elevated call to *make shifts* that together collectively translate to unfamiliar ways of seeing and doing.

I am left wondering: how is *making real* different from *making tangible*? Does the phrase *make room* (to push aside) add anything to the idea to *make space* (to welcome in)? I wonder if to *make towards* is more honest, more emergent, than the phrase to *make right*? With transformative learning, is it possible to *make trouble* at the same time as playfully *making light*? What does it mean to make known in the context of experiential futures as opposed to in an end of year exam? A popular conception of designing might reductively describe the objective to *make things* as driven by an economic imperative to *make profit*. Depending on your intention, you might want to *make conversation*, or *make urgent,* or simply *make memories*. What I did conclude, at least today, was that the brightest star at the centre of a transformative learning constellation should probably be *make meaning*.[3]

---

3  **Kelly**: When I am facilitating a workshop, I think of the process as story-making for meaning-making. The workshop scaffolds the visualising of stories so participants might *make sense* and *make visible* their experiences. The sensing act of making activates embodied ways of knowing and in turn makes visible others' stories. This enabling of collective interpretation in relation to one's own lived experience is what renders meaning across seemingly disparate stories (7, p. 11).

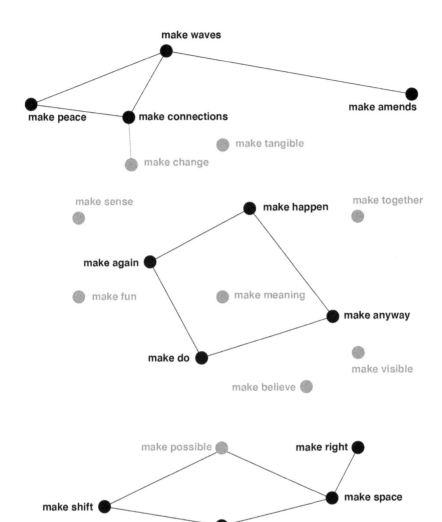

FIGURE 13.2 **Designing Learning Constellation**: Here, an additional 12 makes are noted to the original Making Design constellation. The focus here is on the making moves especially relevant to the designing of learning. I continue to see the wordplay as a heuristic that questions what designing is and could be, reserving my right to be forever troubling what these make (re)configurations say about what design is and what design could be.

Beyond a generative, productive play with this conceptual constellation, any expansive understanding of making needs to ultimately be translated and situated in relation to the design of learning encounters. The following tables retrieve concepts introduced in the earlier chapters to highlight how the learner's intentions, the social interactions and the methods and moves of making come together to design a transformative learning encounter.

**TABLE 13.1** Possible Learning Aims for Designing Transformative Encounters

*Transformative Aims*

| *Individual's Experience* | *Social Encounter* |
| --- | --- |
| Surface tacit beliefs | Retrieve felt memories |
| Interrogate conflicting positions | Make dearly held beliefs visible |
| Discredit false narratives | Label and express emotions |
| Draw agency from lived experiences | Capture diverse lived experiences |
| Reveal a motivating internal why | Scaffold vulnerability |
| Rehearse new ways of being | Cultivate self-awareness |
| Plan to work around challenges | Drive collective investment |
| Reconcile and settle new knowing | Define future action |

**TABLE 13.2** Potential Design Objectives when Designing Learning

*Design Objectives*

| *Individual's Experience* | *Social Encounter* |
| --- | --- |
| Connect shared experiences | Promote chattering |
| Declare irreconcilable assumptions | Foster belonging |
| Interrogate conflicting narratives | Broker sharing |
| Appreciate what you can change | Amplify affect |
| Normalise that change is hard | Frame resonance |
| Embody experience of future action | Draw on collective imagination |
| Believe transformation is possible | Scaffold shared investment |
| Integrate new practices | Prime engagement |

**TABLE 13.3** Design Moves and Methods for Designing Engaging Encounters

*Engagement Strategies*

| *Designing Moves* | *Design Methods* |
| --- | --- |
| Embodying | Visual and experiential metaphors |
| Playing | Story-making |
| Co-creating | Photo-elicitation |
| Reflexive positioning | Card sorting |
| Story sharing | Reflective prompts |
| (de)Futuring | Future scenarios |
| Social imagining | Design games |
| Intention setting | Commitment devices |

As you design your own encounters use Tables 13.1–13.3 as a cheat sheet for reminding you of ideas already introduced. For a more prescriptive approach, you may want to read it horizontally, to consider how an individual's transformative aim might align with objectives of the learning encounter, to reflect on how different engagement moves (for example embodiment) might intersect with an engagement method (like metaphors). Or, you might read it more as an open matrix, looking for serendipitous connections that allow new engagement strategies to emerge from reading across and between the tables.

## 13.3  Engage to Learn from Other(s) Worlds

There is a tension running through the different orientations to making that productively pulls the designer in different directions. Whether that is speculating on future worlds while being grounded in lived experience or learning from a conversation with the materials or diverse stakeholders. The integrative impulse to move between divergent and convergent modes of thinking and doing is core here. The ubiquitous 'Yes And' refrain of improv classes and design thinking workshops underscores the generative value of suspending judgement and building on what is in front of you. However, in a learning space, I often find myself countering with the sobering phrase 'And Yet'. This represents a call to be more critical, to retain my 'Yes And' optimism, yet continue to question my assumptions. To get to a new place of possibility the 'Yes And' whitewashes tensions to affirm potential. To trouble what is desirable the 'And Yet' highlights what might not be reconcilable or preferable. Distinct from a 'Yes, But' which oftentimes forecloses on potential by holding on to what is known, the 'Yes/And/Yet' allows us to sit longer in the liminal space between what is now and what might be. I argue the creative, yet critical, capacity to hold incommensurable ideas and to *make anyway* is the paradoxical move at the heart of designing.

For the designer, educator or researcher, there are dispositional paradoxes and disorienting contradictions that ask of us to reconcile the seemingly irreconcilable. And yet, this resistance to stasis is what gives design its propelling momentum, its transformative agency. However, in wrestling with the paradoxes, there is a refusal to perceive that there is one right way. There might be acknowledgement that a toolkit, for example, offers a gentle way in, yet recognition that transactional methods alone will not lead to the mindset shifts necessary for sustained change. Jung understood the paradox as useful for making sense of the full complexity of our lived experience, engaging with the "union of opposites" as an activity that brings unconscious and conscious processes into conversation with each other.[4]

Even though Jung believed that engaging with paradoxes was the ultimate intellectual challenge, the proposition here is whether the designer's learned

---

4   This webpage links to Jung's collected works to share his thinking on the paradox (8).

capacity to hold the tension of opposites could be designed into the learning experience. Can a learner seeking to make shifts in their own practice be supported by intentionally amplifying the paradoxical tension of 'Yes/And/Yet'?[5] To see the reckoning with as the learning moment, we need to reframe transformation as about more than a move from habit A to habit B. My auto-ethnographic stories might wrongly imply that the moments of disorientation were the starting point. In reality, there is unlikely to be a single genesis for transformation, more a set of priming conditions wrapped around the disorienting dilemma. Similarly, there is no finishing line to cross, more a set of choices of which path to follow next. Transformation instead arrives in small yet profound instalments. Each incremental lesson needs to be understood as happening within a forever curious process of negotiating and renegotiating. This is learning as a liminal, liberating, pedagogic space that invites 'promiscuous', yet intentional wondering (9). And yet, not a passive, holding space, but an animated, promiscuous place. This version of transformative learning does not seek to leave the water to never return, but to learn from being both of the water and the ground.

In WonderLab, we have run many workshops based on the plural worlds that educator and researcher John Holt introduces in his *What Do I Do on Mondays?* book (9). As an early proponent of what would become the unschooling movement, Holt introduces four worlds to help us make sense of what and how we come to know. He also makes clear how hard it is to know what we don't know. On the first day of the Design Rounds, we used a Worlds Workshop (Narrative 8.1 and Figures 2.1 and 8.1) to set intentions of what worlds people hoped to learn from, and on the last day, we reflected on what was actually learned. The following table shows our adaptation of Holt's four worlds (Table 13.4).

I use these worlds as an organising principle for surfacing the paradoxes smuggled into this text by way of practitioner orientations, case study precedents or the practice narratives and vignettes. In their paper on wonder as a feminist pedagogy, Ramos and Roberts explore wonder in the classroom through plurilogue and time-travel (10). Referencing Maria Lugones concept of time-travel and her words to underscore the pedagogical discovery that there are: "worlds

---

5   **Sonali**: I have always been guided by the wisdom of children in my work. Early on in my practice a youth, Donna, who had grown up on the streets in Sacramento critiqued the notion that the way out of struggle was to find one's inner diamond by recalling nurturing memories from the past. Curious as to what Donna was trying to tell me when she implored us not to ignore the pain within, I asked her to tell me more. She simply said, "You need to learn to hold both; grief and joy; day and night; past and present. Life is a paradox; understand it". It took me three years more to really begin to grasp what Donna taught me that day, but eventually with much searching I came to see that no one had easy answers to my questions of how is life a paradox, because this union of opposites is what many of us are running from. The discovery of the paradox as not just a mode of inquiry but as an embodied state to be respected became core to all our work at Dreamcatchers. **Ricardo**: In our work with teachers, Sonali and I made this idea, emotions as paradoxes explicit. We helped them see what Donna already knew, that emotions are not either... or, but rather they coexist with each other. The invitation was for the teachers to inquire further into what paradoxes might be enacted for learners and open a space for staying with the co-existing emotions.

**TABLE 13.4** Worlds We Learn and Live in

| World 1 | Personal | One's inner world. The world inside my skin.★ | A world shaped by beliefs, emotions, mindsets and mental models |
|---|---|---|---|
| World 2 | Private | One's world of experience My world, unique to me.★ | A world shaped by people, place, interactions and encounters |
| World 3 | Possible | One's learned world The world of the possible.★ | A world shaped by information and knowledge outside one's own experiences |
| World 4 | Potential | One's unknowable world The world I cannot imagine.★ | A world shaped by imagination and ignorance, beyond what one knows |

*Holt introduces four worlds. Over the duration of multiple iterations of this workshop colleagues we attempted to name and describe these worlds. The reference to Holt's original language is denoted by the asterisk. World 4, made up of all that is possible that one has not even heard of or imagined, was the hardest for Holt to describe. Design's capacity for speculative inquiry and social imagining offer ways to give shape and texture to the envisaging of these worlds.*

in which those who are the victims of arrogant perception are really subjects, lively beings, resistors, constructors of visions even though in the mainstream construction they are animated only by the arrogant perceiver and are pliable, foldable, file-awayable, classifiable" (10, p. 38). In this way, transformative learning is not something that only happens in world 4 but emerges over time as the learner slips back and forth between the worlds of their own experience and that of others. We learn when we allow our world 3 to connect to another's world 2. When we look into our inner world to make sense of how our lived experiences have shaped us, we can commit to rehearsing new roles and creating new memories. In this way we come to see how recursively transforming world 2 updates world 1. Sharing the beliefs instilled in our personal world 1s might help shed light on what we need from a not yet imagined world 4 (Table 13.5).

These tensions capture a design process that accordions from divergence to convergence and the design disposition to embrace uncertainty by way of productive ambiguity. This is a quest to swim out to the edge of what is possible while being grounded by an ocean floor that is knowable. In this seeking place, a tentative exploration of the contingent and indeterminate invites us to question whether others' experiences might resonate or depart from our own. And yet, the contradiction here, as designers of learning or as learners ourselves, is to fight for our imagination of future world 4s to not be defined by our own restricted, bounded private worlds. We cannot separate the worlds of the learning designer from that of the learner. These paradoxes implicitly declare the value of positioning ourselves within this work while making explicit that we too will be transformed by the work. Bring humility to the limits of your worlds and a curiosity to understand the worlds of your learners. Make a commitment to hold space for

**TABLE 13.5** Yes/And/Yet Designing Learning Paradoxes

| World 1 Personal | • Seek to disrupt established patterns and principles, and yet incrementally shift habits and behaviour<br>• Creatively imagine beyond the constraints, and yet critically consider ethical implications<br>• Forage deeply to name the privilege of your world, and yet concede that some biases are too deep to be seen |
|---|---|
| World 2 Private | • Own your partial perspective, and yet get curious about how your experiences limit your capacity to see others' worlds<br>• Commit to a sense of purpose, and yet flirt with serendipity<br>• Design for the learning of others, and yet be attuned to your own transformation |
| World 3 Possible | • Create a safe place for learning, and yet scaffold for unsettling<br>• Heighten present-moment engagement, and yet bring a consequential perspective<br>• Bring a system-thinking lens to levers for change, and yet an ethical orientation to the entangled relationships |
| World 4 Potential | • Strive to sense another's world, and yet suspend any belief you will ever know<br>• Iterate from a place of not-knowing, and yet be attuned to the limits of what is not-knowable<br>• Frame intentions to shift, and yet trust a process of emergence |

*These paradoxes not only reveal the push and pull within each world but also the liminal space between worlds. When I envisage the worlds, not as independent planets, but as worlds operating in different time and space continuums, it becomes possible to see one world as a portal into another. Any passport to learning through these paradoxes has to see the borders between worlds as distinct yet porous. Knowing has to flow across continents yet be grounded by a critique specific to time and place.*

the diversity of the worlds your learners bring and resist reducing stakeholders or participants to offering just one part of their world for discussion. Create learning experiences that engage with traveling between worlds. The social act of coming together to share beliefs and co-realise our values offers a liminal bridge between our inner worlds and the worlds of possibility. Making mental models visible while unearthing the disconfirming evidence or hard facts that unsettles what we believe creates a revolving door between worlds 1, 2 and 3. The sensorial feedback that comes from envisioning new futures is like a ring road that connects worlds 1, 2 and 4. Yet, work of transformation is not only always a long journey but also the quotidian work that has the learner repeatedly shuttling between one's private world and the potential worlds outside of their orbit. For this is how we ground learning not just in some utopian future but in a preferable tomorrow.

# Bibliography

1  Grocott, Lisa. "Chasing Curiosity: Inquiry-Led Practice in Communication Design." *One and Many Mirrors: Perspectives on Graphic Design Education*, edited by Luke Wood and Brad Haylock, Occasional Papers, 2020, pp. 136–47.
2  Feuerstein, Reuven. "The Theory of Structural Cognitive Modifiability." *Learning and Thinking Styles: Classroom Interaction*, National Education Association of the United States/Better Schools, 1990, pp. 68–134.
3  Agid, Shana. "Worldmaking: Working through Theory/Practice in Design." *Design and Culture*, vol. 4, no. 1, 2012, pp. 27–54, doi:10.2752/175470812X13176523285110.
4  Zaidi, Leah. "Worldbuilding in Science Fiction, Foresight, and Design." *Journal of Futures Studies*, vol. 2, 2019, p. 12, doi:10.6531/JFS.201906_23(4).0003.
5  Snow, Shane. *Dream Teams: Working Together without Falling Apart*. Little, Brown Book Group, 2018.
6  Escobar, Arturo. *Designs for the Pluriverse: Radical Interdependence, Autonomy, and the Making of Worlds*. Duke University Press, 2018.
7  Danko, Sheila et al. "Humanizing Design through Narrative Inquiry." *Journal of Interior Design*, vol. 31, no. 2, 2006, pp. 10–28, doi:10.1111/j.1939-1668.2005.tb00408.
8  Mehrtens, Sue. "Jung on Paradox." *Jungian Center for the Spiritual Sciences: Whole Person Learning in a Jungian Context*, nd.
9  Rantatalo, Oscar and Ola Lindberg. "Liminal Practice and Reflection in Professional Education: Police Education and Medical Education." *Studies in Continuing Education*, vol. 40, no. 3, 2018, pp. 351–66, doi:10.1080/0158037X.2018.1447918.
10  Ramos, Fabiane and Laura Roberts. "Wonder as Feminist Pedagogy: Disrupting Feminist Complicity with Coloniality." *Feminist Review*, vol. 128, no. 1, 2021, pp. 28–43, doi:10.1177/01417789211013702.

# 14

# SEEDING TRANSFORMATION THROUGH DESIGN

## A Designed Approach

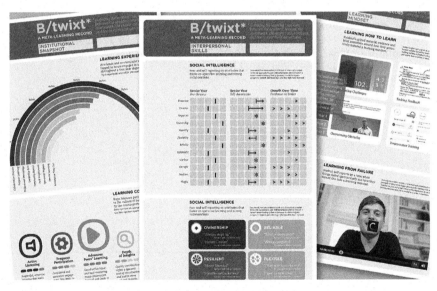

FIGURE 14.1 **B'twixt Meta-Learning Record**: This speculative prop for an alternate present was designed to provoke discussion within learning institutions about alternative ways to record learning. Developed with support from Yi Zhang (Narrative 11.1), the prop came to life out in the wild. When Helen Chen would speak to the prop at conferences – photos were snapped, images tweeted and blog posts written (1; 2). We observed how quickly people grasped our critique of current academic transcripts. Distinct from an executive summary the approximating artefact did more than propose change, but visually summoned the future potential of the opportunity.

DOI: 10.4324/9780429429743-18

There is a recognition running through many models of change introduced (2.4) that an essential part of the journey toward embracing and integrating new behaviour is noticing existing mindsets. Further complicating the more cognitive and behavioural orientations to change are concepts introduced in the previous chapter, like the paradoxes experienced and our limited capacity to know another's world. The focus of this chapter is to translate the broader pedagogical commitments that emerged from pilot projects with partners, then evolved through WonderLab's applied research and have been further crystallised through writing this book.

This chapter introduces SEED (Figure 14.2), four sites of inquiry to hold onto when designing for transformative learning. Think of SEED as pedagogical moves for 'operationalising wonder.' (3, p. 37) Synthesising the lessons from the practice stories, case studies, practice vignettes and personal narratives, of Part II and integrating the keywords of Part III, the SEED metaphor brings a temporal lens to establishing conditions for transformation. The acronym SEED is a heuristic for the work of Surfacing, Envisaging, Experiencing and Driving change. Together the moves draw on the dual orientation of design to be creative and cognitive while recognising the integrative capacity of designing to be speculative and reflective. The temporal orientation holds space for where people have come from, where they are at and where they want to get to. Whereas the garden trellis heuristic of Part III introduced ways to prepare for and grow learning, the following four engagements seed for transformation that takes hold. If the *Making Design* constellation (Figure 13.2) offers *ways* for wondering, SEED offers *temporal sites* for wondering by exploring the subject of inquiry. I begin with the act of surfacing ideas planted in the past, I then consider how we wonder about the future, how we learn from the present moment and plan the next move.

## 14.1 Surfacing Scripts

What might be understood as the contemplation stage in TTM or the 'big assumptions' declared in the Immunity to Change process, the call to bring to the surface our internal scripts signals the importance of recognising that transformative learning requires some wrestling with current thinking. Planted in the past, these internal scripts might be learning mindsets forged from pre-school experiences, cognitive mental models of capitalism, political views unconsciously adopted, assumptions defined by privilege, values embedded in social justice, biases passed down from previous generations, beliefs founded in experienced inequality, philosophical positions internalised from books or dreams defined by oppression. Whatever their origin, these polyvocal, often competing narratives shape our inner world and our actions.

Whereas transmissive knowledge might seek to introduce new information that accumulates alongside existing knowledge, the more audacious objective to transform future actions requires deeper examination of what drives current action. There is a belief here that if we do not reconcile new thinking with old thinking we can thwart sustainable change. The importance of a learner declaring their positions as part of transformative work can signpost the integration work required. For me, the evidence that student-centred learning fails to engage a third of students was not in itself going to change my pedagogical practice. It was formative instead that I examined how my identity as a teacher was wedded to rejecting the teacher-led learning of my design studio education. This realisation that my identity was not tied to student-centred learning as much as a critique of the mentor/student dynamic of the apprentice model allowed me to explore approaches that could reconcile that belief while letting go of my strict adherence to a student-centred approach.

This onto-epistemic work does more than just surfacing tacit beliefs, acknowledging contradictions between what one believes and how one acts or reflecting on where cognitive scripts might come from. In the call to surface recognition that we need to sit with, attend to and de-centre, there are dominant narratives that allow people to see multiple perspectives apart from the internalised scripts we individually follow every day. For Walter Mignolo, the epistemic shift work of de-linking is what affords new epistemologies, different ways of knowing and unfamiliar understandings to emerge. According to Mignolo, de-linking invites an epistemic shift that rejects the modernist principle of the universal project and embraces the pluriversality of other politics, other ethics and other futures (4, p. 453). Might a de-colonial examination of one's lived experience in conversation with embedded modernist narratives allow a different relationship with agency to emerge? What is the role of design in the emancipatory potential of Freire's pedagogical commitment to conscientisation?

The introspective work of examining often tacit assumptions, or stories held so tight we cannot separate them from our identity, can be augmented by design practices that help access or detach from abstract concepts. Mapping and story-making activities allow for a kind of temporary fixing and detachment that allows some ideas to be seen more clearly. Visual and metaphoric ambiguity invite other's interpretations and creative meaning-making. Reflective prompts and improvised moves invite emergence through embodied and critical introspection. In these ways, the say/make/do convivial tools and performative methods of co-design support the elicitation of insights that might not surface if accessed from rational self-examination alone. Although for transformation to become established, this phase of exposing beliefs would need to be revisited throughout the process, as the methods for making beliefs visible are often initial priming activities designed to illuminate the work in front of everyone. In turn, these priming activities can productively normalise shared experiences and reveal a plurality of perspectives. They can create a safe place for sharing while opening up a vulnerability not easily shed. Either way, this work asks of the designer to become more adept at facilitating brave conversations, negotiating difference, minimising alienation and being aware of their own position and biases. Most acutely, if a designer is going to do this work respectfully and with integrity, they need to become attuned to affect. The experience needs to be designed with consideration for the emotions and the feelings that surface in the room, as well as the atmosphere the encounter creates with respect to power, ethics and belonging.

In WonderLab, the work of exposing internal scripts is done through established tools like the break-up letter, customised methods like a mindset storyboard that declares the evolution of mindset, or a photo-elicitation activity that draws on people aligning themselves with an emotional state. Throughout a project, we might play with embodied mapping (like Penny's stand on a continuum, 4.3), or structured debriefs to return to the question of what is being exposed (like Sonali's "what did the activity reveal to you about yourself?" 7.3). The auto-ethnographic writing throughout this book is another discursive strategy that has me examining beliefs through the lens of a specific moment in time. As a Ph.D. community, we have been developing the design research practice narrative as a critical, creative research method for interrogating assumptions in our own work.

You see in Chapter 10 how the work of uncovering scripts intersects with the goal of tilling the soil. The act of (re)framing is supported by the insights that come from surfacing, just as the allegorical work and a commitment to begin from a place of empathy grants access to the multiple kaleidoscopic viewpoints. This is the place where a window into a learner's personal, internal world 1 can help make sense of their private, observable world 2. In taking the time to notice the ground you are working with and establishing the preconditions for change, it becomes possible to trigger the move from pre-contemplation to contemplation, to recognise the big assumptions that need to be reckoned with and to not dismiss the mindsets anchored at the base of the iceberg.

## 14.2 Envisaging Futures

If surfacing scripts is a reflective act that reveals the foundations by which futures are built on, the move to envisage futures is the speculative complementary step for imagining what change can be seeded (Figures 1.1, 3.1, 6.1, 13.1, 15.1). These two moves work in concert, with the promise of the imagined future forever in negotiation with the (in)tangible, experienced past. Similarly, we must acknowledge that our mental models of progress determine the future we anticipate, our well-worn mindsets prescribe our future habits and our values shape the future we aspire to. Recognising the importance of mindset to the field of Transition Design, Lockton and Candy link the work of externalising imaginaries with the need to understand people's existing conceptions of a situation and what mindsets and perspectives accompany those conceptions (5). They argue that it is through making collective and individual imaginaries tangible that they become able to be engaged with, in turn, opening up "vistas—if not always actual maps—towards different futures" (5, p. 911). Here, design can play a particular role in making people "cognisant of the context and cultures where those imaginaries are found", in turn supporting a community to co-create "deeper and more robust visions" (p. 911).

It is therefore critical to understand that shaping futures in this a learning context is not an analytic, predictive or foresight exercise, but a discursive, provocative act of inquiry into the interior lives and everyday texture of human-scaled futures (6). Anne Burdick shares the potential of narrative-based design fiction to support ruminating on individual's interior worlds and the details of everyday life. Interested in attuning to how human and nonhuman relationships are made meaningful, Burdick is concerned with imagining what happens when people make moves in future worlds. Here, design fiction frames inquiry into proximal futures by exploring:

> what will happen? What will people do and what new conditions will their choices give rise to? The answer, of course, depends on the particular people in their particular conditions, or as Le Guin says, "you listen to what the people there tell you."
>
> *(p.87)*

The act of conceptualising alternative futures can prompt participants to examine the injustices or inequities in the current system through. Introducing world-making activities early on in encounters shifts any expectation that the goal of the task is the designed world itself. Instead, they provide the platform for debating the contradictions between the emerging future and the walled past (7). It is possible for the surfacing of scripts and envisioning new futures to be done through the one activity (like a break-up letter to your future self). The intention is to consider plural futures, not to default to the predictably anticipated, nor fall for a utopian future that seemingly erases all inequities. In a paper on feminist anticipation colleagues and I ask "In doing the work to make possible feminist futures more probable, we also ask ourselves: how are we *unmaking* how hard it is, for all of us, to deviate from what is expected?" (8)[1] A consideration for temporal scale can sabotage or help this notion of critical unmaking. It can be liberating to envisage a future a century from now if you seek to detach from present day constraints. Yet, if you want to create some urgency around current realities you might to frame the time scale accordingly. Similarly, having people place the rate of change in perspective can bring to the foreground a pressing concern they wish to push to the future. At the beginning of a professional development session, I once asked design academics to write down what they most thought they needed to teach to prepare students for the future. I then got them to consider

---

1  **Hannah**. Core to this question was our commitment to wondering what feminist moves might amplify the back-talk in ways that allow the designer to tune into different frequencies. We went on to ask a series of questions: Might it be possible to tilt the back-talk of design away from the oppressive systems of the current situation towards supporting how new paths forward might be imagined? How do we reconfigure the tools of design to amplify back-talk in ways that help make the conversation more critical or inclusive? What strategies might support attuning to sensorial ways of knowing, to listening to affect and staying with the trouble of irreconcilable conditions?"

the design education they offered a decade ago (before app stores, snapchat, AI and VR), and got them to reflect on the amount of self-directed learning students who had only recently graduated were having to undertake to stay abreast of change. At the end of the session, we reconsidered what our learning priorities should be given we were not in the business of knowing what will emerge in the decade after they graduate. The answers were completely different as they moved away from design skills and strategies, towards more meta expertise in complex problem-framing, learning how to learn, models for meaningful interdisciplinary collaboration and co-creation strategies. New temporal reference points of timeframe that we are preparing graduates for (beyond the first year out) shifted the purpose that had been driving the educational experience.

The word 'envision' invites the designer to ensure this phase elevates what could otherwise be a verbal, intellectual exercise. Yet, although the term hints at affective, performative, visual and haptic activities that can immediately draw participants into a more holistic engagement with the future, it still seems to privilege what comes next. The choice to say 'envisage' is to respect that what we dream for might well be grounded in old ways from the past,[2] or what we seek to shed will be informed by the present. The straight 'What future do you predict?' question shifts when a visual activity instead explores 'What do you think the future will look like, feel like and work like for different people?' When finding the right words is hard, a selection of rhetorical images might help illuminate 'which futures feel ominous/which futures quicken your heart?'[3] Different strategies for future scenarios work as lures for critical wondering about how a feared future might be transformed into a desired future and vice versa, or whether there is another more just and equitable future you are not anticipating (10). In WonderLab, improvised play like the Playmobil video story (Figure 11.1) is used to reveal a felt experience of the hidden assumptions driving someone's beliefs around what is possible. We use card games to make visible the taken-for-granted assumptions about power, gender, equity, the climate and modernism, for example, that might need to be challenged and unlocked. Elliott's use of the 'futures wheel' can be used to wonder what alternative futures can emerge when core assumptions are rejected (5.3). The 'futures triangle' is another simple tool for holding space for the weight of history, the push of the present and the pull of the future in conceptualising a plausible future. The grounding question throughout is: whose preferred future are you designing for? Laddering a follow-up 'why' to

2   **Lisa**: *Old Ways New* is an Indigenous-led design consultancy that works with a country-centred design method to consider how we might learn from Indigenous past knowledges to envisage more sustainable futures. https://oldwaysnew.com.

3   **Myriam**: Throughout this text, but specifically in this section, I am reminded of Elaine Scarry's cautionary observation that "the vocabulary of 'creating,' 'inventing,' 'making,' 'imagining,' … is usually described as an ethically neutral or amoral phenomenon" and is "in fact laden with ethical consequence" (9, p. 22). Overt and covert violence is made in everything from the words we speak while others are not looking to the nation-states we build.

each of the questions above can be a simple, effective strategy for always return-ing to people's beliefs and blind spots.[4]

The fictional activities in this section align with speculative design specifically (12), and speculative research more broadly. But in the co-creative orientation, there is also a connection to the pedagogical constructivist encounters valued in social interactionist theory (13) and the mutual learning principles of participa-tory design. Furthermore, the philosophical grounding of the social imaginary, enacted through social contracts, values and institutions, troubles the theory and practice behind the premise that in acting in the world, we make the world (14). Threading these interdisciplinary positions together, the world-making practice of storying plausible imaginaries brings a creative form of social constructivism to the relational and systems-based work of designing (15). The work of envis-aging what comes next is not about creating a singular way forward, but more considering an array of deviating paths that allow an "imaginal diversity" to affectively and cognitively inform future decision-making (5, p. 914).

Responding to the creative imagining aspects introduced in Chapter 11, the process of envisioning and evaluating futures is deepened through the process of crafting fictions that spark affective responses. Similar to the co-evolution of the problem and solution principle, the value of envisioning future is generative to the extent new possibilities emerge while simultaneously revealing more critical understandings of the limitations and possibilities embedded in present condi-tions. There is the opportunity for an ambitious world 4 exploration, where everyone is embracing a potential world of unknown unknowns. Stretching to explore someone's world 4 might be conceived to puncture that person's indi-vidual world 2. Or a de-colonial lens might be grounded by exploring parallel possible worlds participants only know through books and media, creating an invitation to more deeply understand what the learned-yet-not-lived in world might be like to inhabit. Again, the most powerful contribution of envisioning might be the ways in which the immersive process of elaboratively encoding and storying a world 3 might, through comparison to one's own, serve to animate, reckon with and re-evaluate an individual learner's personal, internal world 1.

## 14.3 Experiencing Shifts

The exploration of yet-to-be-known worlds and unsettled beliefs seeks to sup-port ruminating on the structures and scripts that no longer serve us. This is a process of unmaking and unlearning as it is crafting something new. Through-out the practice narratives, there are repeated examples that make use of de-sign's hands-on, learning-from-doing disposition. Baked into the recursive, performative practice, there is a commitment to getting feedback from the act of

---

4   **Lisa**: These questions bring a critical, feminist lens to the more foresight orientation of Sohail
    Inayatullah's paper that presents various tools, strategies and specific questions for futures think-
    ing (11).

experiencing, iterating and prototyping. In the context of transformative learning, learner engagement is a key driver. Without engagement, the motivational drive to continue and a sense of agency to invest will likely wane. The social context of collaboration, the relational connection of felt experiences and encounters that introduce a kind of playfulness can amplify not just engagement but the subsequent benefits of belonging, drive and ownership. It is to this configuration of multiple integrated parts that the emphasis on experiential learning is signalled out.

To design encounters that have learners' experiencing the potential of where a transformation might lead them and sensing where the challenges might come from is an example of instructive feedback (15). Just as we can envisage futures and surface scripts simultaneously in one activity, we can consider the experiential component of SEED as enmeshed with the task of making visible hidden social structures and internalised scripts. We can design encounters that intentionally help the learner bump up against what might be previously invisible because it has been normalised. When we seek to transform situations we sometimes only notice what scripts are constraining us as we come up against them (16). This present-moment experiential sensing can spark wonder by attuning to what has come before and being in conversation with what comes next. From interacting with props to embodied role play to structured play-testing, there are a multitude of ways to creatively construct feedback loops for the learner and the teacher/researcher. Transitioning from contemplation towards a preparation for action, this phase moves beyond imagining to an experiential realm of knowing. The shift from a cognitive imagining to a felt experience potentially brings new dimensions to the goal of transformative engagement. The embodied knowing can present an easier path to critiquing something cognitively hard to articulate, a more accessible memory to retrieve later and a brighter memory to motivate change.

However, experiential learning is more than a type of learning activity. In the context of transformative learning, we are talking broadly of learning through doing, with active reflection and purposeful engagement. Real time, in the moment feedback. Offering a design-take on David Kolb's experiential learning cycle, (17) Stuart Candy and Kelly Kornet propose an experiential futures cycle (map, multiply, mediate, mount) that recognises the value of participants feeling their way through a concrete simulated experience of a future scenario (18). Similarly, the embodied work of Roger's Play Gym (Narrative 2.1 and Figure I.1) dives into the felt experience before ending on the debrief. In Kelly's embodied enquiry (7.3.2), the act of learning through doing begins with co-creation before moving into a place of reflecting, observing and thinking through what themes are to be revealed. There is no right place to start this cycle of experiencing. In a transformative context, it seems what is important is the dance between the performative and the purposeful, learning from the feedback that comes from intentionally enacting. Most of the time, as shown in Kolb's cycle, this is a gradual, iterative evolution that needs to be tested in stages and returned to over time.

Whereas standalone foresight or futures can prioritise setting up a way forward or something to move away from, in the transformative agenda, there is another layer of learning that ideally happens. The experiential dimension optimally engages the whole learner, with designed encounters that tap into emotions, phenomena, atmosphere, social interactions, physiological responses and cognitive inquiry. Full spectrum sensorial engagement offers a breadth of opportunities for productive disorientation and desirable difficulty. Creative engagement strategies offer a confluence of feedback from whole-bodied attunement, just as haptic and visual sense-making drives figuring, thinking and remembering. Preparation to transform from one way of being to another requires stepping outside of one's comfort zone. The experiential exercise is part dress rehearsal, a me-but-not-me stage for exploring what comes next. The act of rehearsing, akin to the practice of prototyping, works with the creative risk of stepping into the not-yet-known. For it is in this heightened vulnerable place that certain truths and insights become accessible.

A diverse range of engagement moves create a way for each individual participant to shape the internal motivation to care and/or the perspective to note obstacles in the system or limitations in their own position. To the extent that a shift to the performative is often disoriented and unsettled, an analysis of the design practice narratives in this collection reveals cracks in my previous held beliefs. Whereas once I thought that making – simply designing with my head and hands – was an embodied practice, that thinking now seems a limited repertoire for accessing deeper insights.

My practice has transformed to a place in which I repeatedly draw on strategies that once alienated me. In WonderLab, we regularly use co-creative and performative moves to counter and complement the dominance of cognitive and analytical research methods. Experiential metaphors have been adapted to support critical reflection through an emotion felt in a lived experience so they might wonder how others might feel given their differing perspectives. As an example, working from recent experiences of travel, a teacher recalled the experience of the safety belt sign being left on as if the pilot forgot to wonder what it might feel like for students to feel restrained and forgotten, with no explanation as to why they were being held back. Alibis for play, like Lego and Playmobil, or paper fortune tellers, are established strategies for engaging people with materials that take them back to another time and place, giving them the excuse to engage with different parts of themselves.[5] Repeatedly, we see people initially roll their eyes when they see playful objects upon entering a room and an hour later

---

5   **Alli**: I like to reflect on how the toys we use in these workshops are able to perform in certain ways in certain conditions. A paper triangle sitting alone on a desk might not have the ability to hold the attention of a room, or spark conversations between strangers. Yet, this very same material, when introduced as a way to get to know each other and show connections becomes charged with potential. Suddenly, the passive triangle becomes an active tool for thinking, becoming, introducing and therefore engaging the participants.

animatedly share why the mermaid, knight or construction worker Playmobil is a perfect avatar for how they feel at work. The added layer of the three-act structure in the Playmobil video deepens the improvisational engagement, with sets, scripts and spontaneous action driving serendipitous and mindful insights. WonderLab encounters often begin brief engagements with embodied play to prime participants to attune to their bodies. In framing from the outset, the potential for listening to phenomenological and physiological clues in tandem with critical reflection, we immediately disrupt and disorient learners who might arrive actively disengaged.

Beyond the immersive week-long experiential intensives of WonderLab, we have developed a community where researchers regularly invite each other to run throughs that experientially play-test workshops in development, so the researcher gets useful feedback on areas like unclear instructions, biased materials or more inclusive facilitation moves. The benefit of observing and experiencing being a learner in someone else's workshop is invaluable. Yet, perhaps the researcher-led playdate seems to be our most effective way to gather as a learning community. Distinct the familiar play-test described above, the playdate is built on values of reciprocity and relationality that require the date to be a place where everyone is learning. The basic premise is that a WonderLabber frames a shared challenge facing design researchers as: how do we bring an intention to the data we gather from workshops (video, audio, observational, reflective notes, creative outputs) in strategic ways that still allow emergent insights to be captured? Like asking a friend at a playdate what they'd like to do, the host then asks everyone around the table to reframe the proposition through the lens of their research practice. In real time, the loose structure of the learning encounter is revised to address what interests most people, and we collectively and experientially explore the topic. In the scenario above, Dion presented the idea of a forensic portrait, an equal parts analytical and creative method for interpreting a broad range of data points. We then individually evolve the idea of the forensic portrait, considering what it might mean through the lens of our independent research. At the end of the playdate, Dion is offered a feminist, equity-based, material, co-analysis and translational design (plus more) perspective on his idea. The learning benefits of elevating the relational over the transactional aspect of a learning community of practice go far beyond the deepening of any one person's PhD. As previously mentioned (12.0), we have gone on to design playdates for gathering with other research communities.

Putting the ideas signposted in Chapters 12 and 13 to work, the engagement orientation here is learning through doing, whether with props, prototypes, play-test or pilots. There is recognition that reflection and self-awareness are the active ingredient that ensures the experiencing translates into learning.[6] Attun-

---

6    **Shanti:** This reminds me of Erin Manning's book *The Minor Gesture* (19). I have written about how Manning 'explores the potential of the "minor key" that "does not have the full force of a pre-existing status, or a given structure" (p. 2), but that can unmoor or problematize the major

ing to the feedback, listening to the whole body and reflecting on how insights sit in relation to past or current narratives is how experiential lessons create a porosity between where one is and where one wants to go. Experiential learning translates the other-than-self, detached lessons of world 3 into the I-have-felt, personal experiences of world 2. This shift in learning positions the experiential lesson not as an accumulation of knowledge, but as an evaluation of knowing. In the applied practice of design, the experiential is further shaped by learning in a solution-seeking context. The goal is not to problem solve as such, but for the cognitive, emotional and physiological feedback loops to be in embodied conversation with the often real, sometimes simulated situated contexts so that preferable paths forward might light up.

## 14.4 Driving Intention

The last of the four characteristics that align transformative learning to design focuses on the interventionist impulse of design. With surfacing focused on the past, envisaging on the future, experiencing in real time, this is the temporal site for identifying an immediate course of action. To simply shift mindsets or to stand back and critique the status quo is not the end goal here. Built into SEED is an assumption that transformative change is realised when shifts in scripts translate into shifts in action. This last characteristic weds learning through doing to the importance of implementation. It is an extension of what design thinking refers to as a bias to action. For in addition to the call to experientially surface beliefs and to envision more just futures, the principle on driving transformation recognises the importance of motivations and intentions in fuelling action.

This is also the characteristic that draws most heavily on research from other disciplines. Again, an onto-epistemogical approach is called for here. The final acts of transformation come from knowing and being, coming together to recognise obstacles, create opportunities, channel motivation and foster urgency to ultimately drive commitment. There is an analytical side to this work in the setting of intentions, creating action plans and declaring accountability buddies. Yet, when we see this phase with respect to the themes of Chapter 9, we recognise that the effort is ignited by a more emotional and empowering sense of belonging, agency and internal motivation. Similarly, the mindset lesson of declaring obstacles and challenges in advance is as important as fixing a vision of a desired outcome.

Two theories from psychology are worth noting here: Hazel Markus's concept of Possible Selves (21) and Gabriel Oettingen's theory of mental contrasting (22). For Markus, a cultural psychologist, possible selves are representations

---

structures that it courses through. As she describes it, the minor has a sort of freedom and unpredictability that although "narrated as secondary" has the scope to "initiate the subtle shifts that [create] the conditions for …change" (p. 1). It therefore holds the political potential to unsettle, divert or enable new ways of being and doing. (20)

of individuals' ideas of both what they would like to become, and what they are afraid of becoming. This perspective acknowledges that an individual's cognition, emotions and motivations shape and are shaped by the many cultural contexts they inhabit. Oettingen's research into mental contrasting explores this idea of the future we envisage from the developmental psychology perspective of goal-setting. Oettingen's research is critical of positive psychology's focus on mental visualisations of only desirable futures. It proposes mental contrasting as a reality-bound and solution-focused practice of dreaming. In the app WOOP, (23) Oettingen guides the user through the steps of identifying a wish, declaring an outcome, owning the obstacles and planning how to achieve the goal. According to Oettingen's research, the act of grounding the wish in the reality of how hard it might be to achieve increases the likelihood of achieving the desired outcome. Just as affect and imagination are baked into the first two steps, the last two are grounded by a sobering inquiry into how realistic the dream is and what strategy will be used to work around challenges.

We have adopted variations on this research in learning encounters for organisations interested in channelling people's internal motivation to realise challenging long-term goals. Participants begin by mindfully considering a professional goal they would like to achieve in three to five years, naming what the outcome will be, and how they will know they have achieved what they set out to do. Then, participants wholeheartedly imagine completing it. They visualise the moment of completion and are asked to feel the exhilaration, pride and relief they might experience. The next step is to counter the felt optimism and enthusiasm by concretely identifying all the reasons it might not happen, naming what will get in the way (for example, shifting priorities, self-doubt, inability to delegate, limited resources, lack of management support). There is a moment here to reassess if the goal is realistic and potentially to start over or revise the goal in the face of internal, structural or cultural obstacles. Once the goal seems right-sized and the obstacles surmountable, the move is to intentionally plan how instrumental behaviour can overcome or workaround the often undeclared obstacles. Oettingen calls this 'If/Then' planning. For example, *if* I find the resources are limited, *then* I will review the project scope and resource expenditure rather than table it altogether, or *if* my line manager pushes a new project before this is complete, *then* I will ask to debate the consequences of this project being sidelined to buy more time.

At WonderLab, we have experimented with many variations of how these steps might be navigated. We have designed elaborate, bespoke materials designed for specific institutions, pre-populating the kind of projects, challenges and goals for easy visual reference and mapping of a team's collective work. Or when a more discursive, team-building approach is appropriate, we use embodied, storytelling prompts where people pitch their ambitions to a colleague multiple times until the 'why' of the project narrative aligns with their internal motivation, rather than simply espousing the corporate agenda. Then, people roam the room stopping to pitch an obstacle with a peer so they might co-create the work around strategies. We have also often fallen back on a simple tetrahedron template (printed onto blue sky backgrounds) to allow for a deeper figuring of the foundational purpose (the base), a consideration of what the adjacent component parts are, what projects need to come together (the three sides) and how one face of the tetrahedron relates to the other (the paper tabs that hold it together). These different visual, embodied and material prompts generate artefacts and narratives that allow people to turn desired future fantasies into binding goals that engage with present reality.

In our collaborations with Riverdale Country School and PLUSSED+, Kevin Mattingly always pushed us to integrate the learning post the workshop. The contribution design makes to disrupting professional development as usual in creating what game designers and play theorists would call a 'magical circle' was evident to both of us. Kevin could see that from the moment people entered a room they sensed how it was not a didactic space where they would be preached to. However, his critique of design was often around its implementation. The engagement was strong, the participation productive, the curiosity infectious but the follow through needed more attention. This is where his attention to the science of learning helped us consider the RISE and BEAM research to ensure the engaging experiences became grounded in practice and drove sustained transformation. Emergent neuroscience research reveals the similarities between how we recall the recent past and simulate the near future, identifying the remembering and imagining systems as co-configured (24; 25). Psychologists use the term 'integration' for reconciling this new knowing with the old – the step Mezirow refers to as 'settling'. Tools like the commitment devices that psychology uses to help restrain bad habits or invest in desired habits became an intentional part of how we would close out this work (Figure 13.0). Over the years, Wonder-Lab has experimented with what kinds of commitment devices work in specific contexts or with specific audiences. At WonderLab, we regularly use the website FutureMe.org as the last step in a workshop, (26) creating space for participants to send an email to themselves that they want to read one week, one month, one year from now. This opens space for the learner to choose what kind of email to send to their future selves. Do they channel the wish fulfilment side of WOOP (a celebratory 'we did it and it feels great' email), or dig into the planning phase (setting clear expectations, workarounds and benchmarks) or a witty break-up letter to a limiting belief they want to let go of. Sometimes we get them to consider the kind of email they would normally send and then invite them to try out the opposite to their default approach. The *Archipelago of Possibilities* professional learning game, designed by Isabella Brandalise, Ricardo Dutra Gonçalves, Sophie Riendeau and Ker Thao, alternatively helps teachers create a tangible, encoded representation of the lesson they want to keep front of mind once they return to the classroom (27). One teacher scrunched up a map to remember that teaching should never be led by the lesson plan, another teacher placed the 'souvenir' in her top desk drawer, yet another months later still had his hanging on the rear-view mirror. The project concludes with a metaphoric commitment to how are you going to visit the islands to do the work, with people elaborating on their choices of minesweeper (to push through the school politics), on stilts (to find a new way of walking) or by submarine (so I can go undercover). In *Making Space*, Dion Tuckwell had teachers take polaroids of themselves standing beside the planet constellations they had created of their desired future practice to keep the workshop alive in their imaginary (28).

When Helen Chen and I were keynote speakers at an AAC&U conference, we decided our address (interrupted by a quick interactive 10-minute hands-on photo-elicitation exercise) needed to extend to commitment device postcards for the 1,000 delegates. Collaborating with Alli Edwards, we had delegates choose the type of commitment that would elevate the chance of them taking one idea from the conference and putting it into practice. Our research goal was to see what kind of commitment prompt worked for this community. One postcard invited rumination and reflection for the journey home on what mental model or existing practice the trip to the conference had unsettled. Another was an invitation to draw on the research around accountability and how partnering with a buddy significantly increases the likelihood of following through (29). Yet another detailed the why, when, what and how of a goal and the corresponding 'If/Then' statement to bolster the belief that change could be strategically embraced. We quickly came to see how one postcard completely missed the mark. The postcard that had previously worked well with university students included an attached temporary tattoo. The embodied commitment device came with instructions to apply it the day the person sought to commit fully to the work once back home. This prompt worked for university students making a visible commitment that provoked discussion with peers. But not surprisingly, it was easy to sense that the conference audience of university administrators, although appreciative of the novelty, would not follow through by wearing the tattoo to publicly signal change. For even if some of design's currency lies with the capacity to make the (intended) transformation known, so it might be telegraphed, committed to and evaluated, we must not forget (as we did) to remember the audience and pay attention to what is working for whom.

There are many more structural and cultural changes that support implementation. The ideas above would be complemented by strategies to establish online forums that foster personalised learning communities, or failure fairs that actively seek to shift risk-adverse cultures to ones of experimentation, and the critical role of ongoing coaching and peer mentoring as the learner negotiates the real world of integrating changes. The types of drivers acknowledged in this section speak more directly to the work that can be done in the context of the learning encounter itself, to prime the settling of what has been learned and scaffold the implementation that will result in new practices.

The decision to map the terrain of SEED comes from a belief that design both over claims the extent to which an encounter might have lasting impact on participants and underplays the significance of what happens when we wonder through designing learning. I think of the envisaging and experiencing as the

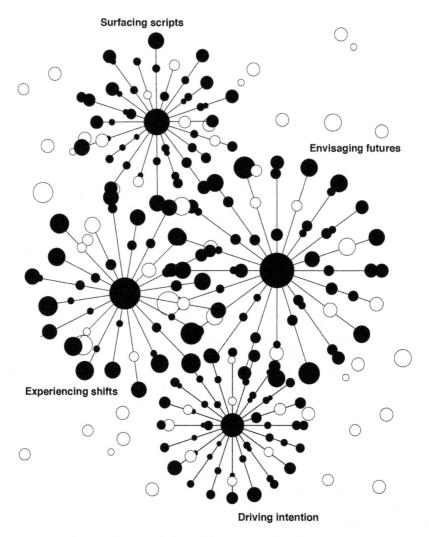

Surfacing scripts

Envisaging futures

Experiencing shifts

Driving intention

FIGURE 14.2 **The Pedagogical Sites of SEED**: The acronym SEED does not evoke a linear process, but more a diaspora of seeds that can travel, not just geographically across terrain, but back and forth in time. Engaging with the past, the future, the present moment and the next steps, the temporal options within SEED allow for small moves and grand gestures, single events and sustained programs for change. More dandelion than acorn, this is less about planting a new behaviour or belief and more an intent to fertilise ways of wondering that support a holistic, integrated approach aligned to the complex nature of shift work.

component parts design most regularly falls back on. And, I see the potential of amplifying our capacity in the experiencing and driving realms. Using extra-rational moves to support the surfacing of what is directing much of our knowing-doing-being and being more intentional in how to implement and integrate change post the encounter seem easy ways into driving change that holds the course.

Circling back to the worlds in 13.3, the emphasis here is how design supports transformation by bringing the participant/learner's lived worlds to the expansive worlds of the possible and the potential. We oftentimes attend to parts of SEED without recognising the extent to which they are all entangled and in need of some separate attention. The transformation may be years in the making, it can be recursive or even perpetual. A conscious interplay between pragmatism and imagination, integration here is not so much a final state, but a moment to pause and consider what wondering should follow.

## Bibliography

1 Chen, Helen et al. "Changing Records of Learning through Innovations in Pedagogy and Technology." *Educause Review*, March, 2016.
2 Grocott, Lisa. "We Get the Behaviour We Reward: The Design of Alternate Records of Learning." *Medium*, 2020.
3 Ramos, Fabiane and Laura Roberts. "Wonder as Feminist Pedagogy: Disrupting Feminist Complicity with Coloniality." *Feminist Review*, vol. 128, no. 1, 2021, pp. 28–43, doi:10.1177/01417789211013702.
4 Mignolo, Walter D. "Delinking." *Cultural Studies*, vol. 21, no. 2–3, 2007, pp. 449–514, doi:10.1080/09502380601162647.
5 Lockton, Dan and Stuart Candy. *A Vocabulary for Visions in Designing for Transitions*, Proceedings of Design Research Society (DRS2018), University of Limerick, Ireland, 1 June 2018.
6 Burdick, Anne. "Designing Futures from the Inside. " *Journal of Futures Studies*, vol. 23, no. 3, 2019, pp. 75–92, doi:10.6531/JFS.201903_23(3).0006.
7 Inayatullah, Sohail. "Can Education Transform?: Contradictions between the Emerging Future and the Walled Past." *Futures and Foresight Science*, vol. 2, no. 1, 2020, p. e27, doi:10.1002/ffo2.27.
8 Korsmeyer, Hannah et al. "Understanding Feminist Anticipation through 'Back-talk': 3 Narratives of Willful, Deviant, and Care-full Co-Design Practices." *Futures*, 2021.
9 Scarry, Elaine. *The Body in Pain*. Oxford University Press, 1987.
10 Dator, Jim. "The Futures of Cultures and Cultures of the Future." *Perspectives on Cross-Cultural Psychology*, edited by Anthony J Marsella et al., Academic Press, 1979, pp. 369–88.
11 Inayatullah, Sohail. "Six Pillars: Futures Thinking for Transforming." *Foresight*, vol. 10, no. 1, 2008, pp. 4–21, doi:10.1108/14636680810855991.
12 Dunne, Anthony and Fiona Raby. *Speculative Everything: Design, Fiction, and Social Dreaming*. The MIT Press, 2013.
13 Kozulin, Alex. *Vygotsky's Educational Theory in Cultural Context*. Cambridge University Press, 2007.
14 Zaidi, Leah. "Worldbuilding in Science Fiction, Foresight, and Design." *Journal of Futures Studies*, vol. 2, 2019, p. 12, doi:10.6531/JFS.201906_23(4).0003.
15 Grocott, Lisa et al. "The Becoming of a Designer: An Affective Pedagogical Approach to Modelling and Scaffolding Risk-Taking." *Art, Design & Communication in Higher Education*, vol. 18, no. 1, 2019, pp. 99–112, doi:10.1386/adch.18.1.99_1.
16 Ahmed, Sara. *On Being Included Racism and Diversity in Institutional Life*. Duke University Press, 2012.
17 Kolb, David. *Experiential Learning: Experience as a Source of Learning and Development*. Prentice Hall, 1984.

18 Candy, Stuart and Kelly Kornet. "Turning Foresight inside Out: An Introduction to Ethnographic Experiential Futures." *Journal of Futures Studies*, vol. 23, no. 3, 2019, pp. 3–22.

19 Manning, Erin. *The Minor Gesture*. Duke University Press, 2013.

20 Sumartojo, Shanti and Matthew Graves. "Rust and Dust: Materiality and the Feel of Memory at Camp Des Milles." *Journal of Material Culture*, vol. 23, no. 3, 2018, pp. 328–43, doi:10.1177/1359183518769110.

21 Markus, Hazel R. and Paula Nurius. "Possible Selves: The Interface between Motivation and the Self-Concept." *Self and Identity: Psychosocial Perspectives*, edited by Krysia Yardley and Terry Honess, Routledge and Kegan Paul, 1987, pp. 157–72.

22 Oettingen, Gabriele et al. "Mental Contrasting and Goal Commitment: The Mediating Role of Energization." *Personality and Social Psychology Bulletin*, vol. 35, no. 5, 2009, pp. 608–22, doi:10.1177/0146167208330856.

23 "Home." *WOOP*, nd, www.woopmylife.org/en/home.

24 Conway, Martin A. et al. "The Formation of Flashbulb Memories." *Memory & Cognition*, vol. 22, no. 3, 1994, pp. 326–43, doi:10.3758/BF03200860.

25 Schacter, Daniel L. et al. "The Future of Memory: Remembering, Imagining, and the Brain." *Neuron*, vol. 76, no. 4, 2012, pp. 677–94, doi:10.1016/j.neuron.2012.11.001.

26 "Write a Letter to the Future." *FutureMe*, 2021, www.futureme.org.

27 McEntee, Kate. "Archipelago of Possibilities: Priming Teachers to Reflect on Intrinsic Motivations for Change." Report, 2016, pp. 1–11, www.iletc.com.au/wp-content/uploads/2016/03/archipelago-report-for-ILETC-project.pdf.

28 Tuckwell, Dion. *Joining Practice Research*, 2021. Monash University, PhD Thesis, doi:10.26180/14533521.v1.

29 Newland, Stephen. "The Power of Accountability." *Association for Financial Counselling & Planning Education*, 2018.

# 15

# SHIFT WORK ELABORATED

## A Contingent Conclusion

FIGURE 15.1  **Climate (in)Action**: This WonderLab workshop, facilitated by Ilya
Fridman and Alli Edwards, translates Kari Marie Norgaard's (1) research into why people informed about climate change still fail to act
and Susan David's research into our inner worlds and our actions (2) by
exploring Alli's research into the agency of materials as co-facilitators.

DOI: 10.4324/9780429429743-19

The previous chapters in this section have revealed practice knowing frameworks and narratives that speak from a place I have come to know intimately, knowing that has been integrated into ways of being. Yet, a commitment to ongoing transformation is going to ask the learner to be disoriented and begin the process of stepping again into the not-yet-known one more. Shift work requires a disposition to learn forever. Just as Mezirow continued to rethink his ideas, I continue to revise my own.[1]

I confidently begin by integrating the connection between Mezirow's ten phases and the SEED framework. I end by tentatively wondering what it would mean to position the design work of transformation as more relational than participatory. I revisit and expand the *Make* constellation (Figure 4.3), further wondering what kinds of making are asked of the designer and what kinds of making emerge from a process of transformation. I ground what the Indigenous narratives showed to me and challenged the very idea that new futures are something to be envisioned anew, not reclaimed from the past. These final wonderings evidence the flux of transformative learning, that change begets more change.

An intentional performance of intellectual humility (2) has called for a promiscuous intermingling of frameworks and models in Part IV. Consider how the perspectives and alternate dimensions bump up against each other as refractions from the turn of a kaleidoscope. Any temporary fixing of these component parts will fail to represent the multi-dimensional, multivariate nature of transformative work. Productively resisting that they ideas become locked into a tidy sequence or typology, these final pages, ensure different parts of the book are juxtaposed and enmeshed. This intermingling brings into focus what aspects of the work are ready to be committed to and what nascent ideas are sources for future wondering disorientation. Use this chapter to note for yourself what knowing feels settled and ready to internalise, and what wonderings keep your curious. Make room for new perspectives to emerge and new potentials to be realised.

## 15.1 Transformative Learning Reconfigured

The concluding move here is to entwine Mezirow's more cognitive and action-oriented phases with the creative *Making Design* constellation (Figure 13.2) and the experiential, affective moves of the SEED practice (Figure 14.2). This intentional interleaving of already introduced concepts brings a kaleidoscopic lens to the translation of ideas about transformative shifts from education, design and psychology (Figure 15.2).

---

1   **Lisa**: In 2000, Mezirow simplified his ten-phase process into a simpler four-part theory. At that point in his work, he distilled the phases down into: elaborating on existing frames of reference, learning new frames, transforming habits of mind and shifting points of view (3).

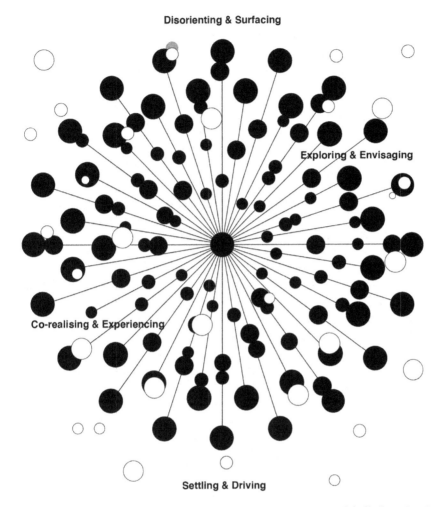

Disorienting & Surfacing

Exploring & Envisaging

Co-realising & Experiencing

Settling & Driving

FIGURE 15.2 **Seeding Shift Work**: Here, the sites of inquiry labelled in SEED and enmeshed with Mezirow's phases of Transformative Learning. In braiding together lessons from design, psychology and education we seek to draw on "reflective and affective wonder" as "an animating force by which the individual can be in constant movement into and out of the imagination, into and out of the conscious and unconscious self" (4, p. 94).

## 15.1.1 Disorienting and Surfacing

In Mezirow's initial moves, there is a commitment to the act of attuning to one's position in relation to the past and present. Mezirow names a disorienting dilemma and a critical assessment of assumptions as the first two phases. This epistemic rumination is the foundation of the surfacing positions aspect of

SEED and the illuminating potential of design to *make sense* and *make visible*.[2] Disorientation works here as the invitation for self-examination and uniting provocation to proactively identify the perspective shift that needs to happen. The stories of practice shared here *make visible* how as researchers and educators we must reckon with our own assumptions just as much as our learners must identify and label their own cognitive wobbles or felt dissonance. Getting curious about what is in conflict, what the tension is, what would be lost and why it matters is how we come to know ourselves, our beliefs, our biases and our assumptions.

Each auto-ethnographic story here further unsettled some epistemic beliefs that I only partially owned in the initial moment of disorientation. You too will have to take the time to unearth, unmake and undo what came up for you when reading stories that resonated, infuriated, challenged or glimpsed perspectives familiar or foreign to your own. My invitation to you is to stop reading and to write your own narrative around a disorienting dilemma that helps you identify foundational assumptions you did not know were there. Make aware your own position, make sense of what you tacitly know, make visible the implications of your practice and you will already be on the way to transforming your practice. As an educator, normalise for learners that this stage is the hardest. Be upfront that this phase will bring emotions to the surface. We cannot go through significant epistemic shifting without bringing up emotions from surprise and shame to loss and optimism.[3] Use play to dive deeper or creative self-distancing to make it easier to stay in the discomfort of critically assessing assumptions. For design, this will challenge the bias to action and resist the impulse to fix problems. Slow down. Be intentional and prepared when stepping into the space of what comes next.

2   **Ricardo**: I think "surfacing" is a good word; however, I think it does not get to the root of awareness. Many times people do not have a conscious understanding of the beliefs they have internalised or the stories they tell themselves. I find make aware a more accurate way of labelling this sensing process of listening to one's body. If we understand intuition as processing multi-sensorial data, then I quite like how bringing awareness feels open to future potential and not just past action. **Sonali**: I understand my facilitation practice as designing for contemplation, a process I initially understood as using artefacts to make visible youth's trauma and dreams. Once I began to integrate the science of learning and more designerly moves it became more intentionally about a practice of meaning-making and memory-making the past and the future simultaneously

3   **Sonali**. As facilitators repeating the same activities, we came to notice that on different days, different emotions surface for the same individual. The more we repeat activities the more space created for sitting with the youths' array of emotions. As facilitators, we learned to live with the tears, to sit with the pain, trauma and loss until it passed. We came to see how on the other side of fears and sorrow, hope could find a home.

## 15.1.2 Exploring and Envisaging

For Mezirow, the phases happen somewhat in a sequence, yet I stand with others who find the "process of perspective transformation to be more recursive, evolving, and spiralling in nature" (5, pp. 43–44). With a focus on considering future behaviour, Mezirow originally saw phases three and four as an exploration of the disorienting dilemma in relation to others seeking to negotiate a similar perspective shift. Yet, if we understand these orientations from a creative perspective, it becomes possible to see how disorientation might follow, not precede, being unsettled by an envisioned future. Creative strategies for exploration address Mezirow's call to relate discontent in a shared space and understand new behaviour. This future inflection is embedded in the SEED commitment to envisage and the invocation to *make possible* to *make fun*. It creates a possible world platform by which people can speculatively engage in, believe in and commit to new ways forward. In sharing an understanding of what is possible with others, Mezirow moves into new territory. In this more generative space, room is made for affect, fictions, reframing and allegory to light up ways that might deviate from what has come before. Transformation, no longer limited to what is known, instead imagines what could be. In this emancipatory space, a more playful disposition is encouraged and a more affective engagement is desired. This perspective shift might be as small as seeing yourself as someone capable of creative writing or bold like envisaging white supremacy as something that is routinely called out in your workplace or as audacious as a country coordinating a commitment to net zero emissions. Whatever the scale, there is no getting around the need for people to engage emotionally if you hope to motivate them to do the shift work required to imagine a different future. Whatever the context, introduce equity pauses to consider how this future might do harm or exclude others. Commit to deviating from futures that lock in power imbalances, perpetuate social injustices and foreclose on self-determination.[4]

For me this transformation required exploring an interpretative role for design as the translator of research from unfamiliar disciplines. The thinking, figuring and discussing we did in developing the 'design research praxis narrative' (DRPN) in WonderLab is an example of an active place where we imagined how a new research method could build on auto-ethnography, the science of emotional granularity and affect theory.[5] For you, find a method that aligns with

---

4   **Stacy:** Self-determination isn't some *thing* a self or a collection of like-minded people possess and exert, but rather actions or doings that take form in relation to other actions and doings. The personal and our evolving understandings of the "auto" in auto-ethnography are what Tony Adams and I (2008) describe as 'relational accomplishments'; this relational, becoming-with orientation to the self acknowledges that any sense of a self or the personal is composed and constituted in and through our subjective, everyday and emergent relationships to other beings and things (6).
5   **Lisa**: The DRPN, first explored in a WonderLab intensive, was refined over time with colleagues Stacy Holman Jones, Hannah Korsmeyer and Alli Edwards. An evolution of the

your motivation to envisage and explore the lessons from the book that might propel you towards new ways of showing up in the world.

### 15.1.3 Co-realising and Experiencing

The experiential orientation design brings to learning and the social interactions at the heart of participatory encounters sits adjacent to three phases Mezirow places further apart. For Mezirow, phase five is the place where there is a self-reckoning with the shame or guilt that might come with looking differently upon old habits or set beliefs. Emotional granularity can be bought to convivial activities where social co-creation promotes a collective space for parallel introspection. Similarly, fictional scenarios, detailed storyboards or analogous spaces offer story-making tools for making emerging tensions, paradoxes and contradictions tangible. The SEED emphasis on embodied rehearsal aligns with Mezirow's commitment to creating space to fail before succeeding. The challenge here is to design encounters that allow people to provisionally, playfully try new roles (phase six) and build competence and confidence through trying out such roles over time (phase nine). Standing with Mezirow, I believe shift work is less hard when supported by deep social relationships. Co-creation that evokes a prototypical mindset invites an interleaving of self-examination with a collaborative commitment to experiential engagement. This whole-of-self reflexive conversation can then attune to the feedback from participatory prototyping, embodied knowing and explicit reflection in and on action. This transition from a cognitive imagining to a felt experiencing cracks open the shared 'aha' moments that come with co-realising.

The transformative opening for me during this period comes from the Design Rounds where I witnessed, engaged in and navigated my emotional response to learning practices unfamiliar to me. Yet, without the trusting, learning environment of the WonderLab intensives, I might have struggled to provisionally role play how to integrate these new insights. The hands-on Design Rounds would unlikely have translated to lasting change without an experimental stage for rehearsing new ways of doing. For you, engaging with wondering questions alone will not be enough. Potential transformation will be heightened by conversations with peers around what narratives are unsettling. Real change might take hold if you intentionally question what needs to be unlearned, if you acknowledge the weight of past choices and find safe places to experiment with

---

auto-ethnographic narratives in this text the DRPN has now been applied to the critical, creative process of accounting for and answering to the embodied, partial perspectives of praxis. **Hannah**: I am curious about how design encounters take shape and shape us in return. So for me, the praxis narrative allowed me to wonder how personal, politicised, perspectives (like feminism) are manifested in and through collaborative, material practice. I could wonder how I, the designer, am also implicated within and affected by material engagements and co-design events. With respect to transformation, I could question the possibilities and constraints in the agency of designers to affect change.

ideas that are equal parts foreign and compelling. Even if event-based encounters do not always afford time to instil confidence or competence, the potential of experiential learning can amplify opportunities for participants to, at the least, build sensorial memory traces that cue the body as to how change might feel.

### 15.1.4 Settling and Driving

In the SEED framework and Mezirow's phases, there is a pragmatic acknowledgement that the work on implementing change requires planning. The intrinsic motivation and intention identified in SEED's driving transformation aligns with Mezirow's planning a course of action and acquiring the knowledge and skills to integrate lessons into practice. Through this lens, the earlier phases position the *make believe* work as part of the pre-contemplation period of this transformational process. In the case studies, the reference to *make believe* acknowledged the power of design to forge prototypes that ask 'what if...?'. Yet, for believing to be internalised we need to convert an imagined possibility into an optimistic commitment. We need to catalyse the motivation and agency of making believe into making change. This is not a once-and-done change, but an intentional settling into new ways of being. Mezirow's final phase involves reintegrating the perspective reframed by the initial disorienting dilemma into one's life. Phase ten underscores this moment of integration is about more than anticipating workarounds to overcome obstacles. This moment of (re)integration is about staying the course. Settling what was once unsettled is change of an onto-epistemological nature, change that calls for a new way of knowing and being. Driving transformation becomes an ongoing commitment to always be unsettling and settling anew. A learning flywheel of continuous curiosity is how we sustain momentum, endure setbacks, keep evolving and drive transformation.[6]

Writing this book, my flywheel was driven by the impulse to interleave three distinct, yet I believe complementary knowledge systems. A multi-method approach forged a translational plan to identify my own worldviews through auto-ethnography, in conversation with science of learning principles, as applied through a creative practice. The intentional epistemic enmeshing of a subjective lens, evidence-based research and practice knowing proved an animating force for driving my own transformation. For you to settle a newfound perspective, identify a specific practice move you want to put into action. The wobble that first knocked you off course will try to remain a stabilising force. Resist defaulting to what is comfortable. Build competency through mindful, deliberate practice. This might be through making a commitment device, planning for how not

---

6   **Lisa**: Jim Collins uses the Flywheel metaphor to describe how change does not come from one single defining action or grand program. The Flywheel metaphor captures the enduring struggle of relentlessly pushing a heavy flywheel, turn upon turn, until a level of momentum activates and breakthroughs are made. www.jimcollins.com/concepts/the-flywheel.html.

to revert to habits and finding an accountability buddy. Normalise a process that rewards discomfort and uncertainty.

This is the area I challenge design to more consciously act upon. The solution-seeking, action-oriented side of design can be quick to fix a problem, yet not consider the implications of new unforeseen challenges. When it comes to creating learning encounters, design can rely too heavily on the in-the-moment energetic high of generative co-creating. We need to more realistically curate experiences that position the event as the beginning and attend more explicitly to the 'what next'. Beyond anchoring a learner's motivation, we must scaffold the next move that integrates the practice shift. Identifying beliefs, dreaming big and creating memorable encounters are only part of the equation. We need to get better at driving transformation home.

## 15.2 A Practice Reclaimed

I am surprised to acknowledge how the auto-ethnographic process of writing in the present about my situated learning from the past has served the transformation process. Design's future-oriented disposition and reflection-in- and on-action had not predisposed me to look to the past. Over the decades, I have told myself quite different stories of my past learning experiences. The focus on retrieving transformative learning experiences allowed previously ignored stories to be bought up from the archives. This literary form of retrieval did more than strengthen my memory traces, it changed the story.

Having lived for decades away from the land of my Indigenous ancestors, I felt untethered from the place and people that grounded my experiences of identifying as a young Māori woman. The act of reflexively revisiting the stand-off with my professor in the final year of my undergraduate degree as well as the total-immersion Māori language class operated on multiple levels. Writing from a temporal distance made space for me to see how my fight was not with my professor alone and more with white supremacy's disinterest in decolonising the curriculum. With this reframing came a perspective shift that allows the lessons to be less personal and more transferable. Candidly writing an affective narrative about how I felt in the Māori elder's office or sitting at the circle with my fellow Māori students bought to the surface my misplaced arrogance *and* how these formative experiences forever changed me. Rosi Braidotti's term 'process-ontology' locates the seemingly epistemic shift asked of me as also calling for an ontological and nomadic process of becoming (7). This attuning to who I was before and who I was afterwards illuminates how profound the disorientation and integration was, while the constellation of subsequent narratives respect shifting as an ongoing process that is always in flux and never done.

If these values became core to the researcher, educator and designer I am today long ago, why am I highlighting the transformative currency of the autoethnographic experience? Simply because the narratives shifted my current perspective on envisaging futures. Much of this book argues for an envisioned future as where new ways, new lessons and new habits will be made clear. Mezirow talks of rehearsing future roles until new knowing settles. The auto-ethnographic narratives signal that perspective shifts might emerge from examining past knowing, past doing and past being. Here is a knowing that is already settled, where the doing and being are hiding in plain sight.[7]

Living in Aotearoa, there were systems, communities, policies and mandates that scaffolded the work of rehearsing the future self I wanted to become. I found myself in a room of peers playfully learning *te reo* because of a cultural commitment and support for stopping the language from dying (Narrative 1.1). Because the university had built anti-racist policies and practices, I had an advocate and did not fail my final year at university (Narrative 3.1). In moving to countries in which the focus on diversity often sidelined Indigenous peoples, I felt stranded. If our identities are shaped by how others see us, then I understood my place as a white Māori in Aotearoa while not knowing how to belong as an Indigenous person in these foreign lands. Back in the playground of my childhood, I could claim my Indigenous self along ancestral lines, yet did not know how to own my lived experiences. If I performed my indigeneity, it felt more political than embodied. Yet, in crafting the auto-ethnographic narratives, I could see how the genesis of those Indigenous lessons had travelled with me. My practice commitments to storytelling, reciprocity, non-verbal communication and metaphoric thinking make evident that these and other Indigenous experiences had settled into my being. The decades long evolution also makes clear that transformation comes in small, yet profound instalments.

Mezirow acknowledges the importance of rehearsing and practicing. Yet, what if the task is as much about unlearning? Might reclaiming past rehearsals be key, like when we primed teachers to think back to a time they had been agents of change? Could we create learning organisations not by framing what new practices, mindsets and processes we need but by remembering the last time we rehearsed chasing curiosity, sought feedback or learned from failure? Time travelling need not be limited to envisioning the future but also envisaging a rehearsal when you knew your mark and your lines. Traveling to the past, for example, a childhood body memory of play, might help people find the courage and wisdom to step onto the stage in this new context. An act of retrospective sense-making could expose anew what is settled yet unclaimed – in turn granting agency to the learner to consciously deploy this past knowing in the future (8).[8]

---

7　**Shanti**: This account of how understanding might move forward as we think about what has already happened really resonates with me. This has a parallel in how I think of the materials created through research processes – as images, texts, conversations and impressions that travel forward with us, never quite finished or closed off. We can think of these artefacts not as 'representing' the past or as 'capturing' something in the world that is separate from us, but rather as lively possibilities that continue to offer potential insight or inquiry as they configure and reconfigure over time.

8　**Lisa**: Reflecting on Mignolo's framing of decolonising the mind, I wonder what it might look like to not centre theoretical cultural constructs when epistemic de-linking. What does

The relational, lived experiences privileged in Indigenous knowing complement the epistemic perspectives of scientific evidence-based data and social research empirical data. I did not set out to do Indigenous auto-ethnography, and
yet I am curious now to trace the ways my whole-body, relational, playful orientation to learning through practice was seeded decades ago. The *8 Ways*[9] project
introduces Aboriginal pedagogical processes as a starting point to be evolved in
conversation with the complex, nuanced specific knowledge of each local community. Of note is how *8 Ways* maps the vectors between ways of valuing, ways
of being, ways of knowing and ways of doing. In this book, the stories and the
science, the purpose and the practices all seek to similarly enmesh the integrative
complexity of the subject.

A conscious attempt to re-link to the *te reo* (language) of my ancestors had me
comparing definitions of what it means to design. In the Oxford dictionary, the
verb 'design' is defined as deciding upon the "look or function" of a building,
garment or object (9). In contrast, the Māori word for design, *whakaahua*, is defined as "to acquire form, transform" (10). The Māori word in a sentence evokes a
poetic lens for considering the shape-shifting agency of designing. *Kātahi ka whakaahua i a ia ki te kererū* in translation becomes "Then he transformed himself into
a pigeon." In reflecting on the transformative journey of authoring this book,
I have moved between intimate narratives and birds-eye views, travelled across
countries and back in time, renounced old mentors and found new collaborators.
I have been changed by the perspective shifts revealed, claimed and internalised.
I have acquired new form.

## 15.3 The Dimensions of Relational Design

Reflecting on times we might fail to be transformed reminds us that rehearsal
spaces are about more than time. They are about values, accountability and commitments. In a sports team, you might learn to acknowledge the assist as much as
the goal scorer, only to shut down that behaviour if the next year your team does
not see the connection between goals and teamwork. You might be celebrated
in one workplace for being a vulnerable leader to be chided in another for the
same behaviour.

Transformative learning sticks when conditions support, reward and respect
the newfound behaviour. For nascent skills to move beyond the budding stage

onto-epistemic de-linking look like? When I think of the Indigenous ways fostered in early
adulthood I wonder what it means to emphasise a re-connecting to those ways of being and
knowing. I am left wondering how, upon learning new ways, I might have been more able to
de-couple from the dominant, at the same time still provincial, script of modernity.

9    The 8ways pedagogical framework includes: Story Sharing, Learning Maps, Non-verbal, Symbols and Images, Land Links (place-based learning), Non-linear, Deconstruct/Reconstruct
(working from wholes to parts) and Community Links. A wooden learning tool is introduced
to facilitate understanding and to bring a cultural orientation to how Aboriginal people learn.
www.8ways.online/about.

into internalised knowing, we need safe, supportive spaces that scaffold the full transition from table read to closing night.

To understand design as an integrative practice is to recognise that there are multiple dimensions at play in any given context. Complex entanglements erased or sanitised by hypothesis testing a single independent variable are equally not well-served by the modern framing of design as productive problem solving. What would it take to deepen design's integrative and interventionist capacity to make in the face of all those interdependent, incommensurate variables? I believe we would need to learn as designers, researchers and educators when to take action, when to pause, when to look to the past, when to unlearn, when to speculate, when to be bold and when to compromise.

In my 20s, Zora Neale Hurston's promise that 'there are years that ask questions and years that answer' resonated with longed for future certainty (11). In my 50s, I would lengthen the sentence to say 'years that answer with more questions'. Beyond reconfiguring what designers *make*, I am now drawn to knottier questions about what design making is in relation to? A co-design practice might begin with a participatory orientation to learning in relation to others, be shaped by a material orientation to inquiry and be grounded by situated contexts – but these are only some of the dimensions the act of designing transformative learning calls for. In previous writing, my co-authors and I ask "The importance of the relational orientation of ...design gestures cannot be dismissed when it comes to engaging in the difficult labour of imagining futures that do not reproduce the everyday inequalities we have become used to" (12, p. nd).

I am now wondering how a *relational* co-design practice might attune to more than the people and the artefacts. The idea of relational learning gives primacy to the school-based relationship between teachers and students to propel motivation and shape curriculum, (13) whereas here I am wondering how relational design might work with the more-than-human and whole-self dimensions. Given the diverse registers design is in relation-with, how might we expansively understand an inter- and intra-relational approach? What does it mean to also be in relation with the mindsets, interactions, movements, affect, the local situation and broader systems? A relational practice would call on the designer to pull back and see the whole, notice the parts, make sense of the connections, acknowledge the mutability, get comfortable with not-knowing, respect the tensions, take care of the planet and be accountable to oneself. A relational orientation to designing would be one that holds space for the sensorial, psychological, social, conceptual, technological,[10] temporal, geographical, political, ethical, cultural, structural and custodial dimensions of our entanglements. My hunch is that a

---

10 **Lisa**: I have questioned whether to use the word material or technological in reference to the role form-making plays in the memory-making, sense-making, meaning-making practice of learning. In a digitally saturated world, we can conflate technologies with digital media, but here I am choosing the term to specifically capture what the technologies serve rather than the material form they take.

paralysis would come from any single project attempting to be in relation to all dimensions simultaneously. Yet, a relational design practice, grounded by situated knowledges, would not hide that the partial perspective is imperfect if privileged, and pragmatic if problematic (14). It seems desirable to hold space for a holistic perspective while honouring, with humility and generosity, that entanglements require multiple ways in, collective action and pluralistic perspectives. The focus here on individual transformational learning has emphasised the sensorial, psychological, social, technological, temporal and conceptual dimensions over others.

However, if the subject had been large-scale technological transformation, then attending to the material, ethical and temporal dimensions would be more urgent. But it is more complex than this. Just as societal transformation cannot happen without individual mental models shifting, individual transformation is restricted by systems and structures that resist change. Avery Gordon's term 'complex personhood' (15, p. 4) paradoxically acknowledges that people are living contradictions. We are always remembering and forgetting, we are self-aware yet in denial, we get stuck and we transform.

For Gordon, the fellow participants at a learning encounter would never, ever be the 'Other', and would always include ghosts of the past that haunt the present. "Complex personhood means that even those who haunt our dominant institutions and their systems of value are haunted too by things they sometimes have names for and sometimes do not. At the very least, complex personhood is about conferring the respect on others that comes from presuming that life and people's lives are simultaneously straightforward and full of enormously subtle meaning" (15, p. 5). Complex personhood enmeshes the stories we tell about ourselves and the stories we tell about society's problems, which in turn challenges any neat narrative that a designer might attend to the sensorial and psychological dimensions without also being in relation with the structural, geographical, cultural, ethical, political and custodial dimensions.

How might honouring complex personhood unsettle how we understand the role participants' play in disclosing explanations of others' complex inner and external worlds? How might a political and structural lens critique the psychological lens on internal motivation (9.4)? What happens when we acknowledge that participation is not by default empowering? How can an ethical and cultural lens caution us to not design learning encounters that pretend to ignore, or seek to transcend, the existence of oppressive systems and colonised imaginations? To apply the idea of complex personhood to the already complex practice of designing learning would be to humbly recognise that any move to work in this hyper-dimensional context will be less than, never enough, yet important all the same. In calling out the inter-relational nature, we invite reflection on how as designers we show up, how we hold ourselves accountable and how we design.

The dimensions given primacy here push and pull design in different directions. The sensorial and conceptual calls on the designer to sit with and translate the felt body of the learner, to engage with and narrate the multi-sensorial

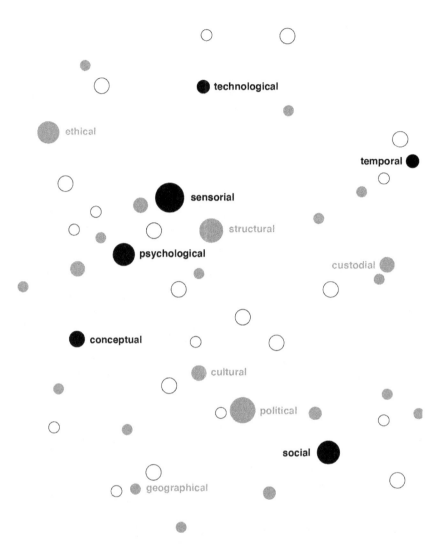

FIGURE 15.3  **The Dimensions of Relational Design**: This nascent idea is a work in progress. Here, I wonder about the complex array of dimensions design work is in relation with – even as we choose to background others. Is the value of acknowledging a breadth of dimensions to be more accountable for what one is not attending to? Or is it to discuss what we mean by the technological, custodial? Or to question how political is distinct from ethical? Or might considering a situation from another relationship angle reveal new tensions? We ran a playdate where the invitation was to identify the relational dimensions people were navigating in their research. The relational design idea was embryonic, yet many questions were generated, the language evolved, even if the wondering continues.

experiences at play in an affective learning environment. The social and technological dimensions in this context catalyses the potential of co-learning by bringing convivial, creative and critical interactions to material encounters with peers, plural perspectives and play. The temporal and psychological dimensions introduce the cognitive, neurobiological processes and the interior emotional landscape in relation to time, reframing how we understand forgetting and remembering, unsettling and evolving, shifting and changing. These six dimensions operate independently and in relation to each other to access the stories we tell ourselves (the mindsets and beliefs we internalise), and the stories we long for (the hopes and dreams we imagine).

However, there is an acknowledgement that in prioritising these dimensions, I can only offer a partial perspective.[11] The decision to focus on an individual's psycho-social engagement at the expense of reckoning with the cultural systems the individual is navigating was made in part because others, more adept than I, are actively examining the ethical, cultural, structural, political, geographical and custodial dimensions of this entanglement.[12] This body of work is indebted to, reliant on and complements the work of these practitioners, scholars and advocates. Those working at the intersection of design and ethics who understand that equitable services, diverse pluralistic perspectives, a culture of care, acknowledgment of trauma and the troubling of power relationships have a lot to contribute to how we deepen learner belonging, agency and self-realisation (18; 19; 20; 21; 22).[13] Indigenous activists like Sadie Red Wing, design institutions like OCAD and Monash University and communities of Indigenous practitioners bring a de-colonial critique, craft design charters and offer ways into indigenising the curriculum, research and practice (23; 24; 25; 26). In turn, Indigenous principles resist Western constructs of land possession and relational

11 **Hannah**: This is a good place to consider what Ahmed would identify as the 'background', being mindful of what we are oriented towards. Also, Bacchi's 'What's the Problem Represented to be?' (WPR) approach to policy analysis demonstrates that "how 'problems' are represented has important effects for what can be seen as problematic, for what is silenced, and for how people think about these issues and about their place in the world." Perhaps this relational design lens asks us to recognise that what we foreground and how we frame situations is really consequential (16, p. 112).

12 **Sean**: Although my research primarily engages with the ethical and structural, I see my relationship with each dimension not as an alignment but rather as a nuanced dialogue with the range of qualities within each. I understand it as relational to the extent that it is useful to articulate the "conditions" by which one dimension is foregrounded. This is where the omission of a historical lens seems problematic. I see bringing a critical consciousness as central to accounting for how history plays out in the present (17). What 21st Century lessons might be learned if design were to un-map the canonical narratives of the discipline and foreground previously excluded aspects of design's past? If we cannot reckon with the role design has played historically, it seems our ability to critically direct the promises embedded in participation are undermined.

13 **Sean**: I wonder if it makes sense for Ethics to be its own dimension given how it's imbricated in everything, especially when engaging with people and places outside of western dominant worldviews and contexts. But then I wonder if perhaps that is true for them all? Maybe owning how entangled they are is the point.

perspectives that privilege place over people, as human geographers remind us of the interdependencies between place-making and atmosphere. Ethnographers, black studies, feminist and queer theorists advance design's understanding: of what a relational practice might be, the import of affect and the sensorial and why one's positionality cannot go unexamined (7; 27; 28; 29; 30; 31; 32; 33; 34).[14] These critiques inform a learner's capacity to surface beliefs, reflexively question assumptions and critically envisage alternate ways of being. The work done on structural impediments to change is deeply interconnected. Operating at the intersection of co-design, systems thinking, STS, HCI and decolonial scholarship are research communities like the Participatory Design Conference and the CoDesign journal that examine the ways in which social, cultural, ecological and political structures might use participation and technologies to enable or constrain individual and collective self-determination (36; 37; 38; 39; 40; 41).

Not every learning encounter can be designed in direct negotiation with these relational dimensions, but we can, at the least, acknowledge the deeper relationality these entanglements reveal. Just as this text sees the mind and body as inextricably connected, these further dimensions cannot be understood in isolation. Our psychological selves are shaped by our socio-cultural and political experiences, and these experiences are sculpted by our technological, structural and geographical interactions, while our interactions are mediated by our sensorial, custodial and ethical responses. These meaning-making experiences, interactions and responses are always in flux with our embodied, lived-in, often unconscious, knowing. What are the implications for transformative practice to see the anticipatory potential of wrestling with these enmeshed dimensions? For an organisation seeking to be anti-racist, how might this hyper-dimensional approach support labelling, owning and acting upon a commitment to diversity, inclusion and belonging? What might a sensorial lived-in knowing experience offer as a motivational driver for change? In what ways might reckoning with internalised racial narratives create space for more ethical social structures? How might technological futures deviate from the structural centring of whiteness? What politicised lens helps us critique a hegemonic value of inclusion over belonging? How might a custodial framing of place-making help shift the workers' understanding of psycho-social care? Perhaps, starting with a generative scan of all dimensions would help assess where the greatest leverage points lie. In owning that some dimensions lie unexamined, one can question the importance of strengthening the fallow relationships. Bringing a prismatic lens to all

---

14 **Lisa**: Threading many of these dimensions Indigenous scholar and activist Leanne Betasamosake Simpson shares Nishnaabeg's research ethics as a practice grounded in "consent, reciprocity, respect, renewal and relationship" (35, p. loc 945). This ethical framework allows for a practice methodology that generates knowledge through "doing or making, relationship, visiting, singing, dancing, storytelling, experimenting, observing, reflecting, mentoring, ceremony, dreaming, and visioning" (35, p. 946).

dimensions makes clear the parallel projects and potential collaborative partners you need for a holistic approach to complex situations.

## In Conclusion

Building on the back of social science research, the contribution of design can be simultaneously small and impactful. If we can design learning encounters that anchor motivation, we can establish a foundation for defining purpose, intentional planning and commitment to future action. If we create spaces that deepen belonging and scaffold productive effort, we can build mastery and foster self-determination. Psychology researchers often study these components independently to gather causal evidence. But as designers, our role is to recognise the virtuous circle animated by activating any one as a lever that deepens learning. We see this cycle of mutual influence when we notice how affect strengthens retrieval practice, analogous thinking can prompt elaborative encoding and how embodied learning might draw on interleaving principles. In recognising the messy, interconnected entanglement of these concepts it becomes possible to see how, together, they amplify a learner's engagement and potential for sustained, meaningful shifts in thinking, doing and being.

Whether we are talking about the future of work, the future of learning or the future of workplaces as learning organisations, making the relational dimensions more robust seems critical. It seems prudent to recognise the limited scope of this work and set about the next phase of inquiry. It seems critical to acknowledge that the inquiry should not stop. It seems appropriate to know the learning will go on forever.

---

## Final Wonderings

As I finish this book, I leave questioning how the *Designing Learning Constellation*, (Figure 13.2) the *SEED* heuristic (Figure 14.2) and *Dimensions of Relational Design* (Figure 15.3) might be iterated on further. Beyond individual pathways to change, what does SEED have to offer when it comes to societal transformation? Is there a design game that helps learning organisations not just identify which relational dimensions to focus on, but also offers moves and methods in support of evolving individual and organisational narratives? When it comes to rethinking the hold modernity has over design education, which *make* wordplays might best critique the dominant script? Lastly, I wonder how experimenting further with the design research practice narrative might hold design researchers more accountable by calling for more critical positioning of ourselves in the work, making our assumptions and values more visible, and deepening our relational capacity to attune to people and place. For me, so many questions are only just coming into focus.

Yet even many of the stories are mine, this book does not centre around me. You were doing your own wondering. Do you leave curious about Indigenous knowing or drawn to the neurobiology of memory traces? At what point did your heart quicken and when did you feel like a belief you held dear was being threatened? Now you are at the end, what do you remember? Are the scientific insights or the case studies from unfamiliar lands easier to recall? Did the macro lens of the practice vignettes and auto-ethnographic stories interleaved throughout stay with you, or did the situated contexts thwart your capacity to see your practice in the stories?

If you remember anything you might recollect that the answer here is not to look back over your notes, but to do the harder work of retrieving from memory. If, as you engaged, you augmented the experience with your own wonderings, diagrams and stories, you will have already encoded and subsequently amplified the residue of thought and strengthened your memories. If it was too hard to over-ride the learned practice of passively reading, there is still time to convert your investment in reading this far into a transformative experience. There are no more words now, only the intention on your part to do the work. Put SEED into action. Begin by identifying your beliefs around how learning happens, envisage where you want this work to take you, go out and experience new ways of learning from and with others and drive your transformation through a commitment to what you do next week. I conclude with an ongoing commitment to wondering disorientation: to seek out the unfamiliar, to let myself be unsettled, to trace new connections and to feel awe. Seeking to not foreclose this inquisitive force of wonder, this book, just like this research, does not end with a full stop but an ellipse, open to the promise of what is still yet to be discovered...

# Bibliography

1 Norgaard, Kari Marie. *Living in Denial Climate Change, Emotions, and Everyday Life.* The MIT Press, 2011.
2 David, Susan A. *Emotional Agility: Get Unstuck, Embrace Change, and Thrive in Work and Life.* Penguin Books, 2016.
3 Kitchenham, Andrew. "The Evolution of Jack Mezirow's Transformative Learning Theory." *Journal of Transformative Education*, vol. 6, no. 2, 2008, pp. 104–23, doi:10.1177/1541344608322678.
4 Grabove, Valerie. "The Many Facets of Transformative Learning Theory and Practice." *Transformative Learning in Action: Insights from Practice. New Directions for Adult and Continuing Education*, edited by Patricia Cranton, Jossey-Bass, 1997, pp. 89–96.
5 Taylor, Edward W. "Building Upon the Theoretical Debate: A Critical Review of the Empirical Studies of Mezirow's Transformative Learning Theory." *Adult Education Quarterly*, vol. 48, no. 1, 1997, pp. 34–59, doi:10.1177/074171369704800104.
6 Adams, T.E and Stacy Holman Jones. "Autoethnography Is Queer." *Handbook of Critical and Indigenous Methodologies*, edited by Norman K Denzin et al., Sage, 2008, pp. 373–90.

7  Braidotti, Rosi. "A Theoretical Framework for the Critical Posthumanities." *Theory, Culture & Society*, vol. 36, no. 6, 2019, pp. 31–61.
8  Mignolo, Walter D. "Delinking." *Cultural Studies*, vol. 21, no. 2–3, 2007, pp. 449–514, doi:10.1080/09502380601162647.
9  "Design." *Lexico*, nd, www.lexico.com/definition/design.
10  "Whakaahua." *Maori Dictionary*, 2021, www.maoridictionary.co.nz/search?keywords=whakaahua.
11  Hurston, Zora Neale. *Their Eyes Were Watching God*. Virago Press, 2018.
12  Korsmeyer, Hannah et al. "Understanding Feminist Anticipation through 'Backtalk': 3 Narratives of Willful, Deviant, and Care-full Co-Design Practices." *Futures*, 2021, In Press, https://doi.org/10.1016/j.futures.2021.102874.
13  Sidorkin, Alexander M. *Learning Relations: Impure Education, Deschooled Schools, and Dialogue with Evil*. Peter Lang, 2002.
14  Haraway, Donna. "Situated Knowledges: The Science Question in Feminism and the Privilege of Partial Perspective." *Feminist Studies*, vol. 14, no. 3, 1988, pp. 575–99.
15  Gordon, Avery. *Ghostly Matters: Haunting and the Sociological Imagination*. University of Minnesota Press, 1997.
16  Bacchi, Carol and Joan Eveline. *Mainstreaming Politics Gendering Practices and Feminist Theory*. University of Adelaide Press, 2010.
17  Tejeda, Carlos and Manuel Espinoza. "Towards a Decolonizing Pedagogy: Social Justice Reconsidered." *Pedagogies of Difference : Rethinking Education for Social Change*, edited by Peter Pericles Trifonas, RoutledgeFalmer, 2003, pp. 1–12. /z-wcorg/, https://openlibrary.org/books/OL15531265M.
18  Vaughan, Laurene. *Designing Cultures of Care*. Bloomsbury, 2019.
19  Wechsler, Jax. "Trauma Informed Design Masterclasses." *Social Design Sydney*, socialdesignsydney.com/masterclasses/.
20  Noel, Lesley-Ann and Marcelo Paiva. "Learning to Recognize Exclusion." *Journal of Usability Studies*, vol. 16, no. 2, 2021, pp. 63–72.
21  "Servdes 2020: Tensions, Paradoxes and Plurality." *ServDes2020*, Online Conference, RMIT University, 2020, www.servdes2020.org.
22  Donahue, Sean et al. *Defining Practices*, 2017, www.definingpractices.com.
23  *Sadie Red Wing*, nd, www.sadieredwing.com.
24  "Indigenous Student Centre." *OCAD University*, nd, www.ocadu.ca/services/indigenous-students.
25  "Wominjeka Djeembana Research Lab." *Monash University*, nd, www.monash.edu/mada/research/wominjeka-djeembana.
26  "International Indigenous Design Charter." *International Council of Design*, 2015, www.ico-d.org/resources/indigo.
27  Harris, Anne M and Stacy Holman Jones. *The Queer Life of Things: Performance, Affect, and the More-Than-Human*. Lexington Books, 2019.
28  Ahmed, Sara. "Queer Use, Lgbtq+@Cam." *YouTube,* uploaded by LGBTQ Cam, 8 January 2019, youtu.be/upkkoFVYfUE.
29  Forlano, Laura et al., editors. *Bauhaus Futures*. The MIT Press, 2019.
30  Mazé, Ramia and Josefin Wangel. "Future (Im)Perfect: Exploring Time, Becoming and Difference in Design and Futures Studies." *Feminist Futures of Spatial Practice*, edited by Meike Schalk and Thérèse Kristiansson Ramia Mazé, AADR and Spurbuchverlag, 2017, pp. 273–86.
31  Cooper, Brittney C. et al., editors. *Crunk Feminist Collection*. Feminist Press, 2017.
32  Smith, Rachel Charlotte et al., editors. *Design Anthropological Futures*. Routledge, 2020.
33  Pink, Sarah et al. *Uncertainty and Possibility: New Approaches to Future Making in Design Anthropology*. Routledge, 2018.
34  Sumartojo, Shanti and Matthew Graves. "Feeling through the Screen: Memory Sites, Affective Entanglements, and Digital Materialities." *Social & Cultural Geography*, vol. 22, no. 2, 2021, pp. 231–49, doi:10.1080/14649365.2018.1563711.

35 Simpson, Leanne Betasamosake. *As We Have Always Done: Indigenous Freedom through Radical Resistance*. Kindle ed., University of Minnesota Press, 2017.
36 Agid, Shana and Elizabeth Chin. "Making and Negotiating Value: Design and Collaboration with Community Led Groups." *CoDesign*, vol. 15, no. 1, 2019, pp. 75–89, doi:10.1080/15710882.2018.1563191.
37 Avram, Gabriela et al. "Repositioning Codesign in the Age of Platform Capitalism: From Sharing to Caring." *CoDesign*, vol. 15, no. 3, 2019, pp. 185–91, doi:10.1080/15710882.2019.1638063.
38 Bonsignore, Elizabeth et al., editors. *Participatory Design for Learning: Perspectives from Practice and Research*, Kindle ed. Routledge, 2017.
39 Agid, Shana et al. "Super Idiotic Creatures (Sic). Keywords in Participatory Design." *Zenodo*, Computer Software, 2021, https://doi.org/10.5281/zenodo.4695510.
40 Akama, Yoko and Shana Agid. *Dance of Designing: Rethinking Position, Relation and Movement in Service Design*, ServDes2018 – Service Design Proof of Concept Conference, 2018, Linköping University Electronic Press, 2018.
41 "Codesign: International Journal of Cocreation in Design and the Arts." *Taylor and Francis Online*, nd, www.tandfonline.com/toc/ncdn20/current.

# INDEX

Note: **Bold** page numbers refer to tables; *italic* page numbers refer to figures and page numbers followed by "n" denote endnotes.

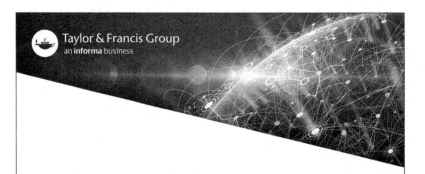

Printed in the United States
by Baker & Taylor Publisher Services